PACKAGE DESIGN *NOW* !

Barnsley College
Honeywell
Learning Centre

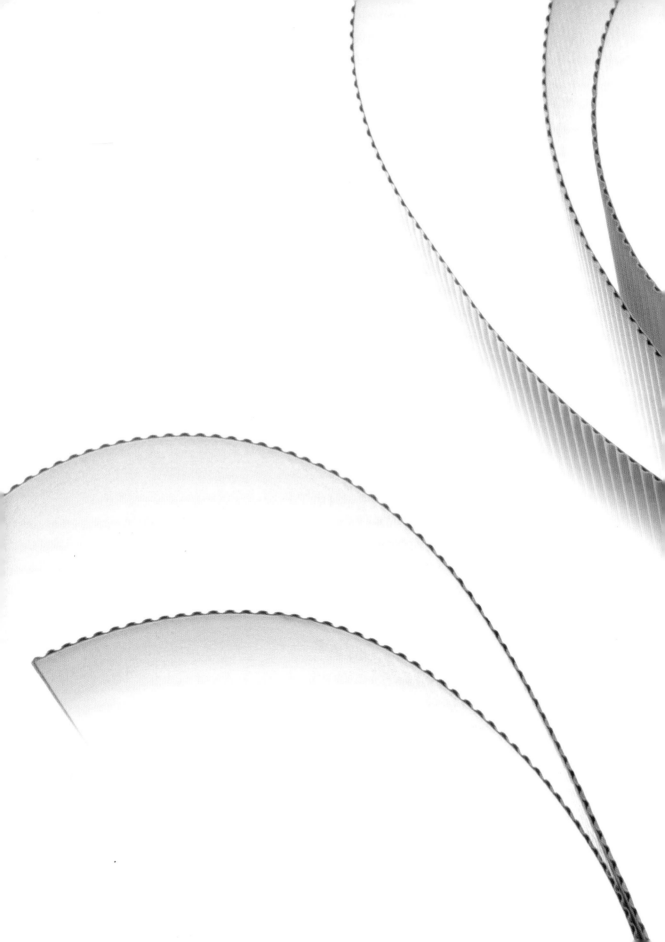

Gisela Kozak
and Julius Wiedemann

PACKAGE
DESIGN
NOW
!

TASCHEN

HONG KONG KÖLN LONDON LOS ANGELES MADRID PARIS TOKYO

INTRODUCTION

PACKAGE DESIGN TODAY

6

CASE STUDIES

CHAPTERS

Introduction
Package Design Today

Gisela Kozak

Cut here... says an icon showing a pair of scissors indicating a dotted line. And you are in the middle of nowhere and without the slightest chance of finding the aforementioned implement within any reasonable distance.

What do you do then? Well... it's down to your own resources and while you try to figure out which part of your anatomy will best serve the function of allowing you to enter into contact with your favourite foodstuff, you realise just how annoying packaging can be.

Tell me that you've never failed to open a yoghurt. That you never ended up with breadsticks on the floor after trying to use both hands to break open the package seal. I'm also sure that among your friends there's one who can open bottles with his teeth... Everyone's got one of those friends.

While I was doing research for my PhD, I found that most of the packages I was studying had been opened, at least once, with the aid of some accessory. Pencils, nail clippers, forks, even screwdrivers figured among the responses. We all probably believe ourselves to be too incompetent to manage to open a package as it's supposed to be done. However, I can tell you... you're not alone!

In his book *Things that make us smart*, Donald Norman says "People err, that is a fact of life. Another fact is that some situations seem as if they were designed to cause errors, especially when their design fails to take human abilities into account."

The most recurrent definitions of packaging mention its role in protecting, preserving, identifying and communicating. For some unknown reason, all these definitions concern the relation between the package and the product; none mentions the relation between the package and the consumer. Personally, I would prefer a definition which included both sides of the equation: the product and the consumer.

Despite the fact that there are several examples on the market that show that the product is not the be-all and end-all of packaging, we still have a long way to go.

Among the best-known examples (and I'm not claiming that they're all successful), of special note is the fact that Japanese law stipulates that packaging must resolve all doubts as to product identity. Shampoo containers, for example, must bear a textured vertical line, which serves to differentiate it from hair conditioner, just by touch. Clearly, this measure benefits the visually impaired, but it also helps all those who wear glasses or contact lenses, but obviously can't do so in the shower or bath.

Other products that were redesigned with a view to enhancing product identity are milk and fruit juice containers. The upper part of the tetra-paks bear either a single or double rounded cut, respectively, identifying the product without the need to read the label. Unfortunately, you don't find out whether the fruit in question is apple or orange until you've tasted it, yet... as I said, it's not all a success story...

And while we're on the subject of not quite getting it right, consider the Japanese law requiring Braille identification of alcoholic drinks. This is all well and good if you hap-pen to read Braille – but the majority of glasses-wearing shoppers don't! And, on top of that, practically all these measures enter the market without a whisper of publicity; consumers only find out by word of mouth.

Another confusing aspect of packaging is what seems to be an entertainment role that has recently come to the fore in the designs produced by branding agencies. In Europe, this is done by means of a startling sense of humour that deprives the products of some of their solemnity, and in Japan, by including comic characters which, to some extent, give the products a more childish image, for some reason obviously deemed necessary. And among products where it's difficult to understand the logic behind the graphic work, we have condoms... strategically illustrated with pictures for children.

Package graphics are renewed much more frequently in Japan than here in the West. For the same reason as they change their electro-domestic appliances way before the end of their useful lives, it just seems that redesign is a must in packaging! Makeovers are periodical and, in the case of many products, carried out on a yearly basis.

But this updating does not only affect graphic aspects, advances are also made in the structural design. Japan is renowned both for its strong cultural roots and its technological advances. If one thing draws attention it is the aggiornamiento or revamping of certain packages which, once upon a time, were developed from natural products.

One of my most treasured souvenirs of Japan is a book on traditional packaging

...ade with natural products such as bamboo
...eaves, bamboo cane, etc. The book, printed
...ome thirty-plus years ago, is a museum
...iece. When living in Japan, I was amazed
...ow the majority of such natural products
...ad been replaced by plastic versions: plastic
...amboo leaves, plastic bamboo canes, etc.
...and I wondered why no one had designed a
...ew style which would be more in keeping
...ith the present-day market rather than
...merely imitating the early materials. Coming
...rom a country whose cultural history totals
...nly centuries rather than millennia, it took
...e a long time to understand how respect
...or culture can also be expressed via the
...esign of packaging.

...In *Package Design Now!*, you will find not
...nly examples of how branding can help a
...roduct to stand out from other products on
...he gondola, but also solutions that have
...een proposed with the aim of making life
...hat little bit easier. And, without any doubt,
...ou're going to leave wishing you could take
...ne or two of these products along with you.
...ither because you like the graphic design,
...he sense of humour, the cultural roots or the
...ractical advantages. I hope that this book
...ill free you from the temptation to include
...ther items that your family considers
...bsolutely vital in this preciously assembled
...and so little understood) personal collection
...f packages. After all, a book takes up less
...pace than 300 packages...

Einleitung
Package Design Today

Gisela Kozak

„Hier aufschneiden", besagt das Piktogramm mit der Schere und weist auf eine gepunktete Linie. Aber leider sind Sie gerade am Ende der Welt und haben natürlich keine Schere dabei und auch keine Chance, eine zu finden.

Was also tun? Nun … Sie sind auf Ihre Fantasie angewiesen, und während Sie gerade herauszufinden versuchen, mit welchem Teil Ihres Körpers Sie der Verpackung wohl am ehesten den heiß ersehnten Inhalt entreißen können, wird Ihnen schmerzlich bewusst, wie nervtötend Verpackungen sein können.

Behaupten Sie jetzt nicht, dass Sie noch nie Probleme beim Öffnen eines Joghurts hatten. Dass Sie die Grissini noch nie vom Boden aufsammeln mussten, nachdem Sie vergeblich versucht haben, die Packung vorsichtig aufzureißen. Ich bin auch sicher, dass sie in Ihrem Freundeskreis jemand haben, der Flaschen mit den Zähnen öffnet … jeder kennt so einen.

Bei den Recherchen zu meiner Diplomarbeit fiel mir auf, dass praktisch jede Verpackung, die ich untersuchte, schon mindestens einmal mithilfe eines kuriosen Hilfsmittels geöffnet worden war. Stifte, Nagelscheren, Gabeln und sogar Schraubenzieher hat man dazu genommen. Wahrscheinlich glauben wir alle, wir seien zu dumm, um die Packung so zu öffnen, wie es vorgesehen ist. Ich kann Ihnen aber versichern, dass es nicht nur Ihnen so ergeht!

In seinem Buch *Things that make us smart* sagt Donald Norman: „Menschen irren, das ist eine schlichte Tatsache. Eine weitere

Tatsache ist aber, dass manche Situationen scheinbar dafür geschaffen sind, Fehler zu provozieren. Dies passiert vor allem dann, wenn niemand daran gedacht hat, die menschlichen Fähigkeiten zu berücksichtigen."

Die am häufigsten verwendeten Definitionen für Verpackung beschreiben ihren Zweck als Schutz, Konservierung, Identifizierung und Kommunikation. Aus unbekanntem Grund beschäftigen sich all diese Definitionen zwar mit dem Verhältnis zwischen Verpackung und Produkt, aber keine einzige mit dem Verhältnis zwischen Verpackung und Verbraucher. Ich würde eine Definition bevorzugen, die beide Seiten, also Produkt und Verbraucher, berücksichtigt.

Obwohl es inzwischen Verpackungen auf dem Markt gibt, die beweisen, dass das Produkt nicht der wichtigste Aspekt für die Verpackung ist, haben wir noch einen langen Weg vor uns.

Unter den bekanntesten Beispielen (und ich sage nicht, dass sie alle von Erfolg gekrönt sind) verdient ein japanisches Gesetz besondere Aufmerksamkeit. Diesem Gesetz zufolge muss jede Verpackung das enthaltene Produkt einwandfrei identifizieren. Shampooflaschen tragen beispielsweise eine vertikale, ertastbare Linie, sodass man das Shampoo schon beim Anfassen von der Pflegespülung unterscheiden kann. Diese Maßnahme hilft Sehbehinderten, aber natürlich auch allen, die auf Brille und Kontaktlinsen angewiesen sind, die sie unter der Dusche nicht tragen können.

So wurden auch die Verpackungen von Milch und Fruchtsäften neu gestaltet, damit

man sie besser unterscheiden kann. Im oberen Bereich der Tetrapacks finden sich einfach und doppelt gerundete Ausschnitte, mit denen man Milch- von Fruchtsaftverpackungen unterscheiden kann, ohne die Aufschrift lesen zu müssen. Um welchen Fruchtsaft es sich handelt, erfährt man allerdings erst beim Probieren, … es sind eben, wie gesagt, nicht alle Entwürfe vollkommen durchdacht …

Da wir gerade bei den Beispielen sind, die nicht perfekt sind: Ein anderes japanisches Gesetz verlangt, dass alle alkoholischen Getränke mit Brailleschrift beschriftet sein müssen. Das ist gut, wenn Sie Braille lesen können, die Mehrzahl der Brillenträger kann dies allerdings nicht! Überdies werden die meisten dieser Maßnahmen eingeführt, ohne dass Verbraucher darüber informiert werden. Nur durch Mundpropaganda erfahren die Konsumenten davon.

Ein weiterer verwirrender Aspekt beim Verpackungsdesign ist der Unterhaltungswert, der in letzter Zeit bei Entwürfen aus Branding-Agenturen stark in den Vordergrund zu treten scheint. In Europa geschieht dies mit einem Humor, der die Produkte weniger ernst darstellt. In Japan setzt man auf witzige Figuren und verleiht den Produkten ein kindlicheres Image. Zu den Produkten, bei denen der Inhalt der grafischen Gestaltung untergeordnet ist, gehören beispielsweise Kondome, die mit kindgerechten Bildern illustriert wurden.

In Japan werden Verpackungen häufiger überarbeitet als in westlichen Ländern. Genau wie man in Japan Elektrogeräte weit vor ihrem eigentlichen Lebensende aus-

uscht, scheint in Japan auch das Redesign *on Verpackungen ein absolutes Muss zu ein! Neugestaltungen werden regelmäßig nd bei vielen Produkten sogar jährlich orgenommen.*

Die Überarbeitung betrifft aber nicht nur ie grafische Gestaltung, sondern auch die Verpackungsformen. Japan ist sowohl für eine starken kulturellen Wurzeln als auch ir technologischen Fortschritt bekannt. Wenn etwas besondere Aufmerksamkeit rweckt, dann ist es die Neugestaltung von Verpackungen, die aus natürlichen Produk- en entwickelt wurden.

Eines meiner meistgeliebten Souvenirs us Japan ist ein Buch über traditionelle Verpackungen aus natürlichen Produkten, ie etwa Bambusblättern, Bambusrohren sw. Das Buch, das vor über 30 Jahren edruckt wurde, ist heute ein Museums- tück. Als ich in Japan lebte, war ich er- taunt, wie viele dieser natürlichen Ver- ackungsmaterialien durch Kunststoff- ersionen ersetzt worden sind. So gibt es Bambusblätter und Bambusrohre aus Plastik sw. Und ich fragte mich, warum niemand ine modernere Verpackung entwickelt hat, ie dem heutigen Markt angemessener wäre, tatt diese frühen Verpackungsmaterialien u imitieren. Als Bürgerin eines Landes, das ur auf Jahrhunderte statt auf Jahrtausende lte eigene Kultur zurückblicken kann, habe h lange gebraucht, um zu verstehen, dass Verpackungsdesign auch ein Ausdruck des espekts für die eigene Kultur sein kann.

Package Design Now! zeigt nicht nur rodukte, die entwickelt wurden, um zwi- chen der Konkurrenz im Regal aufzufallen.

Hier finden sich auch Entwürfe, die uns das Leben etwas erleichtern sollen. Und bestimmt werden Sie auch einige Produkte entdecken, die Sie am liebsten direkt mitneh- men möchten – sei es, weil Ihnen das grafi- sche Design so gut gefällt, oder sei es, weil Ihnen der Humor, die kulturelle Konnotation oder der praktische Nutzen besonders zu- sagt. Ich hoffe, dieses Buch erlöst Sie von der Versuchung, Gegenstände, die Ihre Familie für absolut unverzichtbar hält, in diese sorgfältig zusammengetragene (und so wenig verstandene) persönliche Sammlung von Verpackungen einzuschließen. Schließ- lich beansprucht ein Buch weniger Platz als 300 Verpackungen …

Introduction
Package Design Today

Gisela Kozak

« Découpez ici… », dit l'icône en forme de paire de ciseaux indiquant une ligne de pointillés. Mais vous êtes au milieu de nulle part et sans la moindre chance de trouver l'instrument susmentionné à une distance raisonnable.

Que faites-vous ensuite ? Eh bien… vous vous servez de vos propres ressources et, alors que vous essayez de trouver la partie de votre anatomie qui conviendra le mieux pour accéder à votre nourriture préférée, vous réalisez à quel point les emballages peuvent être agaçants.

Dites-moi que vous n'avez jamais échoué en ouvrant un yaourt. Que vous n'avez jamais fini avec des gâteaux apéritifs partout par terre après avoir essayé d'ouvrir l'emballage scellé à deux mains. Je suis également sûre que, parmi vos amis, il y en a un qui sait ouvrir les bouteilles avec ses dents. Tout le monde a ce genre d'amis.

Alors que je faisais des recherches pour ma thèse de doctorat, je me suis rendu compte que la plupart des emballages que j'étudiais avaient été ouverts, au moins une fois, à l'aide d'un outil de fortune. Stylos, coupe-ongles, fourchettes, même les tournevis figurent parmi les réponses. Chacun d'entre nous se croit probablement trop maladroit pour ouvrir un emballage correctement. Cependant, je peux vous dire que… vous n'êtes pas seul !

Dans son livre *Things that make us smart*, Donald Norman dit : « Les gens se trompent, cela fait partie des choses de la vie. De la même manière, certaines situations semblent avoir été conçues pour induire en erreur, surtout lorsque leur conception ne prend pas en compte les aptitudes de l'être humain ».

Les définitions les plus courantes de l'emballage mentionnent son rôle de protection, de conservation, d'identification et de communication. Pour quelque raison inconnue, toutes ces définitions concernent la relation entre l'emballage et le produit, mais aucune ne fait référence à la relation entre l'emballage et le consommateur. Personnellement, je préférerais une définition prenant en compte les deux côtés de l'équation : le produit et le consommateur.

Bien qu'il y ait déjà sur le marché plusieurs exemples qui montrent que tout ne tourne pas autour du produit, nous avons encore un long chemin à parcourir.

Parmi les exemples les plus connus (ce qui ne veut pas dire qu'ils aient tous eu du succès), mention spéciale à la loi japonaise qui stipule que le conditionnement doit résoudre tout problème d'identification du produit. Les bouteilles de shampooing, par exemple, doivent comporter une ligne verticale en relief, qui sert à les différencier d'un démêlant rien qu'en les touchant. Cette mesure est bien sûr très pratique pour les non-voyants, mais elle aide aussi tous ceux qui portent des lunettes ou des lentilles de contact, inutilisables sous la douche ou dans la baignoire.

Les emballages de lait et de jus de fruit ont aussi été modifiés afin que leur identité soit mieux différenciée. La partie supérieure du Tetra Pak comporte respectivement une ou deux découpes arrondies permettant d'identifier le produit sans avoir à lire l'étiquette. Malheureusement, vous ne saurez si le jus de fruit en question est un jus de pomme ou d'orange que lorsque vous l'aurez goûté mais, comme je l'ai dit, tout n'est pas forcément une réussite…

Et d'ailleurs, en parlant de choses qui ne sont pas très au point, examinons de plus près la loi japonaise qui exige une identification en Braille des boissons alcoolisées. C'est très utile pour ceux qui savent lire le Braille mais, pour la majorité des clients qui ont oublié leurs lunettes chez eux, ça ne servira pas à grand-chose ! Et, surtout, pratiquement toutes ces mesures arrivent sur le marché sans une once de publicité. Les consommateurs doivent les découvrir par le biais du bouche à oreille.

Un autre aspect déroutant de l'emballage est son rôle de divertissement, récemment très en vogue dans les concepts créés par les agences de stratégie de marque. En Europe, cela se manifeste par un sens de l'humour surprenant qui dépossède les produits d'une partie de leur solennité, et au Japon, par l'utilisation de personnages de manga qui donnent aux produits une image plus infantile, jugée nécessaire pour une raison ou pour une autre. Et parmi les produits pour lesquels il est difficile de comprendre la logique derrière le design graphique, nous avons les préservatifs… stratégiquement illustrés de dessins infantiles.

Au Japon, le graphisme des emballages est actualisé beaucoup plus fréquemment qu'ici en Occident. Tout comme ils changent leurs appareils électroménagers avant la fin de leur cycle de vie, il semble que la révision du design soit tout simplement un must

ans l'emballage ! Les changements de look
ont courants et, pour de nombreux produits,
s ont lieu chaque année.

Mais cette mise à jour ne concerne pas
eulement l'aspect graphique, et l'on voit
ussi des avancées en matière de design
tructurel. Le Japon est reconnu dans le
onde entier aussi bien pour ses racines
ulturelles que pour ses avancées technolo-
iques. Si une chose attire l'attention, c'est
aggiornamento, ou la mise au goût du jour
e certains emballages qui, dans une vie
eilleure, avaient été créés à partir de
roduits naturels.

L'un de mes souvenirs les plus précieux du
apon est un livre sur l'emballage tradition-
el, c'est-à-dire à base de matériaux naturels
omme les feuilles de bambou, la canne de
ambou, etc. Le livre, imprimé il y a plus de
0 ans, est une pièce de musée. Lorsque je
ivais au Japon, j'ai été surprise de voir que
a plupart de ces matériaux naturels avaient
té remplacés par des versions en plastique.
es feuilles de bambou en plastique, de la
anne de bambou en plastique, etc. Et je me
uis demandé pourquoi personne n'avait
onçu une nouvelle version qui serait plus
onforme au marché actuel, au lieu de la rem-
lacer purement et simplement. Je viens d'un
ays dont l'histoire culturelle se compte en
ècles, et non en millénaires, et il m'a fallu
u temps pour comprendre que le respect de
a culture peut aussi s'exprimer par le design
emballage.

Dans *Package Design Now* vous ne
rouverez pas seulement des exemples qui
lustrent comment la stratégie de marque
eut aider un produit à se démarquer des

autres produits dans les gondoles. Vous trou-
verez aussi des solutions proposées pour faciliter la vie des consommateurs. Et, sans
aucun doute, lorsque vous refermerez cet
ouvrage, vous aurez une furieuse envie de
posséder plus d'un des produits qu'il présente. Ce sera peut-être le design graphique,
le sens de l'humour, les racines culturelles ou
les avantages pratiques qui vous auront
séduit. J'espère que ce livre vous libèrera de
la tentation d'ajouter de nouveaux éléments
à votre collection personnelle d'emballages
précieusement assemblée (et si peu compri-
se). Après tout, un livre occupe moins
d'espace que 300 emballages…

Case 01
NatureWorks

IDEO – Kara Johnson, Bob Adams,
Joanne Oliver, Pontus Wahlgren

For this conceptual project, the team of experts at the international design consultancy IDEO, explores the use of PLA (polyactic acid), a bioplastic that can be applied to a number of package designs, whilst at the same time respecting the environment. Its immense potential for applications in design can lead to a much more sustainable future for package design.

PLA is a bioplastic with attributes that allow it to be perceived as natural, fresh and beautiful. It is made from natural resources – corn. It is a healthy plastic, something companies are looking for to show they are environmentally responsible. PLA is very versatile and can be injection moulded, formed as a sheet, or be made into a fabric, a thin film or a coating. It can also be embossed – clear or printed. So IDEO explored how to make the most of the unique properties of PLA in four directions:

NATURAL
What if the packaging is as NATURAL as its content?
A bottle of water – clarity; looks and feels like glass.
A bag – made for a snack of potato crisps; foldable sheet and film.

HEALTHY
What if the packaging is as HEALTHY as its content?
A concentrated energy drink – the container is stretch-blow moulded.
A container for Baby Shampoo – easy to open and use.

BEAUTIFUL
What if the packaging is as BEAUTIFUL as its content?
An exclusive perfume – this talc-filled PLA has the feel of ceramic and communicates a feeling of luxury.

FRESH
What if the packaging is as FRESH as its content?
Milk and biscuit for the in-between snack.

NATUREWORKS-PLA AND IDEO SUSTAINABILITY
Sustainability is not always intuitive or immediately understandable. As designers, we have the ability to make it tangible, and, in so doing create the desire for increasingly sustainable solutions within our society. This project gave IDEO an opportunity to explore the issue of sustainability and design in the context of packaging. These packaging concepts tell the story of design and brand opportunities created by the introduction of PLA, a clear, beautiful, stiff bioplastic made from maize and available in high volume.

THE CLIENT
NatureWorks is the first company to offer a family of commercially available polymers derived from 100% annually renewable resources. "Heightened environmental awareness in European countries including Italy, France, Germany, Belgium and the UK has been a key factor in bringing nature-based plastics into the mainstream."
(Dennis McCrew, CEO of NatureWorks).

THE PROCESS
Working with NatureWorks, IDEO began this project by talking to all the people involved in the life cycle of PLA – farmers, non-governmental organisations (NGOs, like Greenpeace and Sierra Club), recycling facilities, converters, designers, brand managers and consumers – so that we could understand their individual perceptions of plastic and the idea of sustainability (or lack thereof). In general, consumers didn't know much about plastic or they didn't know the right stuff about plastic. It was interesting to consider how farmers related to plastic and how they wanted to be part of a system of production that would reduce our dependency on oil for raw materials. Designers didn't see early bio plastics as something that could inspire their designs in a way that was playful, beautiful and sophisticated. Bioplastics were remembered as humble, muted and green and brown. We knew PLA was different and had to find a way to express it, to tell the story. We wanted PLA to be sassy and sexy, transparent, and maybe even orange!

The story of sustainability is emotionally charged. Brands that are already "green" are reluctant to be involved in a solution that is less than perfect. In the US, the commodity market for maize is mostly GMO-based, and this restricted Natureworks' ability to access low cost non-GMO raw materials. And brands that are not "green" don't care about these challenges and do not perceive a fundamental shift that could drive demand for more sustainable products and packaging.

All brands seek success. The definitions for success vary a great deal. Some see success purely as measured by the creation of financial or emotional value. Others measure the value of citizenship and their impact on the environment. A brand's existence relies on its relationship and popularity with consumers. Today, we see brands falling some-

here along this path from "non-green" to
reen". And there will be opportunities to
ove brands along that path as people and
mpanies change.

In the course of this project we collaborat-
with BulldogDrummond, a strategic brand
nsultancy (www.bulldogdrummond.com),
d together we encouraged NatureWorks to
opt a new perspective on their business.
So we focused ourselves on packaging
d used design to tell a story of how this
aterial could create and reinforce brand
lues: a story about people not plastic, a
ory about the opportunity to rethink the
ay we make things.

Credits: IDEO
ara Johnson (materials), Bob Adams
ustainability), Joanne Oliver (design)
mtus Wahlgren (design).

**Bei dieser Konzeptstudie testete
n Expertenteam des internationalen
esign-Beratungsunternehmens IDEO
e Einsatzmöglichkeiten für PLA
olymilchsäure, engl. polylactic acid).
r auf natürlicher Milchsäure basierende
o-Kunststoff kann im Verpackungswesen
elseitig eingesetzt werden, ohne die
nwelt stark zu belasten. Sein großes
nsatzpotenzial kann zur Entwicklung
chhaltiger und umweltverträglicher
erpackungen führen.**

PLA ist ein Bio-Kunststoff, dessen
igenschaften ihn natürlich, frisch und
hön wirken lassen. Er wird aus dem
türlichen Rohstoff Mais hergestellt und

ist somit ein „gesunder" Kunststoff, der
vor allem bei Firmen begehrt ist, die
Umweltbewusstsein groß schreiben. PLA
ist sehr vielseitig einsetzbar. Das Material
eignet sich für Spritzgussverfahren und
kann zu Platten geformt sowie zu Gewebe,
als Folie oder Beschichtung verarbeitet
werden. Es kann bedruckt, geprägt und
durchsichtig hergestellt werden. IDEO
testete unter vier Aspekten, wie die einzigartigen Eigenschaften von PLA vorteilhaft
genutzt werden könnten.

NATÜRLICH
*Was wäre, wenn die Verpackung
genauso NATÜRLICH wäre wie ihr Inhalt?*
Eine Flasche Wasser – Reinheit; sieht aus
und fühlt sich an wie Glas. Ein Beutel – für
Kartoffelchips; faltbarer Karton und Folie.

GESUND
*Was wäre, wenn die Verpackung
genauso GESUND wäre wie ihr Inhalt?*
Ein konzentrierter Energy-Drink –
der Behälter wird im Streckblasverfahren
hergestellt. Ein Behälter für Baby-Shampoo
– einfach zu öffnen und zu verwenden.

SCHÖN
*Was wäre, wenn die Verpackung
genauso SCHÖN wäre wie ihr Inhalt?*
Ein exklusives Parfüm – das mit Talkum
gefüllte PLA wirkt wie Keramik und vermittelt den Eindruck von Luxus.

FRISCH
*Was wäre, wenn die Verpackung
genauso frisch wäre wie ihr Inhalt?*
Milch und Plätzchen für den kleinen Snack
zwischendurch.

NATUREWORKS PLA
UND IDEO NACHHALTIGKEIT
Das Konzept der Nachhaltigkeit ist nicht
immer intuitiv erfassbar oder sofort nach-
vollziehbar. Als Designer können wir es verständlich machen und damit in der Gesellschaft den Wunsch nach immer nachhaltige-
ren, umweltverträglicheren Lösungen
wecken. Das Projekt ermöglichte IDEO, das
Thema Umweltverträglichkeit und Design
im Hinblick auf Verpackungen genauer zu
untersuchen. Diese Verpackungskonzepte
zeigen, welche Möglichkeiten sich im Bereich
Design und Markenidentität durch die
Einführung von PLA ergaben. Das ist ein
durchsichtiger, schöner, fester Bio-Kunststoff, der aus Mais hergestellt wird und in
großen Mengen verfügbar ist.

DER KUNDE
NatureWorks ist das erste Unternehmen,
das eine Reihe von kommerziell verwendba-
ren Polymeren aus 100 % erneuerbaren
Ressourcen herstellt. „Das gesteigerte
Umweltbewusstsein in europäischen Län-
dern wie Italien, Frankreich, Deutschland,
Belgien und Großbritannien hat uns dazu
bewogen, natürliche Kunststoffe für den
Massenmarkt zu produzieren." (Dennis
McCrew, CEO von NatureWorks).

DER PROZESS
Zu Beginn des gemeinsamen Projektes
sprach IDEO zunächst mit allen, die den
Entstehungsprozess von PLA begleiteten –
Landwirte, Nicht-Regierungsorganisationen
(wie z. B. Greenpeace und Sierra Club),
Recycling-Firmen, Weiterverarbeiter,
Designer, Markenmanager und Konsumenten
–, um ihren Standpunkt zu Kunststoff und
ihre Vorstellungen von Nachhaltigkeit zu

analysieren. Im Allgemeinen wussten die Konsumenten nicht sehr viel über Kunststoffe, oder sie waren falsch informiert. Interessant waren die Meinungen der Landwirte über Kunststoff und ihr Wunsch, an einem Produktionssystem beteiligt zu sein, das unsere Abhängigkeit vom Erdöl zugunsten erneuerbarer Rohstoffe reduziert. Designer wiederum assoziierten mit Bio-Kunststoffen vor allem minderwertige Materialien in Grün oder Braun und fanden sie im Hinblick auf Aussehen und Raffinesse wenig inspirierend. Unsere Aufgabe musste also sein, das Neue und Besondere an PLA zu verdeutlichen. Wir wollten, dass PLA frech und sexy ist, transparent und vielleicht sogar orange!

Das Thema Umweltverträglichkeit ist sehr emotionsgeladen. Marken, die umweltbewusst produzieren, sind sehr anspruchsvoll. NatureWorks hatte Schwierigkeiten, preiswerten Nicht-GMO Mais zu finden. Bei dem Mais auf dem amerikanischen Rohstoffmarkt handelt es sich vorwiegend um GMO-Mais (genetisch manipulierte Organismen). Weniger umweltbewusste Marken haben diese Probleme nicht und nehmen auch keine grundlegende Veränderung wahr, die zu einer stärkeren Nachfrage nachhaltig produzierter Produkte und Verpackungen führen könnte.

Alle Marken wollen erfolgreich sein. Doch Erfolg wird unterschiedlich definiert. Manche messen Erfolg an emotional und finanziell geschaffenen Werten, andere an gesellschaftlichen Engagement und an dem Einfluss auf die Umwelt. Die Existenz jeder Marke hängt von ihrem Verhältnis zum Verbraucher und ihrer Beliebtheit ab. Man kann Marken auch auf einer Skala zwischen „grün" und „nicht grün" einordnen. Und da sich Menschen und Unternehmen ändern, wird man auch die

Position eines Unternehmens auf dieser Skala verändern können.

Bei diesem Projekt arbeiteten wir mit dem strategischen Markenberater Bulldog-Drummond. (www.bulldogdrummond.com) zusammen. Wir empfahlen NatureWorks, das Unternehmen aus einer neuen Perspektive zu betrachten.

Wir konzentrierten uns auf Verpackungen und versuchten, mit unseren Entwürfen zu zeigen, wie man mit diesem neuen Material Markenwerte schaffen oder verstärken kann. Im Mittelpunkt stand dabei der Mensch und nicht der Kunststoff.

Quelle: IDEO
Kara Johnson (Materialien), Bob Adams
(Nachhaltigkeit), Joanne Oliver (Design)
Pontus Wahlgren (Design).

Pour ce projet conceptuel, l'équipe d'experts du cabinet de conseil international IDEO explore les utilisations du PLA (acide polyactique), un bioplastique qui se prête à la réalisation de différents types d'emballages respectueux de l'environnement. Son potentiel immense pour des applications dans le domaine du design peut donner à la conception d'emballage un avenir plus écologique.

Le PLA est un bioplastique dont les caractéristiques lui permettent d'être perçu comme naturel, frais et beau. Il est fabriqué à partir d'une ressource naturelle : le maïs. C'est un plastique sain, qualité que les entreprises recherchent pour montrer qu'elles sont respectueuses de l'environnement.

Le PLA est très polyvalent et peut être moulé par injection, pressé en forme de feuille, ou être utilisé sous forme de tissu, de film ou de couche de finition. Il peut être travaillé en relief, transparent ou imprimé. IDEO a donc réfléchi à la façon d'exploiter au mieux les propriétés exceptionnelles du PLA suivant quatre orientations :

NATUREL
Et si l'emballage était aussi NATUREL que son contenu ?
Une bouteille d'eau : transparence ; elle a l'apparence et le toucher du verre. Un sac : pour contenir des chips, feuille et film pliables.

SAIN
Et si l'emballage était aussi SAIN que son contenu ?
Une boisson énergisante concentrée : la bouteille est moulée par soufflage. Un flacon de shampoing pour bébés : facile à ouvrir et à utiliser.

BEAU
Et si l'emballage était aussi BEAU que son contenu ?
Un parfum de luxe : ce PLA mélangé à du talc a le toucher de la céramique et transmet une impression de luxe.

FRAÎCHEUR
Et si l'emballage était aussi FRAIS que son contenu ?
Lait et biscuit comme en-cas.

PLA NATUREWORKS
ET IDEO LA DURABILITÉ
La durabilité n'est pas toujours une question d'intuition, ni immédiatement compré-

nsible. En tant que designers, nous avons possibilité de la rendre tangible, et par là suciter l'envie de solutions de plus en us durables dans notre société. Ce projet a nné à IDEO l'occasion d'explorer la question de la durabilité et du design dans le maine de l'emballage. Ces concepts d'emallage racontent l'histoire des possibilités en atière de stratégie de marque et de design ées par l'apparition du PLA, un bioplasque transparent, rigide et aux qualités thétiques exceptionnelles, fabriqué à partir maïs et disponible en grande quantité.

LE CLIENT

NatureWorks est la première entreprise à ttre sur le marché une famille de polyres dérivés de ressources 100 % renouveles chaque année. « La montée de l'écolosme dans les pays européens, notamment Italie, en France, en Allemagne, en lgique et au Royaume-Uni, a été un facur essentiel pour mettre les plastiques logiques à la disposition du grand public. » ennis McCrew, directeur général de atureWorks).

LE PROCESSUS

En collaboration avec NatureWorks, EO a commencé ce projet en parlant à utes les personnes impliquées dans le cycle vie du PLA – les agriculteurs, les organisions non gouvernementales (des ONG nme Greenpeace et Sierra Club), les ines de recyclage, les convertisseurs, les ecteurs de marque et les consommateurs e façon à comprendre leurs perceptions lividuelles sur le plastique et sur la notion durabilité (ou de non durabilité). En géné-, les consommateurs ne savaient pas nd-chose sur le plastique, ou ne savaient

pas ce qu'il y avait à savoir. Il était intéressant de voir la relation des agriculteurs avec le plastique, et leur volonté de faire partie d'un système de production qui réduirait notre dépendance envers le pétrole pour la fabrication des matières premières. Les designers ne voyaient pas les premiers bioplastiques comme des matériaux pouvant leur inspirer des concepts ludiques, élégants et beaux. Les bioplastiques évoquaient une image de matériau modeste, aux tons vert ou brun sourd. Nous savions que le PLA était différent, et nous devions trouver un moyen d'exprimer cette différence, de raconter l'histoire de ce matériau. Nous voulions que le PLA soit insolent, sexy, transparent, et peut-être même orange !

L'histoire de la durabilité est chargée d'émotion. Les marques qui sont déjà « vertes » ne veulent pas investir dans une solution à moins qu'elle ne soit parfaite. Aux États-Unis, le marché du maïs est principalement composé d'OMG, et cela réduisait l'accès de NatureWorks à des matières premières non modifiées génétiquement et bon marché. Les marques qui ne sont pas « vertes » ne s'intéressent pas à ces défis et ne perçoivent pas non plus le changement fondamental chez le public, qui pourrait entraîner une demande plus importante en produits et en emballages durables.

Toutes les marques recherchent le succès. Les définitions du succès sont très variées. Certains mesurent le succès exclusivement à l'aune de la valeur financière ou émotionnelle. D'autres prennent en compte la citoyenneté et l'impact sur l'environnement. L'existence d'une marque dépend de sa relation avec les consommateurs et de sa popularité. Aujourd'hui, nous voyons certaines marques se positionner quelque part entre

« non vert » et « vert ». À mesure que le public et les entreprises changeront, des occasions vont se créer pour faire avancer les marques sur ce chemin.

Pour ce projet, nous avons travaillé en collaboration avec BulldogDrummond, un cabinet de conseil en stratégie de marque (www.bulldogdrummond.com), et ensemble nous avons encouragé NatureWorks à adopter une nouvelle perspective dans leur activité.

Nous nous sommes donc concentrés sur l'emballage et nous avons utilisé le design pour raconter une histoire sur la façon dont ce matériau pouvait créer et renforcer des valeurs de marque. C'est une histoire sur les gens, pas sur le plastique. Une histoire sur l'occasion de repenser notre façon de faire les choses.

Crédits : IDEO
Kara Johnson (matériaux), Bob Adams
(durabilité), Joanne Oliver (design),
Pontus Wahlgren (design).

A MEANINGFUL CONVERSATION ABOUT DESIGN

NatureWorks and IDEO worked together to explore the power of design to communicate opportunities to a non-technical audience – in advertising, branding, marketing and business. Design creates a tangible conversation about responsibility. PLA is a point of inspiration for brands to rethink material choices to build specific brand attributes. As few people know how to talk about plastic so that it is inspirational and not boring, we invented a language for PLA that appealed to designers and allowed us to look for connections with brands. The introduction of PLA presents a new opportunity to enhance the story of a product or its packaging through a responsible material.

PLA is made from natural ingredients like corn. PLA can compost, burn clean and may be recycled, like materials such as paper – it's NATURAL. PLA does not leach toxic chemicals and is naturally antimicrobial – it's HEALTHY. PLA can be transparent like glass or opaque like ceramic. PLA is easy to twist and fold, it's stiff and noisy. PLA can be easily and deeply embossed – it's BEAUTIFUL.

EIN BEDEUTUNGSVOLLER DIALOG ÜBER DESIGN

NatureWorks und IDEO untersuchten gemeinsam die Möglichkeiten von Design, mit einem nicht-technisch orientierten Publikum aus Werbung, Brand-Marketing und Wirtschaft zu kommunizieren. Design kann einen Dialog über Verantwortung auslösen. PLA ist dabei Anstoß und Inspiration für Marken, ihre Materialwahl zu überdenken und spezielle Markenwerte zu schaffen. Da die Präsentation von Kunststoff meist langweilig ist, haben wir eine neue Sprache für PLA entwickelt, die Designer anspricht und es uns erlaubt, nach Verbindungen mit Marken zu suchen. Denn PLA bietet die Möglichkeit, die Produkt- oder Verpackungslegende durch das umweltbewusste Material zu erneuern und verbessern.

PLA wird aus natürlichen Grundstoffen wie Mais hergestellt. PLA ist ähnlich wie Papier kompostierbar, kann sauber verbrannt werden und ist recycelbar – es ist NATÜRLICH. PLA dünstet keine toxischen Chemikalien aus und hat eine natürliche antimikrobielle Wirkung – es ist GESUND. PLA kann transparent wie Glas sein, aber auch undurchsichtig wie Keramik. PLA ist einfach dreh- und faltbar, es ist fest und geräuschvoll. PLA kann geprägt werden – es ist SCHÖN.

UNE CONVERSATION TRÈS INTÉRESSANTE SUR LE DESIGN

NatureWorks et IDEO ont travaillé ensemble pour explorer la façon dont le design peut aider à faire connaître les atouts du produit à un public non spécialisé – à travers la publicité, la marque, le marketing et les activités commerciales. Le design instaure un dialogue concret sur le thème de la responsabilité. Le PLA peut inciter les marques à repenser leurs choix de matériaux afin de bâtir des attributs de marque spécifiques. Comme peu de personnes savent parler du plastique avec inspiration et sans ennuyer leur public, nous avons inventé pour le PLA un langage qui parle aux designers et qui nous permet de chercher des synergies avec les marques. Le PLA donne une nouvelle occasion d'apporter un plus à la personnalité du produit ou de son emballage, car c'est un matériau responsable.

Le PLA est fabriqué à partir d'ingrédients naturels, comme le maïs. Le PLA peut être composté, brûlé et recyclé, tout comme le papier – c'est un matériau NATUREL. Le PLA ne libère pas de produits chimiques toxiques et est naturellement antimicrobien – c'est un matériau SAIN. Le PLA peut être transparent comme du verre, ou opaque comme de la céramique. Le PLA est facile à tordre et à plier, et il est rigide et sonore. Le PLA est facile à travailler en relief, même avec des reliefs très prononcés – c'est un BEAU matériau.

LEFT: THE SHOPPING BAG

The humble shopping bag sparks conversations about materials. PLA film can be woven to reduce noise and bonded to PLA fabric to create a luxurious handle. This concept integrates fabric and film. Both are NATURAL, from annually renewable natural resources. A fabric handle softens the plastic surfaces of this bag to make it easier to carry.

ABOVE: WATER FOR RESTAURANTS

The water carafe is a symbol of purity and integrity with its thick glass-like structure. PLA imparts no flavour or odour to its contents, so all you taste is the water. This concept is about the clarity of PLA as a bottle. It has thick walls that increase the barrier properties of the packaging and exaggerate the stiffness of the material. It is a pure and NATURAL plastic bottle that looks and feels like glass and can be part of a system of composting.

LINKS: EINKAUFSTASCHE

Eine einfache Einkaufstasche löst einen Dialog über Materialien aus. PLA-Folie kann zur Geräuschreduzierung verwoben und mit PLA-Textilien zu einem luxuriösen Handgriff verbunden werden. Dieses Konzept verbindet Textilfaser und Folie. Beide sind NATÜRLICH, aus erneuerbaren natürlichen Ressourcen. Durch den Stoffüberzug wird der Kunststoffgriff weicher.

OBEN: WASSER FÜR RESTAURANTS

Mit ihrer dicken, glasähnlichen Struktur ist die Wasserkaraffe ein Symbol für Reinheit und Integrität. PLA ist absolut geruchs- und geschmacksneutral, das Wasser schmeckt vollkommen rein. Dieses Konzept zeigt die Durchsichtigkeit von PLA-Flaschen. Die Wandstärke verdeutlicht zugleich die Möglichkeiten des Materials als Verpackung und seine Festigkeit. Es ist eine reine Flasche aus NATÜRLICHEM Kunststoff, die optisch und haptisch wie Glas wirkt und kompostierbar ist.

À GAUCHE: LE SAC À PROVISIONS

Le modeste sac à provisions déclenche des conversations animées sur les matériaux. Le film plastique de PLA peut être tramé pour réduire le bruit et soudé à du tissu de PLA pour créer une anse magnifique. Ce concept associe tissu et film. Les deux sont NATURELS, et fabriqués à partir de ressources renouvelables chaque année. L'anse en tissu rend le plastique plus doux au toucher et le sac plus facile à porter.

CI-DESSUS: DE L'EAU POUR LES RESTAURANTS

La carafe d'eau est un symbole de pureté et d'intégrité, avec ses parois épaisses qui ressemblent à du verre. Le PLA ne donne aucun goût ni aucune odeur à ce qu'il contient, on ne sent que le goût de l'eau. Pour ce concept, ce qui est important c'est la transparence de la bouteille en PLA. Elle a des parois épaisses qui renforcent ses propriétés de protection et la dureté du matériau. C'est une bouteille en plastique pur et NATUREL qui ressemble à du verre et peut faire partie d'un système de compostage.

MILK PUDDING

The pudding mould tells a story about pure healthy packaging and celebrates the ability of PLA to be moulded with tiny details, such as a vanilla flower. Embossing is a feature on the packaging and shows up on the surface of the pudding. The base is thermoformed PLA and the lid metallised PLA. For dairy-based products, the HEALTHY attributes of PLA as a plastic are very relevant to consumers.

PUDDINGFORM

Die Puddingform wird in einer gesunden Verpackung präsentiert und verdeutlicht zugleich, wie gut PLA formbar ist: Sogar feine Details – wie etwa eine Vanilleblüte – treten deutlich hervor. Die Prägung auf der Verpackung findet sich auch auf der Oberfläche des Puddings. Der Boden besteht aus thermogeformtem PLA, der Deckel aus metallbeschichtetem PLA. Besonders bei Molkereiprodukten ist der GESUNDHEITSASPEKT von PLA für die Verbraucher sehr wichtig.

LE DESSERT AU LAIT

Pour ce moule à dessert, ce qui compte c'est le caractère pur et sain de l'emballage. De plus, on a exploité ici les possibilités de travail en relief et tout en finesse du PLA, avec un motif de fleur de vanille. La fleur est travaillée en relief sur l'emballage, et est transférée sur le dessert. La base est fabriquée en PLA thermoformé et le couvercle en PLA métallisé. Pour les produits laitiers, il est très important que les clients sachent que le plastique de l'emballage est SAIN.

POTATO CHIPS

The pleated film is as noisy, crisp, crunchy and fresh as the potato chips inside. The packaging sounds like the product. The concept uses PLA's aesthetic attributes; in particular its crunchy quality to link the consumer to the product inside. The PLA film would be metallised or layered with other plastics to provide adequate barrier resistance. The surface of this bag creates a tactile, multi-sensorial experience – it's BEAUTIFUL.

KARTOFFELCHIPS

Die gefaltete Folie ist genauso geräuschvoll, knackig, knusprig und frisch wie die darin enthaltenen Kartoffelchips. Die Verpackung klingt wie das Produkt selbst. Das Konzept baut auf den ästhetischen Eigenschaften von PLA auf, vor allem auf das knisternde Geräusch, das der Verbraucher sofort mit dem Inhalt assoziieren soll. Die PLA-Folie sollte für eine adäquate Verpackungsleistung und Strapazierfähigkeit mit Metall oder Kunststoff beschichtet sein. Die Tüte erzeugt eine multisensorische Erfahrung – sie ist SCHÖN.

LES CHIPS

Le film plissé est aussi bruyant, croquant, croustillant et frais que les chips de pomme de terre qu'il contient. L'emballage fait le même bruit que le produit. Le concept utilise les attributs esthétiques du PLA, en particulier son croquant, pour jeter un pont entre le consommateur et le produit. Le film de PLA peut être métallisé ou superposé à d'autres plastiques pour apporter une protection adéquate au produit. Ce sac donne des sensations tactiles et multisensorielles – il est BEAU.

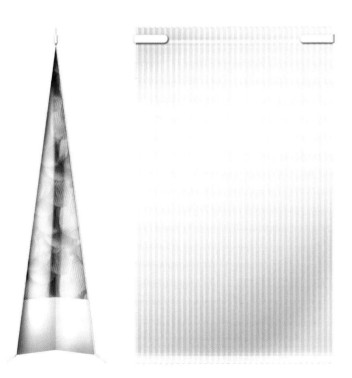

A PERFUME-BOTTLE

The perfume folded paper packaging alludes to the non permanence and disposability of fashion. It's a simple but luxurious packaging for high-end perfume.

The concept of integrating PLA into paper-based folded and sealed packaging technology needs to be explored further, but it is intriguing how this simple technology can be made BEAUTIFUL with the use of PLA on its own or as a laminated or coated layer on paper. A white, talc-filled PLA feels like ceramic and communicates elements of luxury. The PLA material itself provides barrier resistance to aroma preserving the perfume inside. This packaging, if proven technically feasible, could make composting folded packaging possible.

PARFÜMFLASCHE

Die gefaltete Papierverpackung spielt auf die Vergänglichkeit und Schnelllebigkeit der Mode an. Es ist eine einfache, aber luxuriöse Verpackung für ein hochwertiges Parfüm.
Bei dieser Verpackung wird PLA mit Papier kombiniert und mit einer Falt- und Versiegelungstechnologie verarbeitet. Sie zeigt, wie SCHÖN PLA allein oder als Laminier- bzw. Beschichtungsmaterial für Papier gestaltet werden kann. Weißes, mit Talkum kombiniertes PLA fühlt sich wie Keramik an und wirkt luxuriös. PLA selbst bietet eine hervorragende Barriereleistung und versiegelt die zarten Parfümaromen in der Packung. Falls diese Verpackungstechnologien realisiert werden, sind kompostierbare Faltverpackungen möglich.

UNE BOUTEILLE DE PARFUM

Le conditionnement pour parfum en papier plié fait référence au caractère temporel et jetable de la mode. C'est un emballage simple mais splendide pour un parfum de luxe.
Il faut explorer davantage cette idée d'intégrer le PLA à la technologie d'emballage en papier plié et scellé, mais il est fascinant de voir ce que le PLA, utilisé seul, stratifié ou en couche de finition sur le papier peut apporter en termes de BEAUTÉ à cette technologie toute simple. Le PLA blanc et mélangé à du talc ressemble à de la céramique et transmet une impression de luxe. Le PLA en tant que matériau protège l'arôme et conserve le parfum qu'il contient. Si l'on prouve que c'est techniquement faisable, cette solution pourrait permettre le compostage des emballages pliés.

BABY SHAMPOO

This concept links HEALTHY products with healthy packaging and provides a tactile collectible toy for babies to play with while mum bathes them. The packaging reinforces the safe gentle qualities of the product inside.
In this portfolio we have captured PLA's unique attributes and used them to inspire design. The packaging concepts tell a story to NatureWorks' customers that demonstrates how PLA can connect to specific brand values while introducing the idea of small steps towards responsibility.

BABY-SHAMPOO

Dieses Konzept verbindet ein NATÜRLICHES Produkt mit einer natürlichen Verpackung und ist zugleich ein Spielzeug, mit dem Babys spielen können, wenn sie gebadet werden. Die Verpackung unterstreicht die besonderen Eigenschaften des Produkts – Sicherheit und Sanftheit.
In diesem Portfolio haben wir die einzigartigen Eigenschaften von PLA als Inspiration genutzt und sie in innovative Entwürfe umgesetzt. Die Verpackungskonzepte zeigen den Kunden von NatureWorks, wie hervorragend mit PLA bestimmte Markenwerte transportiert und gleichzeitig schrittweise Umweltverantwortung kommuniziert werden können.

LE SHAMPOOING POUR BÉBÉ

Ce concept associe produit SAIN et emballage sain, et peut servir de jouet aux bébés pendant que leur mère leur donne le bain. L'emballage souligne les qualités de douceur et d'innocuité du produit qu'il contient.
Dans ce portfolio, nous avons présenté les avantages exceptionnels du PLA et nous en avons tiré l'inspiration pour créer des emballages. Ces concepts racontent aux clients de NatureWorks une histoire qui démontre que le PLA peut entrer en synergie avec des valeurs de marque spécifiques, tout en introduisant une notion de cheminement vers la responsabilité.

Case 02
Boots Essentials

Steve Gibbons,
founder of Dew Gibbons

Boots Essentials has been a best-selling line for bath and shower at leading British retailer Boots. In this case study, Dew Gibbons, a London-based design office explores the making of the redesign for the whole range of products, which have been on the market for over a decade.

Boots has always recognised how important design is in building perceptions of its brand. And we have been fortunate enough to work with the company, almost continuously, since starting our business in 1997.

This particular project involved a major review of a wide number of product categories. And as the final name suggests it encompassed many of the more basic products that can be purchased at Boots. These included: hair care, bathing, dental care, foot care, eye care, accessories, medicines and first-aid products; in fact, many of the areas that represent the core of the Boots product offer. All told, it encompassed over 500 products divided among 30 or so ranges.

We had license to influence every aspect of the project; so for instance, we were able to recommend not only the colour of the product but also a particular ingredient or fragrance.

Our specific task was to develop a name for this new range, an accompanying visual identity, and packaging designs – both structural and graphic.

We knew from research amongst Boots' consumers that they found it hard to identify the Boots basic offer in-store; and when they did manage to find it they thought it boring and old-fashioned. They also thought it to be more expensive than the supermarkets, but without any additional benefits.

In recent years the supermarkets have overhauled their approach to marketing health and beauty products; massively expanding the ranges of branded products they offer and investing heavily in their own brand ranges.

Our brief was to create a brand that was more stylish than the supermarkets own brand options, easier to find and represented value for money. There was also an additional specific requirement to reduce the current cost of packaging through its life cycle, up to the point it is sold in-store.

We started by auditing all the existing products that fell under the 'basics' umbrella, from both a technical and aesthetic standpoint. We needed to understand the nature of the product and its packaging, and to what extent we could dictate how it could change. For instance, we needed to know if we could change the colour and consistency of a product. Could a hair conditioner be transparent? It could not. How do bottles run down the manufacturer's production line when they are filled? Could we print more colours on the label with little extra cost? We could. All these factors needed to be weighed in the balance as we moved forward with the project.

From a graphic perspective we started with colour. Even though these products are all basics, they need to find a place that stylistically fits in consumers' homes and matches or complements their décor. As a consumer, even if you're buying more basic formulations you'll choose a better looking pack over an ugly one. Simple bold colours will fit with most décors, and with many of the products we were able to offer a choice of colour.

Following the influence of a plethora of lifestyle magazines and TV makeover shows in Britain, consumers are becoming much more interested in how they style their homes, and pay particular attention to everything they put into them. A contemporary, minimal aesthetic is now in the ascendancy, and consumers want products that make a statement about themselves and their taste. Products that might once have been hidden away can now be out on show – both in the bathroom and the kitchen.

We had already decided that we wanted to celebrate colour with this project, and at an early stage explored the possibility of developing a palette of colours that would meet the needs of every product type and category.

Of course colour changes depend on the substance it's applied to, whether it lies on the surface or is embedded in it, and how light refracts through it or reflects on it. So we created a whole spectrum of colours using actual products in clear PVC bottles (the only way to properly appreciate their potential). From these we created, amongst others, palettes for translucent products, for opaque products, and for the male product range.

Next we thought about shape. We needed a family of shapes that could work across a wide variety of packaging formats, and would meet both the aesthetic and functional needs of the project. Given that the number of pack formats had been drastically reduced and individual format volumes had significantly increased, a cost analysis showed that a set of new tools could be built using the 'soft brick' structure across the majority of formats. For those where volumes were too low we were able to source off-the-shelf formats that matched. The 'soft brick' seemed to us to be the perfect solution. It had a contemporary feel, it allowed for a large front face on the shelf (as opposed, for instance, to a cylinder which has poor shelf impact), it was incredibly efficient to pack and transport, and easily ran down the

manufacturer's lines. We also considered all
the various closures, caps, pumps, etc, and
managed to rationalise componentry down
from 44 to 16 items. This made a significant
saving as larger volumes were bought more
cheaply and the whole process became far
less complex to manage. New products could
also be brought far more quickly to market,
by selecting from a reduced inventory of
formats and using easy-to-follow design
guidelines for quick implementation.

*Born in Luton, <u>Steve Gibbons</u> studied at the
Royal College of Art. He set up Dew Gibbons
with fellow creative partner Shaun Dew in 1997
and continues to enjoy working for a variety of
clients, from major multinationals to small not-
for-profit organisations. In its 9 years of trading
Dew Gibbons has won over 50 creative awards.
Current clients include: BBC, Coca-Cola,
Clairol, De Beers LV, Sara Lee Courtaulds,
The Boots Group, Invista, Procter & Gamble
and Vidal Sassoon.*

**Die Produktreihe Boots Essentials der
Drogeriemarktkette Boots hat sich im
Bereich Badeartikel zum Verkaufsschlager
entwickelt. In dieser Fallstudie widmet sich
das Team des Londoner Designbüros Dew
Gibbons den Möglichkeiten eines Neu-
designs für die gesamte Produktlinie, die
seit über einem Jahrzehnt im Handel ist.**

Boots wusste schon immer, wie wichtig
Design für den Aufmerksamkeitswert ihrer
Marke ist. Wir sind stolz darauf, seit Beginn
unserer Tätigkeit 1997 kontinuierlich mit
dieser Firma zusammenzuarbeiten.

Bei diesem Projekt sollte eine Vielzahl
unterschiedlicher Produktkategorien überarbeitet werden. Wie der Projektname bereits
andeutet, handelte es sich dabei um die Basisprodukte (Produkte des täglichen Bedarfs)
von Boots. Dazu zählen u. a. Produkte aus den
Bereichen Baden, Haar-, Zahn-, Fuß- und
Augenpflege, Accessoires, Gesundheit sowie
Erste Hilfe. Diese Bereiche sind das Kern-
geschäft von Boots. Es umfasst über 500
Produkte aus etwa 30 Produktreihen.

Wir konnten alle Aspekte eines Produktes
beeinflussen. So durften wir beispielsweise
nicht nur die Farbe eines Produktes vor-
schlagen, sondern auch einen speziellen
Inhaltsstoff oder eine besondere Duftnote.

Unsere Aufgabe war, einen Namen für die
neue Reihe, eine dazu passende optische
Identität und das Verpackungsdesign
(sowohl die Formen als auch deren grafische
Gestaltung) zu entwickeln.

Umfragen ergaben, dass die Kunden
Schwierigkeiten hatten, die Basisprodukte in
den Boots-Geschäften zu identifizieren, und
diese langweilig oder altmodisch fanden.
Außerdem wurden sie im Vergleich zu den
Konkurrenzprodukten in den Supermärkten
als zu teuer beurteilt. Ein Zusatznutzen war
für die Kunden nicht erkennbar.

In den letzten Jahren haben Supermärkte
ihre Marketingstrategie für Gesundheits-
und Schönheitsprodukte erneuert, ihr Mar
kenangebot stark erweitert und in Eigenmarken investiert.

Wir sollten nun eine Marke kreieren, die
stilvoller war als die Eigenmarken der Supermärkte. Außerdem sollte sie preiswert
und einfacher im Sortiment zu finden sein.
Zusätzlich sollten die Verpackungskosten,
die von der Produktion bis zum Verkauf im
Laden anfallen, reduziert werden.

Zunächst untersuchten wir alle Produkte,
die als Basisprodukte bezeichnet wurden,
unter technischen und ästhetischen Aspekten.
Wir wollten die Eigenart der Produkte und
ihrer Verpackungen verstehen, um festzustel-
len, inwieweit wir sie verändern konnten. So
mussten wir z. B. zunächst klären, ob Farbe
oder Konsistenz eines Produktes geändert
werden kann (ob eine Haarkur z. B. farblos
sein kann – was nicht möglich war –), wie
Flaschen durch eine Abfüllanlage laufen oder
ob wir die Etiketten zu geringfügig höheren
Kosten farbenfroher gestalten konnten.
Letzteres war machbar. All diese Faktoren
mussten während des Projektverlaufs berücksichtigt werden.

Aus grafischer Sicht begannen wir mit
der Farbe. Auch wenn es sich bei den
Produkten um Alltagsprodukte handelte,
mussten sie so gestaltet werden, dass sie
stilistisch die Inneneinrichtung der
Konsumenten ergänzten oder dazu passten. Denn auch bei Alltagsprodukten
greifen Konsumenten eher zu einer schönen als zu einer hässlichen Packung.
Einfache, kräftige Farben passen zu allem,
und für die meisten Produkte konnten wir
eine Farbauswahl anbieten.

Lifestile-Magazine und Renovierungs-
Shows im britischen Fernsehen haben dazu
geführt, dass Konsumenten heute mehr Wert
auf die Einrichtung ihre Häuser und auf kleine Details legen. Das moderne minimalisti-
sche Design hat zur Folge, dass immer mehr
Verbraucher mit den erworbenen Produkten
ihren Geschmack und Stil zum Ausdruck
bringen. Produkte, die früher ein verstecktes
Dasein im Schrank führten, werden nun stolz
im Bad oder in der Küche präsentiert.

Wir entschieden uns bereits früh dafür,
dass Farbe bei diesem Projekt eine bedeu-

tende Rolle spielen sollte. Von Anfang an suchten wir nach Möglichkeiten, eine Farbpalette zu entwickeln, die den Ansprüchen aller Produkttypen und -kategorien gerecht werden würde.

Farben wirken unterschiedlich, je nachdem, mit welchem Material sie kombiniert werden, ob sie auf die Oberfläche aufgetragen oder in ein Material eingebracht werden und ob das Licht vom Material reflektiert wird oder hindurchscheint. Daher entwarfen wir ein ganzes Spektrum an Farben für durchsichtige PVC-Flaschen (um die Farben wirklich beurteilen zu können). Daraus entwickelten wir dann Paletten für durchsichtige Produkte, undurchsichtige Produkte sowie eine Produktreihe für den Herrn.

Dann beschäftigten wir uns mit der Form. Wir benötigten eine Gruppe von Formen, die für verschiedenste Verpackungsformate geeignet war und gleichzeitig den ästhetischen wie auch funktionalen Ansprüchen des Projektes genügen würde. Die Anzahl der Packungsformate sollte drastisch reduziert, die Verpackungsgrößen aber erhöht werden. Eine Kostenanalyse ergab, dass der Bau neuer Maschinen, die die Verpackungsform des „Soft Brick" (weicher Ziegelstein) auf die meisten benötigten Formate anwenden konnte, interessant sein könnte. Für die Formate, deren Volumen zu gering war, konnten wir passende vorkonfektionierte Verpackungen finden. Der „Soft Brick" erschien uns als Ideallösung, da er modern wirkt, im Regal eine große Frontfläche aufweist (im Gegensatz zu einem Zylinder mit schlechter Regalwirkung), im Hinblick auf Verpackung und Transport sehr effizient ist und die Produktionsstraßen problemlos durchlief. Ebenso intensiv untersuchten wir die verschiedenen Verschlüsse, Kappen,

Pumpen usw. und konnten die Komponentenzahl erfolgreich von 44 auf 16 senken. Dies führte zu einer nicht unerheblichen Kostenersparnis, da größere Stückzahlen zu geringeren Preisen bezogen werden konnten und der gesamte Prozess einfacher gestaltet wurde. Außerdem konnten durch die geringere Anzahl an Formaten und durch die klaren Designrichtlinien neue Produkte schneller auf den Markt gebracht werden.

Steve Gibbons wurde in Luton, England, geboren und studierte am Royal College of Art. 1997 gründete er gemeinsam mit Shaun Dew die Agentur Dew Gibbons. Seitdem waren die Partner für eine Vielzahl von Kunden tätig, zu denen multinationale Konzerne ebenso wie kleine Non-Profit-Organisationen gehören. In den neun Jahren ihres Bestehens hat die Agentur Dew Gibbons über 50 Auszeichnungen erhalten. Zu ihren Kunden zählen unter anderem die BBC, Coca-Cola, Clairol, De Beers LV, Sara Lee Courtaulds, The Boots Group, Invista, Procter & Gamble und Vidal Sassoon.

Boots Essentials est une ligne pour le bain et la douche qui rencontre un grand succès dans les magasins britanniques Boots. Dans cette étude de cas, Dew Gibbons, une agence de design londonienne, explore les coulisses du remodelage de toute la ligne de produits, présente sur le marché depuis plus de dix ans.

Boots a toujours eu conscience de l'importance du design dans l'impression que leur marque cause au public, et nous avons eu la chance de travailler avec eux de manière presque continue depuis la naissance de notre agence en 1997.

Pour ce projet, il s'agissait de repenser en profondeur un grand nombre de catégories de produits. Et comme le nom du projet le suggère, cela englobait une grande partie de l'offre de base de Boots, dont les produits de soin capillaire, les produits de bain, de soin dentaire, de soin des pieds, de soin des yeux, les accessoires, les médicaments et les produits de premier secours. En définitive, il s'agissait de plus de 500 produits répartis sur 30 gammes.

Nous pouvions agir sur tous les aspects du projet. Par exemple, nous pouvions recommander non seulement la couleur du produit mais aussi un ingrédient ou un parfum en particulier.

Notre tâche consistait à trouver le nom et l'identité visuelle de cette nouvelle gamme, ainsi qu'à en concevoir les emballages, en termes de structure et de graphisme.

Une étude réalisée auprès des clients de Boots nous a révélé qu'ils avaient des difficultés à identifier les produits de base de Boots en magasin. Et lorsqu'ils arrivaient à les trouver, ils les trouvaient ennuyeux et dépassés. Ils pensaient aussi qu'ils étaient plus chers que les produits des supermarchés, sans pour autant proposer d'avantages supplémentaires.

Ces dernières années, les supermarchés ont modernisé leur approche marketing des produits de santé et de beauté. Ils ont énormément élargi leur offre de produits de marque, et ont beaucoup investi dans les produits de leur propre marque.

Notre mission était de créer une marque plus élégante que les marques des supermarchés, plus facile à trouver, avec un meilleur rapport qualité/prix. Nous devions égale-

ent trouver le moyen de réduire le coût de
mballage tout au long de son cycle de vie,
squ'au moment de la vente en magasin.
Nous avons commencé par analyser tous
s produits existants qui correspondaient
a catégorie des « essentiels » d'un point
vue technique et esthétique. Nous avions
soin de comprendre la nature du produit et
son emballage, et la mesure dans laquelle
us pouvions la faire évoluer. Par exemple,
us devions savoir si nous pouvions changer
couleur et la consistance du produit : un
mêlant peut-il être transparent (non), quel
t le processus de fabrication exact des bou-
illes, et peut-on imprimer plus de couleurs
r l'étiquette sans que cela ne suppose des
ûts supplémentaires importants (oui) ?
us ces facteurs devaient être pris en comp-
au fur et à mesure que nous avancions
ns le projet.
Pour le graphisme, nous avons commencé
r la couleur. Bien que ces produits soient
us des produits de base, ils doivent s'adap-
r au style des intérieurs des consomma-
urs et compléter leur décoration. En tant
e consommateur, même si vous achetez des
roduits de base, vous allez toujours préférer
emballage esthétique plutôt que le
ntraire. Des couleurs simples et vives
nctionnent bien avec la plupart des décora-
ons, et pour de nombreux produits nous
ons pu proposer un choix de couleurs.
Au Royaume-Uni, les magazines de
coration et les émissions de télévision sur
relookage des intérieurs abondent. Les
nsommateurs s'intéressent de plus en plus
la décoration de leur foyer, et sélectionnent
igneusement les objets qu'ils y font entrer.
esthétique minimaliste et contemporaine a
aintenant le vent en poupe, et les consom-
ateurs veulent des produits qui reflètent

leur personnalité et leurs goûts. Les produits
que l'on cachait sont maintenant en exposition permanente, aussi bien dans la salle de
bain que dans la cuisine.

Pour ce projet, nous avions décidé de jouer
la carte de la couleur, et dès le départ nous
avons étudié la possibilité d'élaborer une
palette de couleurs correspondant aux besoins
de chaque type et catégorie de produit.

Bien sûr, pour modifier la couleur il faut
tenir compte de la substance sur laquelle elle
va être appliquée, qu'elle soit posée en
couche de surface ou intégrée à la matière, et
de la façon dont la lumière passe à travers ou
se reflète dessus. Nous avons donc créé tout
un éventail de couleurs en utilisant des
répliques de produits en PVC transparent
(la seule manière d'évaluer correctement leur
potentiel). À partir de là, nous avons créé des
palettes pour les produits translucides, pour
les produits opaques et pour la ligne
masculine, entre autres.

Ensuite nous avons étudié la forme. Nous
avions besoin d'une famille de formes qui
pourrait s'adapter à une grande variété de
formats, et qui répondrait aux critères esthétiques et fonctionnels du projet. Étant donné
que le nombre de formats d'emballage avait
été radicalement réduit, et que les volumes
de chaque format avaient considérablement
augmenté, une analyse de coûts a montré que
l'on pouvait concevoir un nouvel ensemble
d'outils et utiliser la structure de la « brique
molle » pour la majorité des formats. Pour
ceux dont le volume était trop faible, nous
avons pu trouver des formats standard qui
correspondaient à nos besoins. La « brique
molle » nous a semblé être la solution parfaite. Elle a un style contemporain, elle est
bien visible dans les rayons (contrairement
au cylindre, par exemple, qui a une visibilité

réduite et donc peu d'impact), elle est
incroyablement rentable à emballer et à
transporter, et elle se prête très bien à la
fabrication en chaîne. Nous avons également
étudié tous les systèmes de fermeture,
bouchons, pompes, etc. et nous avons réussi
à réduire les accessoires de 44 à 16 articles.
Cela nous a permis de faire des économies
considérables, car le prix à l'unité baisse
lorsque le volume acheté est plus important,
et l'ensemble du processus est beaucoup
moins complexe à gérer. Les nouveaux produits peuvent également entrer beaucoup
plus rapidement sur le marché, car le choix
de formats est plus réduit et il suffit d'appliquer des lignes directrices faciles à suivre
pour une mise en œuvre plus rapide.

*Steve Gibbons est né à Luton et a étudié au
Royal College of Art. Il a fondé l'agence Dew
Gibbons avec son partenaire créatif Shaun Dew
en 1997, et travaille toujours pour des clients
très variés, grandes multinationales ou petites
organisations à but non lucratif. Pendant ses
9 années d'activité, Dew Gibbons a remporté
plus de 50 prix de création. On trouve parmi
les clients actuels de l'agence des sociétés comme
la BBC, Coca-Cola, Clairol, De Beers LV, Sara
Lee Courtaulds, The Boots Group, Invista,
Procter & Gamble et Vidal Sassoon.*

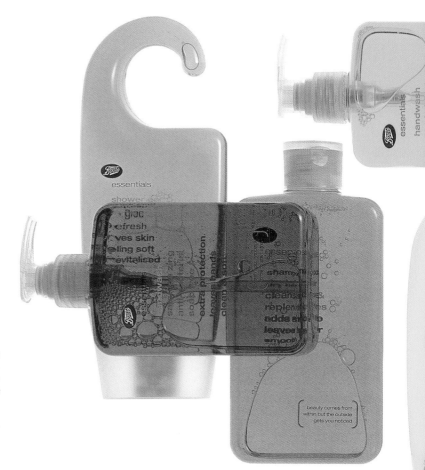

TYPOGRAPHY

*We wanted the typography to be clear, simple
and understated. In controlling the point-of-
sale environment retailers have a big advantage over brand owners. We wanted the Boots
Essentials range to have presence in-store
through its strength of colour presented en
masse. We knew the understated typography
would look sophisticated and stylish in the
home environment.*

TYPOGRAFIE

*Wir wollten eine Typografie, die klar, einfach
und zurückhaltend ist. Einzelhandelsketten
haben gegenüber Markengeschäften den
großen Vorteil, dass sie die Verkaufsumgebung
kontrollieren können. Wir wollten, dass die
Boots-Essentials-Produktreihe allein schon
durch ihre Masse und Farbigkeit auffiel. Die
zurückhaltende Eleganz der Typografie sollte
in der häuslichen Umgebung des Kunden stil-
und geschmackvoll minimalistisch wirken.*

TYPOGRAPHIE

*Nous voulions que la typographie soit
claire, simple et sobre. En ce qui concerne
le contrôle de l'environnement sur le lieu de
vente, les distributeurs ont un grand avantage
sur les propriétaires de marque. Nous voulions que la couleur des produits de la gamme
Boots Essentials, présentés ensemble en
magasin, leur donne de la présence. Nous
savions qu'une typographie sobre donnerait
un résultat élégant et raffiné dans les foyers
des consommateurs.*

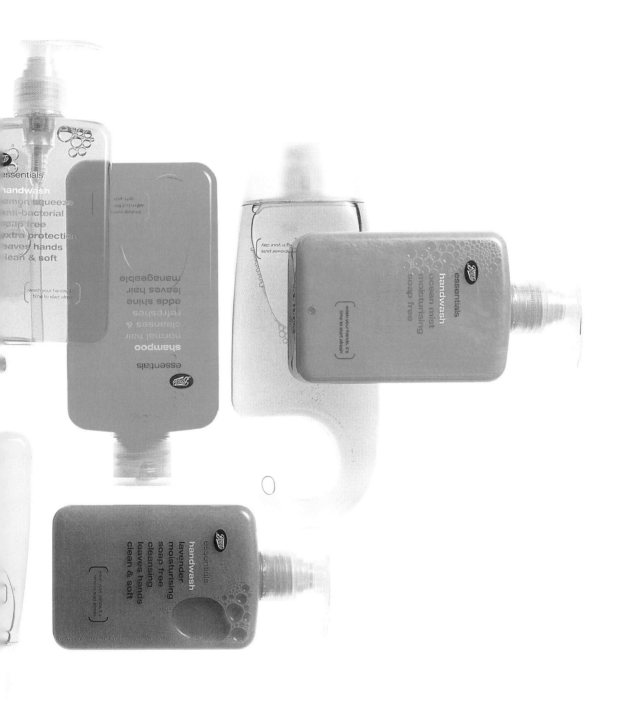

HIERARCHY

Underneath the branding the typography is arranged as a simple hierarchy; first the product name, then its description, then its benefit – all explained in straightforward language.

HIERARCHIE

Unter dem Markennamen ist der Aufdruck in einfacher Hierarchie gegliedert: zuerst der Produktname, dann die Beschreibung, dann der Nutzen – erklärt in einfacher, unkomplizierter Sprache.

HIÉRARCHIE

Sous le nom de la marque, la typographie établit une hiérarchie très simple : tout d'abord le nom du produit, ensuite sa description, puis ses avantages – le tout dans un langage simple et direct.

LANGUAGE

As well as using colour, shape and understated typography to communicate style, we also used language. Each product has its own 'wellbeing' sentence as a footmark, so a dental care pack carries the legend 'smile more, it's catching', a hair care pack says 'beauty comes from within, but the outside gets you noticed', and a bath care pack has the phrase, 'most daily stress is water soluble'.

SPRACHE

Neben Farbe, Form und Typografie nutzen wir auch die Sprache, um Stil zu vermitteln. Als Fußnote trägt jedes Produkt einen Ratschlag für das Wohlbefinden: Bei Zahnpflegeprodukten steht beispielsweise „smile more, it's catching" (lächeln Sie mehr, es steckt an), ein Haarpflegeprodukt trägt die Aufschrift „beauty comes from within, but the outside gets you noticed" (Schönheit kommt von innen, aber durch Ihr Äußeres fallen Sie auf), und ein Pflegebad rät: „Most daily stress is water soluble" (der meiste Stress ist wasserlöslich)

LANGAGE

Tout comme nous avons utilisé la couleur, la forme et une typographie sobre pour exprimer le style des produits, nous avons aussi travaillé sur le langage. Chaque produit a sa petite accroche « bien-être ». Par exemple une boîte de produit de soin dentaire porte la phrase : « souriez davantage, c'est contagieux » ; un produit de soin capillaire : « la beauté vient de l'intérieur, mais l'extérieur vous fera remarquer » ; et pour un produit pour le bain : « le stress quotidien est soluble dans l'eau ».

PERCEPTION
The project has proved to be enormously
successful for Boots with consumers saying
it has changed their perception of the retailer
and has encouraged them to re-evaluate the
Boots own-brand offer. They see Boots Essentials as far more stylish and modern than
Tesco's own brand.

WAHRNEHMUNG

Das Projekt hat sich als äußerst erfolgreich
für Boots erwiesen. Kunden gaben an, sie hät-
ten ihre Meinung über diese Einzelhandels-
kette geändert und das Warenangebot von
Boot genauer betrachtet. Sie halten heute
Boots Essentials für stilvoller und moderner
als die Hausmarke von Tesco.

PERCEPTION

Le projet s'est avéré être un grand succès pour
Boots. Les consommateurs ont déclaré que
leur perception du distributeur avait changé et
qu'ils voyaient l'offre de produits de la marque
Boots sous un nouveau jour. La gamme Boots
Essentials est considérée comme beaucoup
plus élégante et moderne que la marque Tesco.

Case 03
Food to Go

Charlotte Raphael,
Design Chief at Marks & Spencer

Food-to-go is one of the major categories for food retailers in the world. In this case study, Charlotte Raphael, chief designer at leading retailer Marks & Spencer, examines how the company made a turnaround is this area by investing in good and effective package design to completely change the appeal of the product line.

The food to go area was losing market share to contemporary sandwich shops, so the brief required a complete overhaul of the range in terms of brand proposition, customer targeting and in-store experience.

The target audience is predominantly female [72:28] and has a bias towards younger more affluent profiles. These customers are very attracted to new products and prepared to pay for better quality. They're looking for products that are quick and easy to shop for. They're also concerned about the overpackaging of food, especially for the food to go sector, so they are looking for products that address that environmental issue.

The range had to have a clear identity, but we didn't want to create a sub-brand, so we started looking at shapes that could work as identifiers. From a number of natural, organic shapes we arrived at the concentric circle motif. It had the soft, natural qualities we wanted, as well as a simple modernity and the ability to act as a clear identifier.

The circle has been used in a variety of ways across the range. In sandwiches, for example, there was a need for colour coding to distinguish the different types of fillings – meat, fish, poultry or vegetarian – so the circles were used to hold the colours. On juices, where no colour coding was needed, the circles appear as a frosted motif.

Tone of voice was an important part of the design mix and in order to relate to this younger, trendier customer we used a relaxed, friendly tone to communicate messages about our passion for food and our standards in general. On juices, for example, we went for a freshness message: "We don't hang around when we're making this juice… the oranges are squeezed and bottled within 24 hours." On sandwiches, we had the opportunity to communicate an important generic message about the kind of thing that distinguishes us from our competitors.

"We're the only retailer to use free-range eggs in all our products, even in our mayo."

We also knew that this customer took a keen interest in environmental matters, so we tapped into this with messages like these: "You can trust our food to be 100% non GM (we're rated No. 1 retailer by Greenpeace)."

We also used the concentric circle device for copy, enclosing a couple of adjectives that described key flavours within it. So, for example, on an avocado & spinach salad, we used "smooth & nutty". On a duck wrap, it was "rich & succulent". This highlighted the full-flavoured qualities of the product as well as making it even easier for the customer to shop the range – this kind of lunchtime buying has to be fast, and stet the customer information on flavour at a glance really helps.

On front of pack, we stripped the titles right down to the essential ingredients and kept the look very clean by having no subcopy – this was included on back of pack. Doing this enabled us to have a large, clear title which was easy for the customer to read.

The font for our conversational messages was a handwritten script. This gave a friendly, natural impression – as though the sand-

wiches had been made up in somebody's kitchen and just scribbled on.

The team sourced salad bowls made of 50% recycled plastic and juice bottles usin 30% recycled materials. Sandwich boxes u 100% sustainable packaging, with window made from biodegradable cornstarch rathe than plastic and for every four trees that cut down to make the cardboard we plant five more!

We also worked with physical packaging designers to create a new type of box – recently patented – that would help comba the awkwardness of eating a sandwich on go. The innovative solution now features a unique, easy to open "zip" that runs aroun the side of the pack. This allows the pack t open into a flat tray creating your own litt plate from which to eat your sandwich.

Charlotte Raphael was born in London. In 1991 she graduated from Kingston Univer ty with an honours degree in Graphic Design. She joined Marks and Spencer in 1994 and w appointed as Head of Packaging Design in 2(

Produkte für den Direktverzehr erlang im Lebensmittelhandel immer mehr Gewicht. In dieser Fallstudie schildert die Chefdesignerin der britischen Warenhauskette Marks & Spencer, Charlotte Raphael, wie das Unternehme in diesem Produktbereich eine Kehrtwende einleitete, indem es in gute und praktische Verpackungen investiert

Der Bereich „Food To Go" (Snackbereich verlor Marktanteile an moderne Sandwich-

ops. Der Auftrag umfasste daher eine voll-
mmene Überarbeitung der Produktreihe in
zug auf Markenposition, Kundenansprache
d Kauferlebnis im Geschäft.

Die Zielgruppe ist vorwiegend weiblich
(:28) mit einer Tendenz zu einer jüngeren,
hlhabenderen Klientel. Diese Kunden wer-
n stark von neuen Produkten angelockt und
d bereit, für bessere Qualität mehr zu zah-
. Sie suchen nach Produkten, die schnell
d einfach zu kaufen sind. Sie sind aber auch
tisch gegenüber zu viel Verpackungs-
terial, besonders im Snackbereich. Sie
chen nach Produkten, deren Verpackungen
weltverträglich sind.

Die Produktreihe musste eine klare
entität haben, wir wollte aber keine Sub-
arke erzeugen. Daher sahen wir uns nach
rmen um, die als Erkennungsmerkmal
eignet waren. Nachdem wir verschiedene
türliche, organische Formen getestet hat-
, entschieden wir uns schließlich für den
nzentrischen Kreis. Er hat die weiche,
türliche Qualität, nach der wir suchten, ver-
ttelt schlichte Modernität und kann als ein-
utiges Erkennungsmerkmal dienen. Der
eis wird innerhalb der Produktreihe auf
rschiedene Weise genutzt. Bei den
ndwiches benötigten wir beispielsweise eine
rbkodierung, um die verschiedenen Beläge
leisch, Fisch, Geflügel oder Vegetarisches
u unterscheiden, und so wurde der Kreis
terschiedlich eingefärbt. Bei den Säften,
keine Farbkodierung benötigt wurde,
cheint der Kreis als vereistes Motiv.

Auch die Sprache war ein wichtiger
standteil des Designs, denn für diese jün-
re und trendbewusstere Klientel benötig-
wir einen freundlichen, lockeren Tonfall,
die Botschaft der Lebensmittel und die
gemeinen Standards zu vermitteln. Die

Säfte wurden z. B. mit einer Frischenotiz
versehen: „Wir verschwenden keine Zeit,
wenn wir diesen Saft herstellen: Die
Orangen werden innerhalb von 24 Stunden
gepresst und abgefüllt." Bei den Sandwiches
wurde auf den Unterschied zu den
Konkurrenzprodukten hingewiesen:

„Wir sind die einzige Handelskette, die Eier
aus Freilandhaltung in ihren Produkten verwendet, sogar in unserer Mayonnaise."

Da unsere Verbrauchergruppe Wert auf
Umweltbewusstsein legt, wurde auch dieser
Aspekt betont: „Sie können sicher sein, dass
unsere Lebensmittel 100-prozentig nicht gen-
manipuliert sind (wir wurden von Greenpeace
als Nr. 1 im Einzelhandel ausgezeichnet)."

Der konzentrische Kreis kam auch im Text
zum Einsatz, wo er Adjektive umschließt, die
die Hauptgeschmacksnoten beschreiben.
Einen Avocado-Spinat-Salat charakterisierten
wir beispielsweise mit „sanft & nussig", einen
Enten-Wrap als „herzhaft & saftig". Dies ver-
deutlichte nicht nur das Geschmackserlebnis,
sondern erleichterte dem Kunden auch die
Kaufentscheidung – denn der Kauf des Snacks
für die Mittagspause muss schnell erledigt
werden. Die Hauptgeschmacksinformationen
sofort zu erkennen kann dabei hilfreich sein.

Die Vorderseite der Verpackungen wurde
von allen überflüssigen Informationen befreit,
nur der Name und die Hauptzutaten blieben
erhalten. Der Text wurde auf die Rückseite
der Verpackungen verbannt. Dadurch konnten
wir den Produktnamen groß und deutlich
gestalten, sodass er für den Kunden einfach
zu lesen ist.

Als Font für die im Plauderton gehaltenen
Botschaften wurde eine Schreibschrift
gewählt. Dies verlieh den Verpackungen ein
freundliches und natürliches Aussehen – so,
als seien die Sandwiches gerade erst in der

Küche zubereitet und kurz von Hand
beschriftet worden.

Das Team fand Quellen für Salatschüsseln
aus 50 % recyceltem Kunststoff und
Saftflaschen aus 30 % recycelten Materialien.
Die Sandwichverpackungen sind zu 100 %
umweltverträglich, denn das durchsichtige
Verpackungsfenster besteht nicht aus
Kunststoff, sondern aus kompostierbarer
Kornstärke, und für vier Bäume, die zur
Herstellung von Karton abgeholzt werden,
pflanzen wir fünf neue an!

Darüber hinaus haben wir mit Verpackungs-
designern eine neue Art von Karton entwickelt, der kürzlich patentiert wurde. Er sollte den Verzehr eines Sandwiches unterwegs
erleichtern. Die innovative Lösung verfügt
über einen einfach zu öffnenden Aufreißver-
schluss, der um die Verpackung läuft. Die
Verpackung wird so zu einem flachen Tablett
oder Teller, von dem der Kunde sein Sandwich
essen kann.

*Charlotte Raphael wurde in London geboren
und schloss 1991 ihr Grafikdesignstudium an
der Kingston University mit Auszeichnung ab.
Seit 1994 arbeitet sie für Marks & Spencer, wo
sie seit 2004 Leiterin der Abteilung für Verpackungsdesign ist.*

**Les plats à emporter sont une catégorie
très importante pour les magasins d'alimentation du monde entier. Dans cette étude de cas, Charlotte Raphael, directrice du
design pour les magasins Marks & Spencer,
analyse comment l'entreprise a opéré un
changement radical dans ce domaine en
investissant dans des emballages efficaces**

et de qualité afin de modifier l'image de la ligne de produits.

Le secteur des plats à emporter était en déclin à cause des sandwicheries modernes, le projet demandait donc une modernisation profonde de la gamme en termes de proposition de marque, de ciblage de la clientèle et d'organisation dans le magasin.

La cible est constituée majoritairement de femmes [72:28], avec une tendance vers les profils jeunes et financièrement aisés. Ces consommateurs sont très attirés par les nouveaux produits et sont prêts à payer pour une meilleure qualité. Ils cherchent des produits rapides et faciles à acheter. Ils n'aiment pas le suremballage, surtout dans le secteur des plats à emporter, et recherchent donc des produits respectueux de l'environnement dans ce domaine.

La gamme devait avoir une identité claire, mais nous ne voulions pas créer une sous-marque, alors nous avons commencé par chercher des formes qui pourraient servir d'identificateurs. En partant de plusieurs formes naturelles et organiques, nous sommes arrivés au motif des cercles concentriques. Il avait les qualités de douceur et de naturel que nous recherchions, ainsi qu'une modernité simple et la capacité de servir d'identificateur clair.

Le cercle a été utilisé de différentes manières dans la gamme. Pour les sandwichs, par exemple, il fallait un code de couleurs pour différencier les différents types d'ingrédients (viande, poisson, volaille ou végétarien). Les cercles servent donc à afficher les couleurs. Sur les jus de fruits, pour lesquels aucun code de couleurs n'était nécessaire, les cercles apparaissent sur la bouteille sous forme de motif dépoli.

Le ton du discours joue un rôle important dans le design général, et pour nous rapprocher du client jeune et branché que nous ciblons, nous utilisons un ton décontracté et amical pour transmettre un message sur notre passion pour la nourriture et sur nos valeurs en général. Pour les jus de fruits, par exemple, nous avons choisi un message sur la fraîcheur : « Nous ne traînons pas pour faire ce jus d'orange… les fruits sont pressés et mis en bouteille en 24 heures ». Pour les sandwichs, nous avions l'occasion de transmettre un message général important sur le genre de choses qui nous différencie de nos concurrents : « Nous sommes les seuls distributeurs à utiliser des œufs de poules élevées en plein air dans tous nos produits, même dans la mayonnaise ».

Nous savons aussi que notre client cible est soucieux du respect de l'environnement, ce à quoi nous répondons par des messages comme : « Vous pouvez être sûr que ces aliments sont 100 % non génétiquement modifiés (selon Greenpeace, nous sommes le meilleur distributeur) ».

Nous avons aussi utilisé les cercles concentriques pour présenter du texte, avec deux adjectifs qui décrivent les attributs essentiels du produit. Par exemple, pour la salade d'avocat et d'épinards, nous utilisons les termes « doux et noisetté ». Pour un sandwich au canard, c'est « généreux et succulent ». Cela souligne la richesse de la saveur et aide le client à faire son choix parmi les produits de la gamme – ces achats se font souvent à l'heure du repas et doivent être rapides, et recevoir en un coup d'œil des informations sur le goût aide réellement le client.

Sur l'avant du paquet, nous avons limité les titres aux ingrédients essentiels et nous avons privilégié la clarté en éliminant les textes secondaires, qui trouvent leur place au dos, ce qui permet d'avoir un grand titre facile à lire pour le client.

Pour les messages qui s'adressent au client, nous avons utilisé une police de caractères qui imite l'écriture à la main. Cela donne une impression naturelle et bon enfant, comme si les sandwichs venaient d'être faits à la main dans une cuisine et qu'on avait griffonné quelques mots dessus.

L'équipe a trouvé des bols à salade contenant 50 % de plastique recyclé et des bouteilles de jus de fruit contenant 30 % de matériaux recyclés. Les boîtes à sandwichs sont entièrement fabriquées avec des matériaux durables, avec une fenêtre transparente faite d'amidon de blé biodégradable au lieu de plastique, et pour quatre arbres coupés pour faire le carton, nous en plantons cinq !

Nous avons aussi travaillé avec des designers d'emballage pour créer un nouveau type de boîte (récemment breveté) afin de résoudre les inconvénients qu'il y a à manger un sandwich tout en se déplaçant. La solution trouvée, très innovante, consiste en une « fermeture éclair » originale et facile à ouvrir, qui court tout autour de la boîte. La boîte s'ouvre à plat et se transforme en une petite assiette individuelle.

Charlotte Raphael est née à Londres. Elle a obtenu son diplôme de graphisme avec mention à l'université de Kingston en 1991, et est entrée chez Marks and Spencer en 1994, où elle a été nommée responsable du design d'emballage en 2004.

We began by creating a mood board which encapsulated the overall idea, looking at references that conveyed the immediate feel we wanted. The design needed to emphasise that the product was super-fresh so we wanted to create the feel of being in a quality sandwich shop rather than a supermarket. We looked at images of food being freshly prepared, the idea of simple fresh ingredients and hand-scribbled menus on blackboards to show ever-changing choice and seasonal varieties. We liked the idea of creating a more relaxed feel within this area as the customer was younger than our core customer, so the handwritten script enhanced the more relaxed tone of voice. Packaging formats were important and we proposed the idea of using natural substrates together with simple clear packaging that let the product be the visual.

Zunächst haben wir ein Mood Board mit der grundlegenden Idee erstellt und dann nach Referenzen gesucht, die das Gefühl, das wir erzeugen wollten, sofort vermittelten. Das Design sollte die Frische des Produkts betonen und dem Kunden das Gefühl geben, in einem hochwertigen Sandwich-Shop und nicht in einem Supermarkt zu sein. Wir suchten nach Bildern von frisch zubereitetem Essen mit einfachen und frischen Zutaten und handbeschrifteten Speisetafeln, die den Eindruck von wechselndem Angebot und saisonalen Variationen vermitteln. Wir wollten diesen Bereich locker und entspannt gestalten, da die angesprochene Zielgruppe jünger ist als unsere Hauptkundschaft. Die gewählte Schreibschrift betonte den lockeren Tonfall. Ebenso waren die Verpackungsformen wichtig. Wir schlugen einfache durchsichtige Verpackungen aus natürlichen Materialien vor, sodass das Produkt selbst den optischen Eindruck bestimmte.

Nous avons créé une planche de tendances qui représente l'idée générale, en étudiant des références qui transmettaient l'impression que nous souhaitions donner. Le design devait mettre en avant la fraîcheur du produit, alors nous voulions donner l'impression au client de se trouver dans une sandwicherie de qualité, et non dans un supermarché. Nous avons étudié des images de préparation de plats, la notion d'ingrédients simples et frais et des menus écrits à la main sur des tableaux noirs pour montrer le renouvellement perpétuel du choix et les variantes selon les saisons. Nous avons été séduits par l'idée de créer un style décontracté pour notre client cible, plus jeune que notre client moyen habituel, et l'écriture cursive renforçait ce ton. Le format des emballages était très important, et nous avons proposé d'utiliser des supports naturels et un emballage simple et transparent permettant au produit d'être la véritable vedette.

STEP 1

At the first stage we explored several options. We used tone of voice to create a clear identity, whilst also looking at colour coding and use of a unifying substrate across the range.

SCHRITT 1

Zunächst testeten wir verschiedene Möglichkeiten.Wir setzten Sprache zur Schaffung einer eindeutigen Identität ein, experimentierten aber auch mit Farbkodierungen und der Verwendung eines einheitlichen, die gesamte Produktreihe verbindenden Elementes.

ÉTAPE 1

Au premier stade, nous avons étudié plusieurs options. Nous avons utilisé un ton spécifique afin de créer une identité claire, tout en étudiant le code de couleurs et l'utilisation d'un support permettant d'homogénéiser toute la gamme.

STEP 2

We wanted to convey a great passion for good food so we looked at an option using famous quotes relating to food to give a sophisticated twist.

SCHRITT 2

Mit den Produkten wollten wir eine große Leidenschaft für gutes Essen zum Ausdruck bringen und überlegten daher, bekannte Zitate zum Thema Essen zu verwenden, um den Produkten eine gehobene Note zu verleihen.

ÉTAPE 2

Nous voulions transmettre une grande passion pour le « bon manger », c'est pourquoi nous avons étudié l'option des citations célèbres sur le sujet de la nourriture, pour donner un côté raffiné.

STEP 3

We liked the idea of using mmm! to convey the tastiness of the food and thought this might work as an identifier across the range. This also showed the start of using a circle motif as windows or type panels – we felt the use of this organic shape helped convey a natural freshness to the range.

SCHRITT 3

Uns gefiel die Idee, „mmm!" als Zeichen für den guten Geschmack der Lebensmittel und als Erkennungsmerkmal für die gesamte Produktreihe zu verwenden. Hier tauchte auch das Kreismotiv zum ersten Mal auf – als Fenster oder für die Schrift. Die organische Form betonte sehr schön die natürliche Frische der Produkte.

ÉTAPE 3

Nous avons bien aimé l'idée d'utiliser « mmm ! » pour exprimer la saveur des produits, et nous avons pensé que cet élément pourrait servir d'identificateur de la gamme. C'est à ce moment que nous avons commencé à utiliser le motif du cercle sous forme de fenêtre transparente ou de panneau de texte – il nous semblait que cette forme organique aidait à exprimer la fraîcheur naturelle de la gamme.

STEP 4

Sandwich cartons make up the largest section of the range and have the biggest impact in-store, so we focused on how the concentric circle motif would be applied to these. In the early stages we looked at using a soft grey board and more subdued colour. The circles then became a frame for the window, although the constraints of the physical pack dictated an off centre window. We brightened the colours to have greater stand-out in the fridges and the design finally fell into place when we changed the background to a natural brown board.

The final design created great impact on shelf and allowed the window to give focus to the sandwich. Colour coding framed the product to distinguish the type of filling, the brown board gave a natural feel and the colour coding was clear but contemporary. We introduced black sandwich packs for limited edition flavours. Titles are simple and clear and on back of pack the hand script is used to talk about the product while our environmental policy is explained on side of pack, in the hand script again, to retain a friendly approach to the customer.

SCHRITT 4

Da die Sandwichkartons den Hauptbestandteil der Reihe ausmachen und in der Auslage auch am auffälligsten sind, konzentrierten wir uns zunächst darauf, wie das Kreismotiv auf sie angewendet werden könnte. Zunächst verwendeten wir weichen grauen Karton und gedeckte Farben. Der Kreis wurde zum Rahmen des Sichtfensters, musste aber aus verpackungstechnischen Gründen asymmetrisch angeordnet werden. Wir hellten die Farben auf, um einen größeren Aufmerksamkeitswert in den Kühltruhen zu erreichen, und schließlich wurde das Design rund, als wir als Hintergrund natürlich braunen statt eines grauen Kartons wählten.

Das endgültige Design war in der Auslage sehr auffällig und gab durch sein Fenster den Blick direkt auf die Sandwiches frei. Das Produkt wurde von der Farbkodierung umrahmt, die den Belag identifizierte. Der braune Karton vermittelte Natürlichkeit, und die Farbkodierung war klar und modern. Für befristete Belagangebote führten wir schwarze Sandwichverpackungen ein. Die Produktnamen sind schlicht und klar gehalten, auf der Rückseite der Verpackungen finden sich die Produktinformationen in Schreibschrift, und auf der Seite der Packungen erklären wir unser Umweltkonzept. Hier wählten wir ebenfalls die Schreibschrift, um den lockeren Umgang beizubehalten.

ÉTAPE 4

Les boîtes à sandwich constituent la plus grande section de la gamme, et ont également l'impact en magasin le plus fort, c'est pourquoi nous avons beaucoup réfléchi à l'application du motif des cercles concentriques à cette catégorie. Dans les premiers temps, nous avons pensé utiliser du carton gris clair et des couleurs plus sourdes. Puis les cercles sont devenus un cadre pour la fenêtre, bien que les contraintes physiques obligent à excentrer la fenêtre. Nous avons avivé les couleurs pour obtenir une meilleure présence dans les réfrigérateurs, et le design s'est finalement imposé de lui-même lorsque nous avons remplacé le carton gris par du carton brun naturel.

Le design final a beaucoup d'impact en rayon et la fenêtre permet de mettre le sandwich en valeur. Le code de couleurs clair et contemporain encadre le produit et aide à distinguer le type de garniture, et le fond marron donne une impression de naturel. Pour les sandwichs spéciaux en édition limitée, nous avons créé des boîtes noires. Les titres sont simples et clairs, et l'écriture cursive sert à parler du produit au dos de la boîte, tandis que notre politique environnementale est expliquée sur le côté dans la même écriture afin de garder une approche conviviale.

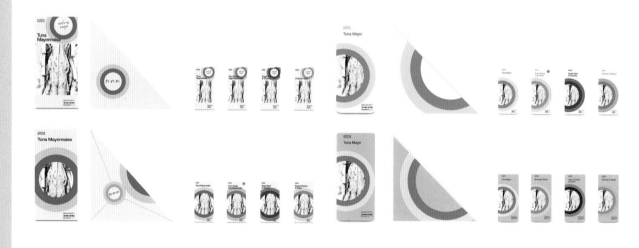

SANDWICH IMAGES

Including demonstration of the zip. The inno-vative "zip" allows the sandwich pack to be opened out to make it easier to eat!

SANDWICH-BILDER

Darunter auch eine Demonstration des Auf-reißmechanismus. Durch diesen innovativen Mechanismus kann die Sandwichverpackung aufgeklappt werden, was das Essen erleichtert!

PHOTOS DES SANDWICHS

Et démonstration du système de fermeture éclair. Cette fermeture innovante permet d'ouvrir la boîte du sandwich, pour qu'il soit plus facile à manger !

DRINKS
The concentric circles have been used in a playful way to suggest sparkling drinks.

GETRÄNKE
Das Motiv des konzentrischen Kreises wird auf spielerische Weise verwendet, um Getränke mit Kohlensäure zu identifizieren.

LES BOISSONS
Les cercles concentriques ont été utilisés sur un mode ludique pour représenter les boissons pétillantes.

CRISPS

Here the concentric circles have been used to create synergy across the crisps range. On crinkle crisps it prints clear on a frosted pack to create a window whilst on handcooked it frames the photograph. Colours used in the bands denote flavours.

CHIPS

Hier erzeugen die konzentrischen Kreise Synergien zwischen den verschiedenen Chips-Produktreihen. Auf „Crinkle Crisps" ist das Kreismotiv aufgedruckt, bei halbtransparenten Packungen bildet es ein Fenster, und auf den „handcooked" (hausgemachten) Chips umrahmt es ein Foto. Bei allen Marken symbolisieren die Farben die Geschmacksrichtung.

LES CHIPS

Ici, les cercles concentriques servent à créer une synergie au sein de la gamme de chips. Sur les chips ondulées le motif est transparent et forme une fenêtre, mais pour les chips cuites « maison », il encadre la photographie. Les couleurs utilisées sur les bandes correspondent aux différents goûts.

Case 04
Information Design for Patient Safety

Colum Menzies Lowe, Head of Design and Human Factors,
NHS National Patient Safety Agency

Colum Menzies Lowe is a leading authority on design in the United Kingdom, where he heads a team at the National Health Service (NHS). In this case study he explains how and why the institution has created a major guideline for package design to improve the safety for patients in the country, through clearer and more accessible design.

The design of medication packaging has a vital role to play in the accurate communication of important information to patients and clinicians alike. However, not until quite recently has the importance of good design been fully appreciated, and more significantly, the potential dangers of bad design.

The NHS National Patient Safety Agency (NPSA) in the United Kingdom has put into place a national reporting system for patient safety incidents, but at this early stage it is not possible to provide a true and accurate figure for the extent of medication errors. This problem is shared by many other countries' healthcare systems. Low reporting rates within the United Kingdom's National Health Service compounds this problem. The true incidence of medication error is believed to be comparable with that of the United States of America where it is estimated that medication errors may occur in as many as 6% of all adult hospital admissions and may lead to roughly 7,000 deaths each year.

In the UK, between January and November 2005, the NPSA received nearly 30,000 incident reports involving medication error, 4% of which had moderate, severe or fatal outcomes. The type of incidents varied from wrong drug, wrong dose and wrong formulation error and an underlying cause for many of these reports was identified as mis-selection. Mis-selection is in part due to the look-alike and sound-alike nature of the information on medication packaging and labelling. This issue was recognised as an important cause of patient harm in the Department of Health's report *Building a Safer NHS for Patients*, in 2001 and in the follow-up report *Improving Medication Safety* in 2004.

The NPSA believes the design of medication packaging should positively assist in the accurate identification and selection of the medicine. This would help to ensure its safe use in practice; and while the industry does currently meet European Union requirements to get a Marketing Authorisation (MA), medicines, unlike medical devices, do not have to undergo any user testing of the final product. Indeed the European Regulator does not require sight of the final design of the product before granting an MA and the product being released on to the market.

The obvious concern is that while some licensed medicines may meet legal requirements they may not be promoting safe use. Subsequently healthcare workers and patients find medicines difficult to identify, especially where the manufacturer's corporate branding is too dominant or has a uniform colour and design for all of their products, or where the legibility of text on the outer packaging is poor and the drug names are similar. This combined with packaging that is difficult to open and close, and an internal blister pack that is difficult to identify once removed from the outer carton, results in a heightened chance of some form of medication error occurring.

Furthermore, some pharmacists believe their role is to purchase medicines as cheaply as possible, and that safety issues, especially ones related to design and manufacturing, are the responsibility of the regulator. The assumption is being made that if it is available to buy, it must be safe to use. But the British Department of Health and the NPSA recommend 'purchasing for safety' where safety in use is considered by purchasers along with price. They also want to indicate to manufacturers the importance of this requirement by purchasing from other suppliers when a product is deemed 'unsafe' in use.

The bottom line is that some information design specifically relating to medication packaging is not totally fit for purpose. All stakeholders need to work in partnership to improve their products, as the adoption of good design is a critical factor in the future progression and development of healthcare in this country. The aim is for design that is appropriately focused on end-user requirements and which aims to simplify the complexity of our current healthcare system.

To this end the NPSA sponsored a one-year research programme from the Helen Hamlyn Research Centre at the Royal College of Art to explore the issue of medication packaging design and to produce simple clear advice for designers and commissioners. Its aim is to support and complement the existing guidance and to help establish a benchmark in good design for the packaging of medicines. I believe this publication goes a long way to setting out the guidelines for achieving this and is a must-read for all designers and manufacturers in medication packaging.

The NPSA publication *Information Design for Patient Safety* is based on and developed from established guidance which it supplements using illustrations of bad and good practice based on real-life exam es. The challenge for the pharmaceutical dustry is to adopt a best practice proach that ensures, as an absolute mini- um, that vital information is clearly legi- e to the relevant user and also stays with edication until the actual moment when it taken by the patient.

Colum Menzies Lowe HND MBA FRSA
1989 Colum graduated from Chelsea School Art where he studied 3D Product Design. In 99 he added an MBA in Design Management m the University of Westminster to his aca- mic credits. After leaving BLDC Colum spent o and a half years as Head of Design at J. nsbury's Homebase Ltd., and just over a year a Partner of Plan Créatif/Crabtree Hall sign Consultants, before taking up his rrent position in November of 2003 at the HS National Patient Safety Agency, where is Head of Design and Human Factors.

Column Menzies Lowe ist eine der chtigsten Autoritäten im Bereich Design Großbritannien und Leiter eines Teams r staatlichen Gesundheitsbehörde tional Health Service (NHS). In dieser llstudie erläutert er, wie und warum die hörde neue und bahnbrechende chtlinien im Bereich Verpackungsdesign rausgegeben hat. Ziel war es, die cherheit der Patienten im Land durch ndeutigere und einfacher zu bedienende rpackungen zu verbessern.

Das Design medizinischer Verpackungen ielt eine bedeutende Rolle bei der Ver- ttlung wichtiger Informationen sowohl an

den Patienten als auch an das klinische Personal. Dennoch sind die Möglichkeiten und Gefahren von Design in diesem Bereich erst seit kurzem allgemein anerkannt.

Die NHS National Patient Safety Agency (NPSA) (Agentur für Patientensicherheit des britischen staatlichen Gesundheits- systems) hat in Großbritannien ein Melde- system für Vorfälle eingerichtet, die den Bereich Patientensicherheit betreffen. Allerdings können noch keine genauen Aussagen über das Ausmaß von Medika- tionsfehlern getroffen werden. Das Problem ist auch in anderen Ländern bekannt. Nied- rige Melderaten erschweren die Situation. Man schätzt, dass Medikationsfehler mit Hochrechnungen aus den USA vergleichbar sind, wo man davon ausgeht, dass bei 6 % der erwachsenen Krankenhauspatienten Fehlmedikationen auftreten, die zu rund 7.000 Todesfällen pro Jahr führen.

In Großbritannien wurden zwischen Janu- ar und November 2005 fast 30.000 Medika- tionsfehler bei der NPSA gemeldet, von denen etwa 4 % mittlere, schwere oder tödli- che Folgen hatten. Die Ursachen hierfür sind falsche Medikamentenwahl, falsche Dosis oder falsche Formulierungen. Als Grund wurde häufig ein Fehler bei der Auswahl (also Fehlgriffe) angegeben. Solche Fehl- griffe kommen u. a. durch große Ähnlichkei- ten bei den Verpackungen, Namen, Beschrif- tungen oder Etiketten der Medikamente vor. Dies wurde im Bericht des Department of Health *Building a Safer NHS for Patients* 2001 sowie 2004 im Folgebericht *Improving Medication Safety* als einer der wichtigsten Gründe für Patientenschäden identifiziert.

Die NHS ist davon überzeugt, dass Medikamentenverpackungen klar identifi- zierbar sein sollten, um dem medizinischen

Personal die eindeutige Wahl des richtigen Medikaments zu erleichtern. Dies könnte bei der Gewährleistung der Patientensicherheit helfen. Die Industrie erfüllt zwar derzeit die Anforderungen der Europäischen Union. Um eine Marketing-Autorisierung (MA) zu erhal- ten, müssen Medikamente allerdings im Gegensatz zu medizinischen Geräten keinem Testlauf mit dem Endprodukt unterzogen werden. Zur Erteilung der MA und für die Markteinführung muss das endgültige Produkt der Regulierungsbehörde nicht ein- mal vorgelegt werden.

Die Gefahr liegt also darin, dass einige lizenzierte Medikamente zwar den rechtli- chen Anforderungen entsprechen, einen sicheren Gebrauch aber nicht fördern. Folglich haben medizinisches Personal wie auch Patienten Schwierigkeiten bei der Unterscheidung vieler Medikamente, beson- ders wenn das Firmenzeichen des Her- stellers zu dominant ist, Farbe und Design einheitlich gestaltet sind, die Lesbarkeit des Verpackungstextes schlecht ist oder die Medikamentnamen sich sehr ähneln. Wenn Verpackungen dann noch schwer zu öffnen und zu schließen sind und Blisterpackungen sich kaum noch unterscheiden, sobald der Karton entfernt wurde, führt das in Kombi- nation zu einer erhöhten Gefahr für Medika- tionsfehler.

Zudem vertreten Apotheker die Auffassung, es sei ihre Aufgabe, Medika- mente so preiswert wie möglich einzukaufen, Sicherheitsfragen seien dagegen Aufgabe der Regulierungsbehörde. Sie gehen grund- sätzlich davon aus, dass die zugelassenen Medikamente auch in ihrer Anwendung sicher sind. NPSA rät aber gemeinsam mit dem britischen Gesundheitsamt, beim Einkauf nicht nur auf den Preis zu achten, sondern auch auf die Sicherheit. In Zukunft wollen die Apotheker der Pharmaindustrie die Bedeutung der Richtlinien vermitteln, indem sie den Lieferanten wechseln, wenn Produkte für „unsicher" erklärt werden.

Nicht jede Art von Kommunikationsdesign ist im Bereich medizinischer Verpackungen geeignet. Alle Beteiligten sollten gemeinsam daran arbeiten, ihre Produkte zu verbessern, da die Einführung von gutem Design ein wichtiger Faktor im Gesundheitswesen des Landes sein wird. Das Ziel ist ein Design, das auf die Bedürfnisse des Endverbrauchers zugeschnitten ist und dazu beiträgt, die Komplexität des derzeitigen Gesundheitssystems zu vereinfachen.

Zu diesem Zweck unterstützte die NPSA ein einjähriges Forschungsprogramm des Helen Hamlyn Forschungszentrums am Royal College of Art, das das Verpackungsdesign für medizinische Produkte untersucht und einfache Richtlinien für Designer und Behörden erstellen soll. Damit sollen die bisherigen Richtlinien ergänzt und eine Bezugsnorm für zweckmäßiges Design im Bereich der medizinische Verpackungen etabliert werden. Ich denke, dass uns diese Publikation unserem Ziel – verbindliche Richtlinien – ein erhebliches Stück näher bringen wird und dass sie für Designer wie Hersteller von medizinischen Verpackungen eine absolute Notwendigkeit darstellen.

Die Publikation *Information Design for Patient Safety* (Kommunikationsdesign für Patientensicherheit) wurde anhand der bestehenden Richtlinien entwickelt. Sie ergänzt diese Richtlinien und präsentiert hierzu Beispiele für schlechtes wie für gutes Design, wie sie derzeit auf dem Markt zu finden sind. Die Herausforderung für die Pharmaindustrie besteht nun darin, diesen Ansatz, der ein absolutes Minimum darstellt, umzusetzen und Sorge dafür zu tragen, dass die wichtigen Informationen für den Anwender deutlich lesbar sind und auch bis zur Einnahme beim Medikament verbleiben.

Colum Menzies Lowe HND MBA FRSA
Colum Menzies Lowe studierte bis 1989 3D-Produktdesign an der Chelsea School of Art. 1999 schloss er das MBA-Studium in Design Management an der University of Westminster ab. Nach seiner Tätigkeit für BLDC arbeitete er zweieinhalb Jahre als Leiter der Designabteilung bei J. Sainsbury's Homebase Ltd. Im Anschluss daran war er etwa ein Jahr lang Partner bei Plan Créatif/Crabtree Hall Design Consultants, bevor er im November 2003 seine derzeitige Stellung als Head of Design and Human Factors bei der NHS National Patient Safety Agency antrat.

Colum Menzies Lowe fait autorité dans le domaine du design au Royaume-Uni, où il dirige une équipe au sein du National Health Service (NHS – le ministère britannique de la Santé). Dans cette étude de cas, il explique comment et pourquoi cette institution a créé un livre de recommandations afin d'améliorer la sécurité des patients grâce à des emballages plus clairs et plus faciles à utiliser.

La conception de l'emballage des médicaments a un rôle vital à jouer dans la bonne communication des informations à l'attention des patients et des professionnels de la santé. Cependant, l'importance d'un design efficace et les dangers potentiels d'un mauvais design ne sont appréciés à leur juste valeur que depuis peu.

L'Agence nationale pour la sécurité des patients (National Patient Safety Agency, NPSA) du ministère de la Santé britannique a mis en place un système national de suivi des incidents liés à la sécurité des patients, mais il est encore trop tôt pour pouvoir fournir des chiffres précis et significatifs sur l'étendue des erreurs de médication. Les systèmes de santé de nombreux autres pays sont concernés par ce problème. Une faible part des incidents réels est déclarée au ministère de la Santé, ce qui complique le problème. La véritable incidence des erreurs de médication peut être comparée à celle des États-Unis, où l'on estime que des erreurs médication se produisent dans 6 % des admissions d'adultes à l'hôpital et pourraient provoquer environ 7 000 décès chaque année.

Au Royaume-Uni, entre janvier et novembre 2005, près de 30 000 incidents concernant des erreurs de médication ont été signalés à la NPSA, dont 4 % ont eu des conséquences modérées, graves ou mortelles. Les différents types d'erreurs portaient sur le médicament, sur la dose ou sur la formulation, et l'une des causes sousjacentes de beaucoup de ces incidents était une erreur de sélection. L'erreur de sélection est en partie due à la similarité visuelle ou verbale des informations imprimées sur les emballages et les étiquettes des médicaments. Le rapport du ministère de la Santé *Building a Safer NHS for Patients* (Bâtir système national de santé plus sûr pour les patients) en 2001, et le rapport de suivi *Improving Medication Safety* (Améliorer l sécurité de la médication) en 2004 reconnaissent que ce problème est un facteur de risque important pour les patients.

La NPSA croit fermement que le design
s emballages de médicaments devrait aider
es identifier et à les sélectionner. Cela
ntribuerait à en garantir une utilisation
ns danger dans la pratique. Bien que le
cteur réponde actuellement aux exigences
l'Union européenne pour obtenir une
torisation de mise sur le marché (AMM),
médicaments, à la différence des appareils
dicaux, ne sont pas obligatoirement sou-
s à des tests auprès des utilisateurs du
oduit final. En effet, l'organisme européen
contrôle n'exige pas de voir le design du
oduit avant d'accorder l'AMM et que le
oduit soit lancé sur le marché.

Cela soulève un problème évident : cer-
ns médicaments autorisés répondant aux
gences de la loi peuvent toutefois ne pas
er dans le sens d'une utilisation en toute
urité. Les professionnels de la santé et
patients peuvent trouver que les médica-
nts sont difficiles à identifier, en particu-
lorsque la marque du fabricant est trop
dominante, lorsque la couleur ou le gra-
sme sont les mêmes pour tous les pro-
ts d'un même fabricant, lorsque le texte
primé sur la boîte est difficile à lire ou que
noms de différents médicaments se res-
blent. Ceci, combiné à un emballage dif-
le à ouvrir et à fermer, et à une plaquette
icile à identifier une fois qu'elle est ex-
ite de sa boîte, augmente les risques
rreur de médication. De plus, certains
armaciens pensent que leur rôle est
cheter des médicaments aussi bon marché
possible, et que les problèmes de sécuri-
en particulier ceux liés au design et à la
rication, relèvent de la responsabilité de
ganisme de contrôle. On présuppose qu'un
duit mis à la vente est un produit dont
ilisation est sans danger. Mais le minis-

tère de la Santé britannique et la NPSA
recommandent « d'acheter en recherchant
la sécurité », c'est-à-dire que les acheteurs
devraient prendre en compte la sécurité tout
autant que le prix. Ils veulent aussi signaler
aux fabricants l'importance de ce critère en
leur demandant d'acheter auprès d'autres
fournisseurs lorsqu'un produit est considéré
comme « dangereux » à utiliser.

Le fond du problème réside dans l'inadé-
quation de certaines informations apparais-
sant sur les emballages des médicaments.
Tous les acteurs doivent travailler
ensemble pour améliorer leurs produits, car
le choix d'un design efficace est un facteur
crucial dans la progression et le développement futurs de la santé dans ce pays. Le
design doit s'adapter aux conditions d'utilisation et tendre à simplifier notre système
de santé actuel.

Pour ce faire, la NPSA a fondé un programme de recherche d'un an au Centre de
recherche Helen Hamlyn du Royal College of
Art afin d'étudier la question du design des
emballages de médicaments et d'élaborer des
recommandations simples et claires à l'intention des designers et des intermédiaires. Le
but est de soutenir et de compléter les
recommandations existantes et de contribuer
à établir un modèle de référence pour l'emballage des médicaments. Je pense que cette
publication présente admirablement bien les
recommandations pour y parvenir et est une
lecture essentielle pour tous les designers et
les fabricants d'emballage de médicaments.

La publication de la NPSA, *Information
Design for Patient Safety* (Le design et l'information pour la sécurité des patients) se
base sur des recommandations établies et les
développe en s'appuyant sur des exemples
réels de bonnes ou de mauvaises pratiques.

Pour l'industrie pharmaceutique, le défi est
d'adopter de bonnes pratiques qui assure-
ront, au minimum, que les informations
vitales seront clairement lisibles pour les utilisateurs concernés et qu'elles resteront disponibles et associées au médicament jusqu'au
moment où il est pris par le patient.

Colum Menzies Lowe HND MBA FRSA
*Colum Menzies Lowe a obtenu son diplôme de
la School of Art de Chelsea en 1989, où il a étudié le design de produits en 3D. En 1999, il a
obtenu un MBA en Gestion de projet à l'Université de Westminster. Après son expérience chez
BLDC, il a occupé pendant deux ans et demi le
poste de responsable du design chez J. Sainsbury's Homebase Ltd et pendant un peu plus d'un
an celui d'associé chez Plan Créatif/Crabtree
Hall Design Consultants, avant de prendre ses
fonctions en novembre 2003 à l'Agence nationale
pour la sécurité des patients du ministère de la
Santé, où il est responsable du design et des facteurs humains.*

*Reference: Building a Safer NHS for Patients,
Improving Medication Safety*, Jan 2004, Page 22.
Bates D, Cullen D, Laird N, Petersen L; et al.
*Incidence of adverse drug events and potential
adverse drug events. JAMA* 1995; 274: Page
29–34. Phillips DP, Christenfeld N, Glynn LM.
*Increase in medication-error deaths between 1983
and 1993. Research letter. Lancet*; 351: Page 643.

Packaging
design checklist

2

Design recommendations
for secondary packaging

The term secondary packaging describes the outer package of a pharmaceutical product. It holds the primary packaging and does not touch the medicine. The combined impact of all design elements, such as colour and typography, should be evaluated.

3

THE MANUAL

These slides showcase the publication
A Guide to the Graphic Design of Medication Packaging, *which serves as a guideline for good design regarding patient safety. The report is constantly updated.*

DAS HANDBUCH

Diese Bilder zeigen die Publikation A Guide to the Graphic Design of Medication Packaging *(Ein Leitfaden für die Gestaltung von Medikamentenverpackungen), die als Richtlinie für gutes Design in Bezug auf die Patientensicherheit dient. Der Bericht wird ständig aktualisiert.*

LE MANUEL

Ces images présentent la publication A Guide to the Graphic Design of Medication Packaging *(Un guide du graphisme appliqué aux emballages de médicaments), qui donne des lignes directrices pour que l'emballage respecte la sécurité des patients. Le rapport est constamment mis à jour.*

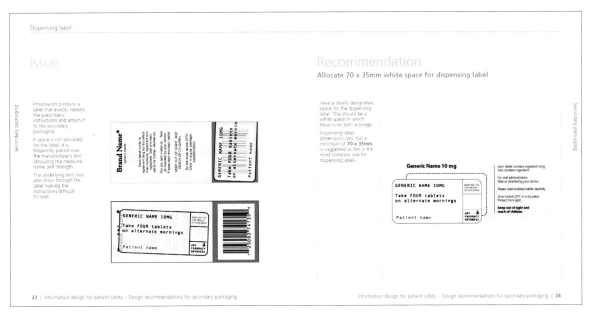

GUIDELINES OUTLINE

Featuring a checklist for a variety of issues, along with a series of recommendations, the report examines every detail of the design produced for medicines.

RICHTLINIEN-ÜBERSICHT

Der Bericht, der neben einer Checkliste für verschiedene Themen auch eine Reihe von Empfehlungen enthält, untersucht jedes Detail der Gestaltung von Medikamenten-verpackungen.

APERÇU DES RECOMMANDATIONS

Ce rapport contient une liste de points à vérifier sur tout un ensemble de sujets, ainsi qu'une série de recommandations. Il analyse tous les détails de la conception d'emballages pour médicaments.

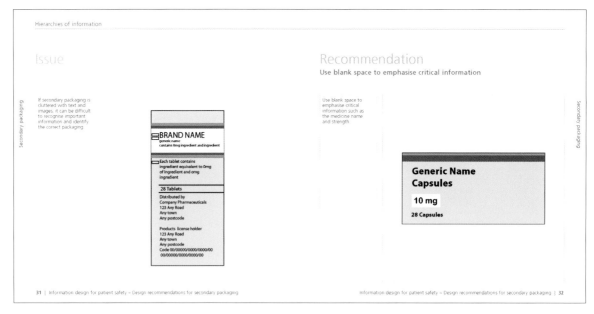

PACKAGE CONCERNS

A wide variety of possibilities in shapes, type of packaging and typography are examined for the packaging of many types of medicines, with practical examples to be adopted and others not to be followed.

DIE WICHTIGKEIT DER VERPACKUNG

Eine Vielzahl an Formen, Verpackungstypen und typografischen Lösungen werden für die Verpackung von ganz unterschiedlichen Medikamenten in Augenschein genommen, mit praktischen Beispielen, die angepasst oder verworfen wurden.

PROBLÈMES LIÉS À L'EMBALLAGE

Un grand nombre de possibilités différentes sont étudiées en termes de forme, de type d'emballage et de typographie pour de nombreuses sortes de médicaments, avec des exemples pratiques à suivre et d'autres à éviter.

Typography

Issue

Recommendation

Create a strong contrast between type and background colour

secondary packaging

Insufficient contrast
between the background
and the type reduces
legibility

There should be a strong
contrast between the
type and background
colours

Dark coloured type (e.g.
black, dark blue) should
be on a light coloured
background (e.g. white,
pale pink, pale yellow)

secondary packaging

Generic Name
Capsules

10 mg

28 Capsules

logo

Generic Name
Capsules

10 mg

28 Capsules

logo

Blister strip

Issue

Recommendation

Match the styles of primary and secondary packaging

Patients taking more
than one medicine, or
the same medicine in
two or more strengths,
must be able to identify
which blister strip
belongs to which packet
because the prescription
instructions are attached
to the secondary
packaging

Mixing packages and
blister strips up could
lead to the patient
taking the wrong
medication or even
overdosing

A product's primary and
secondary packaging
should have an identical
or linked visual style
created through, for
example, colour

BRAND NAME
28 CAPSULES

BRAND NAME

Generic Name
Capsules

28 Capsules

Generic Name

10
m

10
mg

WEBSITE

The full pdf version of the publication Information Design for Patient Safety *is available as a free download from the NPSA website at* http://www.npsa.nhs.uk/health/currentprojects/designforpatientsafety.

WEBSEITE

Die vollständige PDF-Version der Publikation Information Design for Patient Safety *kann auf der Webseite der NPSA kostenlos heruntergeladen werden:* http://www.npsa.nhs.uk/health/currentprojects/designforpatientsafety

SITE INTERNET

La version complète en format PDF de la publication Information Design for Patient Safety *peut être téléchargée gratuitement sur le site Internet de la NPSA* http://www.npsa.nhs.uk/health/currentprojects/designforpatientsafety.

Case 05
Design Effectiveness

Hannah Paterson, Programmes Director,
Design Business Association

In this case study, Hannah Paterson from the Design Business Association (DBA), chooses winners from the institution's yearly Design Effectiveness Awards to highlight practical examples of how companies have created innovative solutions around their package designs to maximise the value of their messages to consumers.

Businesses face different challenges every day, whether it's a downturn in the market, changes in consumer trends, or the task of achieving differentiation in a crowded market place. But what happens when forward-thinking companies put design right at the heart of their strategies to overcome these challenges? The DBA has been running the Design Effectiveness Awards since 1989 to illustrate just this.

We have the case studies that irrefutably prove design can permeate all aspects of a business, by improving profitability, creating new revenue streams, raising a company's profile, building brand recognition and empowering staff to deliver the best results.

The DBA champions design as an enhancement of business growth and there can be no surer evidence of the benefits of design for business than the case studies from the Design Effectiveness Awards. It is the only design award scheme that uses commercial data as key judging criteria, making it the most authoritative and prestigious design awards in the UK.

Without a doubt, design can add value to a business, it can be the ingredient which turns a company around; it can take a poorly perceived brand and turn it into a front runner and it can deliver right back into a business' bottom line. However, it's not all plain sailing to convince businesses to see design as a

vital investment and not a cost, especially when it comes to FMCGs (Fast Moving Consumer Goods), who have tended to put the big budgets behind advertising rather than design; but this is changing. More and more brands trust their design consultancy with the strategic management of their reputation, however it manifests itself.

However, when well-informed companies build business results into the design brief from the outset and unpick the impact from the rest of the marketing mix, the case for design as a critical link in the business process can be resounding; as the following case studies show.

THE THINKING PERSON'S CUPPA

With the relentless rise in the popularity of coffee, how could a niche tea in a huge national market reposition its brand as a top-end product and fight the decline in tea drinking?

Clipper Tea decided it needed a visual overhaul. It faced three challenges in doing this: build distinction, heighten consistency and maintain integrity. Clipper was also adrift without a coherent visual style. William Murray Hamm's new design captures the company's integrity and ethical working practices, boiling the brand essence down to 'the thinking person's cuppa', directing the discreet, sober packaging style. Inspired by journals such as *National Geographic*, each packet also displays a nugget of fascinating information about the region where the tea itself was grown. These references may be about indigenous animals, local histories or traditions.

Introduced to the market between March and December 2001, the most significant result of the redesign was and continues to be the huge increase in sales. In three

years, figures were up an estimated 373 pe cent. Export markets also expanded, from one to 23 countries. Crucially, this increase economic activity has improved the qualit of life and prospects on the fair trade estates that supply the company, bringing fresh investment to communities.

ORGANIC GROWTH

The Organic Milk Suppliers Cooperative (OMSCo) was faced with a very different challenge from that of Clipper – a supply surplus of organic milk, which had led to increasing competition and price pressures from retailers. Looking for a long-term solu tion to build value, OMSCo identified an opportunity for a new premium brand that would lead growth in the organic market. The challenge was to create a product that would communicate the full benefits of an organic alternative, encourage non-organic consumers into the category and repositio the brand as an everyday essential rather than a niche product.

Through packaging design, Blue Marlin delivered a brand that was relevant to con sumers' needs. The 'Altogether Better' nan communicates the taste promise of organic milk, along with its health benefits and greater environmental responsibility. The recyclable bottle, which echoes a tradition: milk churn, is unfamiliar at first but is eas to carry than traditional packaging using t top handle, while the centred rear handle makes it easier to pour.

The graphics avoid traditional organic clicl and instead focus on photography of moment where families enjoy milk together, keeping product mainstream and accessible.

Altogether Better launched in 200 Sainsbury's stores in February 2005.

eekly sales that equate to £1.2 million
r annum mean Altogether Better is nine
r cent up on target and the cumulative
peat purchase rate (the proportion of
ople buying the brand more than once)
s reached 34 per cent within just five
onths after its launch. On current sales
vels the organic milk surplus will be
duced by nearly 2 million litres per year
d cleared in between 12 and 18 months.
e cost of development will be recovered
8 months.

BREAKING THE MOULD

The major paradox in the sanitary care
arket is how to create a product that stands
t but is also discreet. With Kotex's brand
ready poorly perceived and sales declining,
ew strategy was needed to revitalise the
and and overhaul its image without spend-
g any money on product development.
Coley Porter Bell's strategy was to reposi-
n the product as clearly distinct from the
n pro' market, shifting it towards the per-
nal care category. American Kotex packag-
g used a red dot to symbolise menstrua-
n. Up to this point, this was an unspoken
boo in the European market. Coley Porter
ll went all out on the colour red, appropri-
ng assertive symbols like lipsticks, hearts
d spiked heels for the package covers.
All of these businesses have seen a huge
turn on investment from design. To deliver
e value, designers need to get under the
in of their client's business and understand
e context of the project in relation to the
mpany's strategic objectives. By working
th your client to build business objectives
to the design brief at the outset, both par-
s can measure the effectiveness and
pact of your work, leading to stronger,

more long-term relationships. Ultimately this
is where sustainable value comes from.

*Hannah Paterson was born in Wimbledon
(UK) in 1976 and holds a BA in Architecture
from Sheffield University. After finishing her
degree she started work in 1999 at the Design
Business Association (DBA – www.dba.org.uk)
as the Co-ordinator for the Design Effectiveness
Awards. Hannah currently holds the position of
Programmes Director at the DBA and is responsible for delivering all of their events, training
and awards schemes.*

**In dieser Fallstudie präsentiert Hannah
Paterson von der Design Business
Association (DBA) einige Gewinner des
jährlich von der DBA verliehenen Design
Effectiveness Awards. Anhand praktischer
Beispiele erläutert sie, wie verschiedene
Unternehmen innovative Verpackungs-
lösungen genutzt haben, um den Wert
ihrer Botschaft an die Kunden zu steigern.**

Unternehmen müssen sich täglich schwie-
rigen Herausforderungen stellen, sei es
durch konjunkturelle Schwankungen, wechselnde Konsumentenwünsche oder aufgrund
des Überlebenskampfes auf einem gesättig-
ten Markt. Was aber passiert, wenn zukunft-
sorientierte Unternehmen Design zum wichtigsten strategischen Mittel erklären, um mit
diesen Herausforderungen fertig zu werden?
Um dies zu dokumentieren, verleiht die DBA
seit 1989 den Design Effectiveness Award.
Uns liegen Fallstudien vor, die unwider-
legbar beweisen, dass Design alle Bereiche
eines Unternehmens bereichern kann, die

Rentabilität steigert, neue Einkommens-
quellen erschließt, das Ansehen eines Unternehmens erhöht, den Wiedererkennungswert
einer Marke verbessert und die Mitarbeiter
zu besseren Leistungen motiviert.
Die DBA betrachtet Design als Mittel zur
Geschäftsförderung, und welchen besseren
Beweis für die durchschlagende Wirkung von
Design könnte es geben als die mit dem
Design Effectiveness Award ausgezeichne-
ten Projekte? Es ist der einzige Designpreis,
der kommerziellen Erfolg als wichtigstes
Kriterium wertet, was ihn zum aussagekräf-
tigsten und prestigeträchtigsten Designpreis
in Großbritannien macht.
Ohne Zweifel kann Design den Unter-
nehmenswert steigern und einem Unternehmen wieder Schwung verleihen. Es kann
aus einer wenig beachteten Marke einen
Renner machen und einen mageren Umsatz
erhöhen. Allerdings ist es nicht einfach,
Design als eine überlebenswichtige
Investition und nicht nur als einen Kosten-
faktor zu sehen, vor allem, wenn es sich um
FMCGs (Fast Moving Consumer Goods) handelt, bei denen gewaltige Budgets eher in die
Werbung als ins Produktdesign investiert
werden. Hier finden allerdings Veränderun-
gen statt. Mehr und mehr Marken betrauen
ihre Designberater mit dem strategischen
Management ihrer Außenwirkung und lassen
ihnen dabei weitgehend freie Hand.
Wenn aber aufgeklärte Unternehmen
Geschäftsergebnisse von Anfang an in die
Designvorgabe einfließen lassen und die
Präsentation ihrer Produkte aus dem rest-
lichen Marketing-Mix herauslösen, kann
Design als entscheidendes Bindeglied im
Geschäftsprozess phänomenale Resultate
erzielen, wie die folgenden Fallstudien
belegen:

„THE THINKING PERSON'S CUPPA"

Wie kann sich eine Nischen-Teemarke bei der steigenden Popularität von Kaffee auf dem riesigen heimischen Markt als gehobene Marke neu positionieren und gegen den sinkenden Teekonsum ankämpfen?

Das Unternehmen Clipper Tea beschloss, dass es ein neues Erscheinungsbild benötigt. Dabei musste es sich drei Herausforderungen stellen: Es musste Unterscheidungsmerkmale aufbauen, die Konsistenz erhöhen und Integrität schaffen. Zudem fehlte Clipper ein optisch einheitlicher Stil. William Murray Hamms neues Design ist Ausdruck der Integrität sowie der ethischen Geschäftspraxis des Unternehmens, die er mit „The thinking person's cuppa" (die Tasse für den denkenden Menschen) auf den Punkt brachte – dieser Ausspruch verlangt nach einem dezenten und nüchternen Verpackungsdesign. Inspiriert durch Magazine wie National Geographic erzählt nun jede Packung eine faszinierende Geschichte aus der Region, in der der Tee angebaut wird. Diese kurzen Informationen können sich mit der einheimischen Tierwelt, der lokalen Geschichte oder speziellen Traditionen beschäftigen.

Seit seiner Markteinführung zwischen März und Dezember 2001 ist das deutlichste Ergebnis der Umgestaltung eine immense Erhöhung der Verkaufszahlen. Innerhalb von drei Jahren stiegen sie um geschätzte 373 Prozent. Auch der Exportmarkt expandierte auf 23 Länder. Wichtig ist auch, dass der wirtschaftliche Erfolg die Lebensqualität und die Aussichten der Menschen auf den Plantagen, mit denen Clipper Tea fairen Handel treibt, erheblich verbessert und neue Investitionen in die Regionen gebracht hat.

ÖKOLOGISCHER LANDBAU

Die Organic Milk Suppliers Cooperative (OMSCo) sah sich mit einer ganz anderen Herausforderung konfrontiert als Clipper Tea. Ein Überschuss an Biomilch hatte zu starker Konkurrenz und damit zu Preisdruck durch den Handel geführt. Auf der Suche nach einer langfristigen Lösung zur Wertsteigerung entschied man sich, eine neue Qualitätsmarke auf den Markt zu bringen, die dem Biomarkt zu Wachstum verhelfen sollte. Die Herausforderung bestand darin, ein Produkt zu schaffen, das alle Vorteile der alternativen Bioproduktion vermittelt und Kunden anlockt, die keine Bioprodukte kaufen. Das Produkt sollte überdies als Grundnahrungsmittel und nicht als Nischenprodukt positioniert werden.

Mithilfe des Verpackungsdesigns gelang es Blue Marlin, eine Marke zu gestalten, die den Verbraucherwünschen entsprach. Der Name „Altogether Better" verdeutlicht den besseren Geschmack von Biomilch, ihren gesundheitlichen Nutzen sowie ihre Umweltfreundlichkeit. Die recycelbare Flasche, die einer traditionellen Milchkanne nachempfunden ist, mag zunächst ungewohnt erscheinen, ist aber durch den oberen Griff besser zu tragen, und der zweite Griff auf der Rückseite erleichtert das Ausgießen.

Die grafische Gestaltung verzichtet auf die typischen Bioklischees und zeigt stattdessen Familien, die Milch genießen, was das Produkt massenmarktkompatibel und zugänglich macht.

Altogether Better wurde im Februar 2005 in 200 Sainsbury's-Läden eingeführt. Die wöchentlichen Verkaufszahlen belaufen sich auf 1,2 Millionen Pfund im Jahr, damit übersteigt Altogether Better die Erwartungen um 9 Prozent, und der Anteil der Käufer, die die Marke mehr als einmal kaufen, hat innerhalb der ersten fünf Monate nach Verkaufsstart bereits 34 Prozent erreicht. Auf dem derzeitigen Verkaufsniveau kann der Überschuss an Biomilch jährlich um run 2 Millionen Liter reduziert und innerhalb von 12 bis 18 Monaten abgebaut werden. Die Entwicklungskosten werden innerhalb von 8 Monaten eingespielt sein.

KETTEN SPRENGEN

Die große Herausforderung bei Produkte aus dem Bereich der Hygieneartikel besteh darin, sie sowohl auffällig als auch diskret zu gestalten. Da der Bekanntheitswert der Marke Kotex bereits abnahm und die Verkaufszahlen rückläufig waren, war dringend eine neue Strategie nötig, um der Marke ein positives Image zu verleihen, ohne Geld in die Produktentwicklung nvestieren zu müssen.

Coley Porter Bells Strategie bestand dar das Produkt neu zu positionieren. Es wurde aus dem Bereich Hygieneartikel geholt und den Körperpflegeprodukten zugeordnet. Di amerikanische Kotex-Verpackung trug eine roten Punkt, der die Menstruation symbolisierte – bisher ein Tabu auf dem europäisch Markt. Coley Porter Bell konzentrierte sich auf diese rote Farbe und setzte sie in Form von positiven Bildelementen wie Lippenstiften, Herzen und hohen Absätzen im neu Verpackungsdesign um.

All diese Unternehmen sind für ihre Investitionen in Design mit hohen Gewinne belohnt worden. Um wirklich Gutes liefern zu können, müssen Designer das Unternehmen ihrer Auftraggeber genau studiere und das Projekt im Zusammenhang mit de strategischen Zielen des Unternehmens ei ordnen können. Werden gemeinsam mit de

unden von Anfang an wirtschaftliche Ziele
den Designauftrag eingearbeitet, sind die
ffektivität wie auch der Erfolg der Arbeit
r beide Parteien messbar und führen zu
ner intensiveren und längeren Zusammen-
beit. Auf lange Sicht führt genau dies zu
ner nachhaltigen Wertschöpfung.

Hannah Paterson wurde 1976 im englischen
imbledon geboren und absolvierte ein Archi-
kturstudium an der Sheffield University, das
e mit dem BA abschloss. Nach ihrem Studium
ieg sie als Koordinatorin für die Design Effec-
eness Awards bei der Design Business Asso-
ation (DBA – www.dba.org.uk) ein. Derzeit hat
e den Posten Programmes Director bei der
BA inne und ist verantwortlich für die Aus-
chtung aller Veranstaltungen, Lehrgänge und
ward-Programme.

Dans cette étude de cas, Hannah
aterson, de la Design Business
ssociation (DBA), choisit les gagnants
s prix annuels de l'institution, les Design
fectiveness Awards, pour mettre en
leur des exemples pratiques de sociétés
i ont trouvé des solutions d'emballage
éatives afin d'optimiser la valeur du
essage destiné à leurs consommateurs.

Les entreprises font face à des défis diffé-
nts tous les jours, qu'il s'agisse d'une bais-
du marché, d'un changement des ten-
nces de consommation, ou de trouver un
yen de se différencier sur un marché
turé. Mais que se passe-t-il lorsque les
treprises tournées vers l'avenir placent le
sign au cœur de leurs stratégies pour sur-

monter ces défis ? La DBA (Design
Business Association) remet les Design
Effectiveness Awards (les prix de l'efficacité du design) depuis 1989 pour récompenser
ce type d'initiative.

Nous avons des études de cas qui prou-
vent de façon irréfutable que le design peut
pénétrer tous les aspects d'une activité, en
améliorant la rentabilité, en créant de nouvelles sources de revenus, en donnant plus
de prestige à l'entreprise, en faisant
connaître la marque et en donnant au personnel les moyens d'obtenir les meilleurs
résultats possibles.

DBA récompense le design comme outil de
croissance de l'activité, et aucune preuve des
avantages du design pour l'activité des
entreprises n'est plus parlante que les études
de cas des Design Effectiveness Awards.
Dans le domaine du design, c'est le seul système de récompense qui utilise des données
commerciales comme critère de jugement, et
c'est pourquoi ces prix sont les plus sérieux
et les plus prestigieux du Royaume-Uni.

Il ne fait aucun doute que le design peut
ajouter de la valeur à une activité, qu'il peut
être l'ingrédient qui change le destin d'une
entreprise ; grâce à lui, une marque à peine
connue peut se transformer en favorite, et il
peut avoir une grande influence sur les bénéfices de l'entreprise. Et pourtant, ce n'est pas
simple de convaincre les entreprises de voir
le design comme un investissement vital plutôt que comme un coût, surtout en ce qui
concerne les produits de grande consommation, pour lesquels on consacre des budgets
importants à la publicité plutôt qu'au design ;
mais cela est en train de changer. De plus en
plus de marques confient la gestion straté-
gique de leur réputation à leur agence de
conseil en design.

Cependant, lorsque des entreprises bien
informées tiennent compte des résultats
recherchés dès le départ, dans le cahier des
charges du projet de design, et élaborent un
marketing mix cohérent, le design peut jouer
un rôle spectaculaire en tant que lien straté-
gique dans le processus commercial, comme
le montrent les études de cas ci-dessous.

LA TASSE DE THÉ DE LA PERSONNE PENSANTE

Avec la popularité en constante hausse du
café, comment un thé peut-il, sur un marché
national énorme, repositionner sa marque en
tant que produit haut de gamme et lutter
contre le déclin de la consommation de thé ?

La marque Clipper Tea a décidé qu'elle
avait besoin d'une modernisation visuelle.
Pour cela, il y avait trois défis à affronter :
se différencier, améliorer la cohérence et
conserver l'intégrité. Le style visuel de
Clipper manquait de cohérence, ce qui
sapait la stabilité de la marque. Le nouveau
design de William Murray Hamm exprime
l'intégrité de l'entreprise et son éthique, en
résumant l'essence de la marque à « la tasse
de thé de la personne pensante », qui guide
le style de l'emballage, sobre et discret.
Inspiré par des magazines comme National
Geographic, chaque paquet présente aussi
une mine d'informations fascinantes sur la
région d'origine du thé, sur les animaux
autochtones, sur des histoires ou des traditions locales.

Lancée sur le marché entre mars et
décembre 2001, le résultat le plus significatif
de cette révision du design a été, et est toujours, une augmentation considérable des
ventes. On estime que les résultats ont connu
une croissance de 373 % en trois ans. Les
marchés à l'export ont eux aussi progressé,

passant de 1 à 23 pays. Cette augmentation de l'activité économique a également amélioré la qualité de vie et les perspectives d'avenir des domaines qui fournissent Clipper Tea selon les règles du commerce équitable, en permettant de nouveaux investissements.

LA CULTURE BIOLOGIQUE

La Coopérative des fournisseurs de lait biologique (Organic Milk Suppliers Cooperative, OMSCo) était confrontée à un tout autre défi : un surplus de stock de lait biologique, qui avait conduit à une augmentation de la concurrence et à des pressions pour faire baisser les prix de la part des distributeurs. Dans sa recherche d'une solution à long terme pour créer de la valeur, la OMSCo a identifié une occasion de créer une nouvelle marque haut de gamme qui allait permettre de stimuler la croissance du marché biologique. Le défi était de créer un produit capable de communiquer sur les avantages de l'alternative biologique, d'encourager les consommateurs étrangers au biologique à faire ce choix et de repositionner la marque comme un produit essentiel de tous les jours plutôt que comme un produit de niche.

Blue Marlin a créé une marque qui, à travers le design de son emballage, répond aux besoins des consommateurs. Le nom Altogether Better (« entièrement meilleur ») fait référence à la saveur du lait biologique, ainsi qu'à ses bienfaits pour la santé et à sa responsabilité environnementale. La bouteille recyclable, qui évoque un pot à lait traditionnel, semble inhabituelle au premier abord mais est plus facile à porter que les bouteilles courantes, grâce à la poignée du haut, et la poignée située à l'arrière facilite le service.

Le graphisme évite les clichés traditionnels du biologique et préfère montrer des photographies de familles savourant du lait ensemble, pour donner au produit une image grand public et accessible.

Altogether Better a été mis à la vente dans 200 magasins Sainsbury en février 2005. Des ventes hebdomadaires équivalant à 1,2 million de livres sterling par an signifient que Altogether Better a dépassé ses objectifs de 9 pour cent, et le taux cumulatif de répétition de l'achat (la proportion de personnes qui achètent la marque plusieurs fois) a atteint les 34 pour cent dans les cinq premiers mois qui ont suivi le lancement. En se basant sur les ventes actuelles, le surplus de lait biologique diminuera de près de 2 millions de litres par an et sera écoulé entre 12 et 18 mois. Les coûts de développement seront amortis en 8 mois.

CASSER LE MOULE

Le plus grand paradoxe sur le marché des protections périodiques est qu'il faut créer un produit qui se distingue tout en étant discret. La popularité de la marque Kotex était déjà défaillante, et les ventes déclinaient. Il fallait une nouvelle stratégie pour redonner vie à la marque et moderniser son image sans dépenser un sou en développement de produit.

La stratégie de Coley Porter Bell était de repositionner le produit en dehors du marché des protections périodiques, en le plaçant dans la catégorie des produits de soin personnel. L'emballage américain de Kotex utilisait un point rouge pour symboliser la menstruation. Jusqu'à présent, c'était un tabou passé sous silence sur le marché européen. Coley Porter Bell a complètement misé sur la couleur rouge, et a utilisé des symboles tels que des rouges à lèvres, des cœurs et des talons aiguilles sur les emballages.

Toutes ces entreprises ont récolté des retours énormes sur leurs investissements dans le design. Pour créer une véritable valeur ajoutée, les designers devaient comprendre véritablement l'activité de leur client, ainsi que le contexte du projet par rapport aux objectifs stratégiques de l'entreprise. Lorsque l'agence travaille avec son client pour intégrer les objectifs commerciaux au cahier des charges du design dès le départ, les deux parties peuvent mesurer l'efficacité et l'impact du travail de l'agence, ce qui débouche sur des relations plus solides et plus durables. En fin de compte, c'est de l que vient la valeur durable.

Hannah Paterson est née en 1976 à Wimbledon, au Royaume-Uni, et a obtenu un diplôme en Architecture à l'Université de Sheffield. Ell est ensuite entrée à la Design Business Association (DBA – www.dba.org.uk) en 1999 en tant que coordinatrice pour les Design Effectivenes Awards. Hannah occupe actuellement le poste de directrice des programmes chez DBA et est responsable de l'organisation de tous leurs événements et de tous leurs programmes de formation et de récompenses.

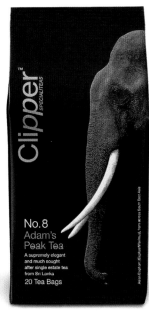

CLIPPER TEA

The first step was to move away from the clichés of tea packet design which reflect the old days of the Empire.

CLIPPER TEA

Der erste wichtige Schritt war, sich von den Teepackungen zu lösen, die auf die Zeiten des Empires anspielten.

CLIPPER TEA

La première étape consistait à s'éloigner du cliché de la boîte de thé nostalgique de la belle époque de l'Empire.

ALTOGETHER BETTER

The packaging is made from materials that preserve 17-day shelf life, has a leak proof cap and is designed to fit into fridge doors.

ALTOGETHER BETTER

Die Verpackung wird aus Materialien hergestellt, die eine 17-tägige Haltbarkeit garantieren. Sie hat einen ausflusssicheren Verschluss, und ihre Form ist passend für Kühlschranktüren entworfen.

ALTOGETHER BETTER

La bouteille est fabriquée à partir de matériaux qui assurent une durée de conservation en stock de 17 jours, elle est dotée d'un bouchon antifuite et est conçue pour être rangée dans les portes des réfrigérateurs.

KOTEX

Identification with Kotex through distinctive packaging rose 780 per cent in Western European markets. Shoppers particularly singled out the 'personal care' angle. They commented that the new packaging showed that Kotex had become more of a beauty product and therefore was a more attractive item to pick off the shelves. In Central Europe the perception of Kotex as a 'feminine brand' increased by 144 per cent.

KOTEX

Durch die auffällige Verpackung wuchs die Identifikation mit Kotex auf dem westeuropäischen Markt um 780 Prozent. Die Käufer lobten vor allem den Aspekt der Körperpflege. Kotex sei nach Ansicht der Käufer zum Schönheitsprodukt geworden und zähle zu den attraktiven Produkten. In Mitteleuropa stieg die Wahrnehmung von Kotex als „feminine Marke" um 144 Prozent.

KOTEX

L'identification à Kotex a augmenté de 780 pour cent sur les marchés d'Europe de l'Ouest grâce à cet emballage différent. Les clientes ont particulièrement apprécié le côté « soin personnel ». Elles ont trouvé que le nouvel emballage montrait que Kotex était devenu plutôt un produit de beauté et qu'on avait donc plus envie de le mettre dans son panier de courses. En Europe centrale, la perception de Kotex en tant que « marque féminine » a augmenté de 144 pour cent.

Case 06
Package Design in Japan

Taku Satoh, founder of Satoh Design

In this essay, Taku Satoh, a leading Japanese product designer based in Tokyo, discourses about his personal vision of the most important factors when developing a package design for the products he works with. With over two decades of experience, Satoh gives an in-depth insight of how a winning package design can be achieved.

When I think about package design, five main points come to mind. I feel that the environment in which a product is created affects the package design of the product in different ways. The first of these five points is the protection of the product, both in matters of storage and shipment. Although this point seems to go without saying, the package of a product must be devised to ensure the product's safety during transportation.

The second point is the easy management of the packaging, in terms of distribution and consumer satisfaction. For example, to help with transportation, the elimination of excess space the package may consume should be taken into consideration; difficulty in opening the package or in the removal of the item, as well as the possibility of incurring an injury to the hands should also be taken into account.

The third point is that the graphic design on the package should adequately convey to the consumer what the contents are. The purpose of package design is to give an added value to the contents of the package; however, I believe that design should not perform this function. Instead of adding something to the value of the contents, I believe that design should make a connection with the product. Therefore, the incorporation of unnecessary elements in the design of the package might make the consumer receive the message incorrectly. Setting aside the special cases of

packages whose contents are deliberately concealed, or as a gift to keep it secret in the present day, where a clear message as to the contents of a package is desired, people will not only stop consuming products with these types of misleading packages but also, if confusing package design increases, they will stop shopping altogether.

The fourth point is attention to environmental care. Perhaps it is not too much to say that, in this age, environmental care should be considered as one of the more important purposes of package design. Before we decide on materials which will not be a burden on the environment, it is essential to verify first why packaging is necessary.

The fifth point is awareness of the media. To put this point into perspective, let us say that there are packages to store a hundred cakes a day and packages for a million bottles of a beverage a day. In the case of the former, the minimum information about the product would suffice; but, in the case of the latter, one must consider other advertising efforts, and so this may not function smoothly at all. In other words, the package itself should be considered as an advertising tool for the item it is representing, and therefore, its design must be conceived by taking this fact into account. Before we come across the product itself, it is through advertising that we will first come to know the product. Bearing this in mind, we must have an idea in advance that will allow us to think in what way we would like to leave an impression upon the mind of the consumer through the package design. A package design that does not leave a lasting impression will prove nonfunctional in terms of advertising.

In summary, let us list these five points once more:

1. Protection of the Product
2. Easy to Manage
3. Clear Conveyance of the Contents
4. Environmentaly Friendly
5. Awareness of Media

Each of these points, of course, is relevant to the others. If we take protection of the contents into consideration, then this affect whether or not excess packaging and usage of unnecessary materials comes into play, i. if we want a plastic bottle to be more easy drink out of then we would logically make the opening bigger, thereby causing us to make the caps larger to fit, thus forcing us use more resources for making those large caps. As small as it may seem, by making just one adjustment, in terms of size, we w ultimately have to use numerous tons of pl. tic to cater for this one change.

Up till now, we have considered these m imum 5 main points of package design; how ever, we must also know that we cannot begin to design the package if we have no idea of what the contents are. Since packag design is the tool of communication by whic we can convey to people the contents of wh is inside the package, we must have a firm grasp of what the product is. Nowadays, ho ever, this simple fact is slowly starting to g overlooked and taken for granted in the cr ation of packages. I feel the ideology, that t purpose of package design should "be fun", too affluent. Since package design is a tool that allows the consumer to see the conten from the outside, we must focus the consic sness of the viewer on what that item is – must adequately guide the viewers mind in the package, not too much, but not too littl

I believe that to discern a "moderate design" is the job of a package designer.

...at is, package design should send an
...pression that unconsciously calls out to
...e consumer; the design should always pull
...e consumer towards the product.
...signers who habitually aim at making
...eir designs fun or interesting seem to be
...getting this fact. I too am engaged in
...signing, and I have really come to under-
...nd this concept. When I begin designing a
...ckage, I first take the time to make sure
...at I have a thorough grasp of what the
...oduct is, I am designing the package for.
...e most important thing is not to begin
...eating an image as one sees fit without
...st knowing the product. So, one must first
...l off this desire to make all designs fun.
...Next, one must ask oneself when thinking
...design of a package for a maker's product:
...at have they produced until now? What is
...hat only they can do? What kind of skills
...they have? What is it that they feel they
...e contributing to society?
...Then, without fail, I travel to the facto-
...s. I listen to the comments of various
...ople in charge and when I see the facto-
...s administrative structure, I understand
...maker's point of view better. When I lis-
...directly to the comments of the engi-
...ers, the feeling of what is involved in
...king the product is conveyed to me. Once
...ave done this, I find numerous things
...ich I too should convey in the message
...t I send through the design of a package.
...king all of these factors into considera-
...n, I begin to edit my design and figure
...the best way to express these elements
...ough the media known as package
...sign. Through this process, I can get
...re thoroughly into the essence of the
...oduct, and I inevitably become able to
...ch on that company's mission.

I have also learnt to understand how certain products are produced continuously for a
long period of time. When we consider this,
and what I have said before, design serves as
tool for guidance. Package design must not
disengage itself from the specific product that
is inside the package. A design need not be so
eloquently displayed – a design which is subtle, to the degree that it is not initially perceived as a design, is what should be sought.

To express this in Japanese, one might use
the word *wakimae*, which is a word that cau-
tions one to consider his position in a situation and display a humble heart. For example, when we wish to warn someone against
their actions we might say, "*tachiba wo wakimaenasai*" (think about your position [in the
situation]). In terms of product design, I feel
that the essence of *wakimae* is also important – an item should be presented as it is.
Therefore, we must also know the essence of
wakimae in the field of design. The designer
should first pose the question of *wakimae* to
himself. I've often thought this, and lately
I've been asking myself how much of this
design isn't necessary – what can be elimi-
nated? As much as possible. I don't try to
make my designs force the viewer to feel
something that isn't there, but rather to
improve the functionality of the package.
This is very difficult, however, but still I
believe this attempt provides a glimpse of
what package design in Japan will be from
this point onwards.

In spite of the fact that package design is
adequately displays the contents of its package, if we are heading towards designs which
don't have any "charm" or "pull," then that
means that the contents didn't have any
"charm" or "pull" to begin with. For products
that have no "charm," to create that "charm"

through the design of a package is to perceive
the design as an added value. I feel that this
is an incorrect utilisation of package design.

Designers who are engaged in package
design should make themselves able to
express the role of a design clearly before
they enter into the creation process. In order
to do this, I think it is important that one
must get to know who and what one is working with, and one must be able to grasp objec-
tively the conditions one was put in when
engaging in any package design project.

*Born in Tokyo in 1955, Taku Satoh graduated
from the Tokyo National University of Fine Arts
and Music, majoring in Design, in 1979 and
later completing a graduate course at the same
university. He initially joined advertising giant
Dentsu before establishing Taku Satoh Design
Office Inc. in 1984. Satoh has designed for
Nikka, Lotte Chewing Gum, Taisho Pharmaceutical, and MEIJI among many others. He
received numerous awards, including the Tokyo
ADC Award, Japan Package Design Award,
New York ADC Award, and Good Design Award.*

In diesem Essay erläutert Taku Satoh, ein führender japanischer Produktdesigner aus Tokio, in einer sehr persönlichen Darstellung, was für ihn die wichtigsten Faktoren sind, wenn er ein neues Verpackungsdesign für ein bestimmtes Produkt entwickelt. Satoh, der mehr als 20 Jahre Erfahrung in dieser Branche aufzuweisen hat, erläutert, wie ausgezeichnetes Verpackungsdesign entworfen werden kann.

Wenn ich an Verpackungsdesign denke, fallen mir fünf wichtige Punkte ein. Ich denke, dass die Umgebung, in der ein Produkt entwickelt wird, das Verpackungsdesign auf unterschiedliche Weise beeinflusst. Der erste Punkt ist die Sicherheit des Produktes im Hinblick auf Lagerung und Lieferung. Auch wenn dieser Punkt kaum erwähnenswert scheint, so muss doch jede Produktverpackung so gestaltet sein, dass sie die Sicherheit des Produktes während des Transportes gewährleistet.

Der zweite Punkt ist die einfache Handhabung einer Verpackung, sowohl beim Transport als auch für den Kunden. So sollte eine Verpackung so gestaltet werden, dass sie gut verstaut keinen zusätzlichen Raum beansprucht. Für den Kunden ist wichtig, dass eine Verpackung leicht zu öffnen und das Produkt einfach zu entnehmen ist. Die Verpackung darf keine Verletzungsgefahren bergen.

Drittens sollte die grafische Gestaltung der Verpackung dem Kunden eine klare Vorstellung vom Produkt vermitteln. Als Zweck für Verpackungsdesign wird oft genannt, dass eine Verpackung ihrem Inhalt einen Zusatznutzen geben sollte. Ich denke allerdings nicht, dass Design diese Aufgabe erfüllen muss. Statt etwas hinzufügen sollte es besser eine Verbindung zum Produkt her-

stellen. Überflüssige Elemente im Design könnten dem Kunden eine falsche Botschaft vermitteln. Lässt man Spezialfälle außer Acht, bei denen der Inhalt einer Verpackung bewusst nicht benannt wird, oder Geschenkverpackungen, die den Inhalt verbergen sollen, wird heute eine klare Bezeichnung des Inhalts verlangt. Die Verbraucher stellen sonst den Konsum solcher Produkte mit missverständlichen Verpackungen einfach ein, und wenn das Verpackungsdesign weiterhin derartig verwirrend bleibt, werden sie den Konsum wahrscheinlich irgendwann ganz einstellen.

Der vierte wichtige Punkt ist der Umweltschutz. In heutiger Zeit ist es bestimmt nicht übertrieben, wenn man sagt, dass Umweltschutz ein wichtiger Aspekt des Verpackungsdesigns sein sollte. Bevor wir uns für ein Verpackungsmaterial entscheiden, das umweltfreundlich ist, sollten wir überlegen, ob überhaupt eine Verpackung notwendig ist.

Der fünfte wichtige Punkt ist ein bewusster Umgang mit unterschiedlichen Mitteln. Lassen Sie uns diesen Punkt an einem Beispiel verdeutlichen: Vergleichen wir eine Verpackung, mit der hundert Kuchen pro Tag verkauft werden sollen, mit einer Verpackung für eine Million Getränke pro Tag. Im ersten Fall reicht ein Minimum an Produktinformation. Im zweiten Fall hingegen müssen andere Werbemaßnahmen ergriffen werden, und das kann alles andere als einfach sein. Hier muss die Verpackung auch als werbewirksames Medium für ihren Inhalt betrachtet werden, ein Punkt, der bereits beim Verpackungsdesign beachtet werden muss. Bevor wir mit dem Produkt selbst in Kontakt kommen, sind wir ihm bereits in der Werbung begegnet. Diese Tatsache muss

klar sein. Es sollten bereits im Vorfeld Test durchgeführt werden, um herauszufinden, welchen Eindruck man mit dem Verpackungsdesign auf den Verbraucher machen möchte. Eine Verpackung, die beim Verbraucher keinen bleibenden Eindruck hinter lässt, wird sich im Hinblick auf ihre Werbewirksamkeit als unbrauchbar erweisen.

Zusammenfassend können diese fünf Punkte folgendermaßen formuliert werden:
1. Schutz des Produktes
2. Einfache Handhabung
3. Klare Vermittlung des Inhalts
4. Umweltfreundlichkeit
5. Bewusster Einsatz der Mittel

Jeder dieser Punkte hat auch Einfluss a die anderen. So kann Produktschutz zusätz ches Verpackungsmaterial oder die Verwendung von unnötigen Materialien erforderlich machen. Wenn wir z. B. eine Plastikflasche so gestalten wollen, dass ma einfacher daraus trinken kann, könnte man die Trinköffnung vergrößern. Dafür müsste aber auch der Verschluss vergrößert werde Somit würde für die Herstellung mehr Material, also mehr Rohstoffe, benötigt. In diesem Fall kann eine winzige Veränderun den Mehrverbrauch von unzähligen Tonne Kunststoff bedeuten.

Bisher haben wir nur die fünf Hauptaspekte des Verpackungsdesigns betrachte Man sollte sich aber auch bewusst machen, dass man ohne klare Vorstellung vom Inha keine Verpackung entwerfen kann. Da Ver packungsdesign ein Kommunikationswerkzeug ist, mit dem wir dem Kunden ein Vorstellung vom Inhalt vermitteln, müsse wir das Produkt genau kennen. Leider wir diese eigentlich selbstverständliche Tatsac heute immer häufiger nicht beachtet und e h vorausgesetzt. Der heutige Trend, dass eigentliche Zweck des Verpackungs-igns Spaß sein sollte, ist mir zu oberfläch-. Da Verpackungsdesign ein Mittel ist, Konsumenten schon von außen einen k auf das Produkt zu gewähren, müssen uns auf die Vorstellung konzentrieren, der Betrachter von diesem Inhalt hat. müssen das geistige Auge des rachters auf angemessene Weise ins ere der Verpackung leiten – nicht zu viel nicht zu wenig.

ch bin davon überzeugt, dass es Aufgabe Verpackungsdesigners ist, ein „modera-Design" zu erstellen. Das heißt, das packungsdesign sollte eine Botschaft ver-teln, die den Konsumenten unbewusst pricht. Das Design sollte den Kunden ner vom Produkt aus ansprechen. Desig-die versuchen, ihr Design verspielt oder ressant zu gestalten, scheinen diese Auf-e zu vergessen. Auch ich bin Designer habe mich mit diesem Konzept einge-d auseinandergesetzt. Wenn ich mit dem wurf einer Verpackung beginne, ver-affe ich mir zunächst ein genaues Bild Produkt. Es ist sehr wichtig, nicht ohne ntnisse über das Produkt zu arbeiten. muss also dem Drang widerstehen, s Design lustig zu gestalten.

ls Nächstes sollte man sich ein paar gen stellen, die das Unternehmen be-fen. Was hat dieser Hersteller bisher luziert? Was kann nur dieser Hersteller en, was sind seine besonderen Fähig-en? Was leistet dieser Hersteller seiner icht nach für die Gesellschaft? ch sehe mir bei jedem neuen Auftrag die Produktionsstätten an. Ich spreche den Verantwortlichen und studiere die waltungsstruktur der Unternehmen.

So kann ich die Sicht des Herstellers besser verstehen. Wenn ich direkt mit den Inge-nieuren spreche, kann ich nachvollziehen, welche Aspekte für die Produktion des Produktes entscheidend waren. Danach habe ich unzählige Punkte, die mein Verpackungs-design vermitteln sollte. Mit diesem Wissen ausgestattet, beginne ich mit dem Entwurf und suche nach der bestmöglichen Umset-zung aller Aspekte in meinem Medium, dem Verpackungsdesign. Auf diese Weise kann ich das Wesen eines Produktes besser ver-stehen und dadurch das Unternehmen und sein Produkt besser vertreten.

Mir ist ebenfalls klar geworden, warum einige Produkte sich über einen langen Zeit-raum behaupten können. Wenn wir uns vor Augen führen, dass Design, wie bereits erwähnt, ein Hilfsmittel ist, den Blick in das Innere zu lenken, darf sich Verpackungs-design nicht vom Produkt lösen. Ein Design muss nicht auffällig sein – unser Ziel sollte eine Gestaltung sein, die so subtil ist, dass sie auf den ersten Blick nicht als Design auffällt.

Im Japanischen würde ich dafür das Wort wakimae wählen. Es bringt zum Ausdruck, dass man seine Position in einer Situation überdenken und ein bescheidenes Herz zei-gen sollte. Wenn wir z. B. jemandem von sei-nem Handeln abraten wollen, sagen wir: „Tachiba wo wakimaenasai" (überdenke deine Position [in dieser Situation]). Aus mei-ner Sicht ist diese Bedeutung von wakimae auch für das Produktdesign wichtig – ein Gegenstand sollte so präsentiert werden, wie er ist. Daher ist wakimae auch für uns Designer wichtig. Der Designer sollte sich immer erst die Frage des wakimae stellen. Ich habe mir diese Frage in letzter Zeit häu-fig gestellt und mich ständig gefragt, wie viel meines Designs überflüssig ist, was ich weg-

lassen kann. Mein Design soll den Betrachter nicht zwingen, etwas zu sehen, was nicht da ist. Ich versuche, die Funktionalität der Verpackung zu verbessern. Dies ist zwar sehr schwierig, aber ich denke, das zeigt, in welche Richtung sich Verpackungsdesign in Japan zukünftig entwickeln wird.

Ziel des Verpackungsdesigns ist, den Inhalt angemessen darzustellen. Heute gibt es einen Trend zu Gestaltungen, die keinerlei Charme oder Anziehungskraft haben, da auch ihr Inhalt bereits keinen Charme und keine Anziehungskraft hat. Entwirft man für ein reizloses Produkt eine reizvolle Verpackung, dann ist das Design ein added value (Zusatz-nutzen). Meines Erachtens ist dieser Einsatz von Verpackungsdesigns nicht korrekt.

Verpackungsdesigner sollten die Rolle eines Designs deutlich zum Ausdruck brin-gen können, bevor sie mit dem kreativen Schaffensprozess beginnen. Dafür ist es mei-ner Meinung nach wichtig, zu wissen, für wen und mit was man arbeitet. Außerdem müssen sich Designer objektiv über die Konditionen klar sein, zu denen sie für ein bestimmtes Projekt beschäftigt wurden.

Taku Satoh wurde 1955 in Tokio geboren und studierte Design an der Tokyo National Univer-sity of Fine Arts and Music, wo er 1979 seinen Abschluss machte. Später absolvierte er einen Graduate-Course an derselben Universität. Zunächst arbeitete er für den Werbegiganten Dentsu, bevor er 1984 seine eigene Firma Taku Satoh Design Office Inc. gründete. Satoh ist u.a. für Nikka, Lotte Kaugummi, Taisho Pharma-ceutical und MEIJI tätig. Er erhielt zahlreiche Auszeichnungen, u.a. den Tokyo ADC Award, Japan Package Design Award, New York ADC Award, and Good Design Award.*

Dans cet essai, Taku Satoh, un grand designer de produits basé à Tokyo, parle de sa vision personnelle des facteurs qui doivent primer dans la création de l'emballage des produits avec lesquels il travaille. Il a plus de vingt ans d'expérience, et nous explique avec une grande subtilité comment obtenir un emballage réussi.

Lorsque je pense au design d'emballage, cinq points principaux me viennent à l'esprit. Je pense que l'environnement dans lequel un produit est créé affecte le design de l'emballage de ce produit de différentes manières. Le premier point est la protection du produit, aussi bien en matière de stockage que de transport. Même si cela peut sembler évident, le conditionnement d'un produit doit être conçu pour assurer sa sécurité durant le transport.

Le second point est la facilité de manipulation de l'emballage en termes de distribution et de satisfaction du consommateur. Par exemple, pour faciliter le transport, il faut prendre en compte l'élimination des espaces vides dus à l'emballage. Il faut aussi penser à la commodité de l'emballage au moment de son ouverture ou de l'extraction du produit, ainsi qu'aux risques de blessures aux mains lors de la manipulation.

Le troisième point, c'est la capacité de l'emballage à communiquer au consommateur la nature de ce qu'il contient de façon adéquate. L'objectif du design d'emballage est de donner au contenu de l'emballage une valeur ajoutée. Cependant, je pense que le design ne doit pas remplir cette fonction. Au lieu d'ajouter quelque chose à la valeur du contenu, je crois que le design doit établir un lien avec le produit. L'ajout d'éléments inutiles au design de l'emballage pourrait donc empêcher le consommateur de recevoir le message

correctement. Si on laisse de côté les cas particuliers des emballages dont le contenu est délibérément tenu secret, ou des cadeaux qui doivent conserver leur mystère, de nos jours les consommateurs veulent que le contenu de l'emballage soit clairement identifié. Non seulement les gens arrêteront de consommer les produits qui utilisent des messages portant à confusion mais si ce type de design d'emballage équivoque se multiplie, ils arrêteront complètement d'acheter.

Le quatrième point est l'attention accordée à la protection de l'environnement. Il n'est sans doute pas excessif de dire qu'à notre époque, la protection de l'environnement doit être considérée comme l'un des objectifs les plus importants du design d'emballage. Avant de choisir des matériaux qui ne représenteront pas un fardeau pour l'environnement, il est essentiel de vérifier d'abord en quoi l'emballage est nécessaire.

Le cinquième point est la prise en compte des médias. Pour expliquer ce point, prenons l'exemple suivant : il y a des emballages qui vont servir pour un volume d'une centaine de gâteaux par jour, et il y a des emballages qui vont servir pour un volume d'un million de bouteilles de boisson par jour. Dans le premier cas, un minimum d'informations sur le produit devrait suffire ; mais, dans le deuxième cas, il faut prendre en compte les autres efforts qui vont être menés dans le domaine de la publicité, et cela ne sera donc sans doute pas aussi simple. En d'autres termes, l'emballage lui-même doit être considéré comme un outil de publicité pour le produit qu'il représente, son design doit donc être conçu en tenant compte de ce fait. Avant de rencontrer le produit lui-même, c'est à travers la publicité que nous ferons sa connaissance. Il faut donc garder cela à l'esprit et

réaliser des simulations qui nous permettron de réfléchir à l'impression que nous voulons laisser au consommateur à travers le design de l'emballage. Un design d'emballage qui n laisse pas une impression durable s'avèrera contreproductif en termes de publicité.

Pour résumer, faisons une liste de ces ci points :
1. La protection du produit
2. La facilité de manipulation
3. La lisibilité du contenu
4. Le respect de l'environnement
5. La prise en compte des médias

Naturellement, chacun de ces points inter agit avec les autres. Si l'on considère la pro tion du contenu, ce point affecte la quantité matériau qui entre en jeu dans la fabricatio de l'emballage. Par exemple, si l'on veut qu'une bouteille en plastique soit plus pratic pour boire directement au goulot, logiqueme on élargit l'ouverture. Le bouchon doit donc être plus grand, ce qui nous force à employe plus de matière première. Dans ce cas, cette petite modification qui paraît toute simple v en fin de compte nous obliger à utiliser plusieurs tonnes de plastique supplémentaires.

Jusqu'à maintenant, nous n'avons pris e compte que ce minimum de 5 points princi paux du design d'emballage. Mais nous ne pouvons pourtant pas commencer le desig de l'emballage si nous n'avons aucune idée la nature du contenu. Puisque le design de l'emballage est l'outil de communication grâce auquel nous pouvons communiquer le contenu, nous devons avoir une bonne compréhension de la nature du produit. Cependant, de nos jours ce simple fait com mence à être négligé petit à petit. J'ai l'im pression que l'idée selon laquelle le design d'emballage doit être « ludique » est trop

pandue. Puisque le design d'emballage est
outil qui permet au consommateur de voir
contenu à partir de l'extérieur, nous
vons focaliser l'attention du consommateur
r la nature de l'article – nous devons gui-
r son attention vers l'intérieur de l'embal-
ge, pas trop, mais suffisamment.

Je pense que le travail du créateur d'embal-
e est de trouver un « design modéré ».
est-à-dire que le design d'emballage doit
erpeller inconsciemment le consommateur ;
design devrait toujours attirer le consomma-
r de l'intérieur et vers le produit. Les desi-
ers qui ont pour habitude de chercher à
ndre leurs emballages ludiques ou intéres-
ts semblent oublier ce fait. Je suis moi aussi
gagé dans le design, et j'en suis arrivé à véri-
blement comprendre ce concept. Lorsque je
mmence à créer un emballage, je prends
bord le temps de m'assurer que j'ai bien
si la nature du produit. Le plus important
de ne pas commencer à créer une image
e l'on pense correcte sans d'abord connaître
produit. On doit donc tout d'abord faire taire
désir de rendre tous les concepts ludiques.
Ensuite, lorsque l'on crée un emballage
ur un fabricant, on doit s'interroger sur
usieurs points. Qu'est-ce que ce fabricant a
oduit jusqu'à maintenant ? Qu'est-il seul
avoir faire ? Quel genre de compétences a-
? Que pense-t-il apporter à la société ?
Puis, sans faute, je visite les usines.
coute ce que plusieurs responsables ont
ire et, lorsque je regarde la structure
ministrative de l'usine, je comprends
eux le point de vue du fabricant. Lorsque
coute directement les histoires des ingé-
urs, une vision de ce qu'implique la fabri-
ion du produit se présente à moi. Une
s que j'ai fait ce travail, je trouve de nom-
ux éléments à inclure dans le message

que j'envoie à travers le design de l'emballage. En tenant compte de tous ces facteurs,
je commence à modifier mon design et à
mettre au point la meilleure façon d'exprimer ces éléments à travers ce support que
l'on appelle design d'emballage. Grâce à ce
processus, j'arrive à mieux pénétrer l'essence du produit, et j'acquiers inévitablement
la capacité de toucher du doigt l'importance
de l'existence de cette entreprise.

J'en suis également venu à comprendre
pourquoi certains produits peuvent être mis
sur le marché sans interruption pendant de
longues périodes. Lorsque l'on examine cela,
et comme je l'ai dit plus haut, le design est
un outil qui guide vers ce qu'il représente. Le
design de l'emballage ne doit pas se détacher
du produit qui est à l'intérieur. Le design n'a
pas besoin d'être étalé ostensiblement – il
faut rechercher un design si subtil qu'il ne
sera pas immédiatement perçu comme tel.

Pour exprimer cela en japonais, on pourrait employer le mot *wakimae*. C'est un mot
qui nous exhorte à tenir compte de notre
position dans une certaine situation et à faire
preuve d'humilité. Par exemple, si l'on souhaite avertir quelqu'un de l'inopportunité de
ses actes, on peut dire, « tachiba wo wakimaenasai » (pensez à votre position [dans la
situation]). En termes de design de produit,
j'estime que l'essence du *wakimae* est également importante – un produit doit être présenté tel qu'il est. Nous devons donc
connaître également l'essence du *wakimae*
dans le domaine du design. Le designer doit
d'abord se poser la question du *wakimae* à
lui-même. Ces derniers temps, j'y ai souvent
pensé, et je m'interroge constamment sur la
nécessité des différents éléments du concept
– qu'est-ce que l'on pourrait éliminer ?
J'essaie autant que possible d'éviter que mes

emballages ne forcent le spectateur à ressen-
tir des choses qui ne sont pas justifiées, et
plutôt d'améliorer la fonctionnalité de l'emballage. C'est très difficile, mais je pense que
cette démarche donne un aperçu de l'avenir
du design de l'emballage au Japon.

Si l'emballage montre son contenu de
façon adéquate, et si l'on aboutit à des emballages sans aucun « charme » ou « attrait »,
alors cela signifie que le contenu n'a aucun
charme ni attrait au départ. Pour les produits qui n'ont aucun « charme », si l'on crée
ce « charme » à travers l'emballage c'est
donc que l'on conçoit l'emballage comme une
valeur ajoutée. Je pense que c'est une utilisation incorrecte du design d'emballage.

Les designers qui sont engagés dans le
design d'emballage devraient se donner les
moyens d'exprimer clairement le rôle de l'emballage avant d'initier le processus de création. Pour ce faire, je pense qu'il est important
d'apprendre à connaître les différents acteurs
avec qui l'on travaille et ce avec quoi l'on travaille, et qu'il faut être capable de comprendre
objectivement les conditions dans lesquelles
on se trouve lorsque l'on s'engage dans un
projet de design d'emballage.

Taku Satoh est né à Tokyo en 1955. En 1979,
il a obtenu son diplôme de design de l'Université
nationale des Beaux-arts et de Musique de Tokyo,
où il a ensuite suivi un programme de troisième
cycle. Il a d'abord intégré les rangs de Dentsu,
le géant de la publicité, avant de fonder Taku
Satoh Design Office Inc. en 1984. Taku Satoh
a créé des concepts pour Nikka, Lotte Chewing
Gum, Taisho Pharmaceutical et MEIJI, pour
ne citer que quelques-uns de ses clients. Il a reçu
de nombreuses récompenses, notamment le prix
Tokyo ADC, le prix Japan Package Design,
le prix New York ADC et le prix Good Design.*

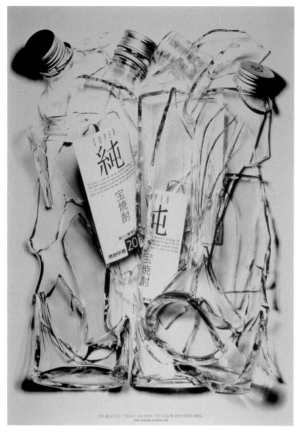

EXHIBITION

Images from the poster exhibition Rebuild, featuring the process through which a product is used. The photographic study comprises of chewing gum packages, soft drink cans, PET (polyethylene terephthalate) bottles and an energy drink package. They remind us that the packages we create eventually become trash.

AUSSTELLUNG

Bilder von der Plakatausstellung Rebuild, die den Prozess verdeutlichen, den ein Produkt durchläuft. Die Dokumentation umfasst die Verpackung eines Kaugummis, eines Softdrinks, eines Energiedrinks und von PET-Flaschen. Sie erinnern uns daran, dass die von uns geschaffenen Verpackungen, schließlich zu Abfall werden.

EXPOSITION

Images de l'exposition d'affiches Rebuild, qui représente le processus d'utilisation d'un produit. Cette étude photographique est composée de paquets de chewing-gum, de canettes de soda, de bouteilles en PET (polyéthylène téréphtalate) et de l'emballage d'une boisson énergisante. Elle nous rappelle que les emballages que nous créons finissent par devenir des déchets.

REBUILD/TAKU SATOH DESIGN OFFICE INC.
1993 LOTTE GUM MINT LINE

REBUILD/TAKU SATOH DESIGN OFFICE INC.
1993 TAISHO PHARM ZENA

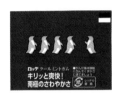

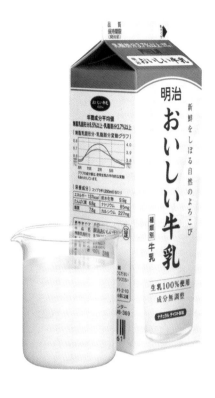

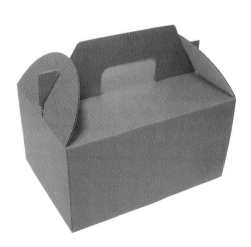

PACKAGES

Clockwise: In this detailed study, all the phases of the COOLMINT chewing gum package are displayed. The Tetra Pak milk carton says "Delicious Milk". Lastly, the traditional cake box made of carton paper.

VERPACKUNGEN

Im Uhrzeigersinn: Diese detaillierte Dokumentation zeigt alle Phasen der Verpackung für den Kaugummi COOLMINT. Der Tetra-Pak-Milchkarton trägt die Aufschrift „Leckere Milch". Schließlich die traditionelle Keksverpackung aus Pappkarton.

EMBALLAGES

Dans le sens des aiguilles d'une montre : cette étude détaillée montre toutes les phases de l'emballage des chewing-gums COOLMINT. La brique de lait Tetra Pak porte l'inscription « Lait délicieux ». Enfin, la boîte de gâteaux traditionnelle, fabriquée en papier cartonné.

Case 07
U'Luvka Vodka Case Study

Sam Aloof, founder of Aloof Design

Sam Aloof is the head of Aloof Design, an award-winning design studio based in London. In this case study, Aloof uses the example of U'Luvka vodka from Poland to explain the step-by-step process for making a completely new product for market.

BACKGROUND

The U'Luvka Vodka brand has been developed by the branding and packaging agency Aloof Design, in close partnership with premium drinks client The Brand Distillery.

CLIENT BRIEF

U'Luvka Vodka is a super premium vodka, needing beautiful and eye-catching packaging, interesting and unique marketing support, and a strong brand name with an extended product range to be developed at a future stage.

In this highly competitive and innovative market place, research shows that consumers want new and better quality products. A strong, cohesive offer across all platforms will lead to rapid growth in product sales.

With the launch of U'Luvka, the new vodka brand will need to become instantly recognisable, changing parameters in its white spirits category and raising the benchmark within the industry.

To emphasise the exclusive nature of U'Luvka, the brand will initially only be available through top trade outlets; 'white hot' bars, clubs, restaurants, hotels, key wine merchants, specialist off licenses and wholesalers.

U'Luvka's carefully managed launch will help to generate aspirational value, engaging a target audience of young to middle-aged professionals across all genders; design and fashion-conscious, urban, discerning, affluent party-goers, as well as the private and corporate luxury gifts market.

Brand recognition will grow through discovery, word of mouth and PR endorsement.

Core Values: genuine, super premium Polish vodka; simple, sexy, feminine and luxurious; aspirational and exclusive; beautiful and stylish; playful and tongue in cheek; authentic – a great Polish heritage.

SUMMARY OF DESIGN STRATEGY

The whole approach in creating U'Luvka has focused on producing something unique and spell-binding – to be technically and visually ground breaking. Throughout the development stages, the technical possibilities of production processes have harmoniously fed the creative decisions, and vice versa.

The bottle and, in particular, its Friendship, Love and Pleasure (FLP) gift packaging, required dedicated development and refinement, challenging preconceptions of what is achievable in using existing mainstream production processes. Aloof had a very clear vision of how the product should develop, and a schedule of prototyping and proofing ensured that maximum potential was gained from the processes specified. U'Luvka has, and will continue to be driven by innovation.

In developing a premium brand, Aloof had to ensure that U'Luvka quickly establishes a pedigree beyond its years. Despite being a new product, the vodka's Polish recipe has genuine heritage, a value that needed to be reinforced throughout. Distilled in Poland, the branding needed to reflect this heritage as well as the diversity of the client's interests – a rich mix of ancient and modern Poland, alchemical philosophy and references to the ideals of the Arts & Crafts movement.

BRANDING & APPLICATION

The type identity was referenced from o[...] of the first recorded Polish typefaces, and sympathetically refined to make it unique and relevant to U'Luvka. A decision was made to keep bottle branding to a subtle minimum, its form and silhouette considere[...] distinct enough to ensure a bottle of U'Luvka is instantly recognisable.

In contrast, the branding of literature, merchandising and packaging is multi-layered. The U'Luvka pattern, drawn by Alo[...] provides the brand's strong unifying element, referencing early 16th and 17th century Polish manuscripts, glassware and period textiles.

Sam Aloof graduated from the University [...] Brighton in 1999 with a BA Hons in Three Dimensional Design for Production. He then showcased his work at New Designers and wo[...] two industry awards for his structural paper packaging and hand-stitched leather products[...] Soon after co-founding Aloof Design with par[...] ner Michelle Kostyrka, Sam began consulting on Tigerprint for Hallmark and Marks & Spencer. His career as designer and creative director has been characterised by an "almost desperate obsession with sheet materials" and[...] the constant desire to achieve perfection.

Sam Aloof ist Leiter von Aloof Design, einem preisgekrönten Designstudio in London. In dieser Fallstudie zeigt Aloof am Beispiel der polnischen Wodka-Mark[...] U'Luvka, wie ein ganz neues Produkt Schritt für Schritt entsteht.

Die Marke U'Luvka Vodka wurde von der
ⸯanding & Packaging-Agentur Aloof
ⸯesign in enger Zusammenarbeit mit dem
ⸯnden The Brand Distillery entworfen.

ER KUNDE

U'Luvka Vodka ist eine gehobene
ⸯualitätsmarke, die eine schöne und auffällige
ⸯrpackung, einen interessanten und einzig-
ⸯtigen Marketing-Support und einen starken
ⸯarkennamen mit einer erweiterten
ⸯoduktreihe benötigt. Letztere soll zu einem
ⸯäteren Zeitpunkt entwickelt werden.

Studien haben ergeben, dass die Kunden auf
ⸯm umkämpften und innovativen Markt neue
ⸯrodukte von besserer Qualität wünschen.
ⸯn starkes Angebot wird zu einer schnellen
ⸯeigerung der Verkaufszahlen führen.

U'Luvka sollte bei der Markteinführung
ⸯrekt als neue Wodkamarke erkennbar sein
ⸯd damit auch für die Konkurrenz im
ⸯreich Spirituosen neue Maßstäbe setzen.
Um die Exklusivität von U'Luvka zu beto-
ⸯn, wird der Wodka anfänglich nur in ausge-
ⸯchten Lokalitäten wie topaktuellen Bars,
ⸯubs, Restaurants, Hotels, ausgesuchten
ⸯeinhändlern, spezialisierten Spirituosen-
ⸯndlern und über den Großhandel vertrieben.
U'Luvkas sorgfältig gesteuerte Markt-
ⸯführung wird einen hohen Begehrlich-
ⸯitswert erzeugen und als Zielgruppe junge
ⸯ mittelalte Berufstätige beiderlei
ⸯschlechts umfassen, die design- und
ⸯdebewusst, urban, anspruchsvoll und
ⸯhlhabend sind und gern auf Partys gehen.
ⸯs weitere Zielgruppe sind gehobene
ⸯschenkemärkte geplant.

Der Bekanntheitsgrad der Marke wird
ⸯrch Mund-zu-Mund-Propaganda und PR
ⸯchsen. Zu vermittelnde Kernwerte: echter

polnischer Qualitätswodka. Einfach, sexy,
feminin, luxuriös. Begehrenswert und exklusiv. Schön und stilvoll. Verspielt und ironisch.
Authentisch, mit großer polnischer Tradition.

ZUSAMMENFASSUNG DER DESIGNSTRATEGIE

Der Ansatz für die Kreation von U'Luvka
konzentrierte sich auf die Schaffung von etwas
Einzigartigem und Fesselndem, das technisch
wie optisch bahnbrechend sein sollte. Bei allen
Entwicklungsphasen haben die technischen
Möglichkeiten immer unsere kreativen Ent-
scheidungen befruchtet und umgekehrt.

Die Flasche und die Friendship, Love and
Pleasure-Geschenkverpackung (FLP) erfor-
derten ein hohes Maß an Entwicklungs- und
Detailarbeit und führte immer wieder dazu,
dass wir die Grenzen des Machbaren in der
industriellen Massenproduktion verschoben.
Aloof hatte eine sehr klare Vorstellung, wie
das Produkt sich entwickeln sollte. Ein
detaillierter Zeitplan für die Erstellung der
Prototypen und deren Endabnahme stellte
sicher, dass aus den ausgewiesenen Pro-
zessen das maximale Potenzial geschöpft
wurde. U'Luvka wurde bisher durch Innovation angetrieben, und so wird dies auch in
Zukunft sein.

Um eine wahre Qualitätsmarke zu schaffen, musste Aloof sicherstellen, dass
U'Luvka sich einen traditionsreichen Ruf
erarbeitete. Denn, obwohl das Produkt neu
ist, geht das Rezept auf ein polnisches
Original zurück, ein Wert, den es zu betonen
galt. Der in Polen destillierte Markenwodka
benötigte ein Branding, das sein polnisches
Erbe widerspiegelte, wie auch die unterschiedlichen Interessen des breit gefächerten
Zielpublikums – eine reiche Mischung aus
historischem und modernem Polen, aus

alchemistischer Philosophie und
Anspielungen auf die Ideale der Arts-and-
Crafts-Bewegung.

BRANDING UND ANWENDUNG

Die Schrift wurde von einer der ersten
dokumentierten polnischen Druckschriften
abgeleitet und mit viel Sachverstand so
umgearbeitet, dass sie einzigartig ist und
sich stimmig in das Konzept von U'Luvka
einfügt. Das Branding der Flasche sollte
minimal gehalten werden, ihre Form und
Silhouette aber so außergewöhnlich sein,
dass eine Flasche von U'Luvka auf den
ersten Blick erkennbar ist.

Einen Kontrast bildet das vielschichtige
Branding der Druckerzeugnisse, des
Merchandisings und der Verpackung. Das
von Aloof für U'Luvka entworfene Muster
ist ein starkes verbindendes Element der
Marke und erinnert an alte polnische
Handschriften, Glaswaren und Textilien aus
dem 16. und 17. Jahrhundert.

1999 schloss <u>*Sam Aloof*</u> *sein Studium des
3D-Designs für Produktion an der University
of Brighton mit einem Prädikatsabschluss ab.
Anschließend stellte er seine Arbeiten bei New
Designers aus und gewann zwei Industriepreise
für seine Papierverpackungen und seine hand-
bestickten Lederprodukte. Kurz nachdem er
gemeinsam mit Partnerin Michelle Kostryka die
Agentur Aloof Design gegründet hatte, beriet er
Tigerprint für Hallmark und Marks & Spencer.
Seine Karriere als Designer und Creative Director ist bis heute geprägt von Perfektion und von
einer großen Begeisterung für Bogenmaterialien.*

Sam Aloof est le directeur d'Aloof Design, un studio de design primé, basé à Londres. Dans cette étude de cas, il utilise l'exemple de la vodka polonaise U'Luvka pour expliquer étape par étape le processus de création d'un produit entièrement nouveau pour sa mise sur le marché.

CONTEXTE

La marque U'Luvka Vodka a été créée par l'agence de stratégie de marque et de packaging Aloof Design, qui a travaillé en étroite collaboration avec le groupe de boissons haut de gamme The Brand Distillery.

LE PROJET DU CLIENT

U'Luvka est une vodka très haut de gamme, et il lui faut un emballage magnifique et séduisant, un marketing original, un nom de marque fort, et une gamme étendue de produits à développer dans le futur.

Sur ce marché très concurrentiel et innovateur, les études montrent que les consommateurs recherchent des produits nouveaux et de grande qualité. Une offre forte et cohérente sur toutes les plateformes mènera à une rapide croissance des ventes du produit.

Avec le lancement d'U'Luvka, la nouvelle marque de vodka devra devenir immédiatement reconnaissable, bouleverser les critères dans la catégorie des alcools blancs et hausser la barre du secteur.

Pour accentuer le caractère exclusif de la vodka U'Luvka, dans un premier temps elle ne sera disponible que dans des points de vente stratégiques : les bars, les discothèques, les restaurants et les hôtels les plus « tendance », et chez des marchands de vins et de spiritueux et des grossistes triés sur le volet.

Le lancement soigneusement travaillé d'U'Luvka permettra de donner au produit une aura de chic, qui séduira une population cible composée d'actifs jeunes ou d'âge moyen, hommes ou femmes, sensibles au design et à la mode, urbains, exigeants, aisés, appréciant la fête, ainsi que le marché des cadeaux d'entreprise de luxe. Le degré d'identification de la marque grandira à travers la découverte, le bouche-à-oreille et l'appui des relations publiques. Les valeurs fondamentales – une véritable vodka polonaise très haut de gamme. Simple, sexy, féminine, luxueuse. Chic et exclusive. Superbe et élégante. Ludique et second degré. Authentique, un grand héritage polonais.

RÉSUMÉ DE LA STRATÉGIE DU CONCEPT

Pour U'Luvka, toute la démarche était concentrée sur la création d'un produit original et envoûtant, techniquement et visuellement révolutionnaire. Tout au long des étapes de développement, les possibilités techniques des processus de production ont nourri les décisions créatives, et vice versa.

La bouteille et le coffret-cadeau « Friendship, Love and Pleasure » (FLP, Amitié, Amour et Plaisir), devaient faire l'objet d'une mise au point et d'un raffinement minutieux, défiant les idées préconçues sur ce que les processus de production traditionnels peuvent faire. Aloof avait une vision très claire du produit, et un programme de prototypage et de tests garantissait que l'on tirerait le meilleur parti des processus spécifiés. Le moteur d'U'Luvka a été et continuera d'être l'innovation.

Pour que la marque acquière un statut haut de gamme, Aloof devait s'assurer que le manque d'ancienneté d'U'Luvka ne serait pas un obstacle pour son pedigree. Bien que le produit soit nouveau, sa recette polonaise représente une véritable tradition, une valeur qui doit être mise en avant. Distillée en Pologne, la marque devait refléter ses racines polonaises ainsi que la diversité des intérêts du public – un riche mélange de la Pologne passée et présente, une philosophie alchimique et des références aux idéaux du mouvement Arts & Crafts.

STRATÉGIE DE MARQUE ET APPLICATION

La police de caractères utilisée vient de l'une des premières polices de caractères polonaises, et a été retravaillée afin de lui donner une personnalité originale et adaptée à U'Luvka. Sur la bouteille, les références à la marque sont maintenues à un minimum, puisque la forme et la silhouette de la bouteille U'Luvka suffisent à la rendre immédiatement reconnaissable.

En revanche, le marquage des documents du merchandising et de l'emballage est tout en superpositions. Le motif U'Luvka, dessiné par Aloof, apporte à la marque un élément fort d'unification faisant référence aux manuscrits, à la verrerie et aux textiles polonais des XVIᵉ et XVIIᵉ siècles.

En 1999, Sam Aloof a obtenu avec mention un diplôme en Design de production en 3D de l'Université de Brighton. Puis il a présenté son travail à l'exposition New Designers et a gagné deux prix, pour son emballage structurel en papier et pour des produits en cuir cousu à la main. Il a fondé Aloof Design avec Michelle Kostyrka le même mois, et a commencé avec Tigerprint pour Hallmark et Marks & Spencer. Sa carrière de designer et de directeur de la création est caractérisée par une « obsession presque désespérée pour les matériaux sous forme de feuille » et un désir constant de parvenir à la perfection.

THE PACKAGING/BRAND BASE COLOUR

Firstly, we developed a U'Luvka colour palette to ensure the right emotive values were being triggered (desirable, luxury, premium). We then carried out three-phase silkscreen proofing on uncoated papers. Fifty paper colours were chosen and each sheet had the same solid magenta screen applied to it. The results were dramatic, as the magenta either reacted with, or enhanced the colour of the paper beneath. Solid magenta on a deep black paper stock was unanimously chosen, and we went through a final refinement of this choice to achieve an exact deep burgundy tone.

DIE VERPACKUNG/GRUNDFARBE DER MARKE

Zunächst entwickelten wir die Farbpalette für U'Luvka, um sicherzustellen, dass die richtigen emotionalen Werte angesprochen werden (begehrenswert, luxuriös, erstklassig). Dann führten wir ein dreistufiges Siebdruck-Proofing auf unbeschichtetem Papier durch. Wir wählten fünfzig Papierfarben aus und ließen je ein Blatt mit 100 % Magenta bedrucken. Die Resultate waren beeindruckend. Das Magenta reagierte entweder mit der Farbe des darunter liegenden Papiers oder verstärkte diese. Wir entschieden uns einhellig für Magenta auf tiefschwarzem Papier. Anschließend wurden letzte Verfeinerungen vorgenommen, um genau den gewünschten tiefen Bordeauxton zu erhalten.

L'EMBALLAGE/LA COULEUR DE BASE DE LA MARQUE

Nous avons tout d'abord élaboré une palette de couleurs U'Luvka pour déclencher les valeurs affectives choisies (désirabilité, luxe, haut de gamme). Ensuite, nous avons réalisé un test en 3 phases de sérigraphie sur des papiers bruts. Une couche identique de magenta a été sérigraphiée sur les 50 couleurs de papier sélectionnées. Les résultats ont été spectaculaires, car le magenta interagissait avec la couleur du papier ou la renforçait. Un magenta uni sur fond noir profond a été choisi à l'unanimité, et nous avons ajusté le résultat jusqu'à obtenir un ton bordeaux profond.

THE PATTERN

The pattern was hand-drawn in sections by the designers at Aloof, referencing early 16th & 17th century Polish manuscripts. It was developed into a repeat, and then underwent a process of distressing. This involved printing the pattern on to a flocked paper to give it some of the characteristics of hand-blocked/period flocked wallpaper. Wood ash was carefully rubbed into the flocked print, and it was then scanned to give us the worn, smoky, fragmented pattern that appears across the brand.
The pattern was then applied to the silk-screened base colour using a shimmering UV varnish. The pattern changes in intensity depending on the angle of light, and ghosts out of view across a panel, merging with the burgundy background. This magical, metamorphic effect very much represents the essence of the brand's values, whilst helping the pack to stand out in POS (Point-of-Sale).

DAS MUSTER

Das Muster wurde zunächst von Aloof-Designern von Hand gezeichnet. Dabei ließen sie sich von alten polnischen Handschriften des 16. und 17. Jahrhunderts inspirieren. Anschließend wurde das Muster zu einem fortlaufenden Rapport entwickelt und dann einem Alterungsprozess unterzogen. Dazu wurde es auf Büttenpapier gedruckt, um ihm die Charakteristika alter handgeschöpfter Papiertapeten zu verleihen. Dann wurde Asche in den Druck eingearbeitet und das Ergebnis anschließend gescannt. So erhielten wir das alte, vergilbte, fragmentierte Aussehen des Musters, das heute die gesamte Marke auszeichnet.
Das Muster wurde schließlich mit glänzendem Lack auf die Grundfarbe aufgetragen. Auf diese Weise ist das Muster je nach Lichteinfall deutlicher oder weniger deutlich zu sehen und verschmilzt mit dem bordeauxfarbenen Hintergrund. Dieser magische, metamorphische Effekt repräsentiert sehr schön die Markenwerte und sorgt für einen hohen Aufmerksamkeitswert.

LE MOTIF

Les designers d'Aloof ont dessiné le motif à la main, en s'inspirant de manuscrits des XVIe et XVIIe siècles. Puis ils l'ont transformé en motif continu, et lui ont fait subir un traitement vieillissant en l'imprimant sur un papier floqué pour lui donner certaines caractéristiques du papier peint ou floqué à la main de l'époque, et en frottant minutieusement de la cendre de bois sur le résultat, qui, une fois scanné, a donné le motif usé, fumeux et fragmenté qui apparaît sur les produits de la marque.
Le motif est appliqué sur la base de couleur sérigraphiée au moyen d'un vernis UV moiré. Le dessin change d'intensité selon l'angle de la lumière et peut disparaître en se confondant avec le fond bordeaux. Cet effet magique et métamorphique représente très bien les valeurs de la marque, et aide l'emballage à se distinguer sur le lieu de vente.

THE BOTTLE

The U'Luvka bottle shape was inspired by glassware designed by Christopher Dresser (British Arts & Crafts Movement) who in turn took his inspiration from Japanese art and philosophy, and the belief that the functionality and beauty of an object should work hand in hand. The bottle as it exists today was the result of 18 months' sourcing before the right manufacturer was found, and a further 18 months of research, development, sampling and testing.

The Cork is encased in glass, manufactured and hand-finished in Portugal. The Brand Distillery circling dragon logo and U'Luvka pattern are applied by hand.

DIE FLASCHE

Die Form der U'Luvka-Flasche wurde durch Glaswaren des Designers Christopher Dresser (britische Arts-and-Crafts-Bewegung) angeregt. Dresser wiederum war von der japanischen Kunst und Philosophie inspiriert, derzufolge Schönheit und Funktionalität eines Gegenstandes Hand in Hand gehen sollten. Bis die heutige Flaschenform entstand und ein Hersteller gefunden war, vergingen 18 Monate, weitere 18 Monate waren für Studien, Entwicklung, Mustererstellung und Proben notwendig.

Der Kork ist in Glas eingelassen und wird in Portugal hergestellt, wobei die Feinarbeiten Handarbeit sind. Das runde Drachenlogo der Destillerie und das U'Luvka-Muster werden von Hand aufgetragen.

LA BOUTEILLE

La forme de la bouteille U'Luvka est inspirée des objets en verre créés par Christopher Dresser (du mouvement Arts & Crafts britannique) qui, lui, s'inspirait de la philosophie et de l'art japonais et qui pensait que la fonctionnalité d'un objet devait contribuer à sa beauté, et vice versa. La bouteille telle qu'elle existe aujourd'hui est le résultat de 18 mois de recherche du fabricant idéal et de 18 autres mois de recherche, de développement et de tests.

Le bouchon est enchâssé dans le verre. Il est fabriqué et fini à la main au Portugal. Le logo des dragons en cercle de The Brand Distillery et le motif U'Luvka sont appliqués à la main.

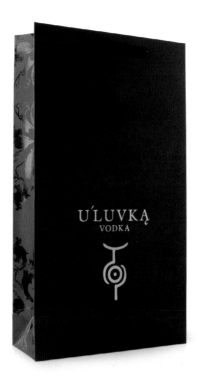

ECONDARY PACKAGING

*Glasses, ice buckets, outer shipping cases, pro-
motional gift bags, etc., sit within a secondary
packaging category, a tier down from the premium FLP gift pack. Design and production
values are shared with the premium pack,
ut budgets, paper and production methods
re more restricted. It was also important
o ensure that the more affordable secondary
ackaging of merchandised goods didn't
ompete with the top tier product.*

SEKUNDÄRVERPACKUNG

*Gläser, Eiskübel, Transportverpackung,
Geschenktaschen für Promotionzwecke usw.
gehören in die Kategorie Sekundärverpackungen, eine Ebene unterhalb der FLP-Geschenk
verpackung. Sie teilen natürlich die Design-
und Produktionswerte der Premiumver-
packung. Budget, Papier und Produktionsme-
thoden sind aber bescheidener. Denn die
preiswerteren Sekundärverpackungen der
Werbemittel sollten keine Konkurrenz zur
hochwertigen Primärverpackung darstellen.*

L'EMBALLAGE SECONDAIRE

*Les verres, les seaux à glaçons, les boîtes exté-
rieures de transport, les pochettes-cadeau pro-
motionnelles, etc. font partie de la catégorie
des emballages secondaires, juste en dessous
du coffret-cadeau FLP haut de gamme. Les
caractéristiques essentielles du design et de la
production sont les mêmes que pour les emballages haut de gamme, mais les budgets, le
papier et les méthodes de production sont un
peu plus économiques. Il était également
important que l'emballage secondaire du merchandising, plus abordable, n'entre pas en
concurrence avec le produit haut de gamme.*

Case 08
Package Materials

Packaging Solutions Advice Group

The Packaging Solutions Advice Group (PSAG) is an industry body that seeks the best solutions for packaging products regarding materials and processes. In this case study, they highlight how five different materials and techniques can be applied to improve the appeal of the content packaged.

Imagine packaging with the allure and sparkle of glistening snowflakes, Christmas wrapping-paper printed with the smell of pine needles, or perhaps the visual appeal of holographic labels.

These and many more special effects are now available, as packaging becomes increasingly complex and sophisticated. It's not just about the 3D form, but also the pigments, inks, and the coatings necessary to achieve exactly the right design solution – one that both protects the contents and attracts consumers. For brand managers and their designers, it's a daunting task to get right. Who do you trust to provide the know-how when your regular packaging convertor may be constrained by the limits of its particular technology and expertise?

One way forward is to consult initially with the makers of the packaging material components such as the supplier of the pigments, or the manufacturer of the casing that forms the structure. These frequently work with each other to achieve new applications of technology across different materials. Many are also keen for brand designers and owners to consult them directly on how to achieve the look they're after, whether it be sparkly, pearl, matt or shiny. This way, brands will be able to access what has until now been a largely untapped expertise, especially if they involve materials suppliers early enough in the design

process. With an estimated 80% of new brand launches failing to meet expectations, brand designers and their clients would do well to get a head start by exploring the full potential of their packaging in order to connect emotionally with the consumer.

Special effects can do just this; achieved with pigments that can add lustre and colour to packaging across a range of materials and printing processes, including under-printing and over-printing. Things have certainly moved on from a century ago when early applications of pearlescence in Paris involved a suspension of guanine crystal membrane produced from fish scales.

Pigment supplier Merck's Miraval pigment uses coated borosilicates to give the effect of a glass flake and is ideal for glitzy and glamorous applications that can lend added value to, for example, packaging. Colorstream® multicolour effect pigments include silicon dioxide platelets that give an iridescent effect. Another Merck range, Xirallic, contains coated aluminium oxide platelets that generate high lustre effects with extreme colour intensity. Iriodin is a pigment based on mica that gives pearl lustre effects from silky to matt and glittery. Meanwhile Biflair, based on bismuth oxychloride, gives a fine and opaque appearance. Lustrous printing results can be achieved using gravure, flexo, screen and offset printing, while pigments can be incorporated into all transparent and semi-transparent plastics using injection mould, extrusion or rotation processes.

When used appropriately with other applications and materials to reinforce the right brand values, such effects can be invaluable in gaining recognition on the shelves. Soft colours with a hint of iridescence, for example, may evoke caring, mild and protective cues,

while shiny fresh colours evoke energy, yout and freshness.

To show brand designers and managers what is possible when these pigments are applied to packaging, several suppliers of packaging materials have worked together t create exemplar pigment effects for two ranges of conceptual products. The results demonstrate what can be achieved when an effect pigment supplier, for example, collabo rates closely with an ink manufacturer.

Well & Wild is conceived for the beverag industry, in particular the soft drinks, alcopops and spirits markets, where product and packaging differentiation is a challenge. The 'Well' products are wellness drinks env sioned as having an enlivening affect on the mind or maybe a positive effect on the skin. The "Wild" products are a group of fun drin for special occasions, perhaps an alcopop or almost dangerous drink that borders on tha thin edge between the acceptable and the unpredictable. For both, shrink sleeve tech nology was chosen and gravure printed usir Merck effect pigments from the Iriodin® an Colorstream® product families, incorporated into Sun Chemical Finelap and Charon ink systems. The plastic caps were mass colour with matching effect pigments.

The second exemplar concept, Wind of Asia, demonstrates pigments that help con vey different moods suited to the healthca sector in Asia. Varieties of Iriodin and Miraval pigments are used to achieve varie pearlescent and shimmery effects for differ ent target markets.

With any packaging concept pigments ar nothing without the wherewithall to apply them, especially for complex branding projects that involve application across a varie of media such as labels, bottles and cans, et achieve this, pigments must be combined a formulation appropriate to the application, whether paper, plastic or tin. That's ere the expertise of ink and coatings suppliers comes in.

There are now alternatives to solvent-ed inks. Sun Chemical has been developing ter-based inks plus energy curable inks, ich have the advantage of containing no atile components as well as offering superi-print quality on the variety of substrates d in flexible packaging. Another exciting v development is the emerging technology romatic inks. A pine needle-smelling gift ap that evokes the smell of Christmas is ng developed by Sun Chemical, who are o working on a drink for a major global nd owner that has a label printed with the matic fragrance of the flower that evokes flavour of the drink.

Consistency of colour and special effect is essential if brand owners want to invest omething new. To tackle the problem of onsistency, there are colour management tems such as SmartColour from Sun mical. These aim to avoid the potential ppointment when packaging is printed fails to live up to the design studio's k-up of the intended effect. Instead, this nique allows brand managers and design-to gain control of variables by seeing what r packaging would look like using various colours and printing techniques. Their sen effect is digitally measured and used application on a variety of substrates to ieve the exact same effect whichever ting process is used – digital, flexography, ography or gravure.

he right pigment and ink is still only part e process. The next is getting it on to the itself. One application that not only per-forms well from a food safety point of view but also achieves a premium look through colour and gloss is Protact. This is a layer of polymer applied to steel packaging in various colours and degrees of opacity. Developed by Corus Packaging Plus, the polymer coatings can be clear to give a premium metal look to the pack or coloured on both the inside and outside of the cans. The polymer surface has considerable decorative potential for high-quality printing, varnishing and embossing across the entire surface. A holographic option helps create aesthetic appeal and can also be an effective anti-counterfeiting solution by incorporating corporate or brand logos into the holographic design.

This scope gives a new perspective to steel packaging, as demonstrated effectively on the tinned packaging for John West Red Salmon, and in particular on the steel packaging for Nicolas Feuillatte Champagne, which shows the visual, premium impact that the holographic technique can provide. A Protact version of the traditional beverage can is also available, as well as peelable and easy open lidded cans. Another advantage is that polymer coated steel cans are 100% recyclable. Also on an environmental note, brand owners can take advantage of Le Carré, a food can which is square. Not only is the can, developed by Corus Packaging Plus, lighter in weight than conventional round cans, it takes up less space in transit and requires 20% less shelf space. Aesthetically, Le Carre can be combined with lithoprint or shrink sleeve labels across its four faces for visual impact on the shelves.

There is also now more scope to achieve shelf differentiation with steel aerosol cans thanks to a new product that allows greater design freedom. 'Buzz' combines a plastic outer reservoir to carry the brand message in any design, pigment, colour and shape in combination with an inner steel aerosol. Developed by Corus Packaging Plus, this increased scope for different outer materials and design is possible because there are no pressure requirements for the outer component.

Designers and brand managers working on products requiring flexible packaging, such as detergent pouches, can also benefit by talking to materials suppliers. These include DuPont Teijin Films, which manufacturers the polyester film Mylar, widely used in food and drink packaging. As well as its robust practical properties for flexible packaging use plus sealant, shrink, holographic, barrier and ovenable films, it also offers excellent optical properties to aid brand recognition.

In the end, it's up to the brand manager and their designer to take the initiative and explore the full potential of their packaging by speaking to the experts who create it.

PSAG

The Packaging Solutions Advice Group (PSAG) is a collaboration of companies that supply the material components that go into packaging, from the pigments to the vessels themselves. Among its members are: Merck – a global pharmaceutical and chemical company which manufactures effect pigment, Sun Chemical – which makes inks, pigments and coatings, Corus Packaging Plus – which supplies packaging steels, and polyester film manufacturer – DuPont Teijin Films. PSAG can be contacted at <www.psag.co.uk>.

Die Packaging Solutions Advice Group (PSAG) ist ein Unternehmen, das die besten Materialien und Herstellungsprozesse für Produktverpackungen sucht. In dieser Fallstudie zeigt sie, wie anhand von fünf verschiedenen Materialien und Techniken die Attraktivität der verpackten Ware verbessert werden kann.

Stellen Sie sich eine Verpackung mit dem Reiz und Glanz von schimmernden Schneeflocken vor, ein Weihnachtsgeschenkpapier mit dem Duft von Tannennadeln oder mit holografischem Effekt.

Die Möglichkeiten moderner Verpackungen werden immer komplexer und technisch raffinierter, sodass heute diese Spezialeffekte möglich sind. Dabei spielt nicht nur die dreidimensionale Form eine wichtige Rolle, sondern auch die Pigmente, Farben und Beschichtungen, die notwendig sind, um genau die richtige Designlösung zu erreichen: Sie soll den Inhalt schützen und gleichzeitig den Kunden anlocken. Für Brandmanager und Designer kann es eine Herausforderung sein, hier den Überblick zu behalten. Und auf wessen Fähigkeiten verlässt man sich, wenn der Stammlieferant für Verpackungen die technischen Anforderungen für eine bestimmte Verpackung nicht erfüllen kann?

Man kann sich im Voraus mit den Zulieferern, wie etwa den Pigmentlieferanten oder den Herstellern der Formen, absprechen. Diese Firmen arbeiten oftmals zusammen, um neue Technologien an verschiedenen Materialien zu erproben. Viele würden es sogar begrüßen, wenn Markendesigner und -inhaber sie bei Fragen zum Aussehen des Materials direkt konsultieren würden, egal ob das Material schillernd, perlmuttfarben, matt

oder glänzend sein soll. So können Marken – besonders, wenn die Materialhersteller schon früh in den Designprozess miteinbezogen werden – von einem großen Fachwissen profitieren, das bisher kaum genutzt wurde. Bei geschätzten 80 % der Markteinführungen, die hinter den Erwartungen zurückbleiben, wären Markendesigner und ihre Kunden gut beraten gewesen, alle potenziellen Verpackungsvarianten auszuloten und sich so einen Vorsprung zu verschaffen, um den Konsumenten emotional anzusprechen.

Spezialeffekte können genau dies erreichen. Mithilfe von Pigmenten kann unter Einsatz unterschiedlichster Druckverfahren, wie z. B. Unterdrucken und Überdrucken, verschiedenen Materialien, Glanz und Farbe verliehen werden. Die Technik hat sich innerhalb des letzten Jahrhunderts stark gewandelt, seit in Paris für die Herstellung und Verwendung von Perlessenz eine konzentrierte Suspension von Guanin-Kristallplättchen benötigt wurde, die aus Fischschuppen gewonnen wurden.

Pigmenthersteller Merck verwendet für seine Miraval-Pigmente z. B. beschichtete Borosilikate, um den Effekt von Glasflocken zu erzielen, die sich besonders für glitzernde Beschichtungen eignen. Solche Beschichtungen können Verpackungen einen besonderen Wert verleihen. Colorstream®-Multicolor-Effektpigmente, die Siliziumoxid-Plättchen enthalten, ergeben einen changierenden Effekt. Xirallic, eine weitere Produktreihe von Merck, enthält Aluminiumoxid-Plättchen, die hochglänzende Effekte mit extremer Farbintensität hervorrufen. Iriodin ist ein Pigment, das zu einem Perlglanzeffekt von seidig über matt bis glitzernd führt. Biflair hingegen, das auf Bismutoxichlorid

basiert, ergibt einen subtilen, seidig matte Glanz. Glänzende Druckergebnisse könner mit so unterschiedlichen Druckverfahren v Tiefdruck, Flexodruck, Siebdruck und Offs druck erzielt werden, während Pigmente durch Verfahren wie Spritzguss, Extrusio oder Rotationspressung in transparente o semitransparente Kunststoffe eingebracht werden können.

Kombiniert man diese Effekte mit ande ren Anwendungen und Materialien, könne sie den Markenwert und die Aufmerksamkeit enorm steigern. Sanfte, leicht irisiere Farben können beispielsweise Assoziation von Milde, Sanftheit und Pflege wecken, während bei leuchtend frischen Farben Energie, Jugend und Frische assoziiert wi

Um Markendesignern und Managern di Möglichkeiten von Pigmenten bei der Ver packung zu demonstrieren, haben sich ver schiedene Zulieferer von Verpackungsmaterialien zusammengeschlossen und ex plarische Pigmenteffekte für zwei Produk linien entwickelt. Die Ergebnisse zeigen, erreicht werden kann, wenn ein Pigmentli ferant z. B. eng mit einem Farbenherstell zusammenarbeitet.

Well & Wild ist für die Getränkeindust konzipiert, besonders für die Bereiche Er schungsgetränke, Alkopops und Spirituos wo Produkt, Verpackung und Differenzie rung eine große Herausforderung darstel Die Well-Produkte sind Wellness-Drinks, z. B. eine belebende Wirkung auf Körper Geist oder eine hautpflegende Wirkung haben könnten. Die Wild-Produkte sind e Gruppe von Fun-Drinks für besondere Ge genheiten: vielleicht ein Alkopop oder ein beinahe gefährliches, hartes alkoholisches tränk. Für die Verpackungen beider Geträ

...rde die Schrumpfschlauch-Technologie ...gesetzt, die im Tiefdruckverfahren mit ...rben der Finelap- und Charon-Farb-...steme von Sun Chemical bedruckt wurden. ...ese wurden mit Effektpigmenten der ...oduktfamilien Iriodin® und Colorstream® ...n Merck versetzt. Die Farben für die ...rschlusskappen wurden ebenfalls mit farb-...n passenden Pigmenten vermischt.

...Das zweite Beispiel hat den Namen Wind ...Asia und veranschaulicht, wie Pigmente ...rschiedene Stimmungen zum Ausdruck ...ngen können: in diesem Fall abgestimmt ...f den asiatischen Gesundheitsmarkt. ...riationen der Pigmente Iriodin und Mira-... werden verwendet, um für unterschiedli-...e Zielmärkte verschiedene Perlmutt- und ...himmereffekte zu erzielen.

...Natürlich benötigen Pigmente ein Medium, ... dem man sie verbinden kann. Die Wahl ... richtigen Mediums ist besonders bei kom-...xen Branding-Projekten wichtig, bei denen ...e Vielzahl unterschiedlicher Medien wie ...ketten, Flaschen, Dosen usw. mit den ...menten kombiniert werden müssen. Daher ...ssen die Pigmente entsprechend der späte-... Anwendung, z. B. für Papier, Kunststoff ...r Blech, in verschiedenen Formeln kombi-...rt werden. Genau hier ist die Kenntnis von ...b- und Beschichtungsspezialisten gefragt. ...Heute gibt es Alternativen zu Farben, die ... Lösungsmittel basieren. Sun Chemical ... wasserbasierte Farben sowie UV-härten-...Lacke entwickelt, die keine flüchtigen ...mponenten enthalten und auf einer Reihe ... Substraten, die für die Herstellung fle-...ler Verpackungen verwendet werden, ...e hohe Druckqualität bieten. Eine weitere ...nnende Entwicklung sind die neuen aro-...ischen Farben. Sun Chemical arbeitet

gerade an einem nach Tannennadeln duften-den Geschenkpapier, das weihnachtliche Gefühle hervorrufen soll. Gleichzeitig gestal-tete Sun Chemical für einen internationalen Getränkekonzern ein Getränkeetikett mit Blütenduft, das an den Geschmack des Getränks erinnern soll.

Die Übereinstimmung von Farben und Spezialeffekten ist ebenfalls von großer Bedeutung, wenn Unternehmen in neue Marken investieren. Um Unstimmigkeiten zu vermeiden, gibt es Farbmanagementsysteme wie etwa SmartColour von Sun Chemical. Sie verhindern Enttäuschungen über Drucker-gebnisse, die mit dem Entwurf des Design-studios nicht übereinstimmen. Diese Technik erlaubt Brandmanagern und Designern eine genaue Kontrolle aller Variablen, denn so kön-nen sie jederzeit prüfen, wie ihre Verpackung bei verschiedenen Farben und unterschiedli-chen Drucktechniken aussehen. Der gewählte Effekt wird dann digital gemessen und auf die verschiedenen Substrate übertragen, damit bei allen Druckprozessen, ob Digitaldruck, Flexodruck, Lithografie oder Tiefdruck, immer dasselbe Ergebnis erzielt wird.

Allerdings ist die richtige Wahl von Pig-menten und Farben weiterhin nur ein Teil des Prozesses. Der nächste Schritt ist die Übertragung auf die Verpackung. Eine Anwendung, die nicht nur hervorragende Ergebnisse auf dem Gebiet der Lebens-mittelsicherheit zeigt, sondern auch ausge-zeichnete Glanz- und Farbergebnisse auf-weist, ist Protact. Es handelt sich dabei um eine Polymerschicht, die in verschiedenen Farben und mit unterschiedlicher Licht-durchlässigkeit bzw. Deckkraft auf Metall-verpackungen aufgetragen wird. Diese von Corus Packaging Plus entwickelte Polymer-

beschichtung kann klar und durchscheinend sein, um einer Verpackung einen luxuriösen Metallglanz zu verleihen, oder farbig, um entweder auf der Innen- oder auf der Außenseite von Konservendosen aufgetra-gen zu werden. Die Polymerbeschichtung hat ein hohes dekoratives Potenzial für qualitativ hochwertige Aufdrucke, Lackierungen oder Gravuren. Auch eine holografische Gestaltung ist möglich und bietet nicht nur einen starken ästhetischen Reiz, sondern auch Schutz vor Markendiebstahl, wenn Markenzeichen oder Logo in das holografi-sche Design eingearbeitet werden.

Dieser Anwendungsbereich verleiht Me-tallverpackungen ganz neue Möglichkeiten, wie z. B. die Konservendose für John West Red Salmon und die Metallverpackung für Nicolas Feuillatte Champagne zeigen: Beide belegen, dass mit einer holografischen Ge-staltung ein hochwertiger optischer Effekt erzielt werden kann. Aber auch traditionelle Getränkedosen und Konservendosen mit ein-fach zu öffnendem Aufreißdeckel aus Protact sind erhältlich. Ein weiterer Vorzug der Konservendosen mit Polymerbeschichtung ist ihre 100-prozentige Recyclebarkeit. Für eine umweltfreundlichere Produktion können Unternehmen die Vorteile von Le Carré nut-zen, einer quadratischen Konservendose. Die von Corus Packaging Plus entwickelte Konservendose ist nicht nur leichter als die üblichen runden Konserven, sie benötigt sowohl beim Transport als auch im Regal bis zu 20 % weniger Platz. Was die ästhetische Gestaltung betrifft, so eignet sich Le Carré für Lithodruck- und Schrumpfschlauch-Etiketten, die auf allen vier Seiten ange-bracht werden können, um in der Auslage für große Aufmerksamkeit zu sorgen.

Dank eines neuen Produktes, das größere Designfreiheiten erlaubt, bieten sich nun auch im Bereich der Aerosoldosen mehr Möglichkeiten zur Differenzierung in den Auslagen. „Buzz" kombiniert einen äußeren Behälter, der Markenzeichen und -botschaft in beliebigen Mustern, Pigments, Farben und Formen tragen kann, mit einem inneren Behälter aus Metall für das Aerosol. Die von Corus Packaging Plus entwickelte Verpackung bietet eine große Anwendungsvielfalt, da der äußere Behälter aus verschiedenen Materialien in unterschiedlichen Designs hergestellt werden kann. Er muss keine Druckbelastung aushalten. Damit sind in diesem Bereich keine Mindestanforderungen zu erfüllen.

Designer und Brandmanager, die gemeinsam an flexiblen Verpackungen arbeiten, wie etwa an Beutelverpackungen für Reinigungsmittel, können ebenfalls vom Dialog mit Materialzulieferern profitieren. Ein solcher Zulieferer ist beispielsweise DuPont Tejin Films, die Hersteller der Polyesterfolie Mylar, die häufig für Getränke- und Lebensmittelverpackungen genutzt werden. Neben ihren robusten praktischen Eigenschaften als flexible Verpackung und als versiegelnde Schrumpf-, holografische, Barriere- und hitzefeste Folie weist sie zudem auch hervorragende optische Eigenschaften auf, mit denen die Markenidentität gestützt werden kann.

Es liegt in der Hand der Brandmanager und Designer, die Initiative zu ergreifen und mit den Experten der Materialindustrie in Dialog zu treten, um alle Potenziale der Verpackungswelt voll auszuschöpfen.

PSAG
Die Packaging Solution Advice Group (PSAG) ist ein Zusammenschluss von Firmen, die Materialkomponenten für Verpackungen von Pigmenten ebenso wie deren Behälter liefern. Zu ihren Mitgliedern zählen unter anderem Merck, ein internationales pharmazeutisches und chemisches Unternehmen, das z. B. Effektpigmente herstellt, Sun Chemical, die Farben, Pigmente und Beschichtungen produzieren, Corus Packaging Plus, ein Hersteller von Stahlverpackungen, sowie der Polyesterfolienhersteller DuPont Teijin Films. Die PSAG kann über www.psag.co.uk kontaktiert werden.

Packaging Solutions Advice Group (PSAG) est un organisme qui mène des recherches sur les solutions, les matériaux et les processus dans le domaine des emballages. Dans cette étude de cas, ils expliquent l'application de cinq matériaux et techniques au bénéfice de l'image du contenu.

Imaginez un emballage qui imite l'éclat des flocons de neige, un papier-cadeau pour Noël qui sent les aiguilles de pin, ou encore une étiquette holographique qui accroche votre regard.

Ces effets et beaucoup d'autres encore sont maintenant disponibles, car les emballages deviennent de plus en plus complexes et raffinés. Il ne s'agit pas seulement des formes en 3D, mais aussi des pigments, des encres et des revêtements nécessaires pour obtenir le résultat idéal : un emballage qui protège son contenu et attire les consommateurs. Pour les marques et les designers, c'est une tâche ardue. Chez qui rechercher le savoir-faire quand votre fabricant d'emballage habituel est limité par sa technologie et sa compétence particulière ?

Le premier pas est de consulter les fabricants de composants de matériaux d'emballage, comme le fournisseur des pigments ou le fabricant du boîtier qui forme la structure. Ils travaillent souvent ensemble pour parvenir à de nouvelles applications technologiques sur différents matériaux. Ils sont aussi nombreux à trouver que les designers et les propriétaires de marque devraient les consulter directement sur la façon d'obtenir le style qu'ils recherchent, scintillant, perlé mat ou brillant. Les marques accèderaient ainsi à une compétence jusqu'à présent inexploitée, surtout si elles impliquent les fournisseurs de matériaux suffisamment tôt dans le processus de design. Environ 80 % des nouveaux lancements de marque n'atteignent pas leurs objectifs. Les designers et leurs clients seraient donc avisés d'explorer tout potentiel de leur emballage afin d'établir un lien affectif avec le consommateur.

C'est justement ce que les effets spéciaux peuvent aider à faire, grâce à des pigments qui ajoutent de l'éclat et de la couleur à l'emballage. Ils sont compatibles avec toute une gamme de matériaux et de processus d'impression, y compris la surimpression et la sous-impression. Les choses ont bien changé depuis le siècle dernier, quand les premiers effets nacrés réalisés à Paris utilisaient une suspension de membrane de cristal de guane produite à partir d'écailles de poisson.

Le pigment Miraval, fabriqué par Merck, utilise des borosilicates pour imiter l'effet d'un éclat de verre et est idéal pour des effets somptueux qui peuvent ajouter de la valeur à, par exemple, un emballage. Les pigments multicolores Colorstream® contiennent des plaquettes de dioxyde de silicium qui donnent un effet irisé. Une autre gamme de pigments de la marque Merck, Xirallic,

ntient des plaquettes d'oxyde d'aluminium
i donnent un brillant et une couleur très
enses. Iriodin est un pigment fabriqué à
tir de mica, qui donne des effets nacrés
eux, mats ou scintillants. Biflair, fabriqué
artir de chlorure de bismuth, donne un
ultat fin et opaque. On peut obtenir des
ultats magnifiques avec l'héliogravure, la
ographie, la sérigraphie ou l'offset, et l'on
it mélanger les pigments avec tous les
stiques transparents et semi-transparents
utilisant un moule à injection ou des pro-
és d'extrusion ou de rotation.
Lorsqu'ils sont utilisés correctement avec
utres applications et matériaux pour ren-
cer les valeurs de la marque, ces effets
vent avoir une valeur inestimable pour
gmenter le degré d'identification de la
rque dans les rayons. Des couleurs douces
c une touche d'irisation, par exemple,
vent évoquer des notions de protection,
douceur et de soin tandis que les couleurs
es et brillantes évoquent l'énergie, la jeu-
se et la fraîcheur.
Pour montrer aux designers et aux
rques les possibilités de ces pigments dans
omaine de l'emballage, plusieurs fournis-
rs de matériaux d'emballage ont travaillé
emble pour créer des exemples d'effets
igment sur deux gammes de produits
ceptuels. Les résultats démontrent ce qu'il
possible de faire lorsqu'un fabricant de
ment, par exemple, travaille en étroite
aboration avec un fabricant d'encre.
La gamme Well & Wild est conçue pour le
teur des boissons, en particulier pour les
rchés des boissons non alcoolisées, des
as alcoolisés et des alcools, pour lesquels
ifférenciation du produit et de l'emballage
un véritable défi. Les produits Well sont
boissons « bien-être » conçues pour sti-

muler l'esprit ou avoir un effet positif sur la
peau. Les produits Wild sont des boissons
festives pour les occasions spéciales. Il peut
s'agir d'un soda alcoolisé, ou d'une boisson
presque dangereuse, à la limite entre ce qui
est acceptable et ce qui est imprévisible.
Pour ces deux catégories, on a choisi des
manchons thermorétractables imprimés à
l'aide des pigments Iriodin® et
Colorstream® de Merck, mélangés aux
encres Finelap et Charon de Sun Chemical.
Les bouchons en plastique sont colorés dans
la masse avec des pigments assortis.

Le second exemple, Wind of Asia, montre
des pigments qui aident à exprimer différentes
notions pensées pour le secteur de la santé en
Asie. Les pigments Iriodin et Miraval sont utilisés pour obtenir des effets nacrés et diaprés
pour différents marchés cibles.

Quel que soit le concept de l'emballage, les
pigments ne sont rien sans leur support, en
particulier pour les projets de stratégie de
marque complexes qui impliquent tout un
éventail de supports tels que les étiquettes,
les bouteilles et les canettes, etc. Les pigments doivent donc être incorporés à une
formule appropriée à chaque support, qu'il
s'agisse de papier, de plastique ou d'acier.
C'est là que l'expérience des fabricants
d'encres et de revêtements entre en jeu.

Il existe maintenant des solutions de rem-
placement pour les encres à base de solvant.
Sun Chemical a créé des encres à base d'eau
ainsi que des encres polymérisables par
apport d'énergie, qui ont l'avantage de ne
pas contenir de composants volatiles tout en
offrant une qualité d'impression supérieure
sur les différents supports utilisés dans les
emballages souples. La technologie naissante
des encres odorantes est aussi un événement
très intéressant. Sun Chemical travaille

actuellement sur un papier-cadeau qui
embaume l'aiguille de pin pour rappeler
l'odeur de Noël, ainsi que sur une étiquette
de boisson parfumée de l'odeur de la fleur
utilisée dans la boisson, pour une grande
marque internationale.

L'uniformité de la couleur et de l'effet spécial est également essentielle pour les
marques qui investissent dans ces nouveautés. Pour résoudre le problème du manque
d'uniformité, il existe des systèmes de gestion de la couleur, comme SmartColour de
Sun Chemical. Ces systèmes visent à garantir que le résultat imprimé correspond exac-
tement à la maquette que l'agence de design
avait présentée. Cette technique donne aux
marques et aux designers plus de contrôle
sur les variables en leur permettant de
visualiser leur emballage selon les encres et
les procédés d'impression utilisés. L'effet
choisi est mesuré numériquement et appliqué
sur différents supports de façon à obtenir le
même effet quel que soit le procédé d'impression utilisé – numérique, flexographie, litho-
graphie ou héliogravure.

La sélection du bon pigment et de la bonne
encre n'est pourtant qu'une partie du processus. L'étape suivante est de les intégrer à
l'emballage lui-même. Protact est un système
qui non seulement fonctionne bien du point de
vue de la sécurité alimentaire, mais dont la
couleur et le brillant donnent également un
résultat de grande qualité. Il s'agit d'une
couche de polymère appliquée sur les emballages en acier, en différentes couleurs et avec
différents degrés d'opacité. Ce revêtement de
polymère créé par Corus Packaging Plus peut
être transparent et donner un fini métallique
de grande qualité, ou bien coloré à l'intérieur
Il a un potentiel esthétique considérable pour
une impression, un vernissage et un travail

en relief de grande qualité sur toute la surface. On peut aussi choisir d'utiliser des hologrammes pour augmenter encore l'attrait visuel du produit, ce qui peut également être une solution efficace pour éviter les contrefaçons en incorporant à l'emballage un hologramme du nom ou du logo de la marque.

Cela ouvre de nouvelles perspectives à l'emballage en acier, comme le démontrent les boîtes de saumon de la marque John West, et en particulier les boîtes en acier du champagne Nicolas Feuillatte, qui montrent bien l'impact visuel que l'holographie peut apporter. Une version Protact de la traditionnelle canette de boisson est aussi disponible, de même que des canettes à ouverture facile. De plus, les canettes en acier à revêtement en polymère sont 100 % recyclables. Toujours dans le domaine de l'environnement, les marques peuvent utiliser Le Carré, une boîte de conserve carrée. Cette boîte, créée par Corus Packaging Plus, est non seulement plus légère que les boîtes rondes habituelles, mais elle prend aussi moins de place pour le transport et occupe 20 % moins d'espace dans les rayons. Du point de vue esthétique, les boîtes Le Carré peuvent être combinées avec des étiquettes lithographiées ou avec des gaines thermorétractables sur les quatre faces pour optimiser leur impact visuel dans les rayons.

Pour les aérosols aussi le champ des possibilités s'est récemment élargi, grâce à un nouveau produit qui donne une plus grande liberté au design. « Buzz » combine un réservoir externe en plastique pour afficher le message de la marque sous n'importe quelle forme, avec les pigments, les couleurs et les formes que l'on souhaite, et un aérosol interne en acier. Ce produit créé par Corus Packaging Plus permet de choisir des matériaux extérieurs et un design différents parce que le composant extérieur n'est soumis à aucune contrainte de pression.

Les designers et les marques qui travaillent sur des produits nécessitant un emballage souple, comme les sachets de lessive, ont également intérêt à interagir avec les fabricants de matériaux, par exemple DuPont Teijin Films, qui fabrique le film de polyester Mylar, très répandu dans les emballages de nourriture et de boisson. En plus de sa commodité et de sa solidité, qui le rendent idéal pour un emballage souple, il est aussi étanche, rétractable, holographique, il peut être mis au four, et il présente également d'excellentes propriétés optiques pour faciliter l'identification de la marque.

En fin de compte, c'est à la marque et au designer de prendre l'initiative et d'explorer tout le potentiel de leur emballage, en parlant avec les experts chargés de sa création.

PSAG

Packaging Solutions Advice Group (PSAG) est une association d'entreprises qui distribuent des matériaux entrant dans la fabrication des emballages, depuis les pigments jusqu'aux récipients eux-mêmes. Parmi ses membres, on peut citer Merck, une multinationale de produits pharmaceutiques et chimiques qui fabrique des pigments, Sun Chemical, qui fabrique des encres, des pigments et des revêtements, Corus Packaging Plus, qui fabrique de l'acier pour le secteur de l'emballage et le fabricant de films de polyester DuPont Teijin Films. On peut contacter PSAG sur le site Internet de l'association, <www.psag.co.uk>.

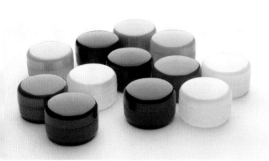

lockwise: Wind of Asia package, Le Carré quared can, the Buzz can, Well & Wild oloured drink bottle, and Nicolas Feuillatte nhanced champagne packaging.

Im Uhrzeigersinn: Verpackung für Wind of Asia, Le Carré und Buzz sowie farbige Getränkeflaschen von Well & Wild und die verbesserte Champagnerverpackung für Nicolas Feuillatte.

Dans le sens des aiguilles d'une montre : l'embalage de Wind of Asia, la boîte de conserve carrée de Le Carré, l'aérosol Buzz, les bouteilles colorées de la boisson Well & Wild et l'emballage de champagne amélioré de Nicolas Feuillatte.

BEVERAGES

ALCOHOLIC

Okumura Akio
Bloom Design
Bravis International
Cahan & Associates
CB'a Design Solutions
Creative XAN Corporation
Design Bridge
Dragon Rouge
Katsunori Hironaka
Jones Knowles Ritchie
Landor Design
Lippa Pearce
Momac.Co. / Right Stuff Co.
P&W Design Consultants
Pearlfisher
PI3
SiebertHead
Strømme Throndsen
Wren & Rowe

The brief: Diageo saw an opportunity to launch a lighter coloured whisky with a smooth and subtle taste, aimed at men in their 20s and 30s. Bloom was tasked with creating a highly distinctive design with strong masculine cues and a contemporary edge.

The design solution: an innovative new bottle shape was created, based on the classic whisky bottle, but with a twist in the form of a diagonal slice feature cut into the front, representative of the clean, crisp, cut-through taste of the whisky. To reinforce the product's quality credentials, the foot of the bottle was embossed with the J&B branding, emphasising category authenticity. The minimalist branding was printed onto a clear label, working to cue clarity of the product and supporting the clear proposition. The design combines quality and brand reassurance with sufficient disruption to cause reappraisal, interrogation and trial.

Der Auftrag: Diageo sah in der Markteinführung eines heller gefärbten Whiskys mit weichem, feinem Geschmack die Chance, die Altersklasse der 20- bis 30-jährigen männlichen Kunden für sich zu gewinnen. Bloom wurde mit der Kreation eines sehr individuellen Designs mit stark maskulinem Unterton und sehr moderner Note beauftragt.

Die Designlösung: Auf Basis der traditionellen Whiskyflaschen wurde eine neue Flaschenform entwickelt, die als Besonderheit eine Vertiefung auf der Vorderseite aufweist, die auf den klaren, reinen und schnittigen Geschmack des Whiskys anspielt. Um die hohe Qualität des Produktes hervorzuheben, wurde der Markenname in den Fuß der Flasche eingeprägt, was gleichzeitig für Authentizität innerhalb der Kategorie sorgt. Die minimalistisch gestaltete Marke wurde auf ein durchsichtiges Etikett gedruckt, was nochmals die Reinheit des Produktes betont und das Verkaufsargument der Klarheit stützt. Das Design vereint Qualität und Markenverstärkung, bricht aber gleichzeitig soweit damit, um Neubewertung und Hinterfragen zu erlauben.

La mission : Diageo avait vu un potentiel dans le lancement d'un whisky de couleur plus claire, au goût doux et subtil, destiné aux hommes d'une vingtaine et d'une trentaine d'années. Bloom a été chargé de créer un design très original, très masculin et contemporain.

La solution design : Une forme innovante de bouteille a vu le jour, basée sur la bouteille de whisky classique, mais avec une touche d'originalité : une découpe en diagonale sur le devant représente le goût pur, franc et original du whisky. Afin de renforcer les signes relatifs à la qualité du produit, la marque J&B est travaillée en relief sur le pied de la bouteille, pour insister sur l'authenticité du produit par rapport à sa catégorie. Le marquage minimaliste a été imprimé sur une étiquette transparente, qui souligne la clarté du produit et renforce le message. Le design combine qualité et consolidation de la marque avec une rupture suffisante pour susciter réévaluation, interrogation et expérimentation.

36+88

&B -6°C

esign: *Bloom Design – Toby
ilson (Structural Designer),
avin Blake, Dan Cornell,
ick Tobias (Graphic Designers);*
ient: *Diageo;* Awards: *Communi-
tion Arts;* Materials: *Cosmetic
nt glass with Roll-On Pilfer
oof closure;* Year: *2005*

CASK NUMBER 26.40
LIMITED EDITION SINGLE
MALT WHISKY
Design: *Lippa Pearce – Harry
Pearce (Designer), John Simmons
(Words);* Materials: *Glass, paper
label stock;* Manufacturing
process: *Blow moulding, litho
printed;* Year: *2004*

BUDOUKA GRAPPA
Design: *Okumura Akio;*
Client: *Katashimo Wine Foods
Japan;* Materials: *Glass, metallic
seal;* Manufacturing process:
Blow moulding, litho printed;
Year: *2003*

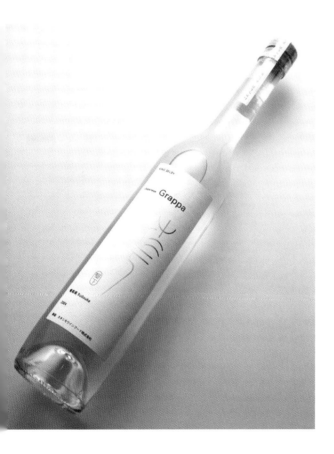

Glenlivet is the original single malt Scotch whisky – being granted the first legal licence in 1824 – and remains the benchmark against which all single malt whiskies are measured. The challenge was to celebrate this unique heritage – "the single malt that started it all" – whilst finding a contemporary expression suitable to both the 21st century and an increasingly global audience. Traditional materials and crafting techniques were married with modern engineering to create innovative packaging solutions which enhance the consumer experience and reinforce the premium brand proposition. Being beautiful is the point of entry for luxury brands. The range of packaging solutions creates a strong proposition for the Glenlivet brand as a whole – original, premium and differentiated from the competition. In addition the packaging creates a sense of autonomy for the individual expressions – 21 year old and Cellar Collection – appropriate to their heritage whilst celebrating the characteristics which make them unique.

Glenlivet ist das eigentliche Original unter den schottischen Single Malt Whiskys, denn die Glenlivet-Destillerie erhielt 1824 als erste eine Lizenz. Und bis heute stellt sie den Prüfstein dar, an dem sich alle anderen Single Malt Whiskys messen lassen müssen. Die Herausforderung bestand nun darin, dieses einzigartige Erbe zu feiern – „the single malt that started it all" (der Single Malt, mit dem alles begann) – und in eine moderne Kommunikation umzusetzen, die sowohl dem 21. Jahrhundert als auch dem wachsenden internationalen Publikum entsprach. Durch die Kombination traditioneller Materialien und alter Handwerkskunst mit moderner Ingenieurstechnik konnte eine innovative Verpackungslösung gefunden werden, die die Erlebnisqualität des Produkts für den Verbraucher erhöht und gleichzeitig die hohe Wertigkeit der Marke stärkt. Schönheit und Eleganz ist für alle Luxusartikel der eigentliche Ansatzpunkt. Das Sortiment an Verpackungslösungen stärkt die Marke Glenlivet als solche, stellt sie als außergewöhnlich und führend heraus und hebt sie damit von der Konkurrenz ab. Darüber hinaus lässt die Verpackung genügend Raum für Individualität – z.B. für den 21 Jahre alten Whisky oder die Cellar Collection – wodurch ihre Tradition und Einzigartigkeit zum Ausdruck kommen.

Glenlivet est le doyen des whiskies single malt : c'est lui qui a obtenu la toute première licence légale, en 1824. Il est toujours la référence contre laquelle tous les whiskies single malt se mesurent. Le défi était de célébrer ce patrimoine unique, « le single malt à partir duquel tout a commencé », tout en trouvant une expression contemporaine adaptée au XXIe siècle et à un public de plus en plus international. Les matériaux et les techniques de fabrication traditionnels ont été associés aux technologies modernes afin de créer des solutions de conditionnement innovantes pour mieux satisfaire les consommateurs et pour renforcer la proposition haut de gamme de la marque. L'esthétique est la voie d'accès des marques de luxe. La gamme de solutions de conditionnement crée une proposition solide pour la marque Glenlivet dans son ensemble originale, haut de gamme et différente de ses concurrentes. De plus, le conditionnement laisse leur autonomie aux différentes versions (21 ans d'âge et Cellar Collection) et reste fidèle à la tradition qui leur est commune tout en célébrant les caractéristiques qui les rendent uniques.

THE GLENLIVET
21 YEAR OLD AND
CELLAR COLLECTION
Design: *Landor Design – Chris*
[...]rt, Kenny Holmes, Lyndon
[...]vey; Client: *Pernod Ricard;*
[...]aterials and process: Light oak
[...]ooden support (debossed/engraved
[...]est to side), magnetic clasp held
[...] leather strap and flush fitting
[...] match box style sliding bottle
[...]lder; Year: *2006*

FUJISANROKU SINGLE MALT
AGED 18 YEARS
Design: *Katsunori Hironaka;*
Client: *Kirin Brewery Company
Limited;* Materials: *Glass, metallic
seal;* Manufacturing process:
Blow moulding; Year: *2005*

KIRIN PURE BLUE
Design: *Momac.Co. / Right Stuff Co.
– Yusuke Moriy, Masafumi Makino
(Designers);* Client: *Kirin Brewery
Co., Ltd.;* Materials: *Glass, plastic
seal, metallic seal;* Year: *2005*

Pearlfisher and Absolut set a new benchmark for the RTD (ready-to-drink) category with Absolut Cut, a drink that capitalises on Absolut's sophistication while adding an edgier attitude. The neck and shoulders of the bottle are modelled on the iconic Absolut shape, and the tall, slim bottle with screen printed graphics highlights the drink's premium status in the RTD category. A raw edge is added with vertical debossed grooves in the glass, giving the hand-held drink a unique tactile feel. Absolut Cut heralds a next generation of pre-mixed drinks and is a cut above in terms of both product and packaging.

Pearlfisher und Absolut setzten mit Absolut Cut neue Standards in der Kategorie der Alkopops (RTD – Ready to Drink). Das Getränk baut dabei auf den kultivierten Ruf von Absolut und fügt seine eigene, prickelndere Note hinzu. Hals und Schulter der Flasche entsprechen der typischen Absolut-Form, und die hohe, schlanke Flasche mit Siebdruckgrafik betont den gehobenen Status des Getränks innerhalb der Kategorie der vorgemischten Alkopops. Die Flasche erhält aber durch die vertikalen Rillen im Glas eine schnittigere Note und ein ganz spezifisches Handgefühl. Absolut Cut ist Vorreiter einer völlig neuen Generation von Mixgetränken, aber forscher in Produkt und Verpackung.

Pearlfisher et Absolut ont établi un nouveau standard dans la catégorie du prêt-à-boire avec Absolut Cut, une boisson qui exploite le raffinement d'Absolut en y ajoutant une attitude plus branchée. Le col et le haut de la bouteille sont calqués sur la silhouette emblématique d'Absolut, et la bouteille longue et fine avec un graphisme sérigraphié souligne le statut haut de gamme de la boisson dans le secteur du prêt-à-boire. Des griffures en relief sur le verre ajoutent une touche sauvage, et donnent à cette bouteille que l'on tient en main lors de la consommation une qualité tactile originale. Absolut Cut annonce une nouvelle génération de cocktails alcoolisés prêts à consommer, et a une longueur d'avance en termes de produit et de conditionnement.

SOMERFIELD VODKA,
SHERRY AND PORT
(GRAPHIC REDESIGN)
Design: *SiebertHead – Paula Macfarlane, Noma Bar (Designers)*; Client: *Somerfield Stores*; Materials: *Glass, metallic seal*; Manufacturing process: *Blow moulding*; Year: *2005*

ABSOLUT CUT
Design: *Pearlfisher – Sean Thomas (Designer)*; Client: *V&S Absolut Spirits*; Awards: *Glasspac Shine Awards UK, Creativity 34 USA, London International Awards*; Materials: *Glass, metallic seal*; Manufacturing process: *Narrow neck press and blow bottle with silk screen graphics*; Year: *2005*

YBOROWA VODKA
esign: *Dragon Rouge –*
phie Romet (Associate General
anager), Patrick Veyssière
reative Director); Awards:
ine & Spirit International Design
card; Materials: *Glass, metallic*
l; Manufacturing process: *Blow*
ulding; Year: *2005*

EFFEN VODKA
Design: *Cahan & Associates –*
Michael Braley (Designer),
Todd Simmons (Bottle Design);
Client: *Planet 10;* Materials: *Glass,*
metallic seal; Manufacturing
process: *Blow moulding;*
Year: *2004*

he creative objective here, from the get-go,
to throw a wrench into the typical alcoholic
erage packaging category. There is a lot of
ieness out there. Consumers know that look
oducts saturated with vintage and aged in
and feel. That works for Scotch. It can be
ndoned for Vodka. Vodka is a mixer. It's
e. Decisions are made by considering many
erent factors: importantly, what the scene is
who else is going to be there, what you are
ring, what kind of music is being spun, and
rall, what vibe the physical space provides.
graphics were skimmed down to the most
c and simplistic level. It is a clear and clean
ifestation of the product itself.

Die kreative Zielsetzung dieses Projekts lautete von Anfang an, mit allen Erwartungen an
die typische Verpackung eines alkoholischen
Getränks radikal zu brechen, da sich vieles
ohnehin schon zu sehr ähnelt. Man kennt den
typischen Look – überladene Verpackungen,
die auf alt und edel getrimmt sind. Das mag
bei Scotch funktionieren. Wenn es aber um
Wodka geht, kann man das alles getrost über
Bord werfen. Wodka ist ein Mixgetränk. Er ist
rein. Bei der Wahl der Bar werden viele unterschiedliche Faktoren mit einbezogen: Wie sieht
die Szene aus, wer kommt in das Lokal, was
trägt man, welche Musik wird gespielt und welche Atmosphäre hat der Laden. Die grafische
Gestaltung wurde so weit wie möglich ver-
schlankt und konzentriert sich auf das Wesent-
liche. Sie ist eine klare und eindeutige Manifes-
tation des Produktes selbst.

Ici, depuis le tout début, l'objectif créatif était
de lancer un pavé dans la mare des bouteilles
de boissons alcoolisées. Il n'y a pas beaucoup
d'originalité dans cette catégorie, on voit toujours la même chose : des produits saturés de
tradition, à l'allure vieillie. Cela fonctionne pour
le scotch, mais l'on peut essayer autre chose
pour la vodka. La vodka sert à faire des cocktails. Elle est pure. Les décisions de consommation sont prises en fonction de nombreux facteurs, et parmi les plus importants : le décor
dans lequel on se trouve, les autres personnes
présentes, ce que l'on porte, le genre de
musique et la vibration générale qui se dégage
de l'espace physique. Le graphisme a été réduit
à son expression la plus élémentaire et la plus
simple. C'est une représentation claire et nette
du produit lui-même.

SHAAZ FIGS AND ORANGE
BLOSSOM LIQUEUR
Design: *CB'a Design Solutions –
Marc Bourges (Designer);* Client:
PERNOD France; Materials: *Glass
bottle, paper;* Manufacturing
process: *Blow moulding;* Year: *2004*

…BAI
…ign: *Design Bridge;* Client:
…m Winery; Awards: *Wine &
…rit International Awards
…nze), Food & Beverage (FAB)
…rds (Finalist);* Materials: *Glass,
…er;* Manufacturing process: *Blow
…lding;* Year: *2005*

LOTUS VODKA
Design: *Cahan & Associates –
Erik Adams (Designer),*
Client: *Delicious Brands;*
Materials: *Glass, metallic seal;*
Manufacturing process:
Blow moulding; Year: *2005*

BAMBARRIA TEQUILA
Design: *P&W Design Consultants,*
Adrian Whitefoord (Art Director),
Lee Newham (Designer & Typogra-
pher); Client: *Wine & Spirits*
International; Awards: *Epica;*
Materials: *Hand blown glass bottle*
with natural cork stopper, inlaid
glass cactus inside bottle, collar
and seal, applied clear label;
Manufacturing process: *Six colour*
printed label, litho; Year: *2005*

N VERACRUZANO

sign: *P&W Design Consultants –*
rian Whitefoord (Art Director),
Newham (Designer & Typogra-
r); Client: *Wine & Spirit Inter-*
ional Ltd; Materials: *Handmade*
ss bottle with uncoated card
m and seal over the top of the
ural cork; Manufacturing
ess: Four-colour printed label,
o; Year: *2005*

Veracruzano is a premium range of Mexican
s from Wine & Spirit International. The pro-
made use of a tall bottle and some small
ns that fitted exactly over the end of the
tle. Some designs used this concept, whilst
ers had a more conservative label. The final
cept used the drum and was wrapped with
oated paper to contrast and emphasise the
gance of the shiny bottle.

Veracruzano ist eine Produktreihe mexika-
nischen Premium-Rums von Wine & Spirit International. Eine elegante hohe Flasche und ein
paar kleine Zylinder kamen zum Einsatz, die
genau über den Fuß der Flasche passten. Im
Design wurden zum Teil die Zylinder verwendet,
zum Teil ein eher konservatives Etikett. Gewählt
wurde schließlich ein Konzept, bei dem der
Zylinder in grundiertes Papier gehüllt ist, um
einen Kontrast zu der glänzenden Flasche zu
erzielen und deren Eleganz zu betonen.

Veracruzano est une marque de rhums mexi-
cains haut de gamme de Wine & Spirit International. Le projet utilise une une magnifique
bouteille allongée ainsi que de petits capu-
chons qui s'adaptent parfaitement à l'extrémité
de la bouteille. Certains concepts de design
utilisaient cette idée, d'autres étaient plus classiques. Le concept choisi utilise le capuchon,
et du papier brut pour créer un contraste avec
l'élégance et la surface brillante de la bouteille.

ALCATRAZ ALE
Design: *Cahan & Associates –*
Sharrie Brooks (Designer);
Client: *Boisset USA;* Materials:
Glass, metallic seal; Manufacturing
process: *Blow moulding, cap press;*
Year: *2005*

MOZELL ART BOTTLE
Design: *Strømme Throndsen*
Design – Nico Widerberg (Designer)
Client: *Ringnes AS;* Awards:
Norwegian Design Council Award
for Design Excellence; Materials:
Glass, metallic cap; Manufacturing
process: *Blow moulding, cap press;*
Year: *2003*

GUINNESS DRAFT
A BOTTLE
Design: *PI3 – Steve Kelsey, Will*
Haskell, Jed O'Brien;
Client: *Diageo;* Awards: *Starpack*
Award; Materials: *Glass bottle, PVC*
shrink sleeve, polypropylene widget
float, steel crown closure;
Manufacturing process: *Glass*
moulding, injection moulding and
line filling and closure; Year: *2005*

STRONGBOW
Design: *Jones Knowles Ritchie;*
Client: *Scottish Courage;* Materials:
Glass, metallic seal; Manufacturing
process: *Blow moulding;* Year: *2005*

SAKE HOURIN
Design: *Okumura Akio;* Client:
Gekkeikan; Materials: *Glass,*
metallic seal; Manufacturing
process: *Blow moulding;* Year: *2002*

APOLLO ALE & LAGER
Design: *Cahan & Associates –
Kevin Roberson (Designer)*;
Client: *Boisset USA*; Materials:
Glass, metallic seal; Manufacturing
process: *Blow moulding*; Year: *20**

This design was an attempt to capture a bit of the spirit and importance of the historic Apollo mission. The blue bottle and simple graphics relate to the vastness of space. This packaging has been positioned to reflect high quality from a sophisticated microbrewery to counter the traditional branding trend.

Mit dieser Verpackung sollten der Geist und die Bedeutung der historischen Apollo-Mission eingefangen werden. Die blaue Flasche und die schlichte grafische Gestaltung spielen auf die unendlichen Weiten des Weltalls an. Die Positionierung spiegelt die hohe Qualität einer Kleinbrauerei wider und setzt sich so von traditionellen Markentrends ab.

Nous avons tenté de capturer un peu de l'esprit et de l'importance de la mission historique Apollo. La bouteille bleue et le graphisme simple font référence à l'immensité de l'espace. Cet emballage a été mis au point afin de refléter la grande qualité d'une micro-brasserie sophistiquée, et dans le but d'aller à l'encontre de la tendance traditionnelle.

The aim of the project was to develop a bottle exclusively for the outdoor life/bar segment.
The physical bottle should function as a communication carrier for the brand's key values
and should support the position of the brand
(i.e. removal of stiffness.) The Ringnes Swing
bottle was the result of a team effort between
Strømme Throndsen Design, led by Jan Hillesland, Rexam Glass and Ringnes.

Das Ziel des Projekts lautete, eine Flasche
zu entwickeln, die exklusiv für das Segment
Outdoor Life/Bar gedacht war. Die Gestalt der
Flasche selbst sollte als Kommunikationsträger
der Kernwerte der Marke fungieren und deren
Positionierung begünstigen (Auflockerung der
Steifheit). Aus der hervorragenden Zusammen-
arbeit von Strømme Throndsen Design mit Jan
Hillesland, Rexam Glass und Ringnes entstand
die Ringnes-Swing-Flasche.

L'objectif du projet était de créer une
bouteille destinée exclusivement au secteur
de la consommation hors du foyer et dans les
bars. La bouteille devait fonctionner comme un
véhicule des valeurs essentielles de la marque
et soutenir sa position (l'abolition de la raideur).
La bouteille Swing de Ringnes est le résultat
d'un travail d'équipe entre Strømme Throndsen
Design, dirigé par Jan Hillesland, Rexam Glass
et Ringnes.

STELLA DEMI ARTOIS
Design: *Jones Knowles Ritchie;*
Client: *Inbev;* Awards:
*Communication Arts Award
of Excellence;* Materials: *Glass,
metallic seal;* Manufacturing
process: *Blow moulding;*
Year: *2004*

RINGNES SWING
Design: *Strømme Throndsen
Design – Jan Hillesland (Designer);*
Client: *Ringnes AS;* Awards:
*Norwegian Design Council Award
for Design Excellence, Organisation
for Visual Communication in
Norway (Gold Visuelt);* Materials:
Glass, metallic cap; Manufacturing
process: *Blow moulding;*
Year: *2005*

Until the launch of G Port, Gilbert's port wines carried the same traditional port image, as with most of the other producers. G Port has therefore been a radically new concept in the port sector. The intention was to create a new brand that made port relevant to a younger, sophisticated and cosmopolitan demographic group, but remain respectful to traditional port values and reflect the high quality of the product. The G Port range consists of six ports: ruby, tawny, white, LBV, 10-year-old tawny and vintage. While those varieties are familiar, the image is something else again. It is bottled in the traditional dark port bottle, and then engraved with a striking stylised "G" logo: each variety wears a distinctive capsule in an easily identified vibrant colour. The varieties are further characterised by their fun and colourful silkscreen lettering.

Gilberts Portweine waren bisher in dasselbe traditionelle Portweingewand gekleidet, das die meisten Produzenten verwenden. G Port ist daher ein radikal neues und bahnbrechendes Konzept auf dem Portweinsektor. Ziel war es, eine neue Marke zu kreieren, die Portwein auch für ein jüngeres, gehobenes und kosmopolitisches Publikum interessant macht, die angesehene Tradition und die Werte des Portweins aber nicht außer Acht lässt und sich dessen hoher Qualität bewusst ist. Die Produktreihe G Port besteht aus sechs Portweinen: Ruby, Tawny, White, LBV, 10-year-old Tawny und Vintage. Die Sorten sind zwar vertraut, das Image ist aber unterschiedlich. Die Portweine werden in traditionelle dunkle Portweinflaschen abgefüllt, dann aber mit dem auffallenden stilisierten „G"-Logo graviert und mit einer farbigen Verschlusskapsel versehen. Jede Sorte erhält eine Kapsel in einer kräftigen, auffälligen Farbe, was sie gut unterscheidbar macht. Ein weiteres Unterscheidungsmerkmal der einzelnen Sorten ist ihre freundliche, farbige Beschriftung.

Avant le lancement de G Port, les portos Gilbert avaient la même image traditionnelle que la plupart des autres portos de producteurs. G Port a donc représenté un concept radicalement nouveau dans le secteur du porto. L'intention était de créer une nouvelle marque qui saurait attirer l'attention d'un groupe démographique jeune, raffiné et cosmopolite, mais qui resterait respectueuse des valeurs traditionnelles du porto et reflèterait la grande qualité du produit. La gamme G Port est composée de six portos : ruby, tawny, blanc, LBV (late bottled vintage, ou vintage embouteillé tard), tawny 10 ans d'âge et vintage. Ces catégories n'ont rien de nouveau, mais l'image est très originale. La bouteille est noire, dans la tradition des bouteilles de porto, mais elle est gravée d'un G stylisé spectaculaire. Chaque variété porte une capsule différente, dans une couleur vive facile à identifier. Les caractères sérigraphiés sur les bouteilles dans un esprit ludique et coloré achèvent de donner du caractère à chaque variété.

About a thousand core range products have been packaged since 2002. CB'a created a new guideline with an original style: graphic structure, colours and visuals. The impact was also created with strong logotypes to affirm the identity of Monoprix. This project belongs to the global strategy of Monoprix who wants to modernise its image to differentiate itself from all the other retailers and reach their urban clients successfully.

Seit 2002 haben rund tausend Kernprodukte eine neue Verpackung erhalten. CB'a entwickelte eine neue Richtlinie und einen originellen Stil inklusive grafischer Struktur, Farben und Visuals. Weitere Aufmerksamkeit wurde anhand starker Wortmarken erreicht, die die Identität von Monoprix untermauern. Das Projekt ist Teil einer weltweiten Strategie, mit der Monoprix sein Image modernisieren und sich von allen anderen Supermärkten absetzen möchte, um seine urbane Kundschaft erfolgreich binden zu können.

Depuis 2002, environ 1 000 produits de cœur de gamme ont reçu un nouveau conditionnement. CB'a a créé une nouvelle ligne directrice au style original : structure graphique, couleurs et visuels. Des logotypes forts affirmant l'identité de Monoprix ont également contribué à l'impact de l'ensemble. Ce projet fait partie de la stratégie mondiale de Monoprix, qui veut moderniser son image afin de se démarquer de tous les autres distributeurs et de mieux atteindre ses clients citadins.

MONOPRIX BRANDS (GLOBAL PACKAGING PROJECT)
Design: *CB'a Design Solutions – Nathalie Jacquot, Philippe Delmotte (Designers)*; Client: *Monoprix*; Awards: *Strategies Packaging Design Prize*; Materials: *various*; Manufacturing process: *various*; Year: *2004*

PORT
Design: *Wren & Rowe – Michael Rowe (Designer)*; Client: *Gilbert's & Co.*; Awards: *Wine & Spirit Design Awards (Gold Medal and "Range of the Year"), Gold Mobius Trophy*; Materials: *Silkscreened glass bottle*; Manufacturing process: *Blow moulding*; Year: *2001*

ROYAL FROG
Design: *Cahan & Associates –*
Erik Adam; Client: *Boisset USA;*
Materials: *Paper;* Manufacturing
process: *Tetra Pak;* Year: *2005*

KIRIN CHU-HI HYOKETSU
Design: *Bravis International ;*
Client: *Kirin Brewery Co., Ltd.;*
Materials: *Aluminium;*
Manufacturing process: *various;*
Year: *2005*

ANDRESEN RESERVE TRIO
Design: *Wren & Rowe – Steve
Younger, Michael Rowe (Designers);*
Client: *J.H. Andresen Sucrs. Ltda.;*
Materials: *Brushed silver tinplate
lid with paper label, black plastic
flock coated tray;* Manufacturing
process: *Logo embossed and
de-bossed onto lid, black and grey
print onto silver tinplate lid,
label foil stamped on black stock;*
Year: *2004*

OTIMA
Design: *Design Bridge;*
Client: *Warre's;* Awards:
*Wine & Spirit Awards (Gold),
Design Effectiveness, Grocery
Advertising Awards;* Materials:
Glass, paper; Manufacturing
Process: *Blow moulding;*
Year: *2000*

STANCIA DEL FUEGO
sign: *Design Bridge;* Client:
cus; Materials: *Glass, metallic*
l; Manufacturing process:
w moulding; Year: *2005*

USEND HÜGEL
sign: *Design Bridge;* Client:
usend Hügel; Materials: *Glass,*
tallic seal; Manufacturing
ocess: Blow moulding; Year: *2005*

GOMEYAMA
Design: *Okumura Akio;* Client:
King Selby; Materials: *Glass,*
metallic seal; Manufacturing
process: *Blow moulding,* Year: *2002*

MATISSE BLENDED MALT
AGED 12 YEARS
Design: *Creative XAN Corporatic*
– Alex Su (Creative Director),
Jillian Cheng (Designer); Client:
Matisse Spirits Company Ltd.;
Materials: *Glass, metallic seal;*
Manufacturing process:
Blow moulding; Year: *2007*

RICARD SPIRIT
Design: *Dragon Rouge;*
Client: *Pernod SA France;*
Materials: *Glass, metallic seal;*
Manufacturing process:
Blow moulding; Year: *2005*

LA RUSTÍA WINE BOTTLE
Design: *SiebertHead;* Client:
Provincia Di Torino; Materials:
Glass, metallic seal; Manufacturing
process: *Blow moulding;* Year: *2003*

I

BEVERAGES

NON ALCOHOLIC

Ana Couto Branding & Design
Bloom Design
Coley Porter Bell
Creative XAN Corporation
Design Bridge
Dragon Rouge
Jones Knowles Ritchie
Kan and Lau Design Consultants
Landor Design
Lewis Moberly
Lloyd (+co)
Metaphase Design Group
Mountain Design
Parker Williams
Pentagram
Ross Lovegrove
Sayuri Studio
Stick Tea
Strømme Throndsen Design
Tin Horse Design Team
Tridimage
Wolff Olins
Ziggurat

P. 114+116

PURE WATER
Design: *Creative XAN Corporatic*
– Alex Su (Creative Director),
Tatsuya Kobayashi (Designer),
Jessy Lee (3D CG); Client: *TAISU*
Enterprise Co., Ltd; Materials:
Polyethylene terephthalate;
Manufacturing process: *Blow*
moulding, injection moulding;
Year: *2005*

This bottle is provided with three round slots at two sides and the lower part of the body, which are used to strengthen the structure and to emphasise the aesthetic effect of adding the finishing touch. The middle part of the bottle's body is provided with a U-shape slot that has the same function as the other three round slots.

Diese Flasche verfügt im unteren Bereich zu beiden Seiten über drei runde Einbuchtungen, die der Flasche Stabilität verleihen, ihre Ästhetik betonen und ihrer Form den letzten Schliff verleihen. Die große, u-förmige Einbuchtung auf dem Flaschenkörper hat dieselbe Funktion.

La bouteille est dotée de trois creux rond sur deux côtés, dans la partie inférieure. Ils servent à renforcer la structure et à souligne l'esthétique en ajoutant une touche finale. L milieu de la bouteille est doté d'un creux en forme de « U », qui a la même fonction que trois creux ronds.

The "S" curve is the element of design, which is formed in one go, simple and clean cut. It provides multiple refraction angles through which the contained "water" magically changes into imposing and powerful water in nature. The turning curves strengthen the structure and protect the bottle from damage or deformation by foreign force. The aluminium foil-sealed opening insures the consistent quality and safety of the contained water. The adoption of polyethylene terephthalate, a kind of reclaimable material, and the design of small-size labels reduce wastes caused by package.

Die „S"-Kurve ist ein Designelement, das einfach und sauber in einem Arbeitsschritt geformt wird. So entstehen verschiedene Lichtbrechungswinkel, die das „Wasser" im Inneren auf magische Weise zum Leben erwecken und es wie Wasser in der Natur wirken lassen. Die geschwungene Form sorgt für Stabilität und schützt die Flasche vor Bruch oder Verformung. Der aluminiumversiegelte Verschluss gewährleistet Qualität und Schutz des Wassers. Durch die Wahl von PET, ein für das Recycling geeignetes Material, und die kleinen Etiketten wird der Abfallanteil der Verpackung reduziert.

La courbe en « S » est l'élément de base du design, simple et défini en un seul geste. Elle donne de multiples angles de réfraction grâce auxquels l'eau de la bouteille se transforme comme par magie en une véritable force de la nature. Les courbes tournantes renforcent la structure et protègent la bouteille des dommages ou déformations provenant d'une force externe. L'ouverture scellée par du papier d'aluminium garantit la qualité et l'hygiène du contenu. L'utilisation de PET, un matériau recyclable, et d'étiquettes de petite taille réduit les déchets causés par l'emballage.

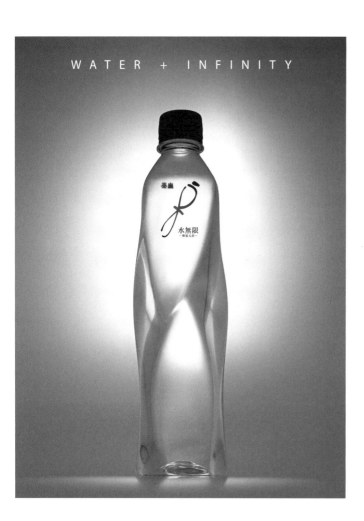

WATER + INFINITY

WATER INFINITY
Design: *Creative XAN Corporation – Alex Su (Creative Director), Tatsuya Kobayashi (Designer), Jessy Lee (3G CG);* Client: *TAISUN Enterprise Co., Ltd;* Awards: *WorldStar (Packaging Excellence), Taiwan Packaging Star;* Material: *Aluminum foil (seal), polyethylene terephthalate;* Manufacturing process: *Blow moulding, injection moulding;* Year: *2004*

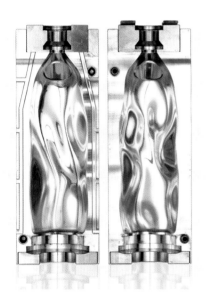

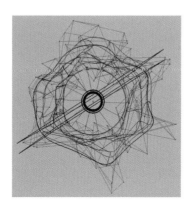

TY NANT WATERBOTTLE
Design: *Ross Lovegrove;* Client:
Ty Nant; Awards: *Bottledwater-world Design Awards;* Materials:
Polyethylene terephthalate;
Manufacturing process: *Blow moulding, injection moulding;*
Year: *2001*

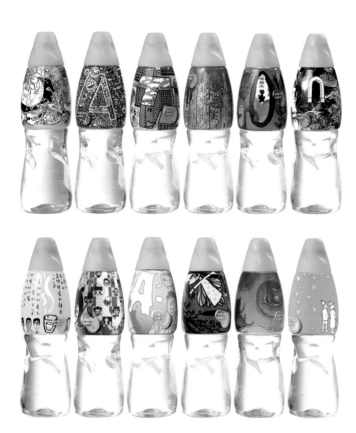

WATSONS WATER
(CENTENNIAL ANNIVERSAR
AND "YEAR OF HONG KONG"
PROJECT)
Design: *Kan and Lau Design
Consultants;* Client: *Watsons Wate*
Awards: *Orient Star Packaging
Design Competition, Hong Kong
Design Awards, Hong Kong
Marketing Awards/TVB Award,
Bottledwaterworld Design Awards
Creativity 33, 15thHong Kong Pri
Awards, Design 03 Shenzhen Shou
Graphic Arts Association of Hong
Kong;* Materials: *Polyvinyl chloric
plastic;* Manufacturing process:
Injection moulding, blow mouldin
Year: *2003*

The innovative packaging design is derived from a combination of gentle water motion and beautiful streamlined human body curves; the new image uplifted the brand identity and elevated its implication of art and enjoyment of life. In celebration of the Centennial Anniversary of Watsons Water in 2003, twelve local artists were invited to create a set of twelve limited edition commemorative bottle labels for Watsons Water. The idea was to use the twelve letters of Watsons Water to convey different themes relating to Hong Kong. This activity successfully utilised a consumer product as a medium to promote local culture. The design concept for the A.S. Watson Group Corporate Brochure utilised a human touch approach and a brisk natural green colour to reflect the nature of its products and the group's corporate culture.

Das innovative Verpackungsdesign leitet sich aus der Kombination sanfter Wasserbewegungen mit den schönen, stilisierten Konturen eines menschlichen Körpers ab. Das neue Design verlieh der Markenidentität einen Aufwärtstrend und betonte die impliziten Inhalte von Kunst und Lebensfreude. Zum 100-jährigen Bestehen von Watsons Water wurden im Jahr 2003 zwölf lokale Künstler eingeladen, in einer limitierten Edition ein Set aus zwölf Jubiläums-Flaschenetiketten für Watsons Water zu entwerfen. Die Idee bestand darin, mit den zwölf Buchstaben, die der Markenname „Watsons Water" enthält, verschiedene Themen aufzugreifen, die mit Hongkong in Verbindung stehen. So wurde mit einem Alltagsprodukt erfolgreich die lokale Kulturszene gefördert. Das Design-Konzept für die Firmenbroschüre der A.S. Watson Group kombiniert die menschliche Anmutung mit einem klaren, natürlichen Grün, um die Natürlichkeit der Produkte und die Firmenkultur des Hauses wiederzugeben.

Le design de ce conditionnement innovant est une combinaison d'ondoiements liquides et de courbes épurées inspirées du corps humain. La nouvelle image revalorise l'identité de la marque et augmente son engagement dans l'art et le plaisir de vivre. Pour célébrer le centième anniversaire de Watsons Water en 2003, 12 artistes locaux ont été invités à créer un ensemble de douze étiquettes commémoratives en édition limitée. L'idée consistait à utiliser les douze lettres de « Watsons Water » pour illustrer différents thèmes liés à Hong Kong. Cette activité a transformé avec succès un produit de consommation en support de promotion de la culture locale. La brochure d'entreprise de l'A.S. Watson Group a été réalisée avec une approche humaine et dans une couleur v vif naturel afin de refléter la nature des produ du groupe et sa culture d'entreprise.

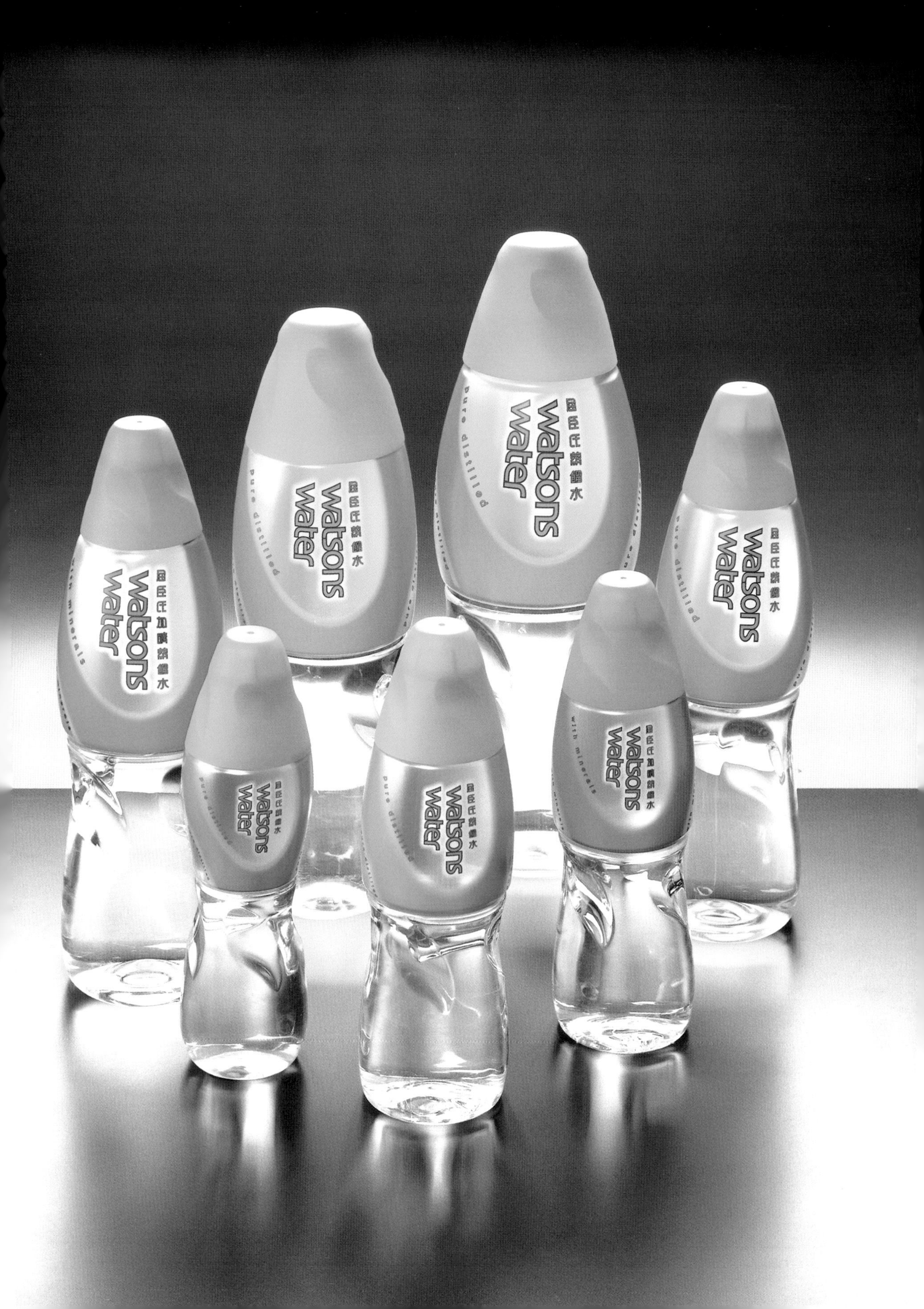
watsons water
屈臣氏蒸餾水
pure distilled
with minerals

PERRIER PET
Design: *Dragon Rouge – Patric Veyssière (Creative director);* Client: *Nestlé Waters;* Materials *Polyethylene terephthalate;* Manufacturing process: *Blow moulding, injection moulding;* Year: *2007*

VITTEL MINERAL WATER
Design: *Dragon Rouge – Sophie Romet (Project Management), Patrick Veyssière (Creative Director);* Client: *Nestlé Waters – Laurent Blum (Marketing International), Marie-Cécile Pellé Lancien (Brand Director), Grégoire Alias (Innovation Director);* Materials: *Polyethylene terephthalate;* Manufacturing process: *Blow moulding, injection moulding;* Year: *2005*

BELU WATER
Design: *Lewis Moberly – Mary Lewis (Art Director, Copywriter), Bryan Clark (Design Director, designer, illustrator, typographer);* Client: *Life Waker UK,* Materials: *Glass, metallic seal;* Manufacturing process: *Blow moulding;* Year: *2005*

EVIAN ORIGINE
Design: *Landor Design – Yannick Lenormand, Thierry Bigard*; Clien *Evian/Danone*; Awards: *Top Com (Bronze) – Prix Spécial de l'Expression, Epica (Bronze), Observeur du design – Cité des Sciences et de l'Industrie de la Villette (Shortlist);* Materials: *Extra-white glass;* Manufacturing process: *Blow moulding;* Year: *200*

MAXENS
(THE FOUR ELEMENTS)
Design: *Landor Design – Ingrid Biraud, Yannick Lenormand;* Client: *Degussa;* Awards: *Grand Prix Stratégies du Design;* Materials: *Polyethylene terephthalate bottles, aluminium caps, transparent plastic boxes;* Manufacturing process: *Blow moulding;* Year: *2003*

SMART WATER
Design: *Lloyd (+ co) – Douglas Lloyd (Creative Director), Andy Boonthang (Art Director);* Client: *Glaceau;* Materials: *Polyethylene terephthalate;* Manufacturing process: *Blow moulding, injection moulding;* Year: *2005*

Challenge: Evian decided to create a new [br]akthrough event bottle to maintain its sta[br] as a trendsetter and the leading plain min[br] water brand. When Evian asked Landor to [br]velop the bottle, there were two challenges: [br] design needed to be beautiful enough to [br]come a collector's bottle, while also convey[br] Evian's values and attributes – the Alps and [br] pure, mineral rich Evian water that has [br]en flowing there from source for over 8,000 [br]rs. The challenge was also technical, since [br]ew bottle would require the creation of a [br]cial production line.

Solution: Landor capitalised on the main icon [br]he Evian identity, the French Alps, by making [br] new bottle into a monolithic, ice-like sculp[br] e of a mountain. To focus attention on the [br]uty of the bottle and the reflections of the [br] pted glass, Landor applied minimal graphics.

Die Herausforderung: Evian beschloss, eine neue, bahnbrechende Flasche auf den Markt zu bringen, um den Status als Trendsetter und Marktführer im Bereich stille Mineralwasser wieder zu festigen. Als Evian mit dem Auftrag an Landor herantrat, stellte sich eine doppelte Herausforderung: Die Flasche musste schön genug sein, um als Sammlerstück zu gelten, und gleichzeitig die Werte und Attribute verkör- pern, für die die Marke Evian steht – die Alpen und das reine, mineralienreiche Evian-Wasser, das hier seit über 8000 Jahren einer Quelle entspringt. Die Herausforderung barg aber auch eine technische Seite, denn die Entwick- lung einer neuen Flasche bedeutete auch die Entwicklung einer neuen Produktionsstraße.

Die Lösung: Landor bediente sich des wich- tigsten Symbols der Evian-Markenidentität (der französischen Alpen) und verlieh der neuen Flasche die monolithische, eisähnliche Silhou- ette eines Berges. Um das Hauptaugenmerk auf die Schönheit der Flasche und die Refle- xionen des geformten Glases zu lenken, hielt Landor die grafische Gestaltung so minimalis- tisch wie möglich.

Le défi : Evian a décidé de créer une bou- teille évènementielle révolutionnaire afin de maintenir son statut de créateur de tendance et de marque numéro un de l'eau plate miné- rale. Lorsque Evian a demandé à Landor de concevoir la bouteille, le défi était double : le design devait être assez beau pour que la bouteille soit un objet de collection, tout en transmettant les valeurs et les attributs d'Evian – les Alpes et l'eau pure d'Evian riche en minéraux qui y coule depuis plus de 8 000 ans. Le défi était aussi technique, puisqu'une nouvelle bouteille requiert la création d'une chaîne de production spéciale.

La solution : Landor s'est servi du principal emblème de l'identité d'Evian, les Alpes fran- çaises, en faisant de la nouvelle bouteille une sculpture monolithique de montagne qui res- semble à une statue de glace. Pour focaliser l'attention sur la beauté de la bouteille et sur les reflets du verre sculpté, Landor a utilisé un graphisme minimaliste.

ICELANDIC GLACIAL WATER
Design: *Design Bridge;* Client:
Icelandic Water Holdings UK;
Materials: *Polyethylene terephtha-
late;* Manufacturing process: *Blow
moulding, injection moulding;*
Year: *2005*

DEEP RIVER ROCK
Design: *Tin Horse Design Team;*
Client: *Coca-Cola Bottlers Ireland;*
Materials: *Polyethylene; terephthalate (bottles), polyethylene stretch
sleeves, industry standard closure;*
Manufacturing process: *Injection
blow moulding (bottle), injection
moulding (lid);* Year: *2005*

LLANLLYR SOURCE;
ORGANIC WATER
Design: *Parker Williams – Paul
Carr, Nicola Benn;* Client: *Llanllyr
Water Company;* Awards: *Bottled-
waterworld Awards – Best Design
in Glass (Winner), Best Label
Design (Commended), Best Overall
Design (Commended);* Materials:
Embossed glass, silkscreen in foil;
Manufacturing process: *Blow
moulding;* Year: *2005*

SDAL BOTTLE
ign: *Strømme Throndsen
ign;* Client: *Ringnes AS;*
ards: *Norwegian Design
ncil Honours Award for
ign Excellence, Organisation
Visual Communication
Norway;* Materials: *Glass;*
ufacturing process:
w moulding;* Year: *2001*

INNOCENT JUICY WATER
Design: *Coley Porter Bell;* Client:
Innocent Drinks; Materials: *Glass,
metallic cap;* Manufacturing
process: *Blow moulding;* Year: *20*

VITAMIN WATER
Design: *Lloyd (+ co) – Douglas
Lloyd (Creative Director), Andy
Boonthang (Art Director);* Client
Glaceau; Materials: *Polyethylene
terephthalate;* Manufacturing
process: *Blow moulding, injection
moulding;* Year: *2005*

23
Design: *Bloom Design – Toby
Wilson (Structural;Designer),
Dan Cornell, Mark Thrush, Polly
Williams (Graphic Designers);*
Client: *Diageo;* Materials:
*Cosmetic flint glass with
Roll-On Pilfer Proof closure;*
Manufacturing process: *Blow
moulding, injection moulding;*
Year: *2004*

NAMACHA GREEN TEA
(PACKAGE RENEWAL)
Design: *Sayuri Studio, Inc. –
Sayuri Shoji, Daiju Aoki, Ryota
Furukawa (Designers);* Client:
Kirin Beverage Corporation;
Materials: *Polyethylene terephtha-
late (bottle), polypropylene (cap);*
Manufacturing process: *Blow
moulding, oriented polystyrene
with gravure printing;* Year: *2005*

SAINSBURY
FLAVOURED WATERS
Design: *Ziggurat – Allison Miguel
(Creative Director), Hayley Bishop
(Designer)*; Client: *Sainsbury
on label packaging*; Materials:
Polyethylene terephthalate;
Manufacturing process: *Blow
moulding, injection moulding,
etc*; Year: *2007*

Design: *Jones Knowles Ritchie*;
Client: *Britvic*; Awards: *DBA
Design Effectiveness Awards
(Finalist), Marketing Week
Effectiveness Awards (Winner)*;
Materials: *Glass, metallic cap*;
Manufacturing process:
Blow moulding; Year: *2004*

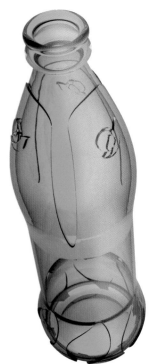

STUDY FOR;
KUAT SOFT DRINK
Design: *Ana Couto Branding
& Design;* Client: *The Coca-Cola
Company;* Materials: *Polyethylen
terephthalate;* Manufacturing
process: *Blow moulding, injection
moulding;* Year: *2006*

Line 1: In this study, asymmetry gives the bottle a light-hearted fun touch designed to appeal to the young.

Line 2: The rounded forms evoke the leaves and fruit of the guarana. The longer layout give the bottle an elegant air.

Line 3: The design of the fruit, which appears in relief on the neck of the bottle, heightens perception of taste. This study also evokes the shape of the leaves and the fruit, reinforcing the natural qualities and dynamism for the Kuat brand.

Linie 1: Bei dieser Studie bekommt die asymmetrische Form der Flasche eine fröhliche Note, die das junge Publikum ansprechen soll.

Linie 2: Die runden Formen spielen auf die Blätter und die Frucht der Guarana-Pflanze an. Die länger gestreckte Form verleiht der Flasche Eleganz.

Linie 3: Mit dem Relief der Frucht auf dem Flaschenhals lenkt dieser Entwurf die Aufmerksamkeit auf den Geschmack. Gleichzeitig erinnert auch dieser Entwurf an die Form von Blättern und Früchten der Pflanze und betont die natürlichen Qualitäten und die dynamische Kraft der Marke Kuat.

Ligne 1 : dans cette étude, l'asymétrie donne à la bouteille une touche ludique et légère, conçue pour séduire les jeunes.

Ligne 2 : les formes rondes évoquent les feuilles et le fruit du guarana. Le dessin plus allongé donne à la bouteille une allure élégante.

Ligne 3 : le dessin du fruit, qui apparaît en relief sur le col de la bouteille, renforce la perception gustative. Cette étude évoque également la forme des feuilles et du fruit, pour souligner les qualités naturelles et le dynamisme de la marque Kuat.

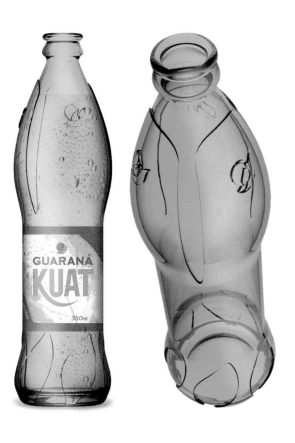

DRAGONFLY ENERGY DRINK
(BRAND IDENTITY, LABEL
DESIGN AND STRUCTURAL
BOTTLE DESIGN)
Design: *Tridimage – Adriana
Cortese, Virginia Gines, Hernán
Braberman (Designers);* Client:
Embotelladora Libélula, Mexico;
Materials: *Polyethylene terephtha-
late;* Manufacturing process:
*Injection-blow moulding,
sleeve label;* Year: *2004*

COCA-COLA LIGHT
LEMON (VISUAL
EXECUTED IN A 0,5 L PET);
Design: *Mountain Design –
Niels Alkema (Designer);* Client:
Coca-Cola Netherlands; Materials:
Polyethylene terephthalate;
Manufacturing process: *Blow
moulding, injection moulding;*
Year: *2005*

GATORADE E.D.G.E.
(ERGONOMICALLY DESI
GATORADE EXPERIENC
Design: *Metaphase Design G
Bryce Rutter, Brad Allen, Jo
Stockdell-Giesler, Scott Port
(Designers), Tony Cenicola
(Photo credit);* Client: *Quake
Awards: *Industrial Design
Excellence Award for Desig
Research (Silver);* Materials
Manufacturing process: *Flat
provides empty bottle stabil
high-speed filling on the pro
line, shrink-wrap labelling,
injection blow moulding;* Ye

PACKAGING GUIDELINES
FOR MINUTE MAID MEXICO
Design: *Ana Couto Branding &*
Design – Ana Couto, Natascha
Brasil, Dalcacio Gama, Danilo Cid,
Raphael Abreu, Vivian Mayrink,
Vian Raco, Clarissa Butelli,
Gabriela Mundim; Client: *Coca*
Cola Mexico; Materials: *Polyethyl-*
ene terephthalate; Manufacturing
Process: *Blow moulding, injection*
moulding; Year: *2006*

SEN
Design: *Wolff Olins – Keshen Teo (Designer);* Client: *Hutchison Whampoa;* Awards: *London International Advertising Awards – Grand Prix (Overall Package Design), Pharmaceuticals Award (Package Design);* Materials: *Smooth uncoated recycled card;* Manufacturing process: *Box construction, litho printed;* Year: *2003*

Wolff Olins created a brand to help cus-
[tome]rs feel comfortable with Chinese medicine
[an]d lend authenticity to the product. As Chi-
[ne]se medicine concerns itself with the balance
[be]tween the body and the natural world, these
[tw]o elements were the essence of the brand
[ide]a: "Living Balance." From this core, the
[stu]dio developed the brand name: Sen
[(th]e Mandarin word for "forest.") The Chinese
[ide]ogram for forest consists of three trees
[pla]ced in triangular formation. The use of this
[im]age lends the packaging cultural and histori-
[cal] references. Moreover, the character of the
[pa]ckaging in one half is counterbalanced by
[the] plainness of the other, so that the product
[de]sign precisely expresses the brand idea,
[mix]ing "balance" with connotations of "living."
[W]olff Olins also designed a store to help
[dra]w people in, give the customer an under-
[sta]nding of Chinese medicine and make them
[feel] comfortable with the products. The first
[Se]n store opened in London in November 2002.

Wolff Olins entwickelte eine Marke, die die
Kunden Zutrauen zur chinesischen Medizin fas-
sen ließ und die dem Produkt Authentizität ver-
lieh. Ein zentraler Gedanke der chinesischen
Medizin ist die Balance von Körper und Natur.
Aus diesem Gedanken bezog das Studio die
Inspiration für das Konzept der Marke: „Gelebte
Balance". Daraus wurde der Markennamen Sen
(das Mandarin-Wort für Wald) entwickelt. Das
chinesische Schriftzeichen für Wald besteht
aus drei Bäumen, die in Form eines Dreiecks
zueinander stehen. Dieses Zeichen verleiht den
Packungen einen kulturellen sowie historischen
Bezug. Zudem wird der Druck auf der einen
Hälfte der Verpackung durch die Schlichtheit
der anderen ausbalanciert, wodurch das Produktdesign das Konzept der Marke widerspie-
gelt, indem es „Balance" mit Konnotationen
des „Lebens" verbindet.

Die von Wolff Olins ebenfalls entworfenen
Ladenlokale sollten Kunden anziehen, Verständ-
nis für die chinesische Medizin vermitteln und sie
damit vertraut machen. Das erste Sen-Ladenlokal
öffnete im November 2002 in London.

Wolff Olins a créé une marque qui aide
les consommateurs à se familiariser avec la
médecine chinoise et apporte de l'authenticité
au produit. La médecine chinoise s'intéresse à
l'équilibre entre le corps et la nature, et ce sont
ces deux éléments qui ont servi de base à l'idée
centrale de la marque : « Living Balance » (équilibre vivant). C'est à partir de cette base que le
studio a conçu le nom de la marque, Sen (le mot
mandarin pour « forêt »). L'idéogramme chinois
représentant la forêt est composé de trois
arbres disposés en forme de triangle. Cette image apporte au conditionnement des références
culturelles et historiques. De plus, la moitié
décorée de chaque boîte est contrebalancée
par l'autre moitié unie, de sorte que le design du
produit exprime précisément l'idée centrale de
la marque, associant « équilibre » et « vie ».

Wolff Olins a également conçu un magasin
afin d'attirer le public, de l'éduquer sur la
médecine chinoise et de le familiariser avec
les produits. Le premier magasin Sen a ouvert
à Londres en novembre 2002.

GEOW YONG TEA
Design: *Kan and Lau Design Consultants;* Client: *Geow Yong Tea Hong (HK) Ltd.;* Awards: *Orient Star Packaging Design Competition, Hong Kong Design Awards, Applied Typography 14, Design 03 Shenzhen Show, Hong Kong Print Awards, Macao Design Biennial;* Materials: *Plastic bag, paper, cardboard, cotton bag;* Manufacturing process: *Folding, glueing, die cut;* Year: *2003*

The repackaging of the gift sets for this century-old tea house in Sheung Wan, Hong Kong, involved deliberately carving the gift boxes with Chinese window patterns, so as to exude the scent of tea, while also setting the mood for the enjoyment of Chinese tea. Different types of tea are identified with different colouring. Most importantly, a seal is designed to avoid counterfeiting.

Die neue Verpackung für die Geschenksets des jahrhundertealten Teehauses in Sheung Wan, Hongkong, wurde bewusst mit traditionellen, geschnitzten chinesischen Fenstern versehen, wodurch sie einerseits verführerischen Teeduft verströmt und andererseits auf den Genuss chinesischen Tees einstimmt. Die verschiedenen Teesorten werden durch eine unterschiedliche Farbgebung gekennzeichnet. Schließlich wurde noch ein Siegel entwickelt, um Fälschungen vorzubeugen.

Pour la réactualisation des coffrets-cadeaux de cette maison de thé centenaire de Sheung Wan, à Hong Kong, on a gravé des motifs de fenêtres chinoises sur les boîtes de façon à laisser l'arôme du thé se répandre, tout en créant une atmosphère propice à la dégustation du thé chinois. Les différentes sortes de thé sont identifiées par différentes couleurs. Surtout, un sceau a été créé afin d'éviter la contrefaçon.

Stick tea is a practical and smart industrial disposable infuser. It is made with a thin aluminium sheet with 450 holes on its surface. It works like a classic infuser used with loose tea. It allows you to obtain an excellent infusion made from the best full leaf tea blends.

Stick tea ist ein praktischer und pfiffiger, für den einmaligen Aufguss entwickelter Wegwerfbehälter aus Aluminiumfolie. Mit seinen 450 feinen Löchern hat er dieselbe Funktion wie das klassische Teesieb für lose Teeblätter. Mit erlesenen Teemischungen gefüllt erlaubt Ihnen der Stick tea den perfekten Teegenuss.

Le Stick tea est une « boule à thé » jetable en forme de bâton, pratique et intelligente. Elle est faite d'une fine feuille d'aluminium percée de 450 trous. Elle fonctionne comme une boule à thé classique utilisée avec du thé en vrac. Elle permet d'obtenir une excellente infusion des meilleurs mélanges de feuilles de thé.

STICK TEA ®
Design: *Stick Tea;* Client: *Stick Tea, Italy;* Materials: *Pure aluminium;* Manufacturing process: *not disclosed;* Year: *2000*

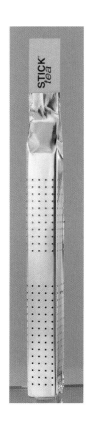

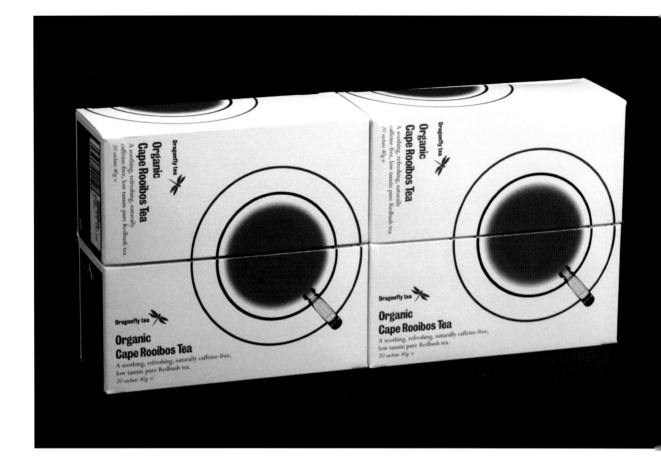

Wistbray launched Dragonfly Tea in 2000, a range of premium organic teas introducing new, modern blends to the UK market. This category has traditionally witnessed a plethora of colourful, ethnic approaches to packaging, making the shelf environment visually chaotic. In order to secure a distinctive, powerful shelf presence, the brand identity and packaging buck the trend, with a very calm graphic approach that lets the quality and clarity of the product speak for itself.

In 2003, Partner David Hillman and Lisa Enebis designed the packaging for Dragonfly's Rooibos natural caffeine-free teas. The packaging for the range of teas creates a strong impact on the shelf, differentiating them from other offerings and reflecting the high quality and heritage of the product. Using clean, clear typography, colour coded to each tea, and a photographic device of wrapping an image around the packaging, the new teas have a powerful presence at point of sale.

Im Jahr 2000 führte Wistbray Dragonfly Tea ein, eine Produktreihe ausgesuchter, biologisch angebauter Tees, die den britischen Markt mit neuartigen und modernen Mischungen bereichern sollten. In dieser Produktkategorie herrschen seit langem sehr bunte Verpackungen mit ethnisch geprägten Mustern vor, wodurch die Auslagen in den Regalen visuell chaotisch wirken. Um also schon im Regal eine auffällige Präsenz sicherzustellen, brachen Produktidentität und Verpackung mit dem Trend und setzten auf einen grafisch sehr ruhigen Ansatz, der die Qualität und Reinheit des Produkts für sich sprechen lässt.

2003 entwarfen die Partner David Hillman und Lisa Enebis eine Verpackung für die von Natur aus koffeinfreien Rooibos-Tees von Dragonfly. Die Verpackung für diese Produktreihe war sehr auffällig, hob sich stark von der Konkurrenz ab und spiegelte die hohe Qualität und die Tradition des Produktes wider. Durch die klare Typografie in unterschiedlichen Farben je Teesorte und eine fotografische Abbildung, die um die Verpackung läuft, erreichte man einen sehr hohen Aufmerksamkeitswert in der Auslage.

En 2000, Wistbray a lancé Dragonfly Tea, une gamme de thés organiques haut de gamme introduisant des mélanges nouveaux et modernes sur le marché britannique. Cette catégorie a souvent été témoin d'une pléthore d'approches ethniques et colorées du conditionnement, qui ont fait des rayons un véritable chaos visuel. Pour assurer au produit une présence originale et bien visible dans les rayons l'identité de marque et le conditionnement vont à contre-courant, avec une approche graphique très modérée qui laisse la qualité et la clarté du produit parler d'elles-mêmes.

En 2003, David Hillman, coassocié, et Lisa Enebis ont conçu l'emballage destiné aux thés Rooibos naturellement sans caféine de DragonFly. L'emballage est très efficace dans les rayons, différencie la gamme des autres produits et reflète sa qualité et sa tradition. Avec une typographie claire et nette, un code de couleur pour chaque type de thé et un traitement original de l'image, avec des photographies qui s'étendent sur plusieurs côtés de la boîte, ces nouveaux thés ont une présence remarquable sur les lieux de vente.

ISTBRAY
RAGONFLY TEA
sign: Pentagram – David
llman (Designer); Client:
stbray; Awards: *Food and*
verage Creative Excellence
ards (Packaging), Organic Food
ards (Commended); Materials:
per, cardboard; Manufacturing
ocess: Folding, glueing, die cut;
ar: 2003

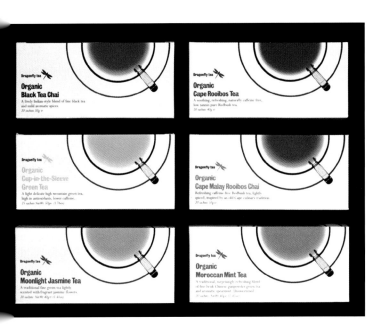

II

ELECTRONICS

& EQUIPMENT

Apple
Design Guys
GAD Design
Industrial Facility
Kornick Lindsay
MetaDesign
Mountain Design
Panasonic Design Company/Matsushita
PDD Group
Stockholm Design Lab.
Taku Satoh Design Office
Tangerine/AIG
Tátil Design

APPLE IPOD SHUFFLE
Design: *Apple;* Client: *Apple Inc*
Materials: *Plastic; Manufacturir*
process: various; Year: *2007*

APPLE IPHONE
Design: *Apple;* Client: *Apple Inc*
Materials: *various;* Manufacturir
process: *various;* Year: *2007*

P. 142
CLARO
Design: *GAD Design – Leonardc*
Araujo (Design Director), Leand:
Saldanha (Designer); Client:
America Movil; Awards: *London*
International Award, IF Design
Award; Materials: *Plastic;*
Manufacturing process: *Blow*
moulding; Year: *2004*

Kornick Lindsay created the packaging for Motorola's Pre-Pay phone offering, encapsulating a V180 phone with all necessary accessories inside a double clamshell design. The structure showcases the product in a clear floating "bubble," while storing the accessories inside an opaque inner shell. The Motorola logo is embossed beneath the phone on the front of the inner shell and on the back. The logo post acts as a guide to position service provider brand graphics and product details.

Kornick Lindsay kreierte für Motorolas Prepaid-Handy V180 eine Verpackung, bei der das Telefon mit allem Zubehör von zwei ineinander sitzenden Kunststoffschalen umhüllt wird. Diese Verpackungsform präsentiert das Produkt, als schwebe es in einer Luftblase, während das Zubehör nicht sichtbar in der inneren Schale verstaut ist. Das Motorola-Logo ist auf der Vorderseite unterhalb des Telefons in die innere Schale eingeprägt und findet sich auch auf der Rückseite. Das Logo dient gleichzeitig als Positionierungshilfe für die Etikettierungsmaterialien und Produktinformationen der einzelnen Netzanbieter.

L'agence Kornick Lindsay a créé l'emballage de l'offre de téléphone portable à carte prépayée de Motorola, en encapsulant un téléphone portable V180 avec tous les accessoires nécessaires dans une double coque. La structure présente le produit dans une « bulle » transparente flottante, tandis que les accessoires sont rangés dans une coque intérieure opaque. Le logo Motorola est travaillé en relief sous le téléphone à l'avant de la coque intérieure, et à l'arrière. Le logo sert de repère pour positionner les graphismes de l'opérateur et les informations sur le produit.

MOTOROLA PEBL
Design: *Kornick Lindsay / Motorola – John O'Connell (Motorola Global Packaging), Luiz Andrade (Motorola Global Image Design);* Client: *Motorola, Silvia Hidalgo (Motorola Global Image Design);* Materials: *Polypropylene, acrylonitrile Butadiene Styrene (ABS);* Manufacturing process: *Injection moulding;* Year: *2005*

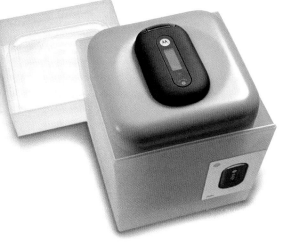

The European mobile network operators E-Plus and kpn have decisively broadened their service with i-mode. MetaDesign has developed its mobile phone packaging as part of a comprehensive brand re-launch. The polystyrene core is suitable for the logo. A translucent film bears the graphics. Extraordinarily cheap materials are used in its production to create an apparently very high value packaging. The use of the polystyrene material as a visible packaging material makes a complex design possible (polystyrene is usually used on the inside of paper packaging to provide a secure storage for the product). This means that the characteristic curved features and bulges of the i-mode brand symbol are transferred to the packaging design. In its two-colour flat print face, the outer covering also shows the characteristic shape of the brand symbol. A complex of transparencies corresponds with the shape of the polystyrene core and focuses the eye on the open i-mode mobile phone. The less attractive components such as the charger, rechargeable batteries or multilingual user's manual are accommodated on the inside of the two-compartment form.

Mit i-mode haben die europäischen Mobilnetzbetreiber E-Plus und die holländische kpn ihren Service entscheidend ausgeweitet. MetaDesign hat die Handyverpackung im Rahmen eines umfassenden Marken-Relaunchs entwickelt. Der Styroporkern ist formal dem Logo angelehnt. Eine lichtdurchlässige Folie trägt die Grafik. In der Produktion außerordentlich günstige Materialien finden hier zu einer sehr hochwertig anmutenden Verpackung zusammen. Die Verwendung des Materials Styropor als sichtbares Verpackungsmaterial ermöglicht ein komplexes Design (gewöhnlich wird Styropor im Inneren von Pappverpackungen zur stabilen Lagerung der Produkte verwendet). Dadurch können die charakteristischen Wölbungen und Ausbuchtungen des i-mode-Markenzeichens auf das Verpackungsdesign übertragen werden. Die Umhüllung zeigt in ihrer zweifarbigen Flächenbedruckung ebenfalls die charakteristischen Formen des Markenzeichens. Eine Vielschichtigkeit von Transparenzen korrespondiert mit der Form des Styropor-Kerns und fokussiert den Blick auf das geöffnete i-mode-Handy. Die weniger attraktiven Packungsinhalte wie Ladegerät, Akkus oder mehrsprachige Bedienungsanleitung sind im Inneren der zweiteiligen Form untergebracht.

Les opérateurs de téléphonie mobile européens E-plus et kpn ont considérablement étendu leurs services grâce à i-mode. MetaDesign a créé l'emballage de leur téléphone portable dans le cadre d'une révision complète de la stratégie de marque. La structure en polystyrène s'adapte bien au logo. Le graphisme est imprimé sur un film translucide. Les matériaux utilisés sont extraordinairement bon marché, mais forment pourtant un emballage qui transmet une impression de grande qualité. L'utilisation du polystyrène en tant que matériau visible permet un design complexe (on utilise généralement le polystyrène pour protéger le produit à l'intérieur de l'emballage lors du stockage). La forme caractéristique du logo de la marque i-mode, avec ses creux et ses bosses, se retrouve dans l'emballage. Le film extérieur, avec son motif bicolore, reprend également le symbole de la marque. Un jeu de transparence avec la structure en polystyrène attire le regard sur le téléphone i-mode présenté. Les éléments moins séduisants, comme le chargeur, les batteries rechargeables ou le manuel d'utilisation multilingue, sont rangés à l'intérieur des deux compartiments de la structure en polystyrène.

I-MODE
MOBILE TELEPHONE
Design: *MetaDesign – Jens-Ole Kracht, Christof Siedel (package design), Jürgen Huber (graphic design)*; Client: *E-Plus, kpn-mob (sister company of NTT DOCOM Japan)*; Awards: *Deutscher Verpackungsdesign Wettbewerb*; Materials: *Polystyrene, polyethylene*; Manufacturing process: *Injection moulding, printing*; Year: *2005*

HELIX
Design: *PDD Group – Miles
Crawley, Martin Kay, Nick Foster,
Chris Taylor (designers);* Client:
PDD Internal Futures Concept;
Materials: *Conceptual;* Manufacturing process: *not in production;*
Year: *2005*

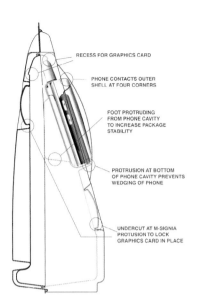

RECESS FOR GRAPHICS CARD

PHONE CONTACTS OUTER
SHELL AT FOUR CORNERS

FOOT PROTRUDING
FROM PHONE CAVITY
TO INCREASE PACKAGE
STABILITY

PROTRUSION AT BOTTOM
OF PHONE CAVITY PREVENTS
WEDGING OF PHONE

UNDERCUT AT M-SIGNIA
PROTUSION TO LOCK
GRAPHICS CARD IN PLACE

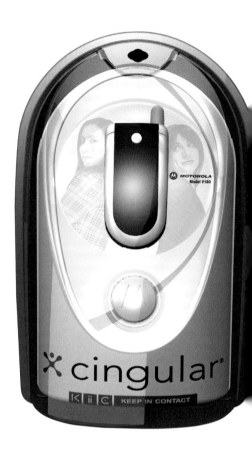

MOTO V-180
Design: *Kornick Lindsay/Motorola
– John O'Connell (Motorola Global
Packaging), Luiz Andrade
(Motorola Global Image Design),
Kornick Lindsay Team;* Materials:
Thermoplastic File; Manufacturing
process: *Thermo Form;* Year: *2005*

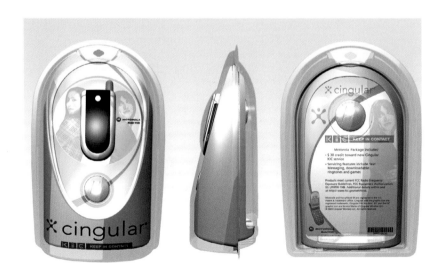

KIA 3220
ESS KIT WITH GIFT)
ign: *Tátil Design – Frederico
i (Chief Designer), Felipe
iar, Fábio Gaspar, Bruno Novo
igner), Alexandre Salgado,
Gelli, Tarso Ghelli (Photo
its);* Client: *NOKIA;* Awards:

*ADG, Brazilian Graphic Design
Biennial, Colunistas Prize,
Brazilian Design Festival;*
Materials: *Polypropylene plates,
ethylene vinyl acetate plates,
magnetised metal catch;*
Manufacturing process:
Trimming and scoring; Year: *2001*

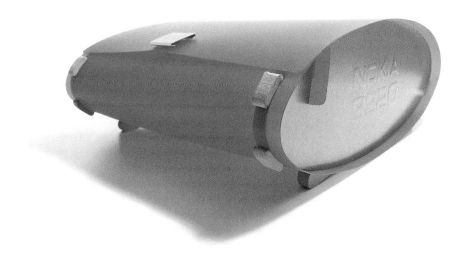

The focus of one aspect of this strategy was a common packaging solution for Iriver's three product ranges. The packs are intended to blend seamlessly with the look and feel of Iriver's stand-alone stores, yet create a strong visual statement when displayed in other retail environments. The lid of the two-part expanded polystyrene box both protects and displays the product. Despite their diminutive size, a typical MP3 Flash player is supplied with a large collection of accessories, software, connectors and power adapters. All these have been carefully fitted into the base of the box without the overall pack becoming bulky. The lid and the base of the box are secured with a large translucent clip. This clip creates a window through which the product can be seen and provides a surface onto which product information can be displayed.

Ein Schwerpunkt dieser Arbeit war, eine einheitliche Verpackung für die drei Produktlinien von Iriver zu entwickeln. Die Verpackungen sollten sich nahtlos in das Design der firmeneigenen Läden einfügen und gleichzeitig hohe Aufmerksamkeit in den Auslagen anderer Einzelhandelsgeschäfte erzielen. Der Deckel der zweiteiligen Styropor-Schachtel dient einerseits als Schutz, andererseits wird darauf das Produkt präsentiert. Trotz seiner geringen Größe wird der typische MP3-Player mit umfangreichem Zubehör, wie etwa Accessoires, Software, Steckern und Netzteil, geliefert. Das gesamte Zubehör ist platzsparend im unteren Teil der Schachtel untergebracht, ohne dass diese dadurch schwer wirkt. Die Schachtel ist in eine große, durchsichtige Kunststoffschale gebettet, sodass das Produkt sichtbar bleibt. Die Produktinformationen befinden sich auf der Kunststoffschale.

L'un des aspects de la stratégie était de créer un concept d'emballage commun aux trois gammes de produits de la marque Iriver. Les emballages sont conçus pour s'intégrer parfaitement au style des magasins Iriver, mais pour se démarquer visuellement lorsqu'ils sont présentés dans d'autres magasins. Le couvercle de la boîte en deux parties, fabriquée en polystyrène expansé, protège et présente le produit. Malgré sa petite taille, elle abrite pour chaque lecteur MP3 un assortiment complet d'accessoires, de logiciels, de connecteurs et d'adaptateurs. Tous ces articles sont soigneusement rangés dans le fond de la boîte et occupent un minimum d'espace. Le couvercle et la base de la boîte sont maintenus par un grand clip translucide. Le clip forme une fenêtre à travers laquelle on peut voir le produit, et offre une surface permettant de présenter les informations sur le produit.

MP3 PLAYER PACKAGING
Design: *Tangerine/AIG –
Mike Woods (Creative Director,
Tangerine), Chris Weightman
(Designer, Tangerine), Tim Fendley
(Creative Director, AIG), Daniel
Freytag (Senior Designer, AIG);*
Client: *Iriver, South Korea;*
Materials: *Expanded polystyrene,
polystyrene;* Manufacturing process:
Moulding, injection moulding;
Year: *2005*

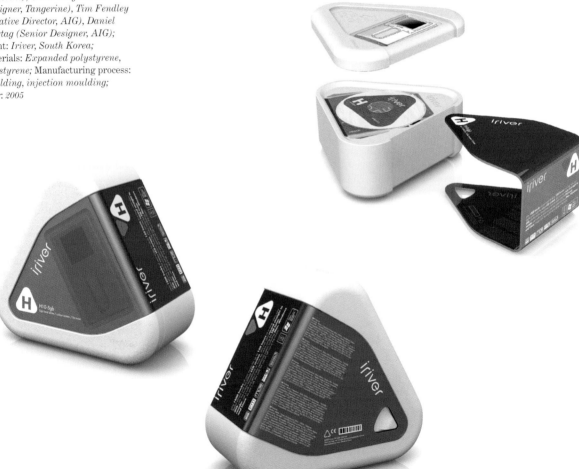

VIRGIN PULSE PACKAGING
Design: *Design Guys – Steve Sikora*
(Creative Director), John Moes,
Paul Amundson (Designers);
Client: *Virgin USA;* Materials:
corrugated paperboard, plastic
clamshells; Manufacturing process:
die cut, litho printing; Year: *2005*

This packaging was designed to speak very directly to the consumer in plain talk as much as possible. Personal electronics are typically sold by technology and esoteric features. Even product names are in code. Design Guys wanted the level of technology to be assumed due to the high quality and care of the presentation. Copy on the package focuses on the benefits of the products themselves, not on getting technical. The paradigm for mass electronics packaging is a plastic clamshell with a printed card sealed inside. While this type of package is protective and functional it tends to look cheap. This packaging intentionally runs opposite to the norm. Virgin Pulse clamshells have an outer paper wrap. This adds extra branding space and allows the opportunity to create multiple gloss and dull textures as opposed to the shiny plastic clamshell alone.

Diese Verpackung sollte den Verbraucher so direkt und eindeutig wie möglich ansprechen. Heimelektronik wird gewöhnlich mit Hinweisen auf seine technologische Ausstattung und mit geheimnisvollen Botschaften verkauft. Sogar die Produktnamen sind wie Codewörter. Design Guys wollten, dass die Präsentation klar die hohe Qualität der Technik vermittelt. Die Verpackungsbeschriftung konzentriert sich auf die Vorteile des Produkts, nicht auf die technischen Details. Eine stereotype Verpackung in der Elektronikbranche besteht aus zwei verschweißten Kunststoffschalen mit einer bedruckten Karte im Inneren. Diese Art der Verpackung hat zwar einen hohen Schutzwert und ist praktisch, wirkt aber schnell billig. Sie bewegt sich bewusst abseits der Norm. Die Kunststoffschalen der Produktreihe Virgin Pulse haben eine Umverpackung aus Papier, auf der es ausreichend Raum für das Markenimage gibt. Verschiedene matte und glänzende Oberflächen auf dem Papier kontrastieren mit dem durchsichtigen Kunststoff.

Cet emballage a été pensé pour parler directement au consommateur, de la manière la plus explicite possible. Normalement, les produits électroniques de grande consommation sont vendus en misant sur leur technologie ou sur des fonctions ésotériques. Même les noms des produits sont codés. L'équipe de Design Guys voulait que le niveau de technologie soit sous-entendu par la qualité et le soin de la présentation. Les textes de l'emballage présentent les avantages des produits en eux-mêmes, et non leur technologie. Pour ce genre de produits, l'exemple type d'emballage est la coque en plastique avec un fond en carton imprimé à l'intérieur. Ce type d'emballage est fonctionnel et protège bien le produit, mais il a tendance à faire bas de gamme. Cet emballage va intentionnellement à contre-courant. Les coques de Virgin Pulse ont un emballage extérieur en papier. Cela donne plus d'espace pour mettre la marque en valeur, et l'on peut ainsi créer des contrastes de texture brillante et mate, plutôt que de n'avoir qu'une coque en plastique brillant.

± CARTON
Design: *Taku Satoh Design Office – Taku Satoh, Ichiji Ohishi;*
Client: *Plus Minus Zero Co., Ltd.;*
Materials: *Cardboard, expanded polystyrene;* Manufacturing process: *Die cut, printing;* Year: *2003*

The project involved a packaging concept and product design for a range of batteries on the Japanese market. A study of the market revealed little differentiation in product and package design for batteries and an overabundance of product information on them. In a radical approach to the assignment Stockholm Design Lab went back to square one to create a design concept that removed all unnecessary information and cluttered graphics from the product. In Japan, batteries are categorised using numbers 1–4. The simple, straightforward design highlights this important piece of product information while sweeping away all irrelevant detail. The batteries are also colour coded as a further aid to identification. The resulting design is a powerful instrument for merchandising and display, with a dynamic effect on sales. As a member of the design team said: "Remove all the non-essentials from packaging for a commodity and interesting things start to happen…"

Dieses Projekt umfasste Verpackungskonzept und Produktdesign für eine Produktreihe von Batterien, die für den japanischen Markt bestimmt waren. Eine Marktstudie ergab, dass Produkt- und Verpackungsdesign in dieser Kategorie wenig differenziert waren und oft ein Überangebot an Informationen boten. Daher entschied sich Stockholm Design Lab für einen radikalen Neuanfang und entwarf ein Konzept, das auf alle überflüssigen Informationen und grafischen Elemente verzichtete. In Japan werden Batterien durch die Zahlen 1 bis 4 kategorisiert. Genau auf diese wichtige Information konzentriert sich das klare Design, während es alle unwichtigen Details weglässt. Zur einfacheren Unterscheidung sind die Batterien zusätzlich farblich gekennzeichnet. So entstand ein kraftvolles Design, das große Aufmerksamkeit erregt, wesentlich zur Verkaufsförderung beiträgt und damit einen dynamischen Effekt auf den Absatz hat. Oder wie ein Mitglied des Design-Teams es formulierte: „Entfernen Sie alle überflüssigen Informationen von einem Gebrauchsgut, und plötzlich tun sich interessante Dinge auf …"

Pour ce projet, il s'agissait d'imaginer un concept d'emballage et un concept graphique pour une gamme de piles sur le marché japonais. Une étude de marché avait révélé que, dans le domaine des piles, l'emballage et le produit étaient très peu différenciés d'une marque à l'autre, et étaient surchargés d'informations. Stockholm Design Lab a abordé sa mission dans un esprit radical, et est reparti de zéro pour créer un concept qui élimine toutes les informations superflues et simplifie le graphisme au maximum. Les piles japonaises sont classées en catégories identifiées par des chiffres de 1 à 4. Le design simple et direct souligne cette information importante et fait disparaître tous les détails inutiles. Les piles sont aussi dotées d'un code de couleurs pour rendre leur identification encore plus facile. Le résultat est un puissant outil de merchandising et de présentation, stimulant pour les ventes. Comme le dit l'un des membres de l'équipe de design : « Supprimez tout ce qui est superflu dans l'emballage d'un produit de base, et des choses intéressantes commenceront à se produire… »

SKUL BATTERIER
ATTERIES
esign: *Stockholm Design Lab;*
lient: *ASKUL;* Materials: *Card-*
oard; Manufacturing process:
ie cut, printing; Year: *2005*

ONCE
Design: *Industrial Facility – Sam*
Hecht (Designer); Client: *Lexon SA;*
Materials: *High impact styrene;*
Manufacturing process: *Injection*
moulded; Year: *2004*

"Once" is a watch formed in vulcanised
bber in either skin colour or grey. Its simplici-
lies in the acknowledgement that setting the
ne and alarm are functions done very rarely
hen compared to the life of the product, and
e learnt by the wearer over a period of time.
is results in the button controls being
sconced within rubber, hidden from view,
d with no expression. The only button that
visible is the display itself, which can be
essed to deactivate the alarm, and also
iminate the display for 3 seconds. To express
s new type of functionality, the packaging
esents itself as a translucent box with a hole
match the watch display. Not only does the
ckaging emphasize the idea of a "one but-
n" watch, but it also turns the watch into a
ck that can sit happily on any horizontal sur-
ce. The investment in the packaging material
d production process is warranted, because
this extended use. Packaging is seen not as
momentary element, but as an integral part
the product's functionality and enjoyment.

„Once" ist eine Uhr aus vulkanisiertem
Gummi, die in Hautfarbe oder Grau erhältlich
ist. Ihr schlichtes Design trägt der Tatsache
Rechnung, dass das Einstellen von Zeit und
Wecker Funktionen sind, die nur sehr selten
verwendet werden. Daher liegen die Einstell-
knöpfe dieser Uhr im Gummi versteckt und
sind nicht markiert. Das einzige sichtbare
Bedienelement ist das Display. Es ist gleichzeitig ein Knopf, der gedrückt wird, um den
Wecker auszuschalten und das Display drei
Sekunden lang zu beleuchten. Diese neue Art
der Funktionalität wurde noch erweitert: Die
durchscheinende Verpackungsschachtel ist mit
einer Aussparung für das Display der Uhr versehen. So kann die Armbanduhr auf jeder hori
zontalen Fläche als Wecker aufgestellt werden.
Dieser offensichtliche Zusatznutzen rechtfertigt
die Investition in das Verpackungsmaterial und
den Produktionsprozess. Die Verpackung ist
hier kein vorübergehend genutztes Element,
sondern ein integraler Bestandteil der
Funktionalität des Produkts.

« Once » est une montre en caoutchouc
vulcanisé de couleur chair ou grise. Le réglage
de l'heure et de l'alarme est une fonction très
rarement utilisée en comparaison avec la
durée de vie du produit, et dont l'utilisateur
apprend à se servir au cours d'une période
déterminée. C'est de cette idée que vient la
simplicité de Once, et elle se traduit par des
boutons de réglage invisibles, incrustés dans
le caoutchouc. Le seul bouton visible est
l'écran lui-même, sur lequel on peut appuyer
pour désactiver l'alarme ou pour illuminer
l'écran pendant 3 secondes. Pour exprimer ce
nouveau type de fonctionnalité, l'emballage est
une boîte translucide avec une découpe qui ne
laisse apparaître que l'écran de la montre. Non
seulement l'emballage souligne l'idée d'une
montre « avec un seul bouton », mais il transforme aussi la montre en une pendule que l'on
peut poser sur n'importe quelle surface hori-
zontale. Le retour sur l'investissement dans le
matériau de l'emballage et dans le processus
de production est garanti, car son utilisation
est de longue durée. L'emballage n'est pas
conçu comme un élément temporaire. Il fait au
contraire partie intégrante de la fonctionnalité
du produit et de son attrait.

EASY-TO-DISTINGUISH
DRY BATTERY PACKAGE
Design: *Keiichi Harada, Noriko Himeda (Panasonic Design Company, Matsushita Electric Industrial Co., Ltd.);* Client: *Matsushita;* Awards: *Osaka Design Center, Japan Packaging Contest, Good Design Award, Kinoshita Prize;* Materials: *Pet film;* Manufacturing process: *Thermal Shrinkage;* Year: *2000*

QOOPAQ
Design: *Panasonic Design Company, Matsushita Electric Industrial ;* Client: *Matsushita;* Awards: *World Packaging Organization, Asian Packaging Federation, Japan Packaging Institute;* Materials: *Expanded polystyrol;* Manufacturing process: *Not disclosed;* Year: *2001*

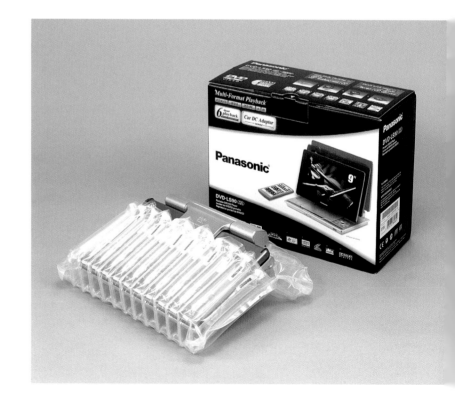

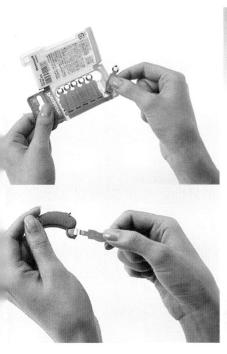

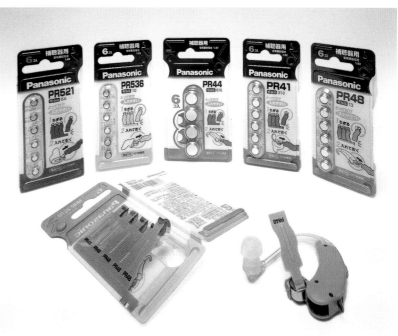

NEW EASY-TO-USE
HEARING AID BATTERY
Design: *Noriko Himeda
Panasonic Design Company,
Matsushita Electric Industrial Co.,
...*); Client: *Matsushita;* Awards:
*... Design Award, Local
Commendation for Invention of
... ki, London International*

*Advertising & Design Awards,
World Star for Packaging
Excellence, National
Commendation for Invention,
Kinoshita Prize;* Materials: *PET;*
Manufacturing process: *Vacuum
Forming;* Year: *2002*

PUSH BRACES
Design: *Mountain Design / Waac's
Design, Rotterdam – Emmy van
Gool (2D Designer, Mountain
Design), Lisa Smith (3D Designer,
WAACS Design);* Client: *NEA
International;* Materials: *Plastic;*
Manufacturing process: *Die cut,
folding;* Year: *2006*

PEPPERED BEEF & POTATO RÖSTI

TENDER BRAISED BEEF IN A CREAMY SAUCE WITH A **KICK** OF PEPPER, TOPPED WITH ROAST MUSHROOMS AND SERVED WITH POTATO RÖSTI

KICK

Waitrose

LINCOLNSHIRE SAUSAGES IN RED WINE

HOMELY LINCOLNSHIRE SAUSAGES IN A RED WINE GRAVY WITH ROASTED HORSE MUSHROOMS

HOME

ROBUST

BELLY OF PORK WITH CARAMELISED APPLES

SLOW ROASTED BELLY OF PORK **RELAXED** IN A CIDER JUS, WITH CARAMELISED APPLE WEDGES

RELAX

Waitrose

BEEF & CHIANTI LASAGNE

LAYERS OF FREE RANGE EGG PASTA WITH A **RICH** BEEF AND RED WINE RAGU, TOPPED WITH A CREAMY CHEESE SAUCE

RICH

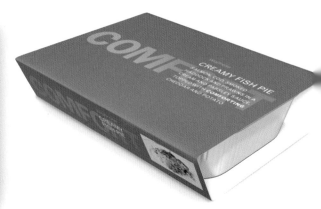

CREAMY FISH PIE

HADDOCK, COD, SMOKED HADDOCK & PRAWNS IN A CREAMY PARSLEY SAUCE TOPPED WITH **COMFORTING** CHEDDAR AND POTATO

COMFORT

OLIVE OIL & BASIL POTATOES

NEW POTATOES **CRUSHED** WITH OLIVE OIL AND BASIL INFUSED OILS

CRUSH

Waitrose

CREAMY MASH

FLAVOURFUL MASHED POTATOES, **LOVINGLY** BLENDED WITH CREAM, BUTTER AND PEPPER

LOVE

III

FOOD

Okumura Akio
Bloom Design
Coley Porter Bell
Creative XAN Corporation
DJPA Partnership
Sato Katsunori
Jones Knowles Ritchie
Lewis Moberly
Marks & Spencer
Metaphase Design Group
Minale Tattersfield & Partners
Morinaga
PDD Group
Pearlfisher
Pentagram
PI3
R Design
slover [AND] company
Strømme Throndsen
Taku Satoh Design Office
Yasuo Tanaka
WSdV Chicago
Ziggurat Brand Consultants

Pearlfisher's revolutionary designs for Waitrose's range of restaurant quality meals dispense with ubiquitous food photography and rely on the power of a single word to tempt customers' taste buds. Heritage and quality is implicit in the Waitrose name, so Pearlfisher was able to steer away from merely describing the food, focusing instead on the emotions that are created or satisfied by eating. Abstract, evocative words capture the essence of each meal – from LOVE for mashed potato to HOME for Lincolnshire sausages. Beautifully designed with clean, simple typography across a spectrum of equally evocative colours, the range is seductive, premium and out of the ordinary. Collectively, on shelf, it has a visual impact way beyond the traditional colour choices of the sector.

Die revolutionären Pearlfisher-Designs für die hochwertigen Mahlzeiten in Restaurantqualität von Waitrose kommen ohne die inzwischen allgegenwärtige Food-Fotografie aus und stützen sich ganz auf die Überzeugungskraft und die Fähigkeit einzelner Worte, die Geschmacksnerven der Kunden anzusprechen. Da der Name Waitrose für Qualität und Tradition steht, brauchte Pearlfisher sich nicht auf die reine Beschreibung des Produkts zu beschränken, sondern konnte sich stattdessen auf die Emotionen konzentrieren, die durch die sinnliche Handlung des Essens hervorgerufen oder befriedigt werden. Abstrakte Wörter bringen das Wesen jeder Speise auf den Punkt – wie etwa LOVE für Kartoffelpüree oder HOME für Lincolnshire Sausages. Die wunderschön gestaltete Produktpalette mit klarer und einfacher Typografie, kombiniert mit einem breiten Spektrum ebenso sinnträchtiger Farben, vermittelt höchste Qualität und ist außergewöhnlich. Das Design geht weit über die traditionelle Farbwahl des Sektors hinaus und beschreitet damit ganz neue Wege.

Les concepts révolutionnaires de conditionnement créés par Pearlfisher pour la gamme plats préparés de qualité restauration de Waitrose font l'impasse sur les omniprésentes photographies alimentaires, et misent sur le pouvoir d'un seul mot pour tenter les papilles gustatives des consommateurs. Le nom Waitrose est synonyme de tradition et de qualité. Pearlfisher a donc pu dépasser la simple description du plat, et se concentrer sur les émotions créées ou satisfaites par l'acte de se nourrir. Des mots abstraits et évocateurs capturent l'essence de chaque plat – LOVE (amour) pour la purée de pommes de terre ou HOME (foyer) pour les saucisses du Lincolnshire. Avec un design magnifique, une typographie claire et simple et des couleurs au grand pouvoir d'évocation, ces produits sont séduisants, haut de gamme et hors du commun. Placés côte à côte sur les rayons, ils ont un impact visuel qui dépasse de loin celui des couleurs traditionnellement utilisées dans le secteur.

WAITROSE READY MEALS
(RESTAURANT
QUALITY MEALS)
Design: *Pearlfisher – Kate Marlow (Designer);* Client: *Waitrose Limited;* Awards: *FAB Awards (Finalist), New York Festivals (Finalist);* Materials: *Incada Excel carton board (Iggesund Paperboard);* Manufacturing process: *Cartons and sleeves printed, UV offset with matt and gloss varnishes, copper colour hot foil logo;* Year: *2005*

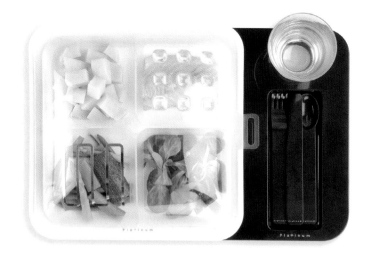

ATINUM
sign: *PDD Group – Miles*
vley, Martin Kay, Dan
dy, Mark Tosey (Designers);
ent: PDD Internal Futures
cept; Materials: *Conceptual*;
nufacturing process: not in
duction; Year: *2004*

he Platinum in-flight food system is an
stigation into how technology might be
e to offer airline passengers a meal cooked
xacting restaurant standards. Cost, time
weight are current factors that work
inst such a notion, so the Platinum project
bines a selection of technologies to see
t could be achieved in the near future.
he product itself comprises of a base unit,
e and a unique, compartmentalised clear
er. Each compartment contains fresh ingre-
ts that are cooked using an induction heat-
process, simultaneously giving steamed,
ed, fried and even chilled foods. Heat ele-
ts are embedded in the base unit and
e to provide the overall cooking effect. In
grill area the metallic loop in the cover pro-
es an additional localised heat transfer to
te a char-grill effect. The steam compart-
t contains replenishable, gel-based water
kets. The chilled compartment is created
g the Peltier effect and is enhanced by
lation in the compartment walls.
he whole process is bound together with
ligent tagging. At ticket purchase each
l choice generates a profile (ultimately
edded in the meal unit) identifying
passenger, meal and bespoke cooking
uctions.

Das Platinum-In-Flight-Food-System soll Flug-
gästen Mahlzeiten auf Restaurantniveau bieten.
Derzeit sind die Kosten, der Zeitaufwand und
das Gewicht für dieses System jedoch noch zu
hoch. Das Platinum-Projekt verbindet aber eine
Reihe unterschiedlicher Technologien, um
zukünftige Möglichkeiten zu testen.

Das Produkt selbst besteht aus einer Basiseinheit, einem Teller und einer einzigartigen, in
Segmente unterteilten, durchsichtigen Abde-
ckung. Jedes Segment enthält frische Zutaten,
die mittels eines Induktionsprozesses gekocht
werden. So kann gleichzeitig gedünstet, gegrillt,
geröstet und sogar gekühlt werden. Die einzelnen Heizelemente sind in die Basiseinheit und
den Teller integriert, um ein gleichmäßiges
Garen zu gewährleisten. Im Grillbereich sorgt
eine zusätzliche Metallschleife in der Abde-
ckung für einen einzigartigen Grilleffekt. Das
Dünstsegment enthält auffüllbare Wasserta-
schen auf Gelbasis. Die Funktion des Kühlseg-
ments baut auf dem Peltier-Effekt auf und wird
durch isolierte Segmentwände verstärkt.

Der ganze Prozess wird durch ein intelligen-
tes Erfassungssystem abgerundet. Beim
Ticketkauf wird mit der Speiseauswahl des
Fluggastes ein Profil erstellt, das Informationen
über den Fluggast, die Essenswahl und zusätzliche Zubereitungswünsche enthält. Während
des Flugs kann das Essen direkt auf Bestellung
gekocht werden, unter Umständen sogar von
den Passagieren selbst.

Le système Platinum de restauration à bord
est une étude sur la façon dont la technologie
pourrait offrir aux passagers de vols aériens un
repas cuisiné selon les mêmes standards de
qualité que dans les restaurants. Actuellement,
les contraintes de prix, de temps et de poids
font obstacle à cette idée. Le projet Platinum
combine donc différentes technologies afin
d'explorer les possibilités pour un futur proche.

Le produit est composé d'une unité de base,
d'une assiette et d'un original couvercle transparent à compartiments. Chaque compartiment contient des ingrédients frais, cuisinés
selon un procédé à induction pouvant donner
simultanément des aliments cuits à la vapeur,
grillés, frits ou même froids. Les éléments
chauffants se trouvent à l'intérieur de l'unité
de base et de l'assiette afin d'obtenir l'effet de
cuisson global. La boucle métallique du couvercle produit un transfert de chaleur localisée
supplémentaire sur la zone du grill afin d'imiter
la carbonisation caractéristique du grill. Le
compartiment à vapeur contient des poches
rechargeables d'eau gélifiée. Le compartiment
froid a été créé à l'aide de l'effet Peltier, et ses
côtés sont isolés.

Tout le processus est géré par un système
d'identification intelligente. À l'achat du ticket,
chaque choix de repas génère un profil qui
sera intégré à l'unité de repas, identifiant le
passager, le repas et les instructions de cuisson sur mesure. Pendant le vol, le repas pourrait être cuisiné à la demande et sans aucun
délai, peut-être par les passagers eux-mêmes.

R Design was briefed to design a range of products to reflect the shop's brand values rather than be product specific. Colour coding everything in black was not only corporate and stylish but made an incredible statement on shelf. Using only colour to indicate product flavour, all the typography was set in the same face and, wherever possible, the same point across the range. This ensured clarity uniformity and stunning good looks.

R Design erhielt den Auftrag, eine Produktreihe zu entwickeln, die mehr die Werte der Kette an sich als die Qualitäten der jeweiligen Produkte betonte. Der Einsatz einer schwarzen Grundfläche für die gesamte Reihe erzeugte nicht nur den Eindruck von Einheit und Eleganz, sondern sorgte auch für Aufmerksamkeit. Farbe wurde nur zur Nennung des jeweiligen Produkts eingesetzt. Soweit möglich wurde für alle Aufdrucke eine einheitliche Schrift verwendet. So entstand eine Produktreihe mit einer klaren, einheitlichen Linie und einem überwältigenden Stil.

R Design a été chargé de concevoir une gamme de produits reflétant les valeurs de la marque du magasin plutôt que de se concentrer sur chaque produit. L'utilisation du noir sur tous les produits donne non seulement une image institutionnelle et élégante, mais aussi une présence incroyable dans les rayons. Seule la couleur indique le goût du produit, et toutes les informations sont imprimées dans la même police de caractères et autant que possible dans la même taille pour tous les produits de la gamme afin de garantir clarté, homogénéité et esthétique.

SELFRIDGES
Design: *R Design – Dave Richmond (Creative Director);* Client: *Selfridges;* Awards: *D&AD, Commercial Arts, London International Awards, Creative Review (Best in Book);* Materials: *Glass, paper, plastic;* Manufacturing process: *Various;* Year: *2004*

CHAMPAGNE
ROSE BRUT
PREMIER CRU
Élaboré à Pargny-Les-Reims par Médot et Cie
France. MA-2851-20-00245
12% Vol 75 cl

CHAMPAGNE
BRUT
produce of France, MA-2851-20-00245,
Élaboré à Pargny-Les-Reims par Médot
et Cie à Reims, France.

CHARDONNAY
VIN DE PAYS
D'OC 2001

MERLOT
VIN DE PAYS
D'OC 2001

RUNNY
HONEY
WITH
HONEYCOMB

CLEAR
RUNNY
HONEY

CRANBERRY
& ORANGE
SAUCE

APPLE
& MINT
SAUCE

BLACK-
CURRANT
JAM

RASP-
BERRY
JAM

MEDIUM
CUT
ORANGE
MARMALADE

ORANGE &
WHISKEY
MARMALADE

Waitrose

ARTICHOKE & GOATS CHEESE

A SMOOTH CREAMY SOUP MADE
WITH JERUSALEM ARTICHOKES AND
ROSARY GOATS CHEESE

Waitrose

BUTTERNUT SQUASH

A SMOOTH SOUP MADE WITH
BUTTERNUT SQUASH AND SEASONED
WITH CRACKED BLACK PEPPER

Waitrose

LOBSTER BISQUE

A FRENCH SYTLE SOUP WITH AN INTENSE
LOBSTER FLAVOUR MADE WITH WHITE
WINE AND DOUBLE CREAM

Waitrose

PEA & HAM

A SMOOTH SOUP MADE WITH
BRITISH PEAS AND SMOKED HAM

Waitrose

MUSHROOM

A RICH CREAMY SOUP MADE WITH
FLAT AND CHESTNUT MUSHROOMS

Waitrose

ITALIAN BEAN

A THICK ITALIAN STYLE SOUP MADE
WITH BEANS, TOMATOES, RED
WINE AND EXTRA VIRGIN OLIVE OIL

The design takes the hero ingredient of each of these soups and presents it as an icon in a minimal photographic style. The ranges are made distinct from each other by using a coloured background for standard soups and a black background for premium. The simplicity of the design differentiates the range in a category filled with colour and illustration, and has exceptional shelf stand-out. It's single-minded, witty and beautiful – design that doesn't need to shout.

Die Hauptzutat jeder dieser Suppe wurde zum Protagonisten des Designs erhoben und mit minimalistischen fotografischen Mitteln porträtiert. Die beiden Produktlinien lassen sich anhand der Hintergrundfarbe unterscheiden, wobei für die Standard-Suppen ein farbiger und für die Premium-Suppen ein schwarzer Hintergrund gewählt wurde. Die Schlichtheit des Designs lässt die Produkte innerhalb ihrer Kategorie, die von opulenten Bebilderungen und Farben geprägt ist, herausstechen und gewährleistet große Aufmerksamkeit. Ein solch eigensinniger, ausgereifter und schöner Entwurf muss nicht auf laute Farben setzen.

Le design prend l'ingrédient phare de chacune de ces soupes et le présente com une icône, avec un style photographique m maliste. Les gammes sont différenciées les unes des autres grâce à un fond de couleu pour les soupes standard et à un fond noir pour les soupes haut de gamme. La simplic du design distingue la gamme dans sa cate rie, où l'on utilise habituellement beaucoup couleurs et d'illustrations, et lui donne une sence exceptionnelle dans les rayons. C'es design résolu, intelligent et beau, qui n'a pa besoin de faire des effets de manche.

WAITROSE SOUPS
Design: *Pearlfisher –*
Kate Marlow (Designer);
Client: Waitrose Limited;
Awards: New York Festivals
Bronze Award and Book Entry);
Materials: Polypropylene
(soup pot), polyethylene (labels);
Manufacturing process:
Injection moulding, web flexo
press; Year: 2005

THE FOOD DOCTOR
Design: *R Design – Creative*
Director: David Richmond,
Designer: Iain Dobson; Client:
The Food Doctor; Materials: *Glass,*
paper, plastic; Manufacturing
process: *Various;* Year: *2005*

SHARWOOD'S NOODLE BOX
Design: *Jones Knowles Ritchie;*
Client: *RHM Culinary;* Materials:
Cardboard; Manufacturing process:
Die cut; Year: *2005*

RAKFISH SMOLKED SALMON
Design: *Strømme Throndsen;*
Client: *Fish Producers of Valdres
region, Norway;* Awards: *Award
Design Excellence by Norwegian
Design Council;* Materials:
Carton; Manufacturing process:
Not disclosed; Year: *2003*

BP WILD BEAN CAFÉ
Design: *Coley Porter Bell;* Client:
BP (British Petroleum) UK;
Materials: *Various;* Manufacturing
process: *Various;* Year: *2005*

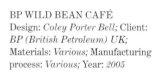

EAT
Design: *Pentagram – Angus Hyland (Partner);* Client: *EAT – Faith & Niall MacArthur;* Awards: *Fab Awards (Winner of Packaging Category);* Materials: *Various;* Manufacturing process: *Various;* Year: *2003*

The proposition highlighted the honesty at the heart of EAT's business – a business that is owned by real people (rather than a corporation) who have a genuine passion for real food and drink. Communication of the proposition was achieved by developing a new logotype and design language, with guidelines for its correct and consistent use across all visual and tangible elements of the EAT brand.

Pentagram developed an all-encompassing brand identity. The new logotype employs a bold sans serif typeface (Akzidenz Grotesk) that communicates the warmth and quality of the brand with clarity and a distinct, contemporary tone. This bold typographical language has been combined with a colour palette of warm, natural, brown hues; with a range of vibrant minor colours for typography and detailing across food packaging, menu boards and other collateral.

Transparenz ist ein wichtiges Motto der Firma EAT, die nicht durch eine anonyme Aktiengesellschaft, sondern noch von Personen geleitet wird, für die Essen und Trinken eine echte Passion ist. Um diesem Motto Ausdruck zu verleihen, wurden ein neuer Firmenschriftzug und eine neue Designsprache mit festen Regeln für eine konsequente Anwendung auf allen Elemente der gesamten EAT-Marke entworfen.

Pentagram entwickelte eine allumfassende Markenidentität. Der neue Schriftzug verwendet eine fette serifenlose Schrift (Akzidenz Grotesk), die mit ihrer Klarheit und ihrer zeitgenössischen Note die Wärme und Qualität der Marke vermittelt. Die Schrift wurde mit einer Palette aus warmen, natürlichen Brauntönen kombiniert und durch eine Reihe leuchtender Farben für Details auf den Verpackungen, Menütafeln und Ähnlichem ergänzt.

La proposition souligne l'honnêteté qui se trouve au cœur de l'activité d'EAT – une entreprise aux mains de vraies personnes (plutôt que d'une société anonyme) qui ont une vrai passion pour les aliments et les boissons authentiques. Pour communiquer cette proposition, on a créé un nouveau logo, un nouveau langage de design, ainsi que des lignes directrices pour assurer leur bonne utilisation et leur cohérence sur tous les éléments tangible et visuels de la marque EAT.

Pentagram a créé une identité de marque globale. Le nouveau logo utilise une police de caractères Bold Sans Sérif (Akzidenz Grotesk) qui transmet la cordialité et la qualité de la marque avec clarté et sur un ton contempor et différent. Ce langage typographique audacieux est combiné à une palette de couleurs brunes, chaudes et naturelles, avec une gamme secondaire de couleurs plus vives pour la typographie et les détails sur le conditionnement des aliments, les menus et autres supports.

WAITROSE CHEESES
Design: *Lewis Moberly –
Mary Lewis (Design Director),
Zoe Green (Designer);* Client:
Waitrose Ltd; Materials: *Paper;*
Manufacturing process:
Die Cut, printing; Year: *2005*

OVER THE MOON
Design: *Ziggurat Brand
Consultants – Allison Miguel
(Creative Director), Hayley Bish*
(Designer); Client: *Dairy Crest;*
Materials: *Plastic;* Manufacturing
process: *Flexo;* Year: *2004*

Waitrose have an impressive and extensive range of cheese from all over Europe. The design had to link disparate shapes and reinforce the provenance of each cheese. Shopping is made easy through simple colour coding by country and a bolder tint circle marks the particular cheese area.

Waitrose vertreibt eine beeindruckende und umfangreiche Auswahl an Käsesorten aus ganz Europa. Das Design musste eine Verbindung zwischen den unterschiedlichen Formen herstellen und gleichzeitig die Herkunft jeder Käsesorte unterstreichen. Der Kauf wird durch eine einfache Farbkodierung für jedes Land erleichtert, und die jeweilige Käseregion wird durch einen Kreis in einem kräftigeren Farbton angezeigt.

Waitrose propose une gamme impression nante de fromages provenant de toute l'Euro pe. Le design devait créer un lien entre les formes disparates et souligner la provenanc de chaque fromage. Un simple code couleu par pays facilite l'achat, et un cercle de cou plus prononcée marque la zone d'origine de chaque fromage.

Drink 'n Crunch is an ergonomically designed vessel with two cups, one inside the other. Fresh milk is poured into the outer cup, and cereal is already in the inner cup. The cereal and milk don't mix until they're in your mouth. As you drink, the cereal rolls out of the inner cup, and the milk flows from the outer cup. You get the right amount of cereal and milk every time for a convenient and healthy breakfast that's always crunchy and never soggy.

Drink 'n Crunch ist ein ergonomisch geformtes Gefäß mit zwei ineinander gesteckten Tassen. In die äußere Tasse gießt man frische Milch, in der inneren befinden sich bereits die Cerealien. Nimmt man nun einen Schluck, rollen die Cerealien aus der inneren Tasse in den Mund und die Milch fließt aus der äußeren Tasse. Beides mischt sich also erst im Mund. Das Mischungsverhältnis von Cerealien und Milch ist bei jedem Schluck ideal, und so erhält man ein praktisches, zeitsparendes und gesundes Frühstück, das immer knusprig und nie matschig ist.

Drink 'n Crunch est un récipient ergonomique avec deux gobelets, l'un à l'intérieur de l'autre. On verse du lait frais dans le gobelet externe, et il y a déjà des céréales dans le gobelet interne. Les céréales et le lait ne se mélangent que lorsqu'ils se retrouvent dans la bouche. Lorsque l'on boit, les céréales tombent du gobelet interne, et le lait coule du gobelet externe. On obtient à chaque fois la bonne quantité de céréales et de lait, pour un petit déjeuner pratique et sain, toujours croustillant et jamais ramolli.

DRINK 'N CRUNCH
Design: *Metaphase Design Group – Bryce Rutter, Marc Hunter, Brian Bone (Designers), Tony Cenicola (Photo credit);* Client: *Kellogg's* Awards: *Red Dot Award, DuPont Special Citation, London International Awards (Finalist), IOPP (Institute of Packaging Professionals) Ameristar, New York Times: Year in Ideas, Good Design Award (Japan);* Materials *Polypropylene, oriented polystyrene, sheet foil;* Manufacturing process: *Injection moulding, reverse rotogravure printing, lamination, printing;* Year: *2003*

SCOOPABLE 1 GALLON SALAD DRESSING FOR THE FOOD SERVICE MARKET
Design: *Metaphase Design Group – Bryce Rutter, Brian Bone, Jeff Feng, Heath Doty (Designers), Colin McRae (Photo credit);* Client: *Kraft;* Awards: *London International Awards, IOPP Ameristar Awards;* Materials: *High density polyethylene;* Manufacturing process: *not disclosed;* Year: *2003*

EXPRESS DAIRIES
(STRUCTURAL PACKAGING)
Design: *Minale Tattersfield &
Partners;* Client: *Express Dairies;*
Materials: *Plastic;* Manufacturing
Process: *Vacuum formed;*
Year: *2005*

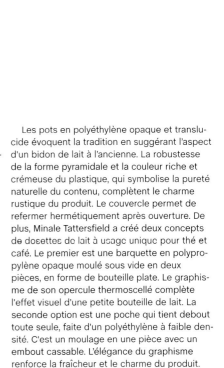

The opaque and translucent polyethylene packs reflect tradition, suggesting the look of old-fashioned milk churn. The solidity of the pyramid shape is strong and sturdy, whilst the rich, creamy coloured plastic suggests the natural purity of the contents inside, completing its homespun appeal. The top is resealable. In addition, Minale Tattersfield produced two concepts for disposable milk sachets for teas and coffees. The first is a two-piece moulding, vacuum-formed, opaque polypropylene tray in the shape of a flattened bottle. It has a heat-sealed tear-off top with graphics that completes the visual effect of a mini milk bottle. The second option is a free-standing pouch made of low-density polyethylene. It is one-piece moulding with a rigid snap-off top. Fresh graphics add to the fresh and appealing nature of the product.

Die opaken, durchscheinenden Polyäthylen-Verpackungen erinnern an altmodische Milchkannen und vermitteln so Tradition. Die Pyramidenformen sind extrem widerstandsfähig, und die kräftige Cremefarbe des Kunststoffs assoziiert natürliche Inhaltsstoffe. Der Deckel ist verschließbar. Zusätzlich entwickelte Minale Tattersfield zwei Wegwerfbehälter für Kaffee- und Teesahne. Der erste ist ein opakes Polyäthylen-Behältnis in Form einer flachen Flasche. Es hat einen Abreißverschluss, dessen Gestaltung die Metapher einer Milchflasche ergänzt. Der zweite Behälter ist ein Gefäß aus Polyäthylen mit geringer Dichte. Er wird in einem Guss gefertigt und besitzt einen festen Abreißverschluss. Die elegante Gestaltung unterstützt den Eindruck von Frische und Appetitlichkeit, den das Produkt bietet.

Les pots en polyéthylène opaque et translucide évoquent la tradition en suggérant l'aspect d'un bidon de lait à l'ancienne. La robustesse de la forme pyramidale et la couleur riche et crémeuse du plastique, qui symbolise la pureté naturelle du contenu, complètent le charme rustique du produit. Le couvercle permet de refermer hermétiquement après ouverture. De plus, Minale Tattersfield a créé deux concepts de dosettes de lait à usage unique pour thé et café. Le premier est une barquette en polypropylène opaque moulé sous vide en deux pièces, en forme de bouteille plate. Le graphisme de son opercule thermoscellé complète l'effet visuel d'une petite bouteille de lait. La seconde option est une poche qui tient debout toute seule, faite d'un polyéthylène à faible densité. C'est un moulage en une pièce avec un embout cassable. L'élégance du graphisme renforce la fraîcheur et le charme du produit.

MARKS & SPENCER
Cheese Balls
Potato & Maize Snacks

...EAT MY GOAL!

MARKS & SPENCER
Spring Onion Sticks
Potato Snacks

...EAT TO THE BEAT

MARKS & SPENCER
Ready Salted Sticks
Potato Snacks

...POLLY WANTS A SNACK

MARKS & SPENCER
Cheese & Onion Waffles
Potato & Cereal Snacks

...LOVE ALL

MARKS & SPENCER
Prawn Cocktails
Maize Snacks

...ANYONE FOR A COCKTAIL?

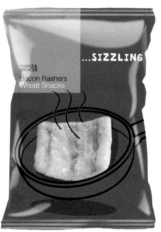

MARKS & SPENCER
Bacon Rashers
Wheat Snacks

...SIZZLING

MARKS & SPENCER
Beef & Onion Rings
Potato Snacks

...FOR THAT SPECIAL SOMEONE ...ME

MARKS & SPENCER
Ready Salted Rings
Potato Snacks

...ONES FAVOURITE SNACK

MARKS & SPENCER
Lightly Salted Triangles
Potato Snacks

...BUZZ OFF THEY'RE MINE!

MARKS & SPENCER
Salt & Vinegar Chiplets
Potato & Maize Snacks

...SEAFOOD AND EAT IT!

MARKS & SPENCER
Spicy Barbeque Twists
Potato Snacks

...A BITE OF PARADISE

MARKS & SPENCER
Cheese Curl
Maize Snacks

...A MONSTER OF A CRISP

MARKS & SPENCER
FLAVOURED SNACKS
Design: *Marks & Spencer –
Charlotte Raphael (Head of
Packaging Design), Andrew Cross
(Senior Designer), Lindsey Webb
(Designer/Illustrator)*; Materials:
not disclosed; Manufacturing
Process: *Flexo*; Year: *2005*

The product range consists of approximately [...] products, so clear product differentiation [...] needed to make the range easy for the [cus]tomer to shop. Unlike most M&S products, [there] were no inherent food values to showcase [the] proposition was one of fun, impromptu [snac]king. The range is mainly aimed at cus[tome]rs with young families, though there are [othe]r customers who buy the snacks for the [nost]algia factor. One thing that separates these [prod]ucts from the rest of the savoury category [is th]at their shapes are all individual. Therefore [it wa]s felt making the product hero and using [the] metallic colours would give each pack a [clear] identity. The playful use of a verbal and [visu]al pun brought a fun element to the pack[agin]g. Mandatory product copy appears in a [sing]le coloured corner panel which is common [to al]l packaging in this category.

Die Palette besteht aus rund 20 Produkten. Daher war es wichtig, dass die Einzelartikel für den Kunden leicht erkennbar blieben. Im Gegensatz zu den meisten anderen Produkten von M&S gab es hier keine besonderen Nährwerte, die man hätte herausstellen können. Die Reihe zielt speziell auf junge Familien, obwohl auch ältere Kunden diese Ware aus Nostalgiegründen kaufen. Die Produkte setzen sich vom Rest der Kategorie „Savoury" durch ihre individuellen Formen ab. Daher entschied man sich, das Produkt zum Star zu machen und jeder Verpackung durch Metallicfarben eine eigene eindeutige Identität zu geben. Die spielerische Kombination aus Wortspiel und Bild verlieh den Packungen zudem einen witzigen Aspekt. Die obligatorischen Produktinformationen finden sich in einer farblich abgesetzten Ecke, die allen Produkten dieser Kategorie gemein ist.

La gamme est composée d'environ 20 produits. Une différentiation claire entre produits était donc nécessaire pour faciliter les achats des consommateurs. Contrairement à la plupart des produits M&S, il n'y avait pas de valeur inhérente à la nourriture à mettre en valeur : on proposait plutôt un en-cas spontané et ludique. La gamme cible essentiellement les clients qui ont de jeunes familles, bien que des clients plus âgés achètent également ces en-cas, par nostalgie. Ce qui démarque ces produits du reste de la catégorie salée, c'est que leurs formes sont toutes individuelles. On a donc estimé qu'en mettant le produit en vedette et en utilisant des couleurs vives et métalliques, on donnerait une identité claire à chaque paquet. L'utilisation d'un calembour verbal et visuel apporte un élément ludique au conditionnement. Les informations réglementaires sur le produit apparaissent dans un simple carré de couleur en coin, comme pour tous les conditionnements de cette catégorie.

Full on Flavour is a new product range of crisps with unique flavour characteristics. The design team was challenged to come up with a design solution that really got the flavour story across and made the range stand out from the rest of the savoury category (though they had to follow industry standard colour coding where applicable.) The target audience was the medium aged and affluent customer, with a willingness to experiment. To get the required stand-out, the range was meant to have a very different look and tone of voice. So, as a contrast to many M&S savoury ranges, the team decided against a fully photographic pack, concentrating instead on the flavour story by using a striking typographic solution. Full on Flavour was created as a product description to encapsulate the unique selling proposition of the range and has since become a registered trademark belonging to M&S.

Full on Flavour ist eine neue Produktreihe mit einzigartigen Geschmackscharakteristika. Die Herausforderung für eine neue Designlösung war, die einzelnen Geschmacksrichtungen zu vermitteln und die Produktreihe von den restlichen Produkten der Kategorie „Savoury" deutlich abzuheben (obwohl man sich bei der Farbkodierung an den Industriestandard halten musste). Die Zielgruppe waren wohlhabende Kunden mittleren Alters, die für neue Produkte aufgeschlossen sind. Um die nötige Aufmerksamkeit zu erregen, sollte die Produktreihe einen eigenen Look und einen besonderen Unterton erhalten. Daher entschied man sich gegen die in dieser Kategorie übliche fotografische Lösung und setzte vielmehr auf eine markante typografische Umsetzung der Geschmacksrichtungen. „Full on Flavour" wurde als Produktbeschreibung entwickelt, die das einzigartige Verkaufsargument der Produktreihe herausstellte. Inzwischen ist „Full on Flavour" eine zu M&S gehörende, registrierte Handelsmarke.

Full on Flavour est une nouvelle gamme d chips aux caractéristiques gustatives unique Le défi de l'équipe était de trouver une solu de design qui transmettrait vraiment l'idée ces goûts et qui démarquerait la gamme du reste de la catégorie salée (tout en respecta les codes couleur du secteur le cas échéan Le public ciblé est d'âge moyen, avec des re nus confortables et une volonté de découvr les nouveautés. Pour mettre en valeur les pr duits de façon adéquate, la gamme devait avoir une allure et un ton différents. C'est p quoi l'équipe s'est éloignée du paquet entiè ment décoré de photos adopté pour de nor breuses gammes salées de M&S, et s'est pl concentrée sur l'idée du goût, grâce à une typographie frappante. Le nom « Full on Fla vour » (plein de goût) avait été créé pour décrire le produit, afin de résumer l'argume de la gamme, et est depuis devenu une marque commerciale déposée de M&S.

'LL ON FLAVOUR
sign: *Marks & Spencer –*
arlotte Raphael (Head of Pack-
ng Design), Andrew Cross
nior Designer), Lindsey Webb
esigner), Lis Parsons (Photogra-
r); Materials: *Not disclosed;*
nufacturing process: *Flexo;*
ar: *2005*

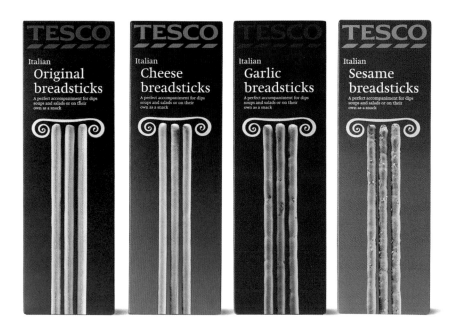

TESCO BREADSTICKS
Design: *R Design – David Richmond (Creative Director), Matt Fowler (Designer);*
Client: *Tesco;* Materials: *Card;*
Manufacturing process: *Not disclosed;* Year: *2005*

MORINAGA FRIED POTATOE
Design: *Sato Katsunori (Art Director/Designer), Shibata Marimo, Kuwata Aya (Designer.*
Client: *Morinaga. Co. Ltd.;*
Materials: *Not disclosed;*
Manufacturing process: *Various;*
Year: *2005*

STRONOMIC ADVENTURES
ign: *Marks & Spencer –*
rlotte Raphael (Head of Pack-
g Design), Andrew Cross
Director/Senior Designer),
sey Webb (Designer);
erials: *Not disclosed;*
ufacturing process: *Flexo;*
: 2005

PRINGLES POP BOX
Design: *PI3 – Steve Kelsey,*
Jed O'Brien, Dave Salmon;
Client: *Procter & Gamble;*
Materials: *Polypropylene;*
Manufacturing process: *Injection*
moulding; Year: *2004*

PRINGLES SINGLE SERVE
Design: *WSdV Chicago;*
Client: *Procter & Gamble;*
Materials: *Polypropylene, foil;*
Manufacturing process: *Thermo-*
form, orm fill seal; Year: *2005*

Pringles is a snack brand enjoyed by all ages, but the iconic tube doesn't always fit consumers' needs. WSdV Chicago was asked to explore how new pack formats could broaden Pringle's appeal by leveraging on snacking occasions such as lunchtime i.e. a lunchbox size, and for those on-the-move. WSdV Chicago identified a large number of occasions with potential, but it was important for any new pack to retain the brand equities consumers have come to expect from Pringles. The Snack Stack is a cost efficient thermoforming that echoes a stack of Pringles in a neat pack.

Pringles ist eine Snack-Marke, die bei allen Altersstufen beliebt ist. Die unverwechselbare Röhre ist aber für die Kunden nicht immer praktisch. WSdV Chicago sollte herausfinden, welche anderen Verpackungsformate sich eigneten, das Pringles-Angebot zu erweitern. Dabei sollten auch Snack-Ideen, wie etwa eine Lunch-Box für die schnelle Mittagspause, berücksichtigt werden. WSdV Chicago konnte viele potenzielle Gelegenheiten für Snacks ausmachen, doch jede neue Verpackung musste unbedingt die Markenwerte vermitteln, die die Käufer von Pringles erwarten. Snack Stack sind kleine Behälter, die die bekannten Pringles-Produkte in einer praktischen Kleinverpackung liefern.

Pringles est une marque d'amuse-gueule que tout le monde apprécie, mais le tube emblématique de la marque n'est pas toujo adapté aux besoins des consommateurs. W Chicago a été chargé de trouver de nouvea formats d'emballage pour rendre les Pringle plus attrayants en exploitant les différentes occasions de grignoter, par exemple le déje uner, avec un emballage format boîte à san wich, et pour les gens qui grignotent entre portes. WSdV Chicago a identifié plusieurs occasions à fort potentiel, mais il fallait que nouvel emballage reprenne les caractéristic de la marque, auxquelles les consommateu se sont habitués. Le Snack Stack est un em lage thermoformé économique à produire, rappelle la fameuse pile de Pringles mais d un format plus compact.

NUTS
sign: *Ziggurat Brand*
nsultants – Allison Miguel
reative Director); Client: *United*
cuits; Awards: *DBA (Design*
siness Association) Design
ectiveness – Branded Packaging
od & Drink) Finalist; Materials:
l; Manufacturing process: *Flexo;*
r: 2004

NATHAN CRISP
sign: *Ziggurat Brand*
nsultants – Allison Miguel
reative Director), Hayley Bishop
signer); Client: *Natural Crisps*
ited; Awards: *GRAMIA*
ocery Advertising & Marketing
ustry Awards) Packaging
ign, Golden Gramia, Design
k Awards, Marketing Design
rds; Materials: *Paper with*
uer, metallised polypropylene,
ethelene; Manufacturing
cess: Flexo; Year: *2004*

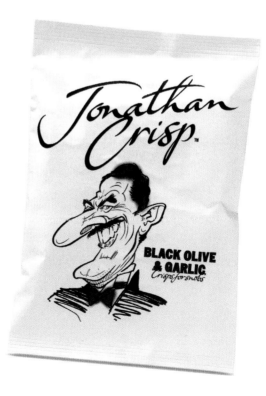

AMOY PREMIUM SOY SAUCE
Design: *DJPA Partnership –
Sara Jones (Creative Director);*
Client: *HP Foods Ltd.;*
Materials: *Glass, foil, metallic seal;*
Manufacturing process: *Litho
printing, blow moulding;*
Year: *2005*

WAITROSE MUSTARDS
Design: *Lewis Moberly – Mary
Lewis (Design Director);* Client:
Waitrose Ltd; Materials: *Glass,
metallic seal;* Manufacturing
process: *Printing, blow moulding;*
Year: *2005*

TAMARIND
Design: *Lewis Moberly – Mary
Lewis (Design Director);* Client:
Tamarind; Materials: *Glass,
metallic seal;* Manufacturing
process: *Printing, blow moulding;*
Year: *2005*

WAITROSE OLIVE OILS
Design: *Pearlfisher – Natalie
Chung (Designer);* Client: *Waitrose
Limited;* Materials: *Tintoretto
Gesso(Manter), glass;*
Manufacturing process: *Printing
(labels), web flexo press;* Year: *2005*

BLACK BOY PREMIUM
Design: *Strømme Throndsen;*
Client: *Rieber & Søn ASA;*
Materials: *Metal box;*
Manufacturing process:
not disclosed; Year: *2005*

Waitrose
COOKS' INGREDIENTS

A SPRINKLE OF
WILD
OREGANO

Waitrose
COOKS' INGREDIENTS

A DASH OF
CHARDONNAY
VINEGAR

Waitrose
COOKS' INGREDIENTS

A GOOD PINCH OF
WILD
THYME

Waitrose
COOKS' INGREDIENTS

EASY ON THE
CHOPPED
CHILLI

Waitrose
COOKS' INGREDIENTS

A SCOOP OF
CARNAROLI
RISOTTO RICE

Waitrose
COOKS' INGREDIENTS

A SPRITZ OF
BALSAMIC
VINEGAR

Waitrose
COOKS' INGREDIENTS

A PINCH OF
ANGLESEY
SEA SALT

Waitrose
COOKS' INGREDIENTS

A SCATTER OF
WILD
BAY LEAVES

Waitrose
COOKS' INGREDIENTS

A HANDFUL OF
FOREST
MUSHROOMS

Waitrose
COOKS' INGREDIENTS

A BUNDLE OF
CINNAMON
STICKS

Waitrose
COOKS' INGREDIENTS

EASY ON THE
DIJON
WHOLEGRAIN MUSTARD

Waitrose
COOKS' INGREDIENTS

A LITTLE BAG OF
BOUQUET
GARNI FOR MEAT

WAITROSE COOKS'
INGREDIENTS
Design: *Lewis Moberly – Mary
Lewis (Design Director), Christian
Stacey, Mary Lewis (Designers and
Copywriters), Christian Stacey,
Mary Lewis, Ann Marshall (Typo-
graphers);* Client: *Waitrose Ltd;*
Materials: *Various;* Manufacturing
process: *Various;* Year: *2005*

S&B SPICE & HERB SERIES
Design: *Taku Satoh Design Office –*
Taku Satoh, Masako Kusakabe;
Client: *S&B Foods, Inc.;* Materials:
Glass, plastic; Manufacturing
process: *Blow moulding, injection*
moulding, Year: *2006*

TESCO HERBS
Design: *R Design – David*
Richmond (Creative Director),
Steve Sheffield (Designer);
Client: *Tesco;* Materials: *Card;*
Manufacturing process: *Not*
disclosed, Year: *2005*

MRS MASSEY'S
Design: *Ziggurat Brand Consultants – Allison Miguel (Creative Director), Andy Audsley (Designer)*; Client: *Nicola Massey*; Awards: *FAB (Food & Beverage Awards) – Packaging Design (Savoury Foods) Winner*; Materials: *Labels, glassware*; Manufacturing process: *Litho print; blow moulding*; Year: *2004*

The brand was first conceived by Mrs. [Ma]ssey herself in her home kitchen in the [Co]tswolds, where it was made to be sold at [far]mer's markets. The products are fantastic, [bu]t she needed an identity and packaging [tha]t reflected the brand – Mrs. Massey and her [cul]inary skills. All of the utensils shot are the [on]es that she actually uses for the range; the [bri]ghtly coloured type reflects her personality, [an]d the copy is the language she uses when [de]scribing her food, "ravishing, perky, bewitch-[ing] ..." Made using premium ingredients, [Mrs.] Massey's range includes dressings, [di]shes, spices and sauces to enhance meals [and] snacks. The design encompasses both the [bra]nd and the owners – vivacious, surprising [and] with a chatty tone of voice. The Mrs. [Mas]sey's brand can now be found selling [suc]cessfully in Fortnum & Mason, Waitrose [and] numerous UK delicatessens.

Die Marke wurde ursprünglich von Mrs. Massey persönlich in ihrer heimischen Küche in den Cotswolds entwickelt und sollte auf den Bauernmärkten der Region verkauft werden. Die Produkte waren hervorragend, doch Mrs. Massey fehlte eine Verpackung und Identität für ihre Produkte, die ihr selbst und ihrem kulinarischen Können entsprachen. Die abgebildeten Küchenutensilien sind Geräte, die sie zur Herstellung ihrer Produkte verwendet. Die freundlichen Farben spiegeln ihre Persönlichkeit wider, und der Text benutzt die Sprache, die sie zur Beschreibung ihrer Produkte verwendet, wie etwa „hinreißend, keck, bezaubernd ...". Zu der aus erstklassigen Zutaten hergestellten Produktpalette von Mrs. Massey gehören Salatsaucen, Relishes, Gewürzmischungen sowie Saucen zur Verfeinerung von Speisen und Snacks. Das lebhafte, überraschende Design steht mit seinem Plauderton sowohl für die Marke als auch für die Besitzer. Die Marke Mrs. Massey's verkauft sich mittlerweile sehr gut bei Fortnum & Mason, Waitrose und unzähligen Feinkostgeschäften in Großbritannien.

La marque a d'abord été conçue par Mme Massey elle-même, dans sa cuisine du Cotswolds, où elle fabriquait ses produits pour les vendre sur des marchés d'agriculteurs. Les produits sont fantastiques, mais elle avait besoin d'une identité et d'un conditionnement pour représenter la marque Mrs. Massey et ses talents culinaires. Tous les ustensiles photographiés sont bien ceux qu'elle utilise réellement pour fabriquer la gamme. Les caractères de couleur vive reflètent sa personnalité et le texte reproduit le langage qu'elle emploie pour décrire ses produits : « enivrant, gai, envoûtant... » Fabriquée à partir d'ingrédients de première qualité, la gamme de Mrs. Massey propose des assaisonnements, des achards, des épices et des sauces pour relever les repas et les en-cas. Le design représente aussi bien la marque que sa propriétaire, avec un ton vif, surprenant et familier. La marque Mrs. Massey's est maintenant disponible à la vente chez Fortnum & Mason, Waitrose et dans de nombreuses épiceries anglaises, où elle rencontre un grand succès.

COFFEE PACKAGE
Design: *Yasuo Tanaka*
(Art Director/Designer); Client:
Arab Coffee; Materials: *Paper, steel;*
Manufacturing process: *Various;*
Year: *1998*

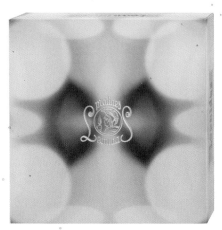

WAITROSE BELGIAN CHOCOLATES
Design: *Lewis Moberly – Mary Lewis (Design Director), Zoe Green (Designer/Illustrator);* Client: *Waitrose Ltd;* Materials: *Paper;* Manufacturing process: *Various;* Year: *2005*

EONIDAS
UXURY PRALINES
esign: *DJPA Partnership – Hans*
uysson (Managing Director),
ra Jones (Creative Director);
ient: *Leonidas, Brussels – Dirk*
cxsens (CEO); Materials: *Card*
ters; Manufacturing process:
rious; Year: *2005*

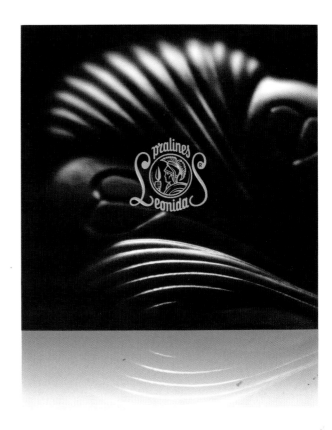

SCAL CAFFET
R ± 0 (FOOD)
ign: *Taku Satoh Design Office –*
u Satoh / Ichiji Ohishi; Client:
s Minus Zero Co., Ltd.;
erials: *Paper;* Manufacturing
cess: *Various;* Year: *2004*

MR KIPLING
Design: *PI3 – Steve Kelsey, J O'Brien;* Client: *Manor Bakeries;* Awards: *Star Pack Award;* Materials: *Polyethylene terephthalate (PET) tubs, card sleeve;* Manufacturing process: *Rotary thermoforming tubs, diaphragm heat sealed, peelable seal layer, card sleeve applied in line with cartooning machine (Sleever International);* Year: *2005*

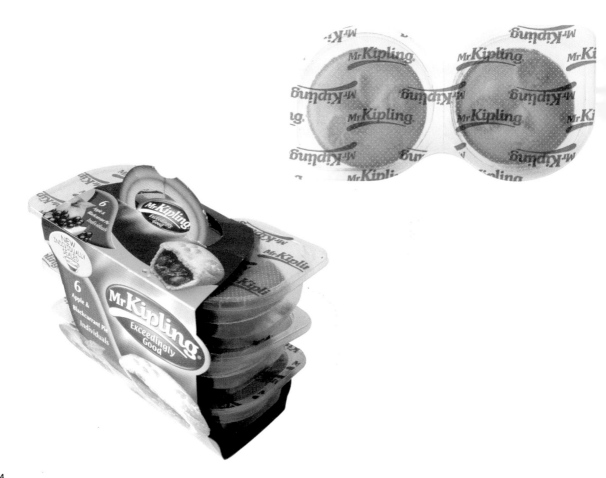

COCOA DELI
Design: R Design – David Richmond
(Creative Director), Iain Dobson,
Scott Keightley; Client: Kinnerton
Confectionary; Materials: Card,
paper, film; Manufacturing process:
not disclosed; Year: 2007

KOEDA BITTER TASTE
Design: Morinaga – Usui Toyoko
(Art Director), Usui toyoko, Saito
Masanori, Tominaga Yuko
(Design); Client: Morinaga.Co.,Ltd;
Materials: Paper; Manufacturing
process: Printing; Year: 2004

DARS
Design: Morinaga – Ootsuka
Takashi (Art Direction), Narabe
Hisako, Tominaga Yuko (Design);
Client: Morinaga.Co., Ltd.;
Awards: Toppan Printing Co., Ltd.;
Materials: Paper; Manufacturing
process: Printing; Year: 2005

DANCING DEER
BAKING COMPANY
Design: *slover [AND] company –
Laura Ljundquist (Illustrator);*
Client: *Dancing Deer Baking
Company;* Awards: *AIGA Best New
Brand, Jacob Javitts Food Show
(Best of Show);* Materials: *Recycled
materials (bleached kraft papers,*
*single-flute corrugated, solid
bleached sulphate box boards,
aluminium caps, polyethylene
terephthalate, food-safe waxed
papers;* Manufacturing process:
*Offset lithography, flexographic
printing, silkscreening;* Year: *2005*

Pie in face / Pie experience

**Blueberry Muffin
Banoffee Pie
Strawberry Cheesecake
Lemon Meringue**

Blueberry Muffin
Banoffee Pie
Strawberry Cheesecake
Lemon Meringue

*Blueberry Muffin
Banoffee Pie
Strawberry Cheesecake
Lemon Meringue*

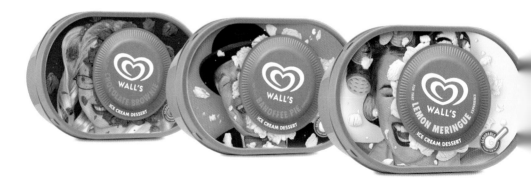

BRITISH HUMOUR

quirky

fcuk

TRADITIONAL

naive

subversive

The Munchies talk to me. They infiltrate my thoughts until I must obey. I try but I cannot resist the sirens of the swedie shop

Devour me

ALL'S ICE CREAM DESSERTS
sign: *Bloom Design – Gavin*
ke, Trish Steel, Nick Tobias
raphic Designers); Client:
ilever Ice Cream and Frozen
ods; Materials: *Polypropylene*
tainer with in-mould label;
nufacturing process: *Various;*
ar: *2005*

Bloom's design solution plays on the irrever- : British sense of humour with traditional tishness and its "custard pie in the face" ntral feature coupled with a set of quirky aracters chosen for their modern family eal. The fun and playful design helps to ct dynamism and modernity into the Wall's nd in a uniquely ownable Wall's way, forcing praisal in the face of stiff own-label com- ition and re-establishing Wall's at the heart he modern British family. In fact, Wall's ed the design so much they built an entire ertising campaign around the design idea.

Blooms Designlösung bedient sich des groben, etwas schlichten und respektlosen britischen Humors, gepaart mit einer Reihe skurriler Gestalten. Das lustige und verspielte Design verleiht der Marke Wall's Dynamik, fordert eine Neubewertung der Konkurrenz und verschafft Wall's wieder einen festen Platz in der modernen britischen Familie. Wall's gefiel die Design-Idee so gut, dass sie eine komplette Werbekampagne daraus entwickelten.

La solution que Bloom a trouvée pour le design joue sur l'irrévérence de l'humour britannique en exploitant les codes britanniques traditionnels et la fameuse « tarte à la crème », ainsi qu'un ensemble de personnages décalés, choisis pour leur succès auprès de la famille moderne. Le design ludique et espiègle aide à donner du dynamisme et de la modernité à la marque Wall's d'une façon toute propre à la marque, force la réévaluation en face d'une concurrence rude de la part des autres marques et redonne à Wall's sa place dans le cœur de la famille britannique moderne. En fait, Wall's aimait tellement le design que toute une campagne publicitaire a été construite autour de cette idée.

The design of the Honey Herbal Jelly bottle has focused in the past on exemplifying the characteristics of the product. This bottle is mainly in the shape of a square because the jelly is in the shape of cubic granules. The effect of the container's design is to reveal the characteristics of the product. The smooth streaming curves round the body of the bottle imply the smooth, elastic, cool texture of the rich granules. The appeal the rich granules have on the taste buds has been successfully integrated into the package design.

Das frühere Design der Flasche von Honey Herbal Jelly konzentrierte sich auf die Produkteigenschaften. Die neue Verpackung trägt hauptsächlich kubische Formen als abstrakte Interpretation von Samenkörnern. Das neue Design verkörpert die eigent-lichen Produkteigenschaften. Die sanfte Kurvenform spielt auf die weiche, elastische Beschaffenheit der Samenkörner an. Der anregende Effekt, den die Körner auf die Geschmacksnerven haben, wurde damit schon im Verpackungsdesign zum Ausdruck gebracht.

Le design de la bouteille Honey Herbal Jelly met l'accent sur l'illustration des caractéristiques du produit. Cette bouteille a une forme carrée parce que la gelée est sous forme de granules cubiques. L'effet recherché dans le design du récipient est de révéler les caractéristiques du produit. Les courbes lisses du corps de la bouteille suggèrent la texture lisse élastique et fraîche des granules savoureuses L'attrait gustatif de ces granules a été intégré avec succès au design du conditionnement.

HONEY HERBAL JELLY
Design: *Creative XAN Corporatio – Alex Su (Creative Director), Tatsuya Kobayashi (Designer), Jesse Lee (3D CG)*; Client: *TAISU Enterprise Co., Ltd.*; Materials: *Polyethylene terephthalate*; Manufacturing process: *Blow moulding, injection moulding*; Year: *2005*

TAIWAN DESSERT
MIXED CONGEE
Design: *Creative XAN Corporatio – Alex Su (Creative Director), Tatsuya Kobayashi (Designer)*; Client: *TAISUN Enterprise Co., Ltd.*; Materials: *Paper, plastic*; Manufacturing process: *Various*; Year: *2005*

FRUIT JELLY
Design: *Okumura Akio;* Client:
Haus Japan; Materials: *Card,*
plastic; Manufacturing process:
Not disclosed; Year: *2002*

IV

HOMECARE

Carré Noir
Karim Rashid
Landor Design
P&W Design Consultants
WSdV Chicago
WSdV London

P. 202+204
METHOD
Design: *Karim Rashid;* Client: *Method Home;* Awards: *IDSA (The Industrial Designers Society of America) Industrial Design Excellence Award (Silver), I.D. Magazine Annual Design Review Design Distinction;* Materials: *Polyethylene;* Manufacturing process: *Blow moulding;* Year: *2004*

FEBREZE AIR EFFECTS
Design: *Landor Design – Amy Sundermann;* Client: *Procter & Gamble;* Awards: *AG Lafley Design Award, P&G Brand Building Awards, AmeriStar Award, Institute of Packaging Professionals, Can of the Year Awards, one of five Best New Household Products in Canada (The National Post, Canadian Living, Coup de Pouce), Package of the Year Award, New Jersey Packaging Executives Cl. The Gold Award – Best New Hou. hold Product Package, New Jers Packaging Executives Club, Nev Jersey Packaging Executives Cl.* Materials: *Aluminium (can), hig density polyethylene (shroud an toupee);* Manufacturing process: *not disclosed;* Year: *2004*

Method would like to rid the world of dirt. [Th]ey create premium homecare products that [ar]e highly effective and safe. All of their prod[uc]ts are naturally derived, biodegradable, [ne]ver tested on animals, and scented with [es]sential oils such as French lavender, [m]agnolia and pink grapefruit.

The challenge was to design packaging that [ke]eps both your design sensibilities and the [en]vironment in mind. Karim designed the [M]ethod line to proudly stand on your counter[t]o rather than be hidden under the kitchen [sin]k. His signature undulating curves and blobs [ar]e extremely ergonomic and user-friendly [aft]er their reincarnation at Method. This makes [cle]aning more fun and more convenient.

Method möchte die Welt vom Schmutz befreien. Daher kreierte das Unternehmen hochwertige Produkte für die häusliche Sauberkeit, die sehr wirksam und sicher sind. Alle Produkte sind aus natürlichen Stoffen, biologisch abbaubar, nie in Tierversuchen getestet und erhalten ihren Duft durch ätherische Öle wie etwa französischen Lavendel, Magnolien oder Grapefruit.

Die Herausforderung bestand nun darin, eine Verpackung zu entwerfen, die sowohl einem hohen Designanspruch als auch dem Umweltbewusstsein der Marke entspricht. Karim hat eine Verpackungslinie entworfen, die zu schön ist, um sie unter dem Spülbecken zu verstecken. Die für seinen Designstil typischen geschwungenen Linien und Blasenformen machen die Method-Flaschen sehr ergonomisch und benutzerfreundlich. So macht das Saubermachen Spaß und fällt leicht.

Method veut débarrasser le monde de la saleté. Cette société a créé des produits d'entretien ménager haut de gamme, très efficaces et sans danger. Tous ces produits sont fabriqués à base d'ingrédients naturels, ils sont biodégradables, ne sont jamais testés sur les animaux et sont parfumés avec des huiles essentielles, comme la lavande française, le magnolia ou le pamplemousse rose.

Le défi consistait à concevoir un conditionnement qui respecterait l'environnement, mais aussi les goûts esthétiques du client. En créant la gamme Method, Karim voulait que les clients posent fièrement les bouteilles sur le plan de travail de la cuisine, plutôt que de les cacher sous l'évier. Les courbes et les formes en goutte caractéristiques de ses bouteilles sont extrêmement ergonomiques et faciles à utiliser. Faire le ménage est maintenant beaucoup plus amusant et pratique.

ARIEL EXCALIBUR
(REDESIGN OF ARIEL
PACKAGING IDENTITY)
Design: *Landor Design – Alex
Durbridge, Gina Keech, Gemma
Ash;* Client: *Procter & Gamble;*
Materials: *Carton board/cardboa[rd]
containers, plastic bottles and
containers;* Manufacturing proces[s]
Lithographic printing; Year: *2005[?]*

DAWN / FAIRY ACTIVE
Design: *WSdV London;* Client:
Procter & Gamble; Materials:
Polyethylene terephthalate;
Manufacturing process: *Injection
stretch blow moulding, polystyrene-
latex / shrink sleeved, injection
moulding (modified pump
mechanism);* Year: *2005*

Recognising that consumer habits are continuously changing, especially with the introduction of the dishwasher, this Active Foam dish wash was created for direct application to either the sponge or the dishes rather than diluted in a sink full of water. WSdV's innovative new pump design automatically foams the concentrated product as it is dispensed. The pack was designed to be multifunctional in that consumers can dispense the product either one-handed, using the ergonomic collar, or in conjunction with the surface top. An additional design challenge was to create an aesthetic that was unique but not alien within the dish wash category, and appropriate to several Procter & Gamble brands in the US and Europe. The design offers a versatile, pure package that highlights the product's unique efficacy through the character of the ergonomic details and delivery surface. The product provides superior grease cutting performance whilst the pump delivery adds dramatic task simplification.

Da sich die Verbrauchergewohnheiten durch die Einführung der Geschirrspülmaschine stark verändert haben, wurde ein Geschirrspülmittel in Form eines Aktivschaums entwickelt, der direkt auf den Schwamm oder das Geschirr aufgetragen wird, statt ihn im Spülwasser zu lösen. Der innovative neue Pumpmechanismus von WSdV schäumt das Konzentrat direkt bei der Abgabe auf. Die Verpackung wurde multifunktional entworfen: Durch ihren ergonomischen Kragen kann sie einhändig bedient werden, nicht nur wenn die Flasche auf der Arbeitsfläche steht, sondern auch wenn man sie in der Hand hält. Zugleich sollte mit dem Design eine neuartige Ästhetik geschaffen werden, die aber in der Kategorie Spülmittel nicht fremd wirken durfte. Überdies sollte die Flasche für mehrere Marken von Procter & Gamble in den USA und Europa verwendbar sein. Das Design bietet eine vielseitige, klare Verpackung, die durch die Details des Pumpspenders und des ergonomischen Kragens einen hohen Praxiswert hat. Das Produkt besticht durch seine starke Fettlösekraft, während der Pumpspender eine große Erleichterung bei der Bedienung darstellt.

Ce liquide vaisselle Active Foam a été créé pour répondre à des habitudes de consommation en constante évolution, surtout depuis l'entrée des lave-vaisselle dans les foyers. Il est conçu pour être appliqué directement sur l'éponge ou sur la vaisselle, plutôt que d'être dilué dans l'évier rempli d'eau. WSdV a inventé une pompe innovante qui fait mousser le produit concentré automatiquement à la sortie de la bouteille. Ce conditionnement a été conçu pour être multifonctionnel, c'est-à-dire que l'utilisateur peut se servir du produit d'une seule main, grâce au col ergonomique, ou bien avec la bouteille posée sur le plan de travail. Créer une esthétique originale sans être étrangère à la catégorie des liquides vaisselle, et adaptée à plusieurs marques de Procter & Gamble aux États-Unis et en Europe, représentait un défi supplémentaire. Ce concept flexible et pur met en valeur l'efficacité du produit à travers le caractère des détails ergonomiques et du système de pompe. Le produit a un pouvoir dégraissant supérieur, et la pompe simplifie considérablement la corvée de vaisselle.

DOWNY SIMPLE PLEASURES
Design: *WSdV Chicago;* Client:
Procter & Gamble; Materials:
Polyethylene terephthalate,
polypropylene; Manufacturing
process: *Blow moulding (bottle),*
injection moulding (cap), in-mou[...]
label (label); Year: 2005

Simple Pleasures was developed to bring new consumers into the fabric enhancer category by offering a fresh emphasis on scents. An innovative packaging approach was required to achieve standout in-store and convey the unique sensorial experiences offered by the product. For maximum differentiation, WSdV recommended tinted PET material for the bottles; a first in the US laundry category. PET offers a brilliant shine and clarity, but does not allow a traditional handle opening, so they developed a necked bottle shape. The shape offers not only an integrated grip, but also a contemporary elegance that perfectly complements the Simple Pleasures positioning.

Simple Pleasures wurde entwickelt, um durch neue frische Düfte neue Kunden anzulocken. Um im Verkaufsraum eine hohe Aufmerksamkeit zu erzielen und die einzigartige Idee der saisonal wechselnden Gerüche zu unterstreichen, war ein innovativer Verpackungsansatz nötig. Zur optimalen Produktdifferenzierung empfahl WSdV gefärbtes PET als Material für die Flaschen – eine absolute Neuheit auf dem amerikanischen Waschmittelmarkt. PET bietet starken Glanz und Klarheit, kann aber nicht mit traditionellem Verschluss hergestellt werden, sodass man eine Flaschenform mit Hals entwickelte. Diese Form bietet gute Griffigkeit wie auch moderne Eleganz und ergänzt somit die Positionierung von Simple Pleasures ideal.

Simple Pleasures a été créé pour attirer [...] nouveaux consommateurs dans la catégori[...] des assouplissants en proposant une nouve[...] approche des parfums. Un conditionnemen[...] innovant était indispensable pour se démar[...] quer en magasin et pour exprimer l'original[...] des sensations proposées par le produit. P[...] une meilleure différenciation, WSdV a recor[...] mandé de fabriquer les bouteilles en PET te[...] té, une première dans le secteur des lessiv[...] aux États-Unis. Le PET offre d'excellentes c[...] tés de brillance et de transparence, mais n[...] permet pas de mettre une poignée sur la b[...] teille, comme c'est la tradition pour ce gen[...] de produits. Ils ont donc créé une bouteille [...] long col. Cette forme offre non seulement [...] prise intégrée, mais aussi une élégance contemporaine qui correspond parfaitemen[...] au positionnement de Simple Pleasures.

LENOR
Designer: WSdV London; Client:
Procter & Gamble, Materials:
High density polyethylene,
polypropylene, Manufacturing
process: *Extrusion blow moulding,*
wet-glue label, injection moulded
closure; Year: *2005*

OUST JOHNSON
Design: *Carré Noir – Béatrice*
Mariotti (Designer), Client:
Johnson Française SA; Materials:
Aluminium, polyethylene;
Manufacturing process:
Various; Year: *2004*

HNSON WISP
sign: *Carré Noir – Béatrice*
riotti (Designer), Client:
nson Française SA; Materials:
uminium, polyethylene;
nufacturing Process: *Various;*
ar: 2005

LY/ECOLIVE
SHING POWDER
sign: *P&W Design Consultants –*
ian Whitefoord (Art Director),
Newham (Design/Typography);
nt: *Donald Cambell;* Awards:
don International Advertising
ard; Materials: *Cardboard,*
on, paper; Manufacturing
cess: *Litho;* Year: *2005*

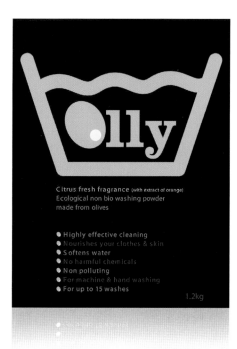

Citrus fresh fragrance (with extract of orange)
Ecological non bio washing powder
made from olives

● Highly effective cleaning
● Nourishes your clothes & skin
● Softens water
● No harmful chemicals
● Non polluting
● For machine & hand washing
● For up to 15 washes

1.2kg

Citrus fresh fragrance
(with extract of orange)
Ecological all purpose cleaner
made from olives

● Dissolves grease & grime on contact
● Anti bacterial
● Anti limescale
● Non harmful chemicals
● Non polluting

500ml

Citrus fresh fragrance
(with extract of orange)
Ecological washing up liquid
made from olives

● Highly effective on grease
● Nourishes your skin
● No harmful chemicals
● Non polluting
● Anti bacterial
● For up to 20 washes

500ml

Citrus fresh fragrance (with extract of orange)
Ecological non bio fabric softener
made from olives

● Softens water
● Nourishes your clothes & skin
● No harmful chemicals
● Non polluting
● For machine & hand washing
● For up to 12 cycles

500ml

LUXURY GOODS

FOOD AND BEVERAGE

Carré Noir
Curiosity
Design Bridge
Dragon Rouge
Coley Porter Bell
Creative Leap
Pearlfisher
Sayuri Studio
Third Eye Design

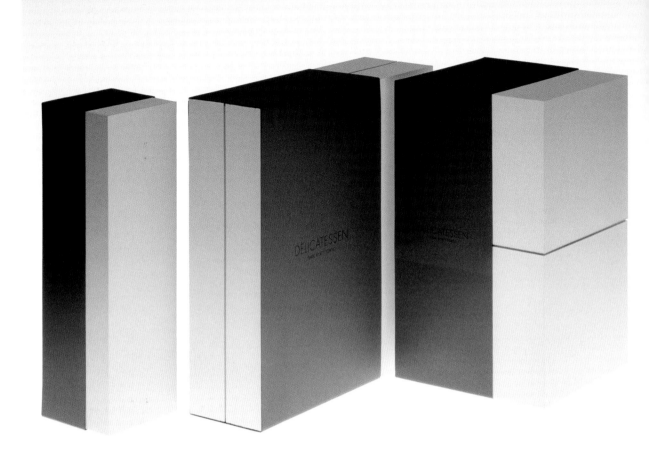

The interior of the Park Hyatt Tokyo is a subtle balance of light and shadow, large plain space and refined detailing. The packaging of the delicatessen is based on the same aesthetic of refinement; a play with light and shadow, simple shapes that will create the appropriate environment for the delis to be presented, wrapped, offered and received.

The white square motif is used as the shape for all items, highlighted with a ray of shadow, an obi (sleeve) in dark shadow green: the food is visible using transparency inside the acrylic boxes, and is protected by a paper wrapping. The visual contrast of light and shadow is expressed in the tactile interaction, with sharp-angled boxes placed into soft fabric bags. The materials are kept as plain as possible with a minimum of printing. The materials themselves reveal their taste and identity with a sense of authenticity and honesty (i.e. you can preview the quality of food presented.) Some original package items were developed like a travel set, a set of transparent boxes connected with an obi and placed into a fabric bag.

Das Park Hyatt Tokyo zeichnet sich durch eine subtile Balance von Licht und Schatten, große offene Räume und elegante Details aus. Das Design der Feinkost-Verpackungen orientiert sich an dieser Ästhetik: Im Vordergrund stehen das Spiel mit Licht und Schatten sowie einfache Formen, die einen adäquaten Präsentationsrahmen für die Delikatessen bieten.

Die Form des weißen Quadrates wird für alle Produkte verwendet. Sie erhält durch einen Obi (eine Banderole) in dunklem Grün einen farbigen Akzent. Durch die Verwendung von Acrylboxen und transparenten Folien bleibt das Essen sichtbar,. Eine Papierverpackung schützt die Produkte. Der optische Kontrast von Licht und Schatten wird durch den Kontrast der eckigen Boxen zu der weichen Textilhülle wiederholt. Die Materialien werden durch einen stark reduzierten Aufdruck so schlicht wie möglich gehalten. Sie sind geschmackvoll und verleihen den Produkten Identität, Authentizität und Transparenz, da die Qualität der Lebensmittel direkt in Augenschein genommen werden kann. Eine Auswahl der verschiedenen Produkte ist als Reiseset mit einem Obi umschlungen und in einer Stofftasche verpackt erhältlich.

L'intérieur du Park Hyatt de Tokyo est un équilibre subtil entre ombre et lumière, vaste espaces dépouillés et détails raffinés. Le con tionnement de l'épicerie fine est basé sur la même esthétique du raffinement, un jeu sur l'ombre et la lumière, des formes simples qui créent l'environnement idéal pour les plats qu seront présentés, empaquetés, offerts et reçu

Le motif du carré blanc est utilisé dans la forme de tous les produits, souligné d'un tra d'ombre, une obi vert foncé : la nourriture es visible par transparence à l'intérieur des boî en acrylique, et est protégée par une ceintu de papier. Le contraste visuel de la lumière de l'ombre s'exprime dans l'interaction tactil avec des boîtes anguleuses placées dans d sacs de tissu doux. Les matériaux sont auss sobres que possible, avec un minimum d'im pression. Ils révèlent leur style et leur identit avec authenticité et honnêteté : vous pouve en déduire la qualité de la nourriture présen tée. Certains produits vendus ensemble ont été conçus comme un nécessaire de voyage un jeu de boîtes transparentes serrées par une obi et placées dans un sac en tissu.

P.212-215
PARK HYATT DELICATESSEN
Design: *Curiosity – Gwenael Nicolas (Designer);* Client: *Park Hyatt;* Materials: *White recycled paper, brown paper, plastic;* Manufacturing process: *Various;* Year: *2005*

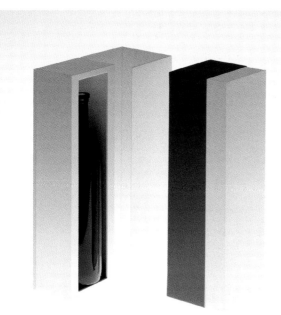

MUMM SPA BOX
Design: *Carré Noir – Béatrice Mariotti (Designer);* Client: *Allied Domecq;* Materials: *Various;* Manufacturing process: *Various;* Year: *2005*

XO COGNAC MARTELL
Design: *Dragon Rouge;* Client: *Pernod Ricard;* Materials: *Glass, metallic seal, paper;* Manufacturing process: *Various;* Year: *2005*

LAPPONIA
Design: *Design Bridge;* Vin & Sprit
Finland; Materials: *Glass, paper;*
Manufacturing process: *Blow*
moulding, printing; Year: *2005*

WILLIAM GRANT'S
FAMILY CASK SELECTION
SCOTCH WHISKY
Design: *Creative Leap;* Client:
William Grant & Sons Internation-
al Ltd; Materials: *Glass, metallic*
ink; Manufacturing process:
Various; Year: *2005*

BALLANTINE'S
Design: *Carré Noir – Béatrice Mariotti (designer)*; Client: *Allied Domecq*; Materials: *Various*; Manufacturing process: *Various*; Year: *2005*

CHIVAS ROYAL SALUTE 38 YEAR OLD 'STONE OF DESTINY'
Design: *Coley Porter Bell*; Client: *Chivas Brothers*; Materials: *Glass, metal, paper*; Manufacturing process: *Blow moulding, printing*; Year: *2005*

KSHOCOLÂT
Design: *Third Eye Design –
Kenny Allan (Designer);* Client:
Kshocolât; Awards: *New York Festivals, Scottish Design Award, DBA
(Design Business Association)
Design Effectiveness Award;* Materials: *Metal, paper;* Manufacturing
process: *Various;* Year: *2004*

ABSOLUT LEVEL
Design: Pearlfisher – Natalie
Chung (Designer); Client: V&S
Absolut Spirits; Awards: Glasspac
Image Award UK (Grand Prix),
Clius USA (Winner), New York
Festivals (Silver), London
International Awards (Finalist),
Creativity 34 (Book entry) USA;
Materials: Extra white flint glass
with heavy base, polished alumini-
um badge; Manufacturing process:
Blow moulding (bottle), robot
applied aluminium badge with
silkscreen graphics; Year: 2004

level™

IMPORTED
VODKA
Spirit of Absolut
40% ALC./VOL. (80 PROOF) 1 LITER

WATERBOTTLE
Design: Sayuri Studio – Sayuri
Shoji; Client: IPSA; Materials:
Glass; Manufacturing process:
Blow moulding; Year: 2006

LUXURY GOODS

JEWELLERY

Aloof Design
Dew Gibbons
Esteban Salgado
The Ad Store

P.222+224

DE BEERS

Design: *Dew Gibbons – Shaun Dew, Steve Gibbons, Suzanne Langley, Sebastian Bergne (Designers);* Client: *De Beers LV;* Awards: *D&AD, LIAA, New York Festivals (Finalist), Communication Arts;*

Materials: *Leather with velvet;* Manufacturing process: *The leather boxes are made individually by Swiss craftsmen, using traditional box and book binding techniques;* Year: *2003*

The power of the De Beers name and a diamond jewellery collection are a potent combination. The De Beers brand launch was a significant development within the luxury retail sector. Dew Gibbons was briefed to create packaging that would rival those such as Cartier, Tiffany and Bulgari. The packaging needed to be timeless and classic but with an intelligent twist—it needed to rival the famous Tiffany "little blue box." The packaging design was inspired by the facets of a cut diamond. The distinctive rhombus form of the morello brown leather jewellery cases and their protective presentation boxes echoed this structure. The rectangular form is classical, but slanting it back by 10 degrees provided the required distinctive twist. The lid for the protective outer presentation boxes falls slightly short of its base, revealing an alizarin pink accent colour running around the box's base. This accent colour is one of the elements developed to be part of the brand's overall identity.

Der berühmte Name De Beers und eine Kollektion mit Diamantschmuck sind eine kraftvolle Kombination. Die Einführung der Marke De Beers war ein bedeutendes Ereignis auf dem Markt der Luxusgüter. Dew Gibbons wurde beauftragt, eine Verpackung zu entwickeln, die es mit hochkarätigen Konkurrenten wie Cartier, Tiffany und Bulgari aufnehmen konnte. Die Verpackung sollte von zeitloser, klassischer Eleganz sein und einen intelligenten Akzent haben – sie sollte mit Tiffanys berühmter „kleinen blauen Schachtel" konkurrieren können. Die kirschrote, lederne Schmuckschatulle ist wie ihre schützende Verpackung in Anlehnung an einen geschliffenen Diamanten rhombenförmig. Die klassische Form in der Schmuckbranche ist die rechteckige Form, doch die Neigung der Seiten um zehn Prozent verleiht der Verpackung hier eine ausgefallene, elegante Note. Der Deckel der schützenden Verpackung umschließt die Schatulle nicht ganz und gibt so einen Blick auf den roten Schatullenboden frei. Diese intensive rote Schmuckfarbe wurde speziell für die Markenidentität entwickelt.

Le nom De Beers et une collection de bijo en diamants sont une combinaison puissant Le lancement de la marque De Beers a repr senté un évènement considérable dans le secteur de la distribution de produits de luxe L'agence Dew Gibbons a été chargée de cré un emballage qui rivaliserait avec celui de Cartier, de Tiffany, et de Bulgari. Il devait être intemporel et classique, mais avec un petit quelque chose en plus – il devait faire concu rence à la célèbre « petite boite bleue » de Tiffany. Le design de l'emballage est inspiré facettes d'un diamant taillé. La forme en losa ge caractéristique des boîtes à bijoux en cu acajou et de leurs boîtes de présentation et de protection rappelle cette structure. La fo rectangulaire est classique, mais l'inclinaiso de 10 degrés vers l'arrière apporte la touche différence recherchée. Le couvercle de la b extérieure de présentation et de protection tombe un peu au-dessus de la base et révèl rose alizarine de la deuxième boîte. Cet acc de couleur est l'un des éléments conçus po former l'identité globale de la marque.

BESPOKE JEWELLERY
PACKAGING FOR JENNY
DYER LONDON
Design: *Aloof Design - Sam Aloof,
Chris Barham, Andrew Scrase
(designers);* Client: *Jenny Dyer
London;* Materials: *Colorplan
Pristine White Fine Linen
embossed, Colorflute, fine bone
china;* Manufacturing process: *One
colour litho print, double faced to
white, die cut and hand glued (outer
box), slipcast moulded from bespoke
form (bone china insert);* Year: *2004*

MANDARINA DUCK
JEWELLERY PACK
Design: *The Ad Store – Rachel
Wild, Natalia Borri (Designers);*
Client: *Mandarina Duck;* Materials:
Various; Manufacturing process:
Not disclosed; Year: *2004*

GEORGINA GOODMAN
GLOVE ENVELOPE
Design: *Aloof Design – Sam Aloof,
Chris Barham (Designers);* Client:
Georgina Goodman Ltd.; Materials:
*Colorplan (Mist Matt, Peregrina
Tungsten);* Manufacturing process:
*Matt laminated, debossed, die cut,
hand glued;* Year: *2002*

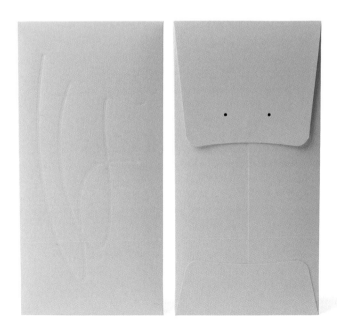

:WELLERY PACKAGING SET
:sign: *Esteban Salgado;* Client:
it disclosed; Materials: *Plastic;*
inufacturing process: *Various;*
:ar: *2005*

LUXURY GOODS

PERSONAL CARE

Marc Atlan
Baron & Baron, Inc.
Guerlain
Karim Rashid
Kosé
Lloyd (+co)
R Design

P.228+230
BURBERRY BRIT
EAU DE PARFUM /
BURBERRY BRIT FOR MEN
EAU DE TOILETTE
Design: *Baron & Baron, Inc. –
Fabien Baron (Designer);* Client:
Burberry; Awards: *Women's –
US FIFI Award for Women's Luxe
Fragrance of the Year, German
FIFI Award for Best Women's
Haute Couture Fragrance, WWD
Breakthrough Product of the
Year – Prestige Fragrance, Men's –
US FIFI Award for Men's Luxe
Fragrance of the Year, UK FIFI
Award for Men's Luxe Fragrance of
the Year, French FIFI Award for
Best Men's Bottle Design, German
FIFI Award for Best Men's
Packaging;* Materials: *Glass;*
Manufacturing process: *Decoration
process (chromography), surlyn
material with tampography
decoration (cap);* Year: *2003*

euphoria
Calvin Klein
eau de parfum spray / vaporisateur
3.4 FL OZ 100 ml ℮
euphoria Calvin Klein

CALVIN KLEIN EUPHORIA
Design: *Baron & Baron, Inc. – Fabien Baron (Designer);* Client: *Calvin Klein;* Materials: *Glass;* Manufacturing process: *Decoration process – chromography; cap – surlyn material with tampography decoration;* Year: *2006*

DAVIDOFF ECHO MAN (ECHO WOMAN)
Design: *Karim Rashid;* Client: *Davidoff;* Awards: *IDSA Industrial Design Excellence Award Bronze;* Materials: *Glass and polypropylene;* Manufacturing process: *Blow moulding (bottle), injection moulding (spray), silkscreened graphics;* Year: *2003*

GUCCI ENVY ME
Design: *Lloyd (+ co) – Douglas Lloyd (Creative Director), Katia Kuethe, Philipp Muesigmann (Art Directors);* Client: *Gucci;* Materials: *Crystal, glass;* Manufacturing process: *Blow moulding;* Year: *2004*

YSL M7
Design: *Lloyd (+ co) – Tom Ford (Creative Director), Douglas Lloyd (Art Director);* Client: *YSL;* Materials: *Glass, plastic;* Manufacturing process: *Injection moulding; blow moulding;* Year: *2002*

GUCCI EAU DE PARFUM
Design: *Lloyd (+ co) – Douglas Lloyd (Creative Director), Alfredo Castro (Art Director);* Client: *Gucci;* Materials: *Glass;* Manufacturing process: *Blow moulding;* Year: *2003*

COMME DES GARÇONS
EAU DE PARFUM
Design: *Marc Atlan;* Client: *Comme des Garçons Parfums;* Awards: *I.D. Magazine Best Packaging of the Year;* Materials: *Silkscreened glass, vacuum packed bottle;* Manufacturing process: *Various;* Year: *1994*

KISSKISS
Design: *Guerlain – Olivier Echaudemaison (Creative Director), Herve Van Der Straeten (Designer);* Client: *Guerlain;* Awards: *Marie Claire – Prix d'Excellence de la Beauté, Edition Jalou – Prix Officiel de la Beauté;* Materials: *Various;* Manufacturing process: *Various;* Year: *2006*

YSL M7 (CLEAN BOTTLE)
Design: *Lloyd (+ co) – Tom Ford (Creative Director), Douglas Lloyd (Art Director);* Client: *YSL;* Materials: *Glass, plastic;* Manufacturing process: *Injection moulding; blow moulding;* Year: *2002*

JOHN VARVATOS
Design: *Lloyd (+ co) – Douglas Lloyd (creative director), Alfredo Castro (art director);* Client: *John Varvatos;* Materials: *glass, leather, chrome;* Manufacturing process: *Various;* Year: *2004*

GUCCI RUSH
Design: *Lloyd (+ co) – Douglas Lloyd (creative director), Alfredo Castro (art director);* Client: *Gucc* Materials: *glass;* Manufacturing process: *Various;* Year: *1999*

JILL STUART
Design: *Kosé – Jill Stuart (creati[ve]
director), Fujio Hanawa (art
director), Akemi Masuda, Chika
Sato, Reiko Futatsuki (designers[)]*;
Client: *KOSÉ Corporation*;
Materials: *ABS, polypropylene,
styrene acrylonitrile, glass, acryl[ic,]
paper;* Manufacturing process:
Various; Year: *2005*

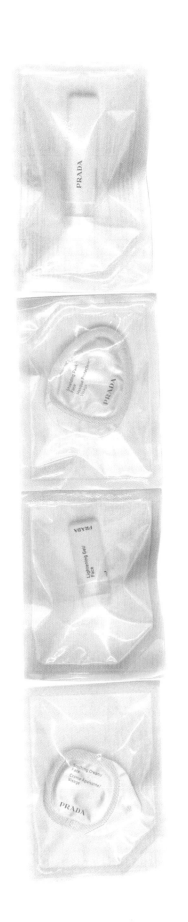
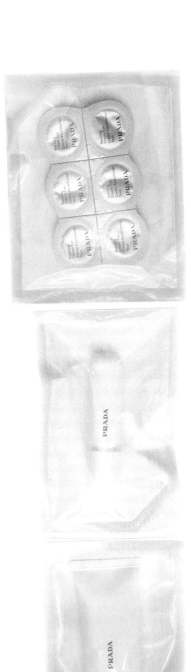

Miuccia Prada created her skincare line to be potent, pure and personal. Meaning that the ingredients had to work efficiently, the products had to be hygienic and travel well. Hence, the skincare products are packaged in their own unique, individual capsules and tubes. Most products in the line come in individually-sealed mono doses that keep out light, air, and bacteria, making them hygienic and fresh. Naturally, these are also available in a multi-dose bottle.

Miuccia Prada hat eine sehr persönliche Hautpflegeserie entwickelt, deren Anspruch hohe Wirksamkeit und Reinheit ist. Die Inhaltsstoffe sollten erstklassig sein. Überdies sollte das Produkt für Reisen geeignet und hygienisch sein. Daher wurden die Hautpflegeprodukte in Einzelkapseln oder -tuben verpackt. Die meisten Produkte der Pflegeserie sind zudem in luftdicht verschweißten Einzelportionen abgepackt, um Licht, Luft und Bakterien fernzuhalten, sodass sie besonders hygienisch und frisch bleiben. Natürlich sind aber auch Flaschen mit mehreren Portionen erhältlich.

Miuccia Prada voulait que sa ligne de soins de la peau soit puissante, pure et personnelle. Il fallait donc que les ingrédients soient efficaces, et que les produits soient hygiéniques et voyagent bien. C'est pourquoi les produits de soin de la peau sont emballés dans des capsules et des tubes individuels. La majorité des produits de la ligne sont emballés en doses individuelles et sont protégés de la lumière, de l'air et des bactéries pour préserver leur hygiène et leur fraîcheur. Naturellement, ils sont aussi disponibles en bouteille multi-doses.

PRADA
MULTIDOSE SKINCARE
Design: *Karim Rashid;* Client:
Prada; Materials: *Polypropylene;*
Manufacturing process: *Injection moulding;* Year: *2000*

JOHN VARVATOS
Design: *Lloyd (+ co) – Douglas Lloyd (creative director), Alfredo Astro (art director);* Client: *John Varvatos;* Materials: *Glass, chrome;*
Manufacturing process:
Not disclosed; Year: *2004*

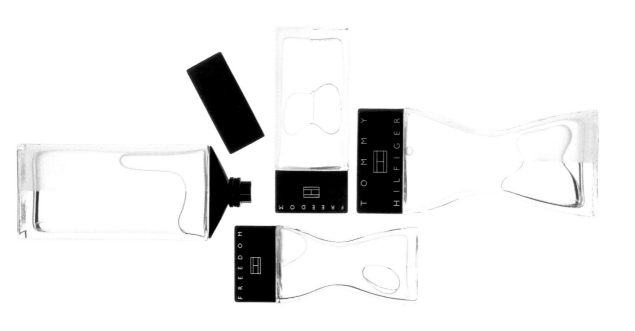

TOMMY HILFIGER
Design: *Karim Rashid;* Client:
Tommy Hilfiger; Materials:
concept; Manufacturing process:
not in production; Year: *2005*

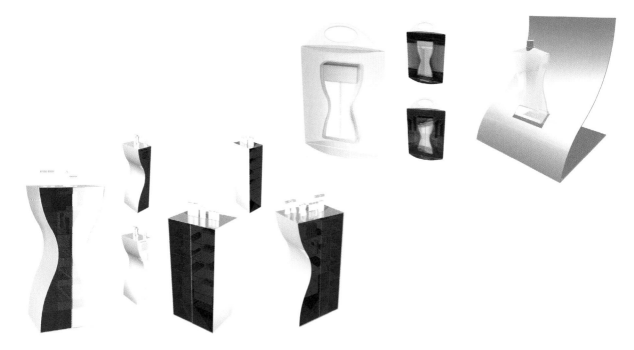

V

LUXURY GOODS

OTHERS

Curiosity
Helmut Jahn
Pentagram
Andrée Putman
Tom Sachs
Sayuri Studio

Sayuri Studio wanted to make an original concept shopping bag for Pleats Please, not a cliché shopping bag. All shopping bag venders turned down the offer on the grounds that manufacturing this package would be too costly and technical difficulties would arise. Sayuri Studio finally found a specialist vender of plastic with an affiliate factory in China to produce the bag.

Das Sayuri Studio wollte für Pleats Please eine wirklich originelle Einkaufstasche entwickeln, die sich von den üblichen Modellen deutlich abhebt. Alle Taschenhersteller erteilten eine Absage mit dem Argument, die Herstellung sei zu kostenintensiv und technisch zu kompliziert. Schließlich fand das Sayuri Studio einen Kunststoffspezialisten, der mit einer Fabrik in China zusammenarbeitet und die Tasche produzierte.

Sayuri Studio voulait créer un concept original de fourre-tout pour Pleats Please, différent des sacs que l'on a l'habitude de voir. Tous les fabricants de sacs ont refusé l'offre, alléguant que la fabrication de ce sac coûterait trop cher et causerait des difficultés techniques. Sayuri Studio a finalement trouvé un fabricant spécialisé dans le plastique avec une usine en Chine pour produire le sac.

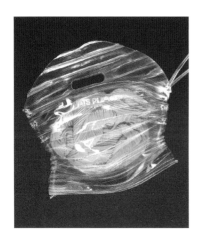

PLEATS PLEASE
LIMITED EDITION SHOPPING
BAG (ISSEY MIYAKE)
Design: *Sayuri Studio – Sayuri Shoji, Atsuko Suzuki (Designers)*; Client: *Issey Miyake USA, Inc.*; Awards: *I.D. Magazine Design Distinctive Award, New York and Tokyo Art Directors Club, Graphis Design Annual*; Materials: *Polypropylene with vinyl tube*; Manufacturing process: *Hand scored materials*; Year: *2002*

FINO PREMIUM
TOUCH SHAMPOO
Design: *Sayuri Studio – Akiko Jinnai, Sayuri Shoji, Hanako Oda, Yumiko Letsugu (Designers);* Client: *Shiseido Fine Toiletry;* Awards: *Tokyo Art Directors Club;* Materials: *Polyethylene, polyethylene terephthalate, carton (pearlised carton stock);* Manufacturing process: *Blow moulding, injection moulding, offset printing;* Year: *2005*

LANGFORD
Design: *Pentagram – John McConnell (Former Partner);* Client: *Langford & Co;* Materials: *Paper;* Manufacturing process: *Various;* Year: *2001*

LOUIS VUITTON (SHOP
OPENING INVITATION)
Design: *Curiosity – Gwenael
Nicolas (Designer)*; Client: *Louis
Vuitton (Japan)*; Materials: *Acrylic,
resin, paper*; Manufacturing
Process: *Various*; Year: *2006*

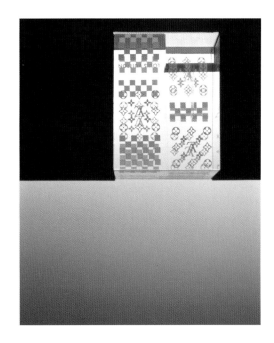

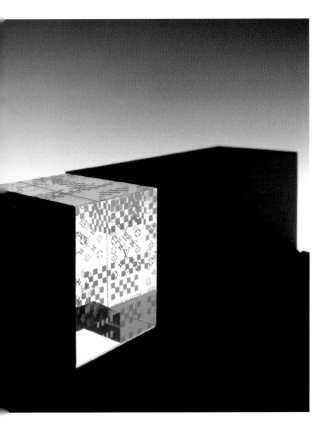

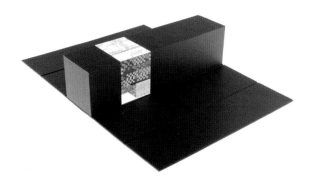

This package was designed as the opening
invitation for the main shop in Tokyo. The shop
is situated in their new building and the acrylic
object showing an image of the building was a
gift for their guests. In line with the "building"
concept, the logo and marks were printed on
the object to create an unusual reflection, and
the use of cubes adds an aura of anticipation
to attract guests to visit the shop.

Die Verpackung wurde zur Eröffnung der
neuen Hauptfiliale in Tokio entworfen. Die Filiale ist in einem neu erbauten Gebäude untergebracht. Das Acrylobjekt mit dem Bild des
Gebäudes wurde den geladenen Gästen als
Geschenk überreicht. In Anlehnung an das
Gebäudekonzept wurden Logo und Markenzeichen so auf das Objekt gedruckt, dass sie
ungewöhnliche Reflexionen ergeben. Die
Verwendung von kubischen Elementen lenkt
die Neugierde der Gäste auf die neue Filiale.

Cet emballage a été conçu pour servir
d'invitation à l'occasion de l'ouverture de la
boutique principale à Tokyo. La boutique est
située dans leur nouveau bâtiment, et l'objet
en acrylique montrant une image de l'im-
meuble était un cadeau pour les invités.
En accord avec le concept de « bâtiment »,
le logo et les marques ont été imprimés sur
l'objet de sorte à donner un effet inhabituel,
et les cubes ont été utilisés de sorte à donner
un avant-goût aux invités, et à leur donner
envie de visiter la boutique.

MONTBLANC
HELMUT JAHN
Design: *Helmut Jahn;* Client:
Montblanc; Materials: *Acrylic;*
Manufacturing process:
Not disclosed; Year: *2005*

MONTBLANC
TOM SACHS
Design: *Tom Sachs;* Client:
Montblanc; Materials: *Various,*
Manufacturing process:
Not disclosed; Year: *2005*

MONTBLANC
ANDRÉE PUTMAN

Design: *Andrée Putman;* Client:
Montblanc; Materials: *Wood;*
Manufacturing process:
Not disclosed; Year: *2005*

More than any other brand, Montblanc embodies "The Art of Writing." The culture of writing is its domain, its core competency. Founded on one of the oldest forms of human culture, writing, the company feels it has a moral and cultural duty to confront the global problem of illiteracy. In 2005, Montblanc in cooperation with UNICEF, launched a very special worldwide campaign: 149 prominent personalities—including Mikhail Gorbachev, Harry Belafonte, Luciano Pavarotti, Bianca Jagger and Vivienne Westwood—agreed to take part by revealing their thoughts on the value and importance of writing. These handwritten reflections under the slogan "Sign up for the right to write" were sold at an international auction in spring 2005 with all proceeds, as well as a donation from Montblanc of US\$ 4,810 for each of the 149 statements (a figure chosen as a reference to the height of Mont Blanc itself), given to the "UNICEF Initiative Against Illiteracy."

Montblanc steht mehr als jede andere Marke für „Die Kunst des Schreibens". Die Kultur des Schreibens ist das Betätigungsfeld der Marke, sozusagen ihre Kernkompetenz. Begründet in einer der ältesten Ausprägungen menschlicher Kultur, im Schreiben, fühlt sich die Firma moralisch und kulturell verantwortlich, etwas gegen das weltweite Problem des Analphabetismus zu unternehmen. 2005 rief Montblanc daher in Zusammenarbeit mit UNICEF eine ganz besondere weltweite Kampagne ins Leben: 149 berühmte Persönlichkeiten, darunter Michail Gorbatschow, Harry Belafonte, Luciano Pavarotti, Bianca Jagger und Vivienne Westwood, erklärten sich bereit, ihre ganz persönlichen Gefühle und Gedanken zu Wert und Wichtigkeit des Schreibens festzuhalten. Diese handschriftlichen Notizen wurden im Frühjahr 2005 bei einer internationalen Auktion unter dem Motto „Sign up for the right to write" versteigert. Der Erlös wurde von Montblanc um eine Spende von 4.810 US-Dollar (der Wert entspricht der Höhe des Montblancs) für jedes der 149 Schriftstücke aufgestockt und der „UNICEF Initiative Against Illiteracy" (UNICEF-Initiative gegen Analphabetismus) überreicht.

Plus que toute autre marque, Montblanc incarne « l'art de l'écriture ». La culture de l'écriture est son domaine, sa compétence principale. L'entreprise, fondée sur l'une des formes de culture humaine les plus anciennes, pense qu'il est de son devoir moral et culturel de combattre le problème de l'analphabétisme. En 2005, Montblanc a, en coopération avec l'UNICEF, lancé une campagne mondiale très spéciale : 149 personnalités (dont Mikhail Gorbachev, Harry Belafonte, Luciano Pavarotti, Bianca Jagger et Vivienne Westwood) ont accepté d'y participer en révélant leurs réflexions sur la valeur et l'importance de l'écriture. Ces pensées écrites, rassemblées sous le slogan « Sign up for the right to write » (Signez pour le droit d'écrire) ont été vendues lors d'une vente aux enchères internationale qui s'est tenue au printemps 2005 et dont tous les profits, ainsi qu'un don effectué par Montblanc de 4 810 dollars (ce chiffre est aussi la hauteur du Mont Blanc) pour chacune des 149 déclarations, ont été versés à l'Initiative contre l'analphabétisme de l'UNICEF.

KANEBO YUSUI

LOOSEN BARRIER
LOTION II

KANEBO YUSUI

OIL TREATMENT

VI

PERSONAL CARE

& BEAUTY

Alloy

Marc Atlan

CB'a Design Solutions

Coley Porter Bell

Curiosity

Dew Gibbons

Dragon Rouge

DJPA Partnership

Forme Design Office

Fuseproject

Jones Knowles Ritchie

K2 Design

Kosé

Lewis Moberly

Lippa Pearce

PDD Group

Pearlfisher

PI3

Pola

Pure Equator

R Design

Karim Rashid

Sayuri Studio

SiebertHead

slover [AND] company

SS Studio

Stockholm Design Lab

Yasuo Tanaka

Tátil Design

The Ad Store

Tin Horse Design Team

Toyo Seikan Kaisha

WSdV Chicago

WSdV London

Hana Zalzal

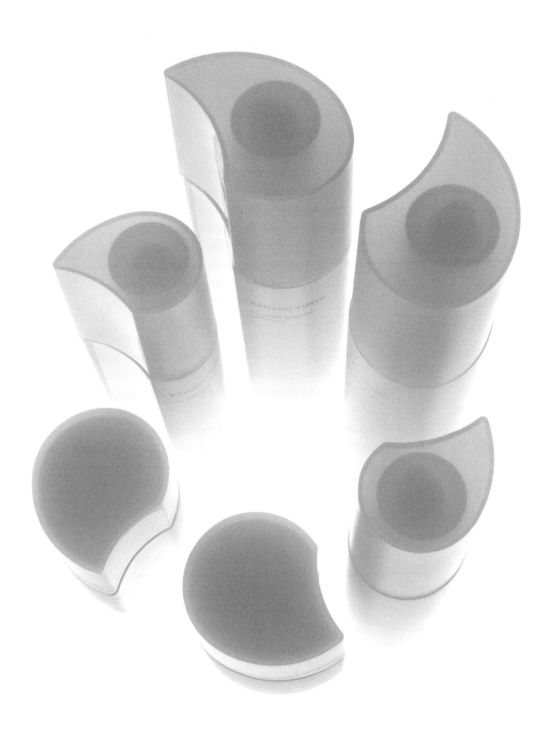

Yusui is the skincare line for Kanebo and the concept is to moisturise the skin to look fresh. Following the concept, the bottle shape is asymmetrically curved, which actually feels easy and soft to hold. Using total line as a process, the bottle can be arranged in a circle to look like a flower.

Yusui ist eine Hautpflegelinie von Kanebo, die der Haut Feuchtigkeit und damit einen frischen Look verleiht. Um dieses Konzept zu verdeutlichen, wurde die Flasche in asymmetrischer Form gestaltet. Sie liegt angenehm und sanft in der Hand. Die gesamte Produktlinie erhielt diese Flaschenform, sodass mehrere Flaschen kreisförmig zu einer Blütenform angeordnet werden können.

Yusui est la ligne de soins de la peau de Kanebo. Son concept : hydrater la peau et donner un teint frais et reposé. La bouteille, en accord avec ce concept, suit une courbe asymétrique qui la rend facile et agréable à prendre en main. Disposées en cercle, les bouteilles de toute la ligne de produits forment une fleur.

256+258

USUI
Design: *Curiosity – Gwenael
Nicolas (Designer);* Client:
Kanebo Cosmetics; Materials:
Plastic; Manufacturing process:
Not disclosed; Year: *2004*

PRODIGY HELENA
RUBINSTEIN
Design: *CB'a Design Solutions –
Hadi Amini (Designer);* Client:
Prestige et Collections; Materials:
Glass; Manufacturing process:
Not disclosed; Year: *2004*

POLA ESTINA ALVITA
Design: *Pola – Takeshi Usui (Art
Director), Chiharu Suzuki, Takashi
Matsui, Kazuhiko Kimishita
(Designers);* Client: *Pola Cosmetics,
Inc.;* Awards: *London International
Awards;* Materials: *Polypropylene;
acrylonitrile butadiene styrene,
polyethylene;* Manufacturing
process: *Injection moulding,
blow moulding;* Year: *2005*

OLA WRINKLE
HOT ESSENCE
esign: *Pola – Takeshi Usui
Art Director)*, *Nobuyuki Shirai
Designer)*; Client: *Pola Cosmetics,
c.*; Awards: *Japan Packaging
ontest, New York Festivals
inalist)*; Materials: *Glass,
olypropylene*; Manufacturing
rocess: *Plastic injection*;
ear: *2005*

OWSHED
esign: *Pearlfisher – Sarah
dgeon (Designer)*; Client:
ho House Hotels*; Materials:
gh density polyethylene (bottles),
w density polyethylene (tubes),
lypropylene (closures, glass jars),
lyethylene (labels, card sleeves)*;
anufacturing process: *Narrow web
xo printing (labels)*, *UV offset
ho prnting (sleeves)*; Year: *2001*

Pearlfisher designed a new identity and
ckaging for Cowshed, a brand created at the
house spa of Babington House, an exclusive
glish country hotel. The design is inspired by
interiors of Babington House and uses wall-
er patterns of differing colours and tex-
es to echo the natural ingredients and bene-
of each product. Each range – skincare,
, spa and men's – is differentiated by its
n colour scheme and set of designs. A
se of Englishness is created by the wallpa-
theme and its countryside patterns, and
by the warm and unconventional humour
he pack copy. The result is a unique brand
t brings the casual elegance of Babington
he bathroom.

Pearlfisher verlieh Cowshed, der exklusiven
Hausmarke der Wellness-Oase im britischen
Luxus-Landhotel Babington House, eine neue
Identität und Verpackung. Das Design ist
durch das Interieur von Babington House
inspiriert und verwendet Tapetenmuster in
verschiedenen Farben und Texturen, um die
natürlichen Ingredienzien und Vorzüge der
Produkte herauszustellen. Jede der Produktreihen – Hautpflege, Öle, Wellness und Herren-
kosmetik – besitzt eine eigene Farbpalette
und ein eigenes Muster. Tapetenmuster und
ländliche Motive, aber auch der warmherzige
und unkonventionelle Humor verleihen den
Produkten einen typisch englischen Charakter
und bringen die legere Eleganz von Babington
House ins Badezimmer.

Pearlfisher a conçu une nouvelle identité et
un nouveau conditionnement pour Cowshed,
une marque créée dans le centre de remise en
forme de Babington House, un luxueux hôtel
rural anglais. Le design est inspiré de la décoration de Babington House et utilise des motifs
de papier peint de différentes couleurs et textures pour évoquer les ingrédients naturels et
les qualités de chaque produit. Chaque gamme
– soins de la peau, huiles, produits issus du
thermalisme, ligne masculine – a son propre
thème de couleurs et ses propres motifs. Le
thème du papier peint et les motifs cham-
pêtres donnent aux produits une identité typi-
quement anglaise, renforcée par l'humour cha-
leureux et décalé des textes. Le résultat est
une marque unique qui fait entrer l'élégance
décontractée de Babington dans la salle de
bain du consommateur.

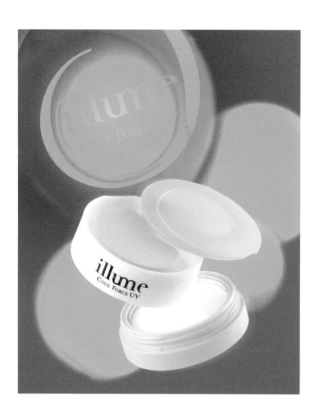

ILLUME COOL FORCE UV
Design: *Forme Design Office,
Inc. – Akiko Ashiwa (Art Direc…
Procter & Gamble Far East, Inc…
Kazuki Fujiwara, Yuko Hirai
(Designers);* Client: *Procter
& Gamble Far East, Inc.;* Award
*London International Advertisi…
Awards – Package Design /
Cosmetics (Finalist);* Materials:
Resin, sponge; Manufacturing
process: *Injection moulding, bl…
moulding;* Year: *2004*

MEA
Design: *R Design – David Richmond (Creative Director), David Gray (Designer);* Client: *Debenhams;* Materials: *Glass, paper, plastic, metal;* Manufacturing Process: *Various;* Year: *2000*

miracle mea™
Essential Skincare kit

Visibly reduces fine lines and wrinkles in 8 weeks
to reveal a younger looking you

mea

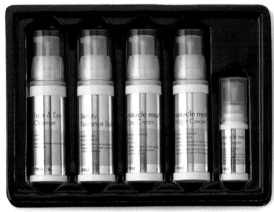

Beauty
Radiance
Balm

· Radiant Vitality
· Illuminates the skin

Instantly tightens and revitalises
tired fatigued skin to reveal
a glowing, smooth complexion

mea

Beauty
Radiance Balm

· Radiant Vitality
· Illuminates the skin

Instantly tightens and revitalises tired
fatigued skin to reveal a glowing,
smooth complexion

mea

Moisture
Day Lotion

· Oil Free
· Shine Control

Instant matte look whilst
providing vital hydration

mea

Moisture
Day Lotion

· Oil Free
· Shine Control

Instant matte look whilst
providing vital hydration

mea

ACTION SUBLIME PACK
Design: *The Ad Store – Rachel*
Wild, Natalia Borri (Designer);
Client: *Daviness – division*
Comfort Zone; Materials:
Plexiglass; Manufacturing
process: *Not disclosed;*
Year: *2002*

SK-II SKIN CARE COSMETICS
Design: *Forme Design Office,*
Inc. – Akiko Ashiwa (Art Director,
Procter & Gamble Far East, Inc.),
Kazuki Fujiwara, Yuko Hirai
(Designers); Client: *Procter &*
Gamble Far East, Inc.; Materials:
Plastic; Manufacturing process:
Not disclosed; Year: *2005*

SK-II LXP SKIN CARE
COSMETICS
Design: *Forme Design Office,*
Inc. – Akiko Ashiwa (Art Director,
Procter & Gamble Far East, Inc.)
Kazuki Fujiwara, Yuko Hirai
(Designers); Client: *Procter &*
Gamble Far East, Inc.; Materials:
Plastic, glass, metal; Manufacturing
process: Not disclosed; Year: *2005*

DAVINESS – COMFORT
ZONE – LINEA MAN
Design: *The Ad Store – Rachel
Wild, Natalia Borri (Designers);*
Materials: *Plexiglas (for the base);*
Manufacturing process:
Not disclosed; Year: *2005*

The Ad Store Italy has created the concept of image corresponding with the packaging and its stand for the line Man, the first Comfort Zone line entirely dedicated to men. Plexiglas is used to exemplify the main Comfort Zone characteristics, such as the minimal, clean look. At the same time, while using quite thick panes, the idea of something strong, robust and masculine has been conveyed. The use of transparencies and colours helps to soften the whole look, while preserving the image and keeping the elegance of the line.

The Ad Store Italy hat das Imagekonzept und die entsprechende Verpackung für Man entworfen, die erste Produktlinie von Comfort Zone, die sich ausschließlich an Männer richtet. Um die wichtigsten Charakteristika, wie den minimalistischen, reinen Look von Comfort Zone zu verdeutlichen, wurde Plexiglas verwendet. Durch das dicke Material vermittelte das Produkt gleichzeitig Stärke, Robustheit und Männlichkeit. Durch die Wahl transparenter Materialien und Farben wird der Gesamteindruck gleichzeitig gedämpft und weicher, ohne das maskuline Image einzubüßen, und wahrt zugleich die Eleganz der Produktlinie.

The Ad Store Italy a conçu l'image correspondant au conditionnement et au présentoir de la ligne Man, la première ligne de Comfort Zone entièrement consacrée aux hommes. L'utilisation du plexiglas illustre les caractéristiques principales de Comfort Zone, comme pureté et le minimalisme. En même temps, l'épaisseur des plaques véhicule une idée de force, de robustesse et de masculinité. L'utilisation de la transparence et des couleurs aide à adoucir l'ensemble, tout en préservant l'image et en conservant l'élégance de la ligne.

MEN EXPERT L'ORÉAL
Design: CB'a Design Solutions –
Géraldine Roussel (Designer) ;
Client: L'oreal OAP ; Materials:
stickers (labels), paper, plastic;
Manufacturing process:
not disclosed; Year: 2004

KORRES FACE CARE
(UNISEX SOPHISTICATED
CONTAINERS)
Design: *K2 Design – Yiannis
Kouroudis (Creative Director),
Chrysafis Chrysafis (Art Director),
Dimitra Diamandi (Graphic
Designer), Stavros Papayiannis
(Photo credits);* Client: *Korres;*

Awards: *Ermis (Bronze) Face Care
Packaging category (Greek Association of Advertising & Communication Companies);* Materials: *Plastic,
paper;* Manufacturing process:
various; Year: *2004*

Korres Natural Products has invested in
sophisticated and luxurious containers that
use airbackless technology in some of the face
care products such as the Wild Mango butter
and the Absinthe shaving cream. The containers are a system of three parts: the outside
plastic cylinder, the pump and the attached
shrinkable bag, which contains the bulk-
product. When the product is used, no air is
allowed to get back into the bag and in contact
with the product. Therefore, the product's safety has increased, while fewer preservatives are
used in the formula. The cylinder is transparent
to allow eye contact with the product, while
much information is printed on it.

Korres Natural Products hat für einige seiner
Gesichtspflegeprodukte, wie etwa für Wild Mango Butter und für Absinthe Shaving Cream,
hochwertige, elegante Behälter entwerfen lassen, deren innovative Technologie verhindert,
dass die Produkte mit Luft in Kontakt kommen.
Die Gefäße bestehen aus drei Komponenten:
dem äußeren Kunststoffzylinder, einer Pumpe
und einem daran befestigten, flexiblen Kunst-
stoffbeutel, der das Produkt enthält. Auf diese
Weise wird die Produktsicherheit erhöht, und
zugleich sind weniger Konservierungsstoffe
notwendig. Der Kunststoffzylinder ist transparent und erlaubt so, die Füllmenge zu kontrollieren, gleichzeitig ist er aber mit umfangrei-
chen Produktinformationen bedruckt.

Korres Natural Products a investi dans des
flacons sophistiqués et luxueux qui utilisent la
technologie « airbackless » (anti-retour d'air)
pour certains soins du visage tels que le beur-
re de mangue sauvage et la crème de rasage
à l'absinthe. Le système est composé de trois
éléments : le cylindre extérieur en plastique, la
pompe et le sachet rétractable qui lui est atta-
ché, contenant le produit en lui-même. Lorsque
l'on utilise le produit, l'air ne peut pas rentrer
dans le sachet et ne peut donc pas entrer en
contact avec le produit. C'est pourquoi le produit est encore plus sûr, bien que la formule
contienne moins de conservateurs. Le cylindre
est transparent pour permettre à l'utilisateur
de voir le produit, mais de nombreuses informations y sont imprimées.

KORRES
COLOURED PENCILS
Design: *K2 Design – Yiannis Kouroudis (Creative Director), Chrysafis Chrysafis (Art Director, Dimitra Diamandi (Graphic Designer), Stavros Papayiannis (Photo credits);* Client: *Korres;* Awards: *Votre Beauté magazine – Prix de Beauté;* Materials: *Paper, plastic;* Manufacturing process: *Not disclosed;* Year: *2005*

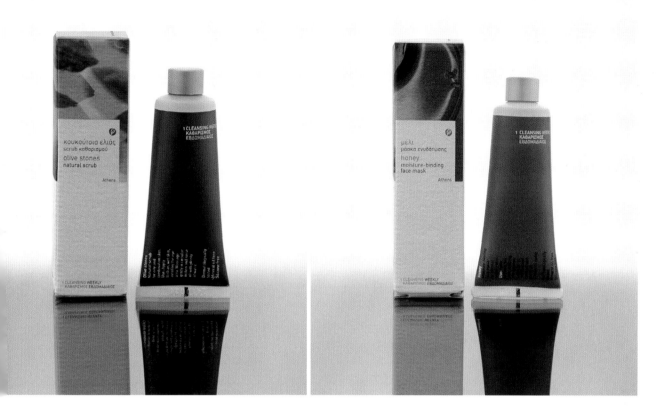

KORRES FACE CARE
(UNISEX SOPHISTICATED
CONTAINERS)
Design: *K2 Design – Yiannis
Kouroudis (Creative Director),
Chrysafis Chrysafis (Art Director),
Dimitra Diamandi (Graphic
Designer), Stavros Papayiannis
(Photo credits);* Client: *Korres;*

Awards: *Ermis (Bronze) Face Care
Packaging category (Greek Association of Advertising & Communication Companies);* Materials: *Paper,
plastic;* Manufacturing process:
Not disclosed; Year: *2004*

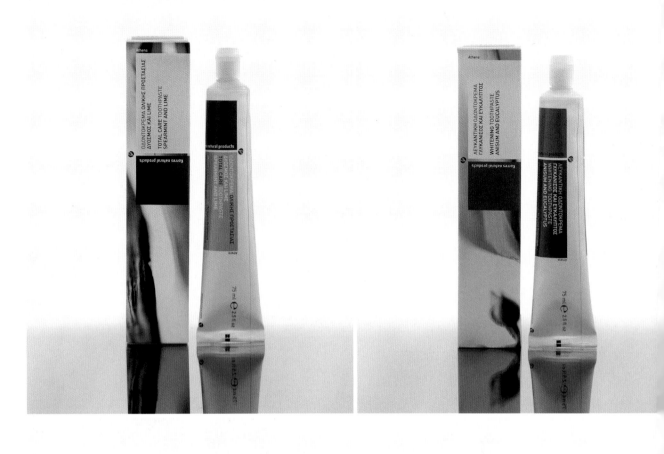
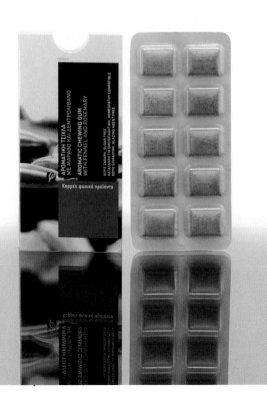
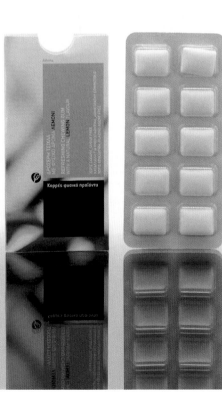

TOTAL CARE TOOTHPASTE
Design: *K2 Design – Yiannis Kouroudis (Creative Director), Chrysafis Chrysafis (Art Director), Dimitra Diamandi (Graphic Designer), Tasia Voutyropoulou (Photo credits);* Client: *Korres;* Materials: *Paper, plastic;* Manufacturing process: *Not disclosed;* Year: *2004*

AROMATIC CHEWING GUM
Design: *K2 Design – Yiannis Kouroudis (Creative Director), Chrysafis Chrysafis (Art Director), Dimitra Diamandi (Graphic Designer), Tasia Voutyropoulou (Photo credits);* Client: *Korres;* Materials: *Paper, plastic;* Manufacturing process: *Not disclosed;* Year: *2004*

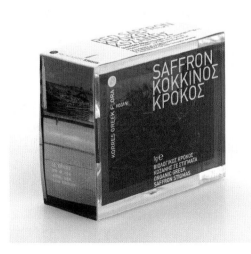

KROKOS (KORRES GREEK FLORA)
Design: *K2 Design – Yiannis Kouroudis (Creative Director), Chrysafis Chrysafis (Art Director), Dimitra Diamandi (Graphic Designer), Tasia Voutyropoulou (Photo credits);* Client: *Korres;* Materials: *Paper, plastic;* Manufacturing process: *Not disclosed;* Year: *2004*

KROKUS (MOUTHWASH NATURAL PROTECTION)
Design: *K2 Design – Yiannis Kouroudis (Creative Director), Chrysafis Chrysafis (Art Director), Dimitra Diamandi (Graphic Designer), Tasia Voutyropoulou (Photo credits);* Client: *Korres;* Materials: *Paper, plastic;* Manufacturing process: *Not disclosed;* Year: *2004*

POND'S
Design: *Tin Horse Design Team;*
Client: *Unilever;* Materials: *Poly-*
propylene, polyethylene terephtha-
late, glass (jars), high density poly-
ethylene (bottles), polypropylene
(closures), shrink sleeve

(labels), polyethylene, self-adhesive
(labels); Manufacturing process:
Bi-injected two-colour closures,
injection blow moulding (jars),
blow moulding (bottles);
Year: *2005*

Beauty, without apology, exists between myth and reality. In development the concept was referred to as "Enigma," an intentional play on the illusiveness of beauty, and the sculptural expression explores notions of belief, myth and faith in physical form and structure. Cool, white softened geometry is interrupted only by the presence of a pool of colour which is immersed in the surface of the pack. The pool's coloured high gloss, transparent and reflective surface is in high contrast to the silky, soft feel of the pack's skin. The contrasting surfaces have been designed to invite sensual touch and discovery. The pebble-like form which narrows toward the base achieves a delicate balance and poise, an expression of both the fragility and the wonder of beauty.

Schönheit liegt irgendwo zwischen Mythos und Realität. In der Entwicklungsphase wurde das Konzept „Enigma" (Rätsel) genannt, eine bewusste Anspielung auf die Unwirklichkeit der Schönheit. Zudem wurden bildhauerische Umsetzungen getestet, um die unterschiedlichen Vorstellungen und Mythen über Schönheit physisch und strukturell darzustellen. Die kühle, weiße, abgerundete Geometrie wird nur durch einen Farbtropfen durchbrochen, der in die Oberfläche der Packung eingelassen ist. Die hochglänzende Farbe, Transparenz und reflektierende Oberfläche des Tropfens bildet einen scharfen Kontrast zur seidigen, weichen Oberfläche der restlichen Verpackung. Die kontrastierenden Oberflächenstrukturen sollen zum Berühren und Erkunden einladen und neugierig machen. Durch die sich nach unten verjüngende, an einen Flusskiesel erinnernde, weiche Form wird eine delikate Balance erzielt, die sowohl die Zerbrechlichkeit als auch das Zauberhafte der Schönheit vermittelt.

La beauté, sans apologie, existe entre le mythe et la réalité. C'est pourquoi, pendant s phase de développement, le concept s'appe « Enigma », un jeu intentionnel sur le caractè illusoire de la beauté. Nous avons aussi utilis la sculpture pour explorer les notions de croyance, de mythe et de foi dans la forme physique et dans la structure. La géométrie froide, blanche et douce n'est interrompue q par la présence d'une flaque de couleur affl rant en haut du pot ou de la bouteille. La sur ce de la flaque, très brillante, transparente e réfléchissante, tranche avec la texture douc et soyeuse du récipient. Ce contraste des te tures invite à l'exploration tactile et à la déc verte sensuelle. La forme de galet, qui se ré cit vers la base, d'une harmonie et d'une gr délicates, est une expression de la fragilité du miracle de la beauté.

ORIFLAME COSMETICS
Design: *Stockholm Design Lab;*
Client: *Oriflame;* Materials:
Concept; Manufacturing process:
Not in production; Year: *2005*

OIL OF OLAY
Design: *PI3;* Client: *Procter & Gamble;* Materials: *Polypropylene (container), carton (sleeve);* Manufacturing process: *Thermoforming, injection moulding;* Year: *2005*

OLAY DAILY FACIALS CLARITY
Design: *WSdV Chicago;* Client: *Procter & Gamble;* Materials: *Polypropylene;* Manufacturing process: *Blow moulding (bottle), injection moulding (cap), pressure sensitive (label);* Year: *2005*

OLAY REGENERIST
Design: *WSdV Chicago;* Client: *Procter & Gamble;* Materials: *Polypropylene;* Manufacturing process: *Blow moulding (bottle), injection moulding (cap); pressure sensitive (label);* Year: *2005*

Regenerist is an undoubted scientific advance; the range needed packaging that demonstrated and empowered this message. The pack structures needed to build an ownable Olay aesthetic without undermining the Olay heritage. The secondary packs expand the tiny bottles' shelf presence, facilitate transparency and layering in the graphics, and guarantee stop-and-look shelf standout in the skincare aisle. The consumer benefit is that lotion and serum are easy to handle, despite their small size, for close-up application to the face. The cream pack features one handed operation, and the airless mechanisms bring a thick cream product to the consumer without the product mess that is typical of crème products in a traditional jar. Product application is clean and easy and the locking pump travels well.

Regenerist ist zweifellos ein wissenschaftlicher Fortschritt. Die Produktserie benötigte eine Verpackung, die dem Kunden diese Botschaft deutlich vermittelte. Die Verpackungsform musste auf der Olay-eigenen Ästhetik aufbauen, ohne die Olay-Traditionen zu untergraben. Die Sekundärverpackungen erhöhen den Aufmerksamkeitswert der kleinen Flaschen im Regal und erlauben durch ihre Transparenz eine mehrschichtige grafische Gestaltung. So fallen sie in jedem Hautpflege-Regalsortiment sofort auf. Ein klarer Vorteil für den Verbraucher ist, dass sich Lotion und Serum trotz der kleinen Behälter sehr gut auf die Haut auftragen lassen. Die Creme-Verpackung kann mit einer Hand bedient werden. Durch den Vakuummechanismus kann der Verbraucher die dickflüssige Creme sauber entnehmen (ohne das Cremetöpfchen zu verschmieren). Das Produkt lässt sich einfach und sauber anwenden, und durch den Verschlussmechanismus ist die Pumpflasche auch für die Reise geeignet.

Regenerist est une avancée technologique incontestable : la gamme avait besoin d'un conditionnement qui reflèterait et renforcerait ce message. La structure du conditionnement devait correspondre à l'esthétique et à la tradition d'Olay. L'emballage secondaire renforce la présence du petit flacon dans les rayons, permet d'utiliser la transparence et plusieurs couches dans le graphisme, et incite les clientes à s'arrêter pour regarder de plus près. Pour la consommatrice, l'avantage est que la lotion et le sérum sont faciles à manipuler et à appliquer malgré leur petite taille. La crème peut s'appliquer d'une seule main, et le mécanisme sous vide d'air donne une crème épaisse, sans les inconvénients et le désordre typiques des crèmes en pot traditionnelles. Le produit s'applique proprement et facilement, et grâce au système de blocage de la pompe, il est pratique à transporter.

AROMATIC BODY WASH 木

LISTEN T

EQUILIR
Design: *Curiosity – Gwenael Nicolas (Designer);* Client: *Kanebo Cosmetics;* Materials: *Glass, aluminium, plastic;* Manufacturing process: *Various;* Year: 2005

To protect the oil from the damaging effects of daily light, the glass bottle had to be deeply tinted and thus looks similar to that of a medicine bottle. The cone shape is designed to convey an air of elegance and the convex base gives it rhythmic movement and makes use of a relaxing image.

Um das Öl vor schädlichem Tageslicht zu schützen, musste das Flaschenglas dunkel getönt werden, sodass das Gefäß wie eine Medizinflasche aussieht. Die Konusform vermittelt Eleganz, und der konvexe Boden verleiht der Flasche Rhythmus und wirkt gleichzeitig beruhigend.

Pour protéger l'huile des effets nocifs de la lumière, la bouteille en verre devait être teintée d'une couleur très sombre, comme un flacon de médicament. Sa forme conique lui confère une grande élégance, et sa base convexe lui donne du rythme tout en projetant une idée de relaxation.

Lippa Pearce was approached to create a brand identity for Naked, a new toiletries range from the "Enormous Yes Company." The new range, which incorporates a selection of products from bath foams and body scrubs to face washes and mood candles, uses wit and humour as a main component of the design to convey the playfulness and essence of the brand. With names like "Angelica in the Altogether," "Rose with no Clothes," "Grapefruit Unveiled," and "Starflower Stark Naked" the title of each product perfectly illustrates the purity and natural ingredient of the range. The thinking behind Naked was to introduce a very natural and honest product to the market; a product that has nothing to hide. Lippa Pearce took the already devised brand name and worked on producing a design which reflected Naked's "what you see is what you get" philosophy.

Lippa Pearce wurde gebeten, eine Markenidentität für Naked, eine Serie von Toilettenartikeln der „Enormous Yes Company", zu entwickeln. Die neue Produktlinie, zu der eine Reihe von Badezusätzen, Körperpeelings, Gesichtsreinigern und Duftkerzen gehört, verwendet spritzigen Humor als wichtigstes Designmerkmal und setzt damit auf das Element der Verspieltheit. Die einzelnen Namen wie „Angelica in the Altogether", „Rose with no Clothes", „Grapefruit Unveiled" und „Starflower Stark Naked" vermitteln die Reinheit des Produkts und die Natürlichkeit der Bestandteile der gesamten Produktlinie. Der Gedanke hinter Naked war, ein sehr unverfälschtes und ehrliches Produkt auf den Markt zu bringen, das nichts zu verbergen hat. Lippa Pearce erarbeitet mit dem bereits festgelegten Markennamen ein Design, das die Philosophie des Produkts – „Sie bekommen, was Sie sehen" – ideal wiedergibt.

L'agence Lippa Pearce a récemment été chargée de créer l'identité de la marque Naked une nouvelle gamme de produits de toilette de la société « Enormous Yes Company ». Le concept de la nouvelle gamme (qui comprend une sélection de produits depuis les bains moussants et les gommages corporels jusqu'aux nettoyants du visage et les bougies d'ambiance) est centré sur l'ironie et l'humour afin d'exprimer l'espièglerie et l'essence de la marque. Avec des noms comme « Angelica in the Altogether », « Rose with no Clothes », « Grapefruit Unveiled » et « Starflower Stark Naked », l'appellation de chaque produit illustre parfaitement le caractère pur et naturel de la gamme. L'idée de Naked était de mettre sur le marché un produit très naturel et honnête, un produit qui n'a rien à cacher. Lippa Pearce a pris le nom de la marque, déjà existant, et a cherché à créer un design reflétant la philosophie de Naked « ce que l'on voit, c'est ce que l'on obtiendra ».

NAKED (BRAND IDENTITY)
Design: *Lippa Pearce – Harry Pearce (Art Director), Richard Wilson;* Materials: *Clear self-adhesive labels;* Manufacturing process: *Flexo printed;* Year: *2005*

MISS FRANCE
Design: *CB'a Design Solutions – Pierre Rhodes (designer);* Client: *Endemol;* Materials: *Various;* Manufacturing process: *Various;* Year: *2005*

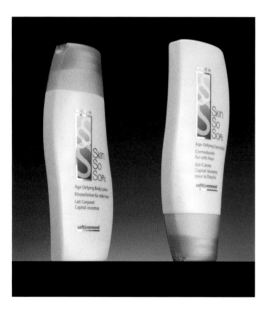

AVON –
SENSES & SKIN SO SOFT
(STRUCTURAL REDESIGN)
Design: *SiebertHead – Hai Tran
(Designer)*; Client: *Avon*; Materials:
High density polyethylene, polyethylene terephthalate; Manufacturing
process: *Injection moulding and
blow moulding*; Year: *2005*

RADOX SHOWER, BATH
AND HANDWASH (REDESIGN
Design: *DJPA Partnership – Sara
Jones (Designer)*; Client: *Sara Lee
Household and Body Care UK*;
Materials: *Polystyrene-latex clear
plastic labels*; Manufacturing
process: *Not disclosed*; Year: *2004*

PALMOLIVE THERMAL SPA
Design: *Dragon Rouge;* Client:
Palmolive; Materials: *Not disclosed;*
Manufacturing process: *Not disclosed;* Year: *2005*

RMK COLLECTION KIT
(SUGAR COLOR)
Design: *Sayuri Studio – Sayuri
Shoji, Fuyumi Sakamoto, Yumiko
Ietsugu (Designers);* Client: *Equipe,
Inc.;* Materials: *Chip board stock,
silver foil paper, polypropylene,
aluminum pouch, glass;* Manufacturing process: *Various;* Year: *2005*

The outside container is translucent, allowing the contents to be viewed easily. Bright colours call attention to the most unique feature of the packaging, the airless inside pocket. This container is packaged inside a starch foam outer box, which is entirely soluble in water and is certified non-transgenic. This is the first time this innovative material has been applied in the cosmetics world. Within the container, an internal pocket envelops the product in a vacuum seal. The vacuum provides optimum protection and preservation of the natural product inside, retaining its proper restitution and freshness. The view of the product inside the pocket within the container visually demonstrates the preciousness and naturalness of the product as a whole.

Der äußere Behälter ist durchsichtig und gibt den Blick auf das Produkt frei. Leuchtende Farben lenken die Aufmerksamkeit auf das herausstechendste Merkmal der Verpackung: die luftdicht verschlossene, innere Tasche. Der Behälter wird in einem Karton aus Stärkeschaum verpackt, der aus garantiert nicht genverändertem Mais hergestellt wird und vollständig in Wasser löslich ist. Das Vakuum garantiert optimalen Schutz und optimale Haltbarkeit des Naturprodukts und bewahrt dessen Wirkkraft und Frische. Der ungehinderte Blick auf das Produkt im Vakuum des Behälters verdeutlicht gleichzeitig, wie natürlich und hochwertig das Produkt ist.

Le flacon extérieur est transparent, et permet de voir le contenu aisément. Les couleurs vives attirent l'attention sur l'élément le plus original du flacon, la poche sous vide à l'intérieur. Ce flacon est emballé dans une boîte extérieure en mousse d'amidon, entièrement soluble dans l'eau et certifiée non transgénique. C'est la première fois que ce matériau innovant est utilisé dans le secteur des cosmétiques. À l'intérieur du flacon, le produit est scellé sous vide dans la poche interne. Le vide assure une restitution optimale du produit naturel en conservant sa fraîcheur. La vue du produit dans la poche, à l'intérieur du flacon, démontre visuellement la valeur et la qualité naturelle du produit dans son ensemble.

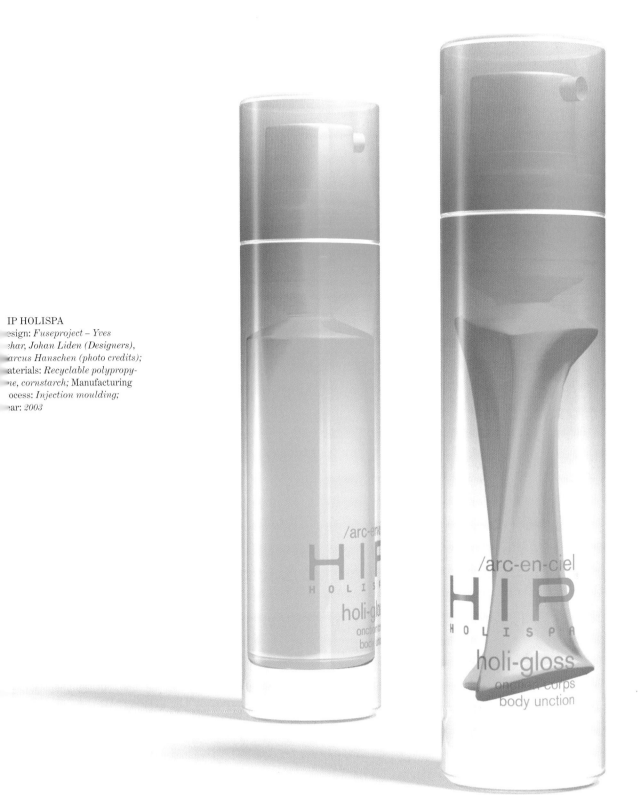

IP HOLISPA
esign: *Fuseproject – Yves*
har, Johan Liden (Designers),
arcus Hanschen (photo credits);
aterials: *Recyclable polypropy-*
ne, cornstarch; Manufacturing
ocess: *Injection moulding;*
ar: *2003*

WAITROSE UMI
Design: *Pearlfisher – Natalie Chung (Designer);* Client: *Waitrose Limited;* Awards: *UK Marketing Design Award, UK DBA Design Effectiveness Award;* Materials: *Polyethylene terephthalate (bottles), low density polyethylene* *(metalised tubes, labels), polyethylene (closures), glass (jars and bottles), Aluminium (containers), cardboard (sleeves);* Manufacturing process: *web flexo printing, offset litho printing;* Year: *2006*

BATH & BODY
COLLECTION SEPHORA
Design: *Not disclosed;* Client:
Sephora; Materials: *Plastic;*
Manufacturing process:
Not disclosed; Year: *2007*

The design brief called for iconic packaging to reflect the Original Source brand proposition: strong, honest and confident. Although the project encompassed a complete redesign of both the graphics and structure, the design of the structure became the key driver with the graphics following its lead. In the early stages of the rigorous design process, workshops with end users explored brand associations and structural cues. These were followed up with in-depth focus groups to determine and validate directions for the design. The selected concept incorporates both humanistic and natural elements. The strong upright tapering form is striking in elevation and can be carried across all elements in the range. Its stance is eager, with the boldly cut polished face angled towards the consumer. The touch surfaces are etched and tactile for better grip in the wet and create a strong contrast with the front face.

Die Aufgabe lautete, eine symbolträchtige Verpackung zu gestalten, die das Markenimage von Original Source reflektiert: stark, aufrichtig und souverän. Das Projekt erforderte ein komplettes Neudesign sowohl der grafischen als auch der formellen Gestaltung, wobei die Form das Schlüsselelement bildete, dem die Grafik zu folgen hatte. Bevor jedoch ein neues Design entworfen wurde, ermittelte man in Workshops mit Verbrauchern zunächst Markenassoziationen und strukturelle Probleme. Dann wurden Zielgruppenstudien durchgeführt, um die Anforderungen für das neue Design festzulegen. Das ausgewählte Projekt beinhaltet sowohl humanistische als auch natürliche Elemente. Die kräftige, sich nach oben verjüngende Form wirkt positiv aufstrebend und lässt sich auf alle Artikel der Serie anwenden. Das Produkt wirkt durch die polierte, dem Anwender zugeneigte Fläche positiv erwartungsvoll. Die Griffflächen sind mattiert, sodass sie auch nass einen guten Halt bieten, und kontrastieren auffällig mit der Frontseite.

Le cahier des charges précisait que le conditionnement du produit devait être emblématique et refléter le message de la marque Original Source : force, authenticité et assurance. Le projet supposait une transformation aussi bien du graphisme que de la structure, mais la conception de la structure est vite devenue centrale, et le graphisme a suivi. Dans les premiers stades du rigoureux processus de création, des ateliers ont été conduits avec des utilisateurs afin d'explorer les associations inspirées par la marque ainsi que les attentes structurelles. Des groupes d'étude ont ensuite déterminé et validé les idées conceptuelles.

Le concept sélectionné allie humain et naturel. La forme puissante, droite et fuselée est frappante de verticalité et peut être appliquée à tous les éléments de la gamme. Elle transmet de l'enthousiasme, avec sa face avant polie à coupe audacieuse. Les surfaces de préhension sont rugueuses et tactiles afin d'assurer une meilleure prise dans l'eau, et créent un fort contraste avec la face avant.

ORIGINAL SOURCE
PERSONAL CARE RANGE
Design: *Alloy – Nina
Warburton (Design Team Leader);*
Client: *PZ Cussons;* Materials:
Polypropylene; Manufacturing
process: *Blow moulding, injection
moulding;* Year: *2005*

BATHING OIL
Design: *Yasuo Tanaka (Art
Director/Graphic Designer);*
Client: *Package land;* Materials:
Plastic; Manufacturing process:
Not disclosed; Year: *2001*

PUCELLE
Design: *Forme Design Office –*
Yuko Hirai (Art Director), Ruriko
Nomura, Chizuru Yoshitsugu
(Designers); Client: *Mandom Corp.;*
Materials: *Resin, shrink film, paper,*
blister pack; Manufacturing process:
Blow moulding, injection moulding;
Year: *2005*

NATURA KID
(REDESIGN PROPOSAL AND
PACKAGING CONCEPT)
Client: *Tátil Design – Frederico
Gelli (Chief Designer), Bernardo
Eckardt, Patricia Larica, Fernanda
Caboia, Eduardo Câmara (Photo
credits);* Client: *Natura;* Materials: *Low density polyethylene, expanded
polyurathane, low density
polypropylene;* Manufacturing
process: *Blow moulding, injection
moulding;* Year: *2000*

Inspired by baby bottles, toys and teething
rings, Tátil developed an ergonomic packaging
line to offer comfort and fun to the kids. During
and after its use, each packaging turned into
a toy in order to stimulate imagination and
games. This redesign included ring toss, soap
bubbles, inflatable soap dishes, funny shaped
sponges and lots of colours.

Inspiriert durch Babyflaschen, Babyspiel-
zeug und Beißringe für zahnende Babys entwickelte Tátil eine ergonomische Verpackungslinie, die Kindern Spaß machen und ein
wohliges Gefühl vermitteln soll. Die Verpackungen lassen sich in Spielzeuge verwandeln,
die die Fantasie der Kinder anregen und das
Spielen fördern. Dazu zählen Wurfringe, Seifen-
blasen, aufblasbare Seifenschalen und lustige
Schwämme in vielen Farben.

Tátil a mis au point une ligne ergonomique,
inspirée des biberons, des jouets et des
anneaux de dentition, pour offrir confort et
amusement aux enfants. Pendant et après utilisation, chaque produit se transforme en jouet
pour stimuler l'imagination et les jeux. Ce remodelage incluait un jeu d'anneaux, des bulles de
savon, des porte-savons gonflables, des
éponges rigolotes et beaucoup de couleurs.

BOOTS BOTANICS
Design: *Lippa Pearce – Harry Pearce (Art Director), Joke Rasch (Designer);* Materials: *White carton board with white label paper stock for the labels;* Manufacturing process: *Flexo;* Year: *2005*

UYURA BODY WASH
esign: Sayuri Studio –
kiko Jinnai, Sayuri Shoji,
umi Hayashida, Daiju Aoki
Designers); Client: *Shiseido*
ine Toiletry; Materials:
olyethylene, polypropylene;
anufacturing process: In-
ould label, silkscreen;
ear: 2005

OLAY BODY – QUENCH
Design: *WSdV London;*
Client: *Procter & Gamble;*
Materials: *Polypropylene (cap),*
high density polyethylene (bottle);
Manufacturing process: *Blow*
moulding, injection moulding,
label-pressure sensitive wrap-
around; Year: *2005*

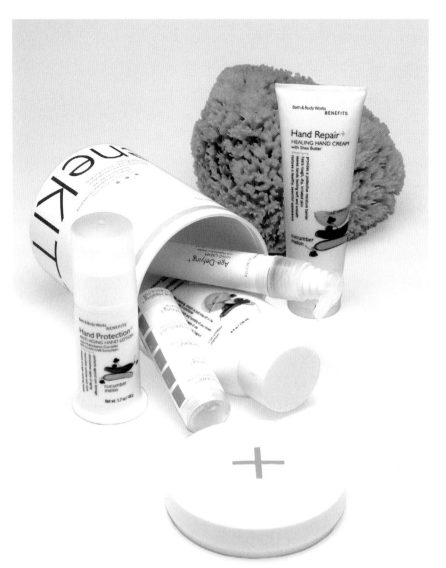

BENEFITS
(BATH & BODY WORKS)
Design: *slover [AND] company –*
Beth Galton (Photographer); Client:
Bath & Body Works; Materials:
Plastic, paper (fully recyclable
materials); Manufacturing process:
Various; Year: *2005*

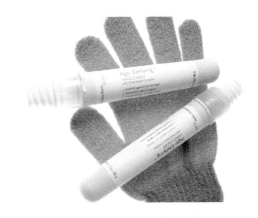

Bath & Body Works PLEASURES

vetyver

2 scented soaps

8 OZ 228 G

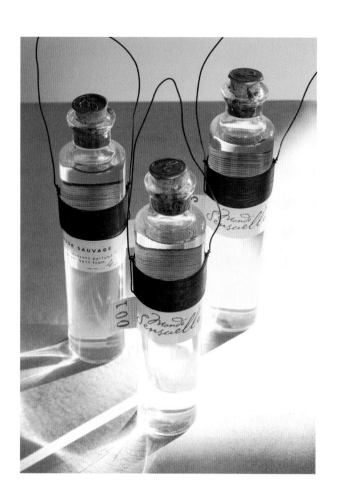

MONDE SENSUELLE BATH
& BODY COLLECTION
Designer: *slover [AND]
company;* Client: *Bath & Body
Works;* Materials: *Glass, paper;*
Manufacturing process: *Offset
lithography, embossing,
silkscreening, blow moulding;*
Year: *2005*

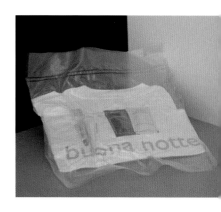

STARHOTEL
NIGHT COMFORT KIT
Design: *The Ad Store – Rachel Wild, Natalia Borri (Designers);* Client: *Starhotels;* Materials: *Various;* Manufacturing process: *Various;* Year: *2005*

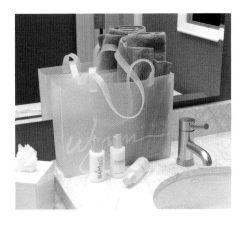

DESERT BAMBU
WYNN LAS VEGAS
(IN-ROOM AMENITIES)
Design: *slover [AND] company;*
Client: *Wynn Las Vegas, USA;*
Materials: *Various;* Manufacturing
Process: *Various;* Year: *2005*

TESCO SPA BODY THERAPY
Design: *R Design – David Richmond (Creative Director), Iain Dobson, Sarah Bustin (Designers).* Client: *Tesco;* Materials: *Glass, paper labels, metal lids, plastic;* Manufacturing process: *Various;* Year: *2006*

SCO FINEST CLASSIC
ALTH AND BEAUTY RANGE
sign: *R Design – David Rich-
nd (Creative Director)*, *Sarah
stin (Designer)*; Client: *Tesco*;
terials: *Various*; Manufacturing
cess: *Various*; Year: *2005*

GRADATION BOTTLE
Design: *Toyo Seikan Kaisha, Ltd;*
Client: *Toyo Seikan Kaisha, Ltd;*
Materials: *Polypropylene, poly-
ethylene;* Manufacturing process:
Blow moulding; Year: *2005*

HILOU
esign: *Fuseproject – Yves Behar*
(designer), Marcus Hanschen
(photo credits); Materials: *Low*
density polyurethane, acrylonitrile
butadiene styrene, coated polyethy-
lene; Manufacturing process: *Blow*
moulding, injection moulding;
Year: 2005

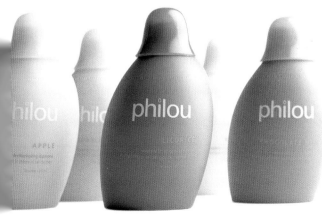

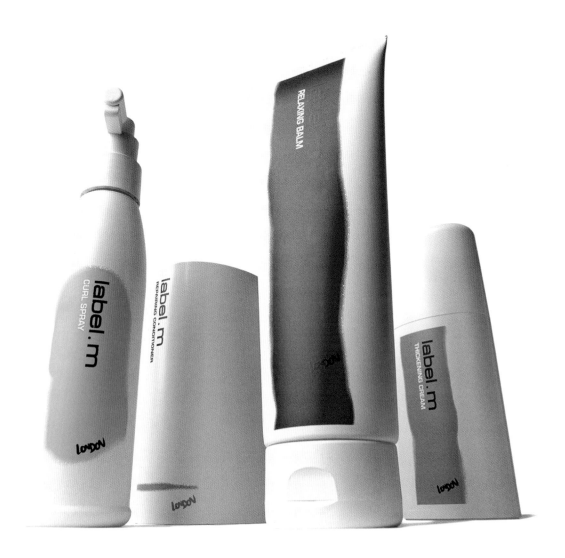

The Mascola family wanted to create a range so unique in both product and packaging that it would truly become a world success; a range that would challenge what consumers had come to expect from hair care products and that would create a ripple in the industry. That range is Label M. The bottle design came about after in-depth research into bottle structures leading to the choice of a structure with no apparent lid. The challenges, which involved overcoming the perceived high costs of production, were worth taking in order to deliver a finished product that would be both unique and innovative. Pure Equator, the design office, sourced the world for bottle manufacturers who were willing to share their vision, settling finally on a company from Florida whose passion for finding the right solution, no matter how difficult, matched their own. Through consultation it was concluded that with an outer sheath that encased the bottle, the teardrop shape could successfully be created in one piece yet still retain the strength that is paramount for successful production.

Die Familie Mascola hatte es sich zum Ziel gesetzt, eine in Verpackung und Produkt einzigartige Linie herauszubringen, die alle Erwartungen des Kunden an Haarpflegeprodukte übertreffen und ein Welterfolg werden sollte. Das Ergebnis ist Label M. Der Entwurf der Flasche entstand nach intensiven Untersuchungen diverser Flaschenformen. Das daraus resultierende Design ist eine Flasche ohne erkennbaren Verschluss. Ein Teil der Herausforderung bestand darin, die hoch erscheinenden Produktionskosten durch ein hervorragendes Produkt zu kompensieren, das sowohl einzigartig als auch innovativ ist. Zunächst aber suchte Pure Equator, das Designbüro, auf der ganzen Welt nach einem Flaschenhersteller, der bereit war, seine Vision zu teilen. Schließlich fand es eine Firma in Florida, die gewillt war, mit ihm eine perfekte Lösung zu suchen, unabhängig davon, wie groß die Schwierigkeiten waren. Schließlich wurde beschlossen, die Tropfenform mittels einer äußeren Hülle, die die Flasche umschließt, in einem Stück herzustellen, sodass die Flasche die für eine erfolgreiche Produktion notwendige Festigkeit behielt.

La famille Mascola voulait créer une gamme tellement unique, aussi bien par ses produits que par leur conditionnement, qu'elle serait un véritable succès mondial. Une gamme qui dépasserait ce que les consommateurs attendent aujourd'hui des produits capillaires, et qui aurait des répercussions dans le secteur. Cette gamme, c'est Label M. La bouteille est le résultat d'une recherche en profondeur sur les structures de bouteilles, à partir de laquelle on a choisi une structure sans couvercle apparent. Il a fallu surmonter l'obstacle de coûts de production élevés. Cela valait la peine, car le produit fini présenté est à la fois unique et innovant. L'agence de design Pure Equator a cherché dans le monde entier des fabricants de bouteilles disposés à partager sa vision, et a finalement choisi une entreprise de Floride dont la passion pour trouver la bonne solution, peu importe la difficulté du projet, correspondait à la sienne. De leur réflexion commune, il est ressorti qu'avec une gaine recouvrant la bouteille, on pourrait fabriquer d'une pièce la forme de larme tout en conservant la solidité primordiale pour la production.

LABEL M
Design: *Pure Equator – David Rogers (Creative Director), Sam Masters (Senior Designer);* Client: *Toni & Guy;* Awards: *London International Awards (Best Toiletries Packaging), Cream Awards (Bronze – Best Packaging), Mobius (Certificate for Creative Excellence);* Materials: *Plastic;* Manufacturing process: *Blow moulding, injection moulding;* Year: *2005*

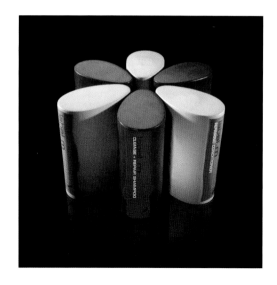

SEAH HAIRSPA
Design: *Lewis Moberly – Mary Lewis (Design Director), Sarah Cruz, Mary Lewis (Designers);* Client: *Schwarzkopf Professional;* Materials: *Plastic;* Manufacturing process: *Blow moulding, injection moulding;* Year: *2003*

STEPHEN KNOLL
COLLECTION
Design: *Kosé – Tatsuo Kannami (Creative Director), Fujio Hanawa (Art Director), Yoshimi Iguchi, Rieko Morita, Naoko Akai (Designers);* Client: *KOSÉ Corporation;* Materials: *Polyethylene terephthalate, polypropylene, TPX®, polyethylene, metal, aluminium, styrene acrylonitrile, paper;* Manufacturing process: *Injection moulding; blow moulding;* Year: *2005*

DANIÈLE RYMAN

Design: *Dew Gibbons – Shaun Dew, Steve Gibbons, Jacqui Owers (Designers);* Client: *The Boots Group;* Awards: *London International Advertising Awards (Finalist), Starpack (Bronze);*

Materials: *Soft touch uncoated board (Delos Cloud White);* Manufacturing process: *Lithographic printing, hot foil stamping, semi-gloss finish;* Year: *2004*

Danièle Ryman, whose bespoke aromatherapy skincare treatments are followed by an exclusive worldwide clientele, wanted to bring her expertise to a broader market. Dew Gibbons was briefed to create an identity and packaging for the new Danièle Ryman range of facial and body products to reflect the brand's high-end skincare positioning. The design office created a distinctive, uplifting pack shape; a unique colour – natural mink – and simple, elegant typography endorsed with Danièle's signature. Designed to clearly stand-out from the shelf as a crafted product from a skincare expert, the innovative outer pack is complimented by an elegant inner container. Transparent, it allows the focus to remain on the natural ingredients and extracts.

Danièle Ryman, deren maßgeschneiderte Aromatherapie-Hautpflegeprodukte sich weltweit einer exklusiven Anhängerschaft erfreuen, wollte ihre Produkte einem breiteren Markt zugänglich machen. Dew Gibbons wurde damit beauftragt, der neuen Danièle-Ryman-Produktreihe von Haut- und Körperpflegemitteln eine Identität und Verpackung zu geben, die der gehobenen Positionierung der Marke entsprechen. Das Design-Studio entwarf eine Verpackung mit auffälliger, ansprechender Form und einzigartiger Farbe – Natural Mink (Nerz natur) –, die als schlichten, eleganten Schriftzug die Signatur Danièle Rymans trägt. Das Design sorgt für Aufmerksamkeit und verdeutlicht den exquisiten Charakter der Produkte. In der innovativen Verpackung steckt ein elegantes Gefäß, dessen Transparenz den Fokus auf die natürlichen Ingredienzien und Extrakte lenkt.

Danièle Ryman, dont les soins de la peau s[ ] mesure à base d'aromathérapie sont prisés p[ ] une clientèle prestigieuse dans le monde entier, voulait appliquer son expertise à un marché plus vaste. L'agence Dew Gibbons fu[ ] chargée de créer l'identité et le conditionnement de la nouvelle gamme de soins pour le visage et pour le corps de Danièle Ryman, et[ ] devait ce faisant traduire le positionnement haut de gamme de la marque. Le bureau d'études a créé un conditionnement différen[ ] et tonique, avec une seule couleur – vison naturel – et une typographie simple et éléga[ ] te portant la signature de Danièle. Conçu po[ ] se détacher clairement dans les rayons et p[ ] être immédiatement identifiable comme un produit réalisé avec art par un expert en soin[ ] de la peau, l'emballage extérieur innovant contient un flacon élégant qui lui fait écho. Transparent, il laisse la vedette aux ingrédi[ ] et extraits naturels employés.

COVERGIRL OUTLAST
Design: *WSdV Chicago;*
Client: *Procter & Gamble;*
Awards: *HBA International
Packaging Design Awards
(winner);* Materials: *High-density
polyethelene, polypropelene;*
Manufacturing process: *Injection
blow moulding; injection moulding,
silk screen;* Year: *2004*

POLA THE MAKE B.A.
Design: *Pola – Takeshi Usui (Art
Director), Takashi Matsui, Yushi
Watanabe, Kazuhiko Kimishita,
Emi Yabusaki (Designers);* Client:
Pola Cosmetics, Inc.; Awards:
IF Design Award; Materials:
*Acrylonitrile butadiene styrene,
arsenic, polypropylene,
polyethylene, aluminium, glass;*
Manufacturing process: *Injection
moulding;* Year: *2005*

MOLTON BROWN
COLOUR COSMETICS
Design: *Jones Knowles Ritchie;*
Client: *Molton Brown;* Materials:
Not disclosed; Manufacturing
process: *Not disclosed;*
Year: *2005*

CARGO COLORCARDS™
Design: *Hana Zalzal;* Client:
CARGO Cosmetics; Materials: *Card stock, metallic box;* Manufacturing process: *Pressing;* Year: *2004*

CARGO LIQUID FOUNDATION
Design: *Hana Zalzal;* Client:
CARGO Cosmetics; Materials:
Laminate foil pouch; Manufacturing process: *flexographic printing;*
Year: *2004*

CARGO GLOSSYGREETINGS™
Design: *Motiv-8 Communications/ Hana Zalzal;* Client: *CARGO Cosmetics;* Materials: *Card stock printed with lip gloss blister inserted;* Manufacturing process: *Press print and hand assembled;* Year: *2005*

CARGO DAILYGLOSS™
Design: *Hana Zalzal;* Client: *CARGO Cosmetics;* Awards: *CPC Packaging Design Award, Brand Packaging Award;* Materials: *Foil backed blister pack, laminated thermofoils;* Manufacturing process: *Form fill, seal press;* Year: *2004*

CARGO ColorCards™ are ultra-portable, uper-flat, single-use cards of powder eye adows. Each decorative tin holds 28 Color- rds™ made up of 7 of CARGO's most famous e shadow colours (with 4 of each colour in ColorDeck). Each tin also includes playing rds with application tips.

CARGO ColorCards™ sind sehr praktische, ultraflache Karten mit Lidschattenpuder. Jede der dekorativen Blechdosen enthält 28 Color-Cards™ mit bis zu sieben der beliebtesten Lid-schatten von CARGO (vier von jeder Farbe in einem ColorDeck). Außerdem enthält die Dose Spielkarten mit Gebrauchsanweisungen.

CARGO ColorCards™, ce sont des cartes de fard à paupières à usage unique, ultra portables et extra plates. Chaque boîtier, en fer blanc très décoratif, contient 28 ColorCards™ composées des 7 fards à paupières les plus prisés de la marque CARGO (4 de chaque couleur dans un ColorDeck). Chaque boîtier inclut aussi des cartes à jouer avec des conseils d'application.

FASIO
Design: *Kosé – Tenji Motoda
(Art Director), Emiko Saito,
Shigeru Yamasaki (Designers)*;
Client: *Kosé Corporation*; Awards:
*Worldstars for Packaging, Japan
Packaging Contest, AsiaStar*;
Materials: *Acrylonitrile butadiene
styrene, polypropylene, polyethyl-
ene terephthalate, styrene acryloni-
trile, metal, paper*; Manufacturing
process: *Blow moulding; injection
moulding*; Year: *2004*

VISÉE
Design: *Kosé – Fujio Hanawa
(Creative Director), Yoshimi Iguch
(Art Director), Naoko Yokokura
(Designer)*; Client: *Kosé Corporation*; Materials: *Styrene acrylonitrile, acrylonitrile butadiene
styrene, polypropylene, glass,
metal*; Manufacturing process:
*Blow moulding; injection
moulding*; Year: *2003*

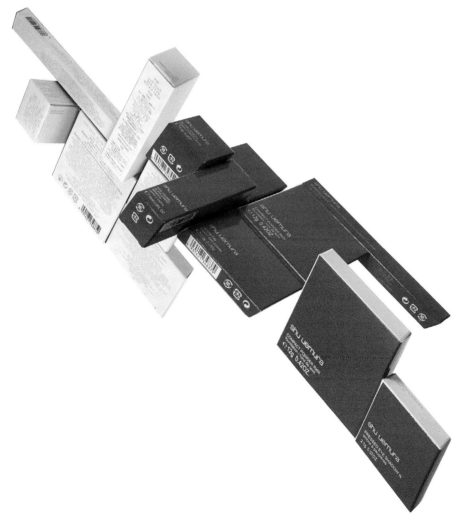

MEA
Design: *R Design – David Richmond (Creative Director), David Gray (Designer);* Client: *Debenhams;* Materials: *Glass, paper, plastic, metal;* Manufacturing process: *Various;* Year: *2000*

SHU UEMURA COSMETICS
Design: *Sayuri Studio – Sayuri Shoji;* Client: *Shu Uemura;* Materials: *Glass, paper, plastic, metal;* Manufacturing process: *Various;* Year: *2006*

ESTÉE LAUDER PRIME FX
Design: *Sayuri Studio – Sayuri Shoji, Yumico Ietsugu, Nobuto Wakada (Designers);* Client: *Esteé Lauder & Companies;* Materials: *Polyethylene, polypropylene, anodised metal,* Manufacturing process: *Various;* Year: *2005*

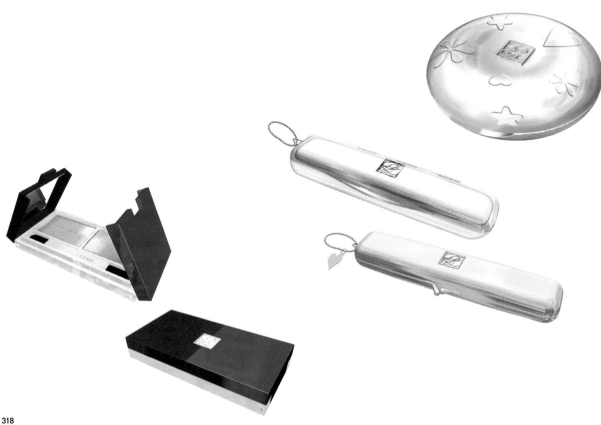

**LOVELY
FROM SARAH
JESSICA PARKER**
Design: *Not disclosed;* Client:
Coty; Materials: *Glass, metal;*
Manufacturing process:
Blow moulding; Year: *2005*

**BOUDOIR
FROM VIVIENNE WESTWOOD**
Design: *Not disclosed;* Client:
Coty; Materials: *Glass, metal;*
Manufacturing process:
Blow moulding; Year: *1998*

**LIVE
FROM JENNIFER LOPEZ**
Design: *Not disclosed;* Client:
Coty; Materials: *Glass, metal;*
Manufacturing process:
Blow moulding; Year: *2005*

COMME DES GARÇONS
COSMETIC LINE
Design: *Marc Atlan;* Client:
Comme des Garçons Parfums;
Materials: *Various;* Manufacturing
process: *Various;* Year: *1994- 2000*

Setting itself apart from what jurors called the "blobular" packaging, so common among avant-garde perfumeries, the bottle and case for Shiseido's 5S adeptly combine hard and soft in a single packaging aesthetic. Angular without appearing sharp, the translucent plastic pieces work together to suggest a mysterious and tactile form. Whether viewed through the outer package or alone, the frosted lavender bottle seems to float in space without revealing its interior walls, the pump or the perfume inside. The vessel itself can be set down in several positions, depending on the user's preference or mood. Yet the piece's function is neither hidden nor difficult to understand, and it's comfortable to hold and use. Stronger and easier to ship than glass, the plastic doesn't need cardboard reinforcement or inserts to protect it, which allows the bottle and case to work together without additional printed pieces. The material also enabled Rashid to create the bottle's unusual five-pointed shape (to reflect the 5S name).

Flasche und Verpackung für das neue Shiseido 5S setzen sich wohltuend von dem ab, was die Juroren mit „Kleckserei" bezeichneten. Das provokative Design verbindet harte und weiche Konturen geschickt zu einer stimmigen Verpackungsästhetik. Die eckigen, jedoch nicht kantigen, durchscheinenden Kunststoffelemente fügen sich harmonisch zu einem geheimnisvollen und handlichen Körper zusammen. Sowohl in der Verpackung als auch ohne Verpackung scheint die milchige Flasche frei im Raum zu schweben. Ihr Inneres, die Pumpe und das Parfüm, wird jedoch dem Blick nicht preisgegeben. Die Flasche kann ganz nach Belieben in unterschiedlichen Positionen aufgestellt werden. Die Funktion des Gefäßes ist aber in allen Positionen eindeutig, und seine Funktionalität wird nicht eingeschränkt. Der Kunststoffbehälter ist nicht nur einfacher zu transportieren als eine Glasflasche, sondern auch stabiler, und muss daher nicht durch eine zusätzliche Pappverstärkung oder einen Einleger geschützt werden. Flasche und Verpackung können so ohne weitere bedruckte Teile frei miteinander harmonieren. Erst das innovative Material ermöglichte Rashid die Gestaltung dieser einzigartigen fünfeckigen Flasche. Der Name 5S greift die Form des Gefäßes auf.

Se démarquant de ce que les jurés appellent le conditionnement « blobulaire » (des formes coulantes), si courant dans la parfumerie d'avant-garde, la bouteille et l'étui audacieux du 5S de Shiseido allient merveilleusement les matières rigides et souples dans l'esthétique globale du conditionnement. Angleuses sans paraître agressives, les pièces de plastique translucide s'assemblent pour suggérer une forme mystérieuse et tactile. Qu'on la regarde directement ou à travers l'étui, la bouteille couleur lavande givrée semble flotter dans l'espace sans révéler ses parois internes, sa pompe ou le parfum à l'intérieur. On peut la poser de différentes façons, selon la préférence ou l'humeur de chacun. Sa fonction n'est pourtant jamais cachée ni difficile à comprendre, et elle est agréable à tenir en main et à utiliser. Plus solide et plus facile à transporter que le verre, le plastique n'a pas besoin d'être protégé par des renforts en carton. Cela permet de laisser le tandem bouteille et étui fonctionner sans éléments imprimés supplémentaires. Ce matériau a également permis à Rashid de créer la forme inhabituelle de la bouteille, avec ses cinq sommets (faisant écho au nom 5S).

METASENSE
Design: *Karim Rashid;* Client: *5S
Shiseido;* Awards: *I.D. Magazine –
Annual Design Review (Design
Distinction & Best of Category);*
Materials: *Polypropylene;* Manu-
facturing process: *Blow moulded
(bottle), injection moulded (case);*
Year: *2001*

PERFUME 09
Design: *Fuseproject – Yves Behar,
Johan Liden, Geoffrey Petrizzi
(Designers), Robert Schlatter,
Marcus Hanschen (Photo Credits);*
Materials: *Polyurethane rubber,
glass;* Manufacturing process: *Not
disclosed;* Year *2002*

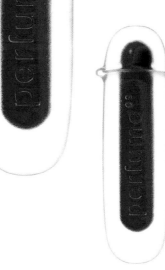

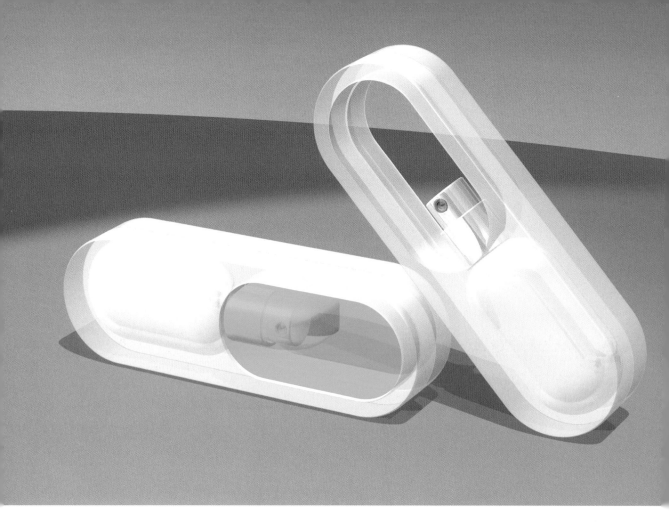

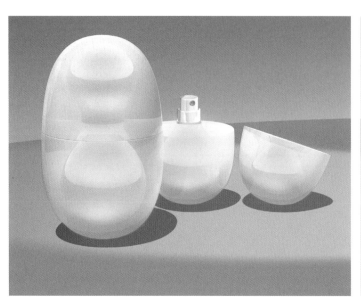

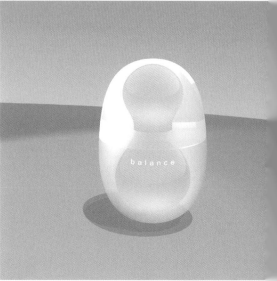

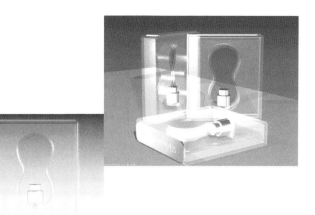

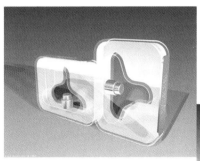

PRESCRIPTIVES
Design: *Karim Rashid;* Client:
Not disclosed; Materials: *Concept;*
Manufacturing process:
Not in production; Year: *2004*

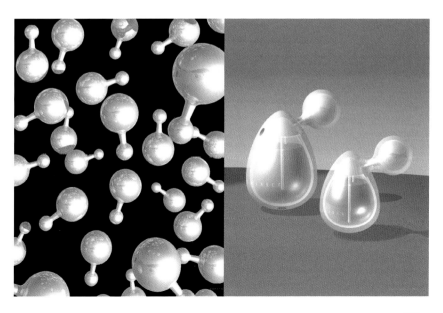

MICHELINE ARCIER
Design: *R Design – David Richmond (Creative Director), Charlotte Hayes, Suzanne Langley (Designers);* Client: *Micheline Arcier;* Materials: *Glass, Card, Paper;* Manufacturing process: *Various;* Year: *2006*

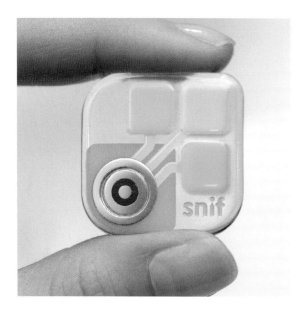

SNIF
Design: *PDD Group – Miles Hawley, Dan Brady, Mark Tosey (Designers)*; Client: *PDD Internal Futures Concept*; Materials: *Conceptual*; Manufacturing process: *Not in production*; Year: *2005*

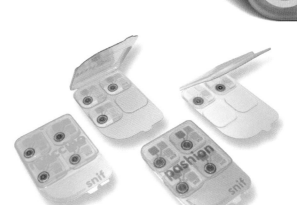

The SNIF fragrance device can be placed anywhere on the body. Dual sensors monitor both the body conditions of the wearer and environmental change. These readings can then be processed to calculate, combine and release optimal levels of scent. The fragrance range is sensitive to skin balance and will naturally complement the user's body. A more alkaline skin type might use a more acidic-based fragrance to provide natural balance, and vice versa. When combined with other aspects of skin chemistry the device will deliver scent that is genuinely and individually inspired by the wearer. Because SNIF is as much an accessory as it is a fragrance it has immense branding potential; for the first time a fragrance product could be visible on the body it perfumes.

Der SNIF-Duftspender kann überall am Körper getragen werden. Zwei Sensorsysteme überwachen sowohl die Körperfunktionen des Trägers als auch die Bedingungen der Umgebung. Die Messungen werden verarbeitet, und aus den Ergebnissen errechnet der Duftspender dann die optimale Menge an abzugebendem Duftstoff. Alle Düfte der Duftpalette reagieren auf das empfindliche Gleichgewicht der Haut und können sich auf natürliche Weise dem Träger anpassen. Basische Hauttypen sollten für eine natürliche Balance einen eher säuregeprägten Duft verwenden und umgekehrt. Kombiniert mit anderen Aspekten der Hautchemie und äußeren Einflüssen liefert der Duftspender einen einzigartigen, allein auf den Träger abgestimmten Duft. Da SNIF sowohl ein Accessoire als auch ein Duftspender ist, hat es ein immenses Markenpotential. Zum ersten Mal könnte ein Produkt der Parfümindustrie sichtbar am Körper getragen werden.

Le dispositif SNIF peut se placer n'importe où sur le corps. Un double capteur contrôle le paramètres corporels du porteur et les modifications de l'environnement. Ces lectures peuvent ensuite être traitées pour calculer, combiner et libérer des doses de parfum optimales. La gamme s'adapte à la nature de la peau de l'utilisateur, et complète naturellement son corps. Un type de peau alcalin pourra utiliser un parfum plus acide afin de rétablir l'équilibre naturel, et inversement. Combiné avec d'autres aspects de la chimie de la peau, l'appareil délivrera un parfum véritablement inspiré par chaque porteur. SNIF étant un accessoire tout autant qu'un parfum, son potentiel en termes de stratégie de marque est immense. Pour la première fois, un produit de parfumerie peut être vu sur le corps qu'il parfume.

Invent Your Scent for The Body Shop, took the idea of creating your own personalised fragrance and turned it into a simple and understandable concept in-store. Success was dependent on translating the complexities of the idea "layering scents" into something straightforward and clearly understood by the multicultural audience of young consumers worldwide. Therefore, each element of the design programme – the name, brand identity, in-store presentation and packaging – needed to communicate the product's proposition in the simplest, most direct and appealing way. The design used language, the bottle shape and a spectrum of colour to simplify the product idea and to manage the hierarchy of in-store communication. The bottles, with their concave recesses, allowed the different scents to "interlock," communicating the product concept of mixing fragrances. The clamshell design for the sampler kit with its stylish shape and semi-translucent nature of the material made it an ideal gift item.

„Invent Your Scent" für die Body-Shop-Kette griff die Idee auf, eine ganz persönliche Duftnote kreieren zu können, und verwandelte die Idee in ein einfach verständliches Verkaufskonzept. Wichtig für den Erfolg des neuen Produkts war, die komplexe Kunst der Duftzusammenstellung in ein Konzept umzusetzen, das der jungen, multikulturellen Zielgruppe rund um den Globus einen einfachen Zugang ermöglichte. Daher mussten alle Designelemente, wie Name, Markenidentität, Präsentation in den Filialen und Verpackung, die Idee des Produkts so einfach, verständlich und ansprechend wie möglich vermitteln. Entsprechend wurden Sprache, Flaschenform und Farbpalette ausgewählt, um eine einfache Kommunikation in den Verkaufsstellen zu ermöglichen. Die konkave Einbuchtung an den Flaschen erlaubt es, die Gefäße harmonisch aneinanderzureihen, und führt bildlich noch einmal das Konzept der Kombination vor. Das ausgefallene Design, die elegante Form und die transparente Qualität machen das Sampler Kit zu einem attraktiven Geschenkartikel.

Le projet « Inventez votre parfum », pour The Body Shop, est parti de l'idée de créer un parfum personnalisé, mais avec un concept simple à utiliser en magasin. Le succès dépendait de la traduction de la complexité de l'idée – « superposer des senteurs » – en quelque chose de très simple, compréhensible pour le public multiculturel des jeunes consommateurs du monde entier. C'est pourquoi chaque élément du programme de conception (le nom, l'identité de la marque, la présentation dans les magasins et le conditionnement) devait communiquer la proposition du produit de la manière la plus simple, la plus directe et la plus attrayante possible. Le design utilise le langage, la forme de la bouteille et un éventail de couleurs pour simplifier l'idée du produit et pour gérer la hiérarchie de la communication en magasin. Les bouteilles, avec leurs renfoncements concaves, permettent « d'emboîter » les différentes senteurs, et transmettent l'idée de mélange des parfums. La boîte « coquille » choisie pour le kit d'échantillons, élégante et semi-translucide, en fait un cadeau idéal.

INVENT YOUR SCENT
Design: *Dew Gibbons – Shaun Dew, Steve Gibbons, Christian Eves (Designers)*; Client: *The Body Shop*; Awards: *D&AD, London International Advertising Awards (Finalist), One Show (Finalist)*; Materials: *Glass, polypropylene*; Manufacturing process: *Blow moulding, injection moulding*; Year: *2005*

329

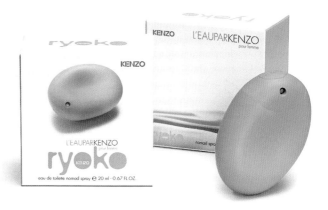

KENZO RYOKO
Design: *Karim Rashid;*
Client: *Kenzo;* Materials:
Polypropylene; Manufacturing
process: *Injection moulding,
lacquering;* Year: *2007*

Smooth as silk, the Ryoko can be slipped into a pocket or nestled in the palm of the hand like a caress. Their unique design, to the eye and to the touch, makes them instant objects of desire. A specially designed neoprene pouch envelops them, keeping them safe. Each fragrance, with Flower, Summer, Air, l'Eau par Kenzo, or Kenzo pour Homme, is easily identifiable by the coloured pebble. Karim Translated Kenzo's existing range of perfumes into one line of small travel size bottles while giving each fragrance its own identity. The allover pebble design of the Ryoko makes it uniquely tactile and friendly. There is no fixed approach to handling the bottle.

Ryoko kann in die Tasche gesteckt oder wie ein Handschmeichler in der Handfläche gehalten werden. Das optisch und haptisch einzigartige Design macht Ryoko so begehrenswert. Eine speziell entwickelte Haut aus Neopren umhüllt die Parfümbehälter und schützt sie. Jede Duftnote wie etwa Flower, Summer Air, l'Eau par Kenzo oder Kenzo pour Homme hat ihre eigene Farbe. Mit diesem Design entwickelte Karim für die bestehende Parfümkollektion von Kenzo eine Reisekollektion mit kleinen Behältern und verlieh jeder Geruchsnote ihre eigene Identität. Das kieselförmige Design von Ryoko macht die Produktreihe so attraktiv und handlich. Es gibt keine festgelegte Handhabung für diese Parfümflasche.

Doux comme de la soie, Ryoko se glisse dans une poche ou se dépose au creux de la main comme une caresse. Son design unique, à l'œil et au toucher, le rend irrésistible. Une peau en néoprène créée tout spécialement l'enveloppe et le protège. Chaque fragrance, Flower, Summer, Air, l'Eau par Kenzo ou Kenzo pour Homme, s'identifie facilement par la couleur de son galet. Karim a transposé la gamme de parfums Kenzo en une ligne de petits flacons de voyage tout en donnant à chaque fragrance sa propre identité. La conception unique de la surface du galet le rend sensuel et invitant. Il n'y a aucune façon prédéterminé de prendre le flacon en main.

Coley Porter Bell was appointed to revamp the Kotex brand, which in European markets was in serious decline, had a weak image and was seen as outdated. The research identified that women are enjoying a surge in pride in being female and this became the opportunity to move Kotex away from the strictures of the san-pro category. Packaging was a key factor in bringing this new brand standing to life. The design solution made bold use of red with beacons of modern femininity, i.e. migrating symbols from the world of beauty and fashion and using the language and humour women share with each other. The bold symbols appear on a clean white background to make the packaging uncluttered and a thing of beauty.

Kotex hatte auf dem europäischen Markt ein schwaches Image und verlor immer mehr an Bedeutung, und so erhielt Coley Porter Bell den Auftrag, der Marke ein vollkommen neues Gesicht zu verleihen. Marktforschungen ergaben, dass die europäische Frau wieder stärker ihre Weiblichkeit betont. So konnte Kotex aus der starren Kategorie der Hygieneartikel herausgenommen werden. Die Designlösung bediente sich mutig der Farbe Rot, kombinierte sie mit Symbolen moderner Weiblichkeit, die aus der Welt der Kosmetik und Mode stammen, und orientierte sich sprachlich an jener Art von Humor, den Frauen untereinander pflegen. Die Symbole erscheinen auf der Verpackung auf rein weißem Untergrund, sodass diese übersichtlich und fast wie ein Modeartikel wirkt.

L'agence Coley Porter Bell a été chargée de repenser la marque Kotex. Elle était en sérieux déclin sur les marchés européens, et avait une image médiocre et dépassée. La recherche menée a mis en évidence une forte augmentation de la fierté que les femmes éprouvent à appartenir à leur sexe. C'était l'occasion pour Kotex de s'affranchir des contraintes du strict hygiénisme. Pour insuffler une vie nouvelle à cette marque, le conditionnement était essentiel. La solution choisie fait une utilisation audacieuse du rouge et des symboles de la féminité moderne, en reprenant les codes du monde de la beauté et de la mode et en utilisant le langage et l'humour féminins. Ces symboles audacieux apparaissent sur un fond blanc immaculé, faisant du paquet un objet dépouillé et esthétique.

KOTEX
Design: *Coley Porter Bell;*
Client: *Kimberly Clark;* Materials:
Various; Manufacturing process:
Not disclosed; Year: *2005*

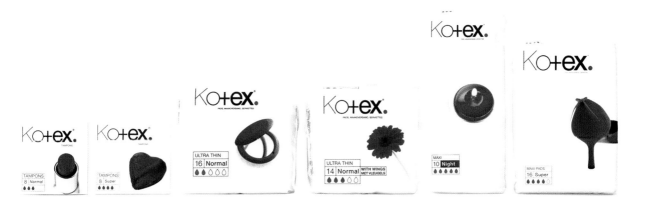

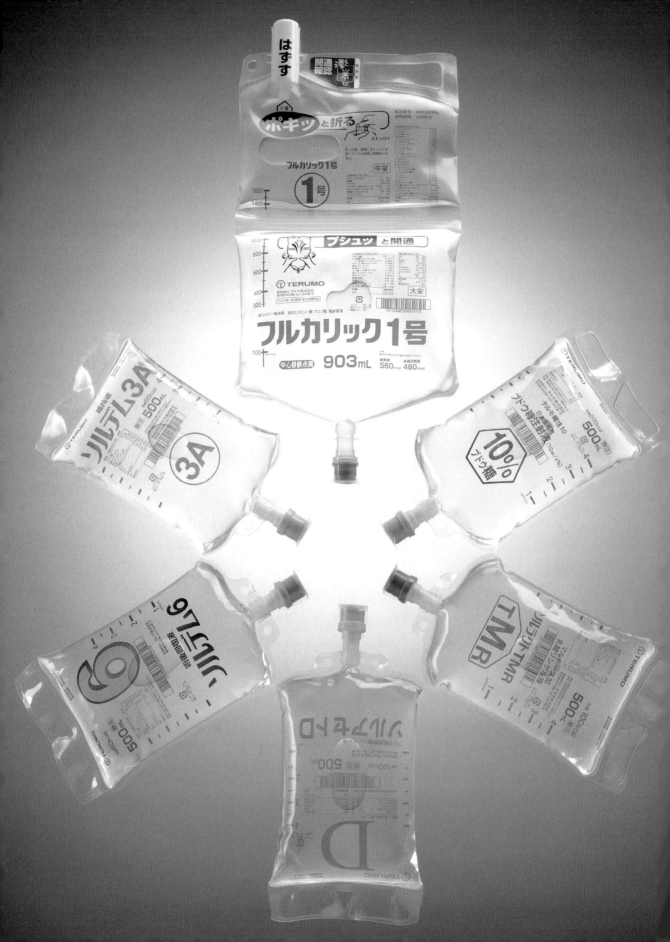

VII

PHARMACEUTICAL

Creative Leap
Pearson Matthews
PI3
SiebertHead
Terumo
Tin Horse Design Team

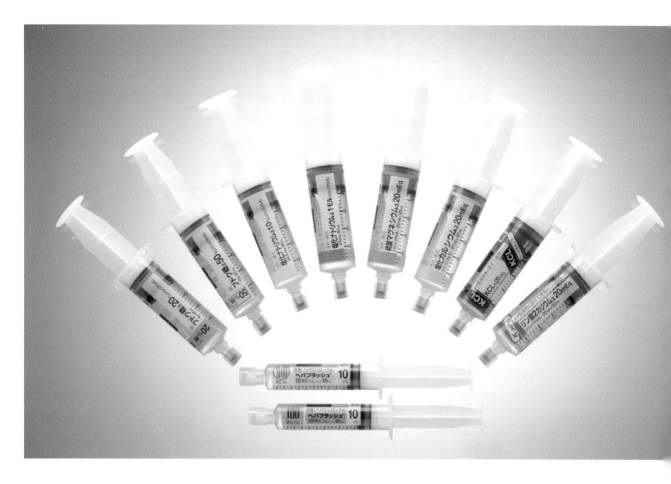

P. 332
SOFT BAG FOR INFUSION
Design/Client: *Terumo;* Awards:
Good Design Award; Materials:
EVAC, rubber; Manufacturing
process: *Not disclosed;* Year: *2003*

P. 334
SYRINGE
Design/Client: *Terumo;* Awards:
Good Design Award; Materials:
*Polypropylene, thermoplastic
elastomer, rubber;*

Manufacturing process:
Not disclosed; Year: *2003*

Clinical Design Ltd. invented an ingenious yet simple, kinked tube dose control mechanism, but also recognised that this new technology had to be as seductive as it is clever. The Tin Horse design team worked closely with the pharmaceutical engineering team at The Technology Partnership, creating a compact, user-friendly external envelope that optimised the technology, the appearance and the user experience. Breath actuation has the potential to provide greatly enhanced patient care but the cost of complex devices can seriously limit patient access. The vision from the start was to use this simple technological innovation to smash the paradigm that breath actuation is expensive. Our FMCG (Fast Moving Consumer Goods) experience enabled us to balance the need for low cost, with genuinely user-friendly and appealing design.

Clinical Design Ltd. entwickelte ein geniales und zugleich einfaches neues Dosierungssystem mit einer geknickten Röhre. Die neue Technologie sollte aber nicht nur praktisch, sondern auch ansprechend sein, um sich auf dem Markt durchzusetzen. Die Designer von Tin Horse arbeiteten eng mit den Ingenieuren von The Technology Partnership zusammen und entwickelten eine kompakte, benutzerfreundliche äußere Hülle, die sowohl die Technologie als auch die Form und Bedienung optimierte. Die Nutzung von Inhalationshilfen kann die Pflege der Patienten stark erleichtern, die Kosten der komplizierten Geräte beschränkt jedoch den Kreis der Nutznießer auf eine kleine Gruppe von Patienten. Dieses Projekt will mit seiner einfachen technologischen Innovation das Vorurteil entkräften, dass Inhalationshilfen teuer sein müssen. Unsere Erfahrung mit FMCG (Fast Moving Consumer Goods) ermöglicht uns, das Kostenniveau niedrig zu halten und dennoch ein benutzerfreundliches und ansprechendes Design zu entwickeln.

Clinical Designs Ltd. a inventé un mécanisme de contrôle de dosage muni d'un tube coudé, à la fois simple et ingénieux, mais savait également que cette nouvelle technologie devait être aussi attrayante qu'ingénieuse. L'équipe de design de Tin Horse a travaillé en étroite collaboration avec l'équipe d'ingénieurs pharmaceutiques de Technology Partnership. Ils ont créé une enveloppe externe compacte et conviviale qui optimise la technologie, l'apparence ainsi que l'expérience de l'utilisateur. L'activation respiratoire permet d'améliorer l'état du patient de manière significative, mais le coût des appareils complexes peut constituer un obstacle pour le patient. L'idée de départ était d'utiliser cette innovation technologique simple pour en finir avec l'idée qu'un appareil respiratoire est trop cher. Notre expérience dans les produits de grande consommation nous a permis de créer un appareil convivial au prix abordable et au design attrayant.

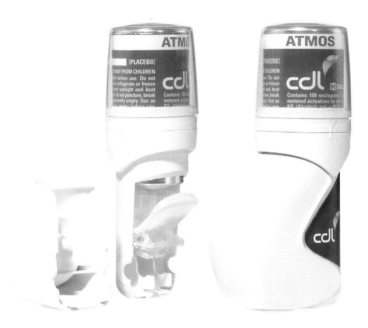

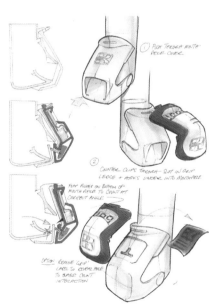

(1) PUSH THROUGH MOUTH PIECE COVER.

(2) COUNTER CLIPS THROUGH - SLOT IN GRIP LEDGE + HOOKS UNDER INTO MOUTHPIECE

FLAT PUSHES ON BOTTOM OF MOUTH PIECE TO COUNT AT CORRECT ANGLE

OPTION: REMOVE 'GRIP' LABEL TO OVERRIDE TO BLOCK COUNT INTERACTION

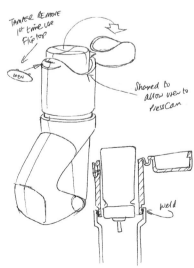

TAMPER REMOVE 1st TIME USE Flip top

OPEN

Shaped to allow use to press Can

weld

-HALER

esign: *Tin Horse Design Team;*
lient: *Clinical Designs Ltd;*
wards: *Medical Futures Best*
ommercial Proposition, Medical
utures Best Improvement to
atient Care; Materials:
olypropylene actuator parts,
ink" valve polypropylene and
etal self adhesive polyethylene
bels, aluminium standard
etered dose aerosol can;
anufacturing process:
jection moulding with part
ser weld assembly; Year: *2005*

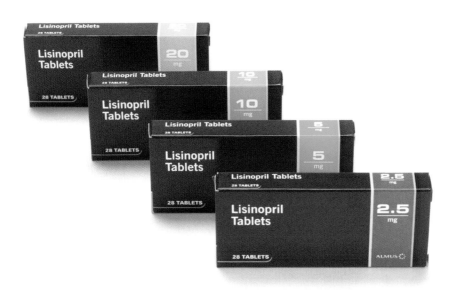

ALMUS
Design: *Creative Leap;* Client:
Alliance Unichem Plc; Awards:
*DBA Design Effectiveness Award
(Winner);* Materials: *Carton;*
Manufacturing process: *Not dis-
closed;* Year: *2004*

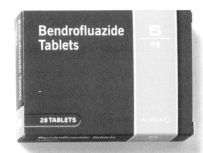

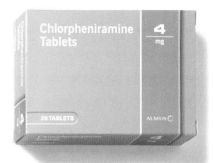

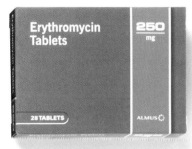

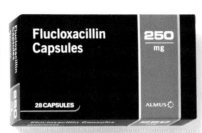

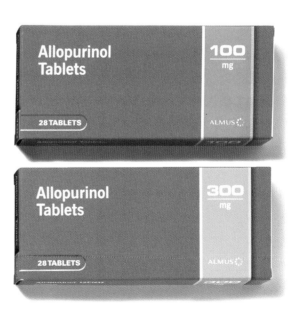

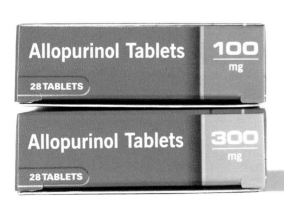

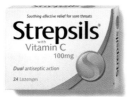

STREPSILS (GLOBAL
PACKAGING)
Design: *Creative Leap;* Client:
Boots Healthcare International;
Awards: *London International
Awards (Finalist);* Materials:
Various; Manufacturing process:
Not disclosed; Year: *2004*

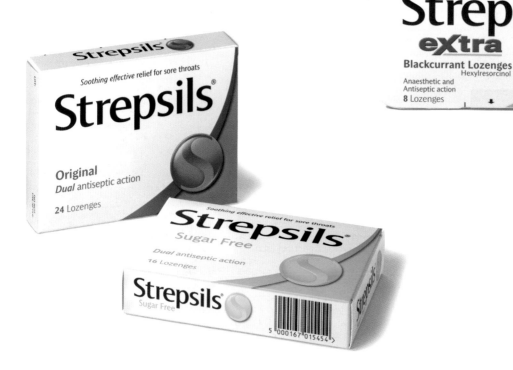

NUROFEN MOBILE PACK
Design: *Pearson Matthews;* Client:
*Boots Healthcare International /
Crookes Healthcare;* Awards: *OTC
Bulletin Awards for OTC Market-
ing Innovation of the Year, Best
New OTC Packaging;* Materials:
Acrylonitrile butadiene styrene;
Manufacturing process: *Injection
moulding;* Year: *2002*

Boots Healthcare International have long recognised that, within the boundaries of a "box" construction, the conventional use of cardboard is less than ideal in terms of quality, consumer friendliness, experience and added-value. Market research has shown that having to carry a pack of pain relief tablets around can be frustrating as the pack often gets damaged or is too big to fit into one's pocket or handbag. In fulfilling this demanding brief, BHI with Pearson Matthews have developed the smart "Mobile Pack" – accommodating a standard 12-tablet blister, which meets the durability and portability a consumer needs whilst also aligning with the Nurofen brand essence and personality. The pack consists of three high quality silver injection-moulded ABS plastic components. The front and rear case-halves are "snapped" together, trapping the hinged-lid closure in place. The lid-clip has a reassuring audible and tactile "click" when closed. There is now no need for an outer cardboard box – the pack is visible and stands alone at point of purchase. The Mobile Pack was developed from initial sketches and concept models, through CAD, regulatory approval, tooling, moulding and filling to stock-in-ware-house in just 19 weeks and went on sale nationwide at the beginning of September 2002.

Boots Healthcare International hatte bereits seit langem erkannt, dass Kartonverpackungen weder benutzerfreundlich sind noch einen sonstigen zusätzlichen Nutzen aufweisen. In einer Umfrage beklagten viele Verbraucher, die Schmerztabletten mitführen müssen, dass die Verpackungen oft beschädigt werden und zu groß für Hosen- oder Handtasche sind. Den Verbraucherwünschen und -bedürfnissen entsprechend entwickelte Pearson Matthews das praktische „Mobile Pack", das eine handelsübliche Blisterpackung mit zwölf Tabletten fasst, den Stabilitäts- und Tragbarkeitsansprüchen der Konsumenten entspricht und zur Marke Nurofen passt. Die Packung besteht aus drei hochwertigen, spritzgussgeformten ABS-Kunst-stoffkomponenten. Vorder- und Rückseite werden aufeinander gesteckt und halten so den Scharnierdeckel. Der Deckel schließt mit einem vertrauenerweckenden, hör- und fühlbaren Klicken. Eine Kartonumverpackung ist nicht mehr erforderlich. Die Verpackung hat einen hohen Aufmerksamkeitswert in den Regalen. Das „Mobile Pack" wurde von den ersten gezeichneten Entwürfen über Konzeptmodelle, CAD-Zeichnungen, gesetzliche Genehmigungs-verfahren, Werkzeug- und Formherstellung bis hin zur ersten Fabrikfertigung in nur 19 Wochen entwickelt und ging Anfang September 2002 in den Verkauf.

Il y a longtemps que Boots Healthcare International s'est aperçu que, pour la fabrication des boîtes, l'utilisation traditionnelle du carton est loin d'être idéale en termes de qualité, de commodité, d'impression générale et de valeur ajoutée. Des études de marché ont montré qu'il peut être frustrant de devoir porter sur soi une boîte de comprimés antidouleur car, en plus de s'abîmer facilement, la boîte est souvent trop grande pour tenir dans la poche ou le sac à main. Pour y remédier, BHI et Pearson Matthews ont créé le « Mobile Pack » intelligent – une plaquette standard de 12 comprimés, à la fois solide et pratique à transporter, et qui respecte l'essence et l'identité de la marque Nurofen. L'étui se compose de trois éléments en plastique ABS de haute qualité, moulés à injection et de finition argentée. La face et le dos du boîtier sont clipsés ensemble et maintiennent le couvercle à charnière en place. Ce dernier se ferme en se clipsant et émet un « clic » sonore et tactile rassurant. La boîte externe en carton n'est désormais plus d'aucune utilité. L'étui est suffisamment visible et est présenté tel quel dans les points de vente. Le Mobile Pack a été conçu d'après des croquis et des modèles conceptuels, puis est passé par les étapes de conception assistée par ordinateur, approbation réglementaire, outillage, moulage, remplissage et mise en entrepôt, tout cela en seulement 19 semaines. Il a été mis en vente à l'échelle nationale au début du mois de septembre 2002.

IMIGRAN
Design: *PI3 – Steve Kelsey, Jed O'Brien, Dave Salmon;* Client: *Glaxo-SmithKline;* Awards: *Starpack Award;* Materials: *Polypropylene;* Manufacturing process: *Injection moulded components, inline filling and closure;* Year: *2005*

CLEVERNAME
Design: *Pearson Matthews;* Client: *Helen Hamlyn Research Centre / Design Business Association;* Awards: *DBA Design Challenge for Inclusive Design (Winner);* Materials: *Cardboard;* Manufacturing process: *Stamped, bent, folded and glued;* Year: *2004*

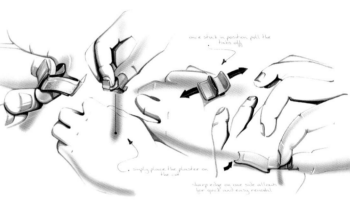

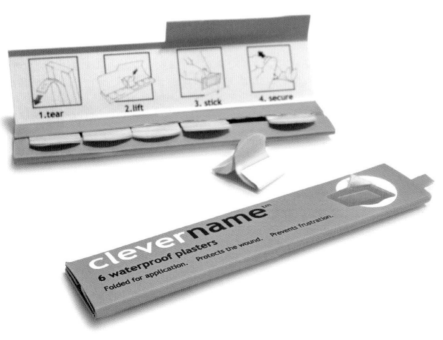

CLEARBLUE
Design: *Pearson Matthews;* Client:
Unipath; Materials: *Polystyrene;*
Manufacturing process: *Injection
moulded;* Year: *2004*

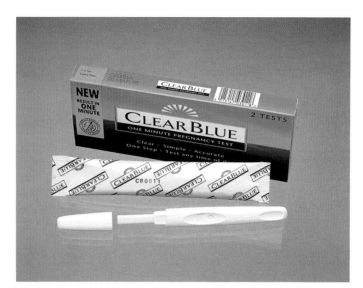

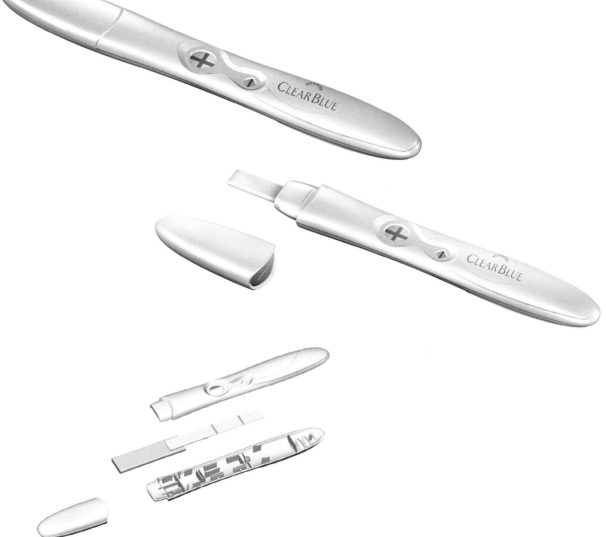

SiebertHead identified a need for pharmaceutical packaging that is easy to open for older consumers as well as consumers with disabilities, whilst being inaccessible to children. The intelligent pharmaceutical packaging, Pharmassist uses biometric scanning, a multi-sensory reminder system, a visual display and audio information system to communicate with the patient. When the pharmacists dispense medicine they will programme the Pharmassist with the patient's prescription data. The pharmacist will also scan the patients' fingerprint, which will be used as the key to open the pack. When it is time for the patients to take their medicine the Pharmassist will alert them. Once the patient's fingerprint is confirmed by the biometric scanner, the Pharmassist will release the correct dosage of the medicine.

SiebertHead erkannte den Bedarf, Medikamente einerseits für Kinder unzugänglich aufzubewahren, andererseits aber älteren und behinderten Menschen eine einfache Handhabung zu ermöglichen. Die intelligente Medikamentenverpackung Pharmassist verwendet ein biometrisches Scanverfahren, ein multi-sensorisches Erinnerungssystem, ein visuelles Display und ein Audio-Informationssystem, um mit dem Patienten zu kommunizieren. Bei Abgabe eines Medikaments gibt der Apotheker alle notwendigen Daten für den Patienten in das Gerät ein und scannt den Fingerabdruck des Patienten, der als Schlüssel fungiert, um Pharmassist zu öffnen. Wenn der Patient seine Medikamente nehmen muss, wird er vom Pharmassist alamiert. Hat der Patient sich durch seinen Fingerabdruck auf dem Scanner identifiziert, gibt der Pharmassist exakt die benötigte Dosis des Medikaments ab.

SiebertHead a identifié le besoin d'un conditionnement pharmaceutique facile à ouvrir pour les personnes âgées ou souffrant d'un handicap, mais hors de portée des enfants. Le conditionnement pharmaceutique intelligent Pharmassist est doté d'un scanner biométrique et d'un système de rappel multisensoriel ainsi que d'un système d'affichage visuel et d'information sonore pour communiquer avec le patient. Au moment de délivrer les médicaments, les pharmaciens pourront programmer les données de l'ordonnance du patient sur Pharmassist. Ils scanneront également l'empreinte digitale du patient, qui servira de clé pour ouvrir la boîte. À l'heure de la prise du médicament, Pharmassist préviendra le patient. Une fois l'empreinte du patient reconnue par le scanner biométrique, Pharmassist fournira la dose prescrite.

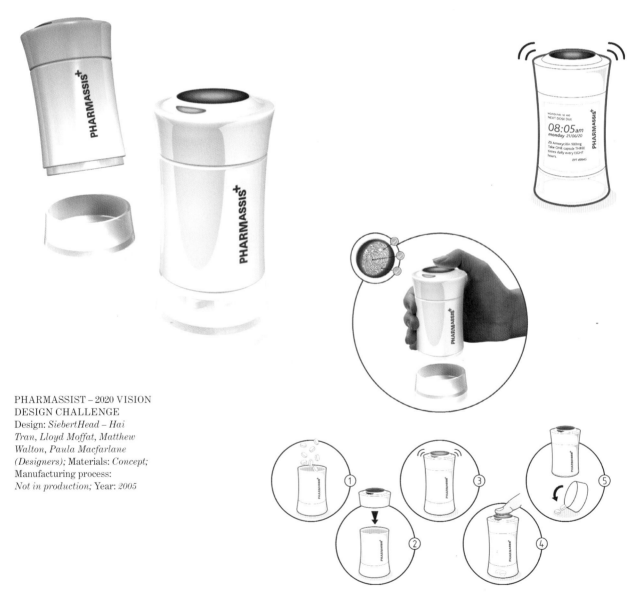

PHARMASSIST – 2020 VISION
DESIGN CHALLENGE
Design: *SiebertHead – Hai Tran, Lloyd Moffat, Matthew Walton, Paula Macfarlane (Designers);* Materials: *Concept;* Manufacturing process: *Not in production;* Year: *2005*

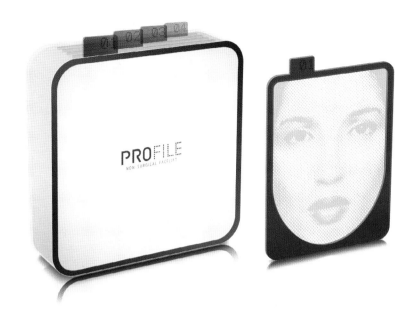

PROFILE – 2020 VISION
DESIGN CHALLENGE
Design: *SiebertHead – Hai
Tran, Lloyd Moffat, Matthew
Walton, Paula Macfarlane
(Designers);* Materials: *Concept;*
Manufacturing process: *Not in
production;* Year: *2005*

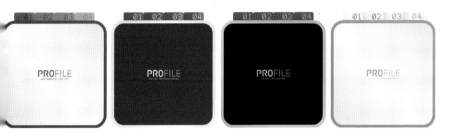

SiebertHead had recognised how society increasingly gives more importance to youth and beauty than age and maturity and thought there will be a future demand for in-home facelifts. The Profile range of non-surgical facelift products allows for effects previously only achievable with surgery to be performed at home through the application of a facemask. The active ingredients in Botox and collagen are printed directly onto a nanometric film in the shape of a facemask. The mask is placed directly on the face and the arrangement of the active ingredients on the nanometric film enables precise absorption through the skin. The temperature self-regulating packaging of the nanometric films prevents the infiltration of microorganisms. Slide activation aperture securely seals the slides inside the container. Internal rollers are inset just beneath the aperture doors to apply activation gel to a slide as it exits the container.

SiebertHead beobachtete den gesellschaftlichen Trend, dass Jugend und Schönheit immer größere Bedeutung beigemessen wird, während Alter und Reife an Stellenwert verlieren. Man schloss daraus, dass es einen wachsenden Bedarf an Gesichtsliftings für den Hausgebrauch geben wird. Die Produktreihe Profile bietet in Form einer Gesichtsmaske hautstraffende Effekte, die bisher nur durch Operationen erlangt werden konnten. Die Maske wird direkt auf das Gesicht aufgetragen. Die Aufbringung des Wirkstoffs auf einen nanometrischen Film erlaubt die gezielte Absorption durch die Haut. Die Verpackung des nanometrischen Films, die die Temperatur selbst reguliert, verhindert das Eindringen von Mikroorganismen. Die Trägerfolien sind innerhalb des Behälters durch einen Aktivierungsschlitz sicher versiegelt. Erst beim Herausziehen wird durch Rollen direkt unterhalb des Schlitzes ein aktivierendes Gel auf die Träger aufgetragen.

Sieberthead a remarqué que la société accorde de plus en plus d'importance à la jeunesse et à la beauté, plutôt qu'à l'âge et à la maturité. L'agence a donc pensé qu'il y aurait dans le futur une demande pour les liftings faciaux à domicile. La gamme de liftings faciaux non chirurgicaux Profile permet d'obtenir les effets qui ne s'obtenaient auparavant que par le biais de la chirurgie, à domicile et au moyen d'un masque à appliquer sur le visage. Les principes actifs du Botox et du collagène sont imprimés directement sur un film nanométrique qui prend la forme d'un masque. Le masque se pose directement sur le visage, et la disposition des ingrédients actifs sur le film nanométrique permet une absorption précise à travers la peau. Le conditionnement des films nanométriques est doté d'un système automatique de régulation de la température, et empêche l'infiltration de microorganismes. L'ouverture coulissante scelle les films dans leur récipient. À l'intérieur, des rouleaux sont insérés juste en dessous des ouvertures afin d'appliquer le gel d'activation sur le film à sa sortie du récipient.

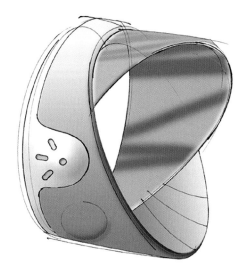

SOLUTIONS FOR THE
VITAMINS MARKET – 2020
VISION DESIGN CHALLENGE
Design: *Pearson Matthews;* Client:
*Packaging Innovation Show 2004
– 2020 Vision Design Challenge;*
Materials: *Various;* Manufacturing
process: *Various;* Year: *2004*

Project description: Focusing on user benefits to demonstrate how a user-centred approach can drive innovation for commercial benefit. Using scenario-based business tools to generate solutions that answer real consumer needs, focusing on the vitamin market sector. Four different solutions for four different people, buying vitamins for four different reasons:

vitaWear: A tablet-storing bracelet with technology to monitor and advise the wearer of their vitamin levels through a discreet colour-changing band.

vitaBadge: Is a variation on the bracelet, which is worn on the skin, automatically monitoring and administering vitamins transdermally.

vitaCup: A cup with a personalised recipe of vitamins printed onto the surface fill the cup with water and the vitamins are released to form a drink.

vitaMix: A cartridge system with up to five vitamins in powder form combines with a low cost test device that measures vitamin levels within the body and then doses at precise levels.

Projektbeschreibung: Fokussierung auf den Nutzen für den Verbraucher, um zu zeigen, wie ein auf den Anwender konzentrierter Ansatz Innovation und kommerziellen Erfolg fördern kann. Entwicklung von Lösungen, die an Konsumentenbedürfnissen orientiert sind, unter Verwendung von individuell angepassten Geräten. Konzentration auf den Vitaminpräparatsektor. Das führt zu vier unterschiedlichen Lösungen für vier unterschiedliche Menschentypen, die Vitamine aus vier unterschiedlichen Gründen kaufen:

vitaWear: Ein Armband mit Tablettenfach und einer Technologie, die den Vitaminhaushalt des Trägers überwacht und ihn durch eine diskrete, die Farbe wechselnde Markierung darüber informiert.

vitaBadge: Eine Variation des Armbandes, die direkt auf der Haut getragen wird, den Vitaminhaushalt kontrolliert und ihn durch direkte Vitaminabgabe in die Haut reguliert.

vitaCup: Ein Becher mit einer auf den Kunden zugeschnittenen Vitaminmischung. Füllt man Wasser in den Becher, lösen sich die Vitamine, und man erhält ein Vitamingetränk.

vitaMix: Ein Kartuschensystem mit bis zu fünf Vitaminen in Pulverform, kombiniert mit einem preiswerten Testsystem. Zunächst wird der Vitaminbedarf des Körpers bestimmt und dann die entsprechende Dosis gemischt.

Description du projet: Se concentrer sur l'intérêt de l'utilisateur pour démontrer en quoi une approche centrée sur celui-ci peut conduire à une innovation et à des bénéfices commerciaux Utiliser des instruments stratégiques basés sur des scénarios afin de générer des solutions qui répondent à de réels besoins des consommateurs. Se concentrer sur le marché des vitamines. Quatre solutions différentes pour quatre types de personnes, qui ont quatre raisons différentes d'acheter des vitamines :

vitaWear: Ce bracelet contient les comprimés et est doté d'une technologie permettant de contrôler les niveaux de vitamines du porteur, et de le prévenir au moyen d'une bande discrète qui change de couleur.

vitaBadge: C'est une variante du bracelet, il se porte sur la peau et contrôle et administre les vitamines automatiquement à travers la peau.

vitaCup: Il s'agit d'un gobelet à la surface duquel est imprimé un cocktail de vitamines personnalisé. Il suffit de remplir le gobelet avec de l'eau et les vitamines se diluent pour former une boisson.

vitaMix: C'est un système à cartouches qui peut contenir jusqu'à cinq vitamines en poudre. Il comporte un test bon marché qui mesure les niveaux de vitamines du corps puis effectue un dosage précis.

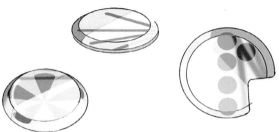

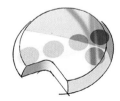

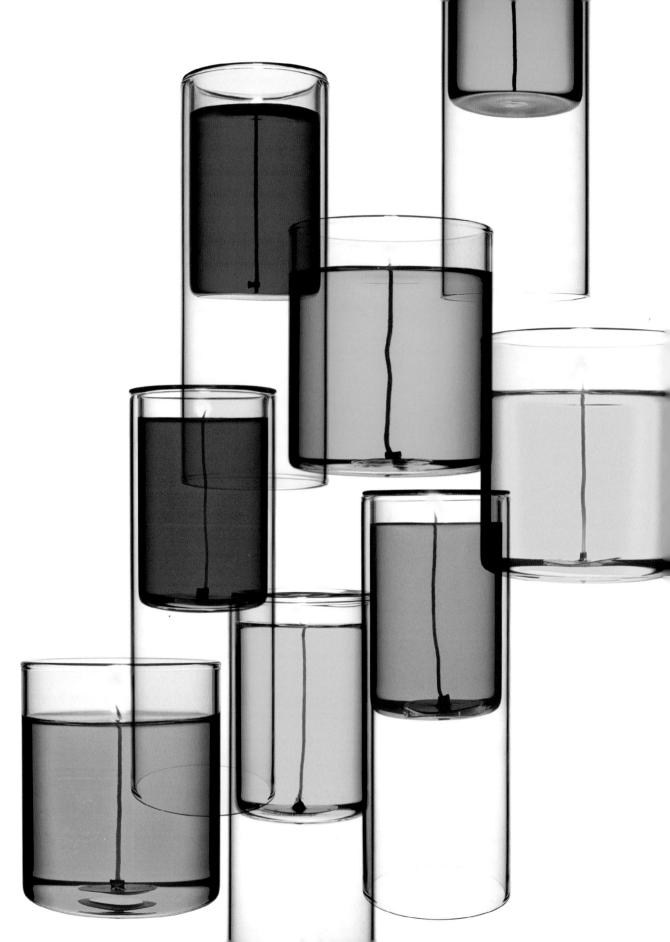

VIII

STORE

& RETAIL

Okumura Akio
Aloof Design
Alloy
CB'a Design Solutions
Design Guys
Elmwood
Lippa Pierce
Sayuri Studio
Stockholm Design Lab
Tana–X
Yosua Tanaka
Tin Horse Design Team

P. 346+348

CANDLE 0015/ 0017
Design: *Sayuri Studio
– Sayuri Shoji, David Seidler
(Designers);* Client: *Sephora, USA*
Awards: *American Institute of
Graphic Arts Design Annual,
Graphis Annual;* Materials: *Glass
clear acetate;* Manufacturing
process: *Extrusion, silkscreen;*
Year: *2002*

FELISSIMO CARTON BOX
Design: *Sayuri Studio, Inc.
– Sayuri Shoji, Yoshiko Shimizu
(Designers);* Client: *Felissimo;*
Award: *I.D. Magazine (Design
Distinction Award);* Materials:
Corrugated paper; Manufacturing
process: *Printing;* Year: *2002*

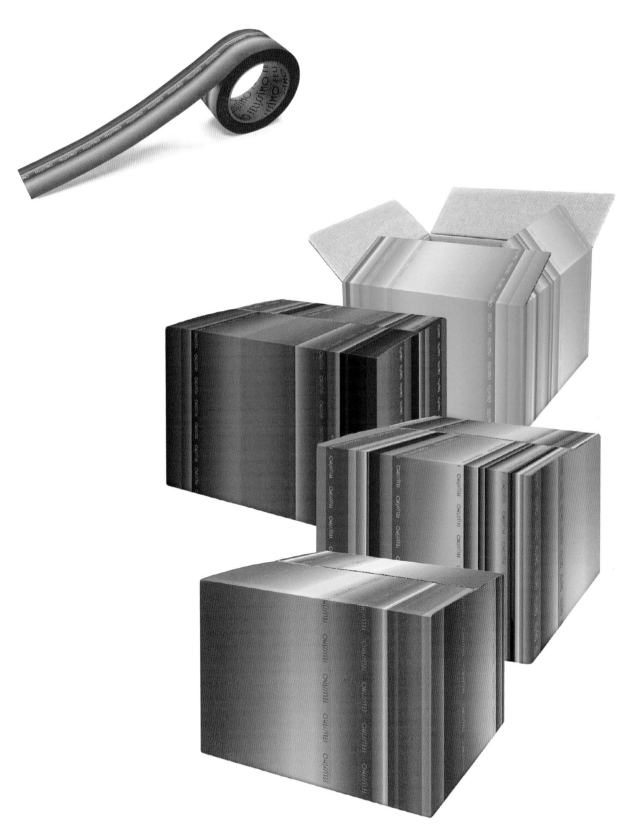

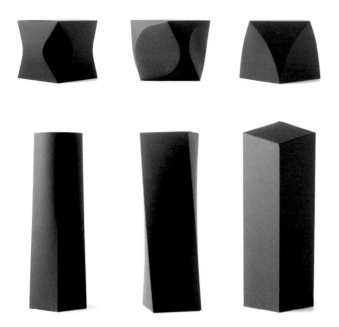

ALOOF PACK DESIGNS
IN-HOUSE STRUCTURAL
PACK DESIGNS
Design: *Aloof Design (© 2005 Aloof
Design retain the copyright and
reproduction rights to the work
shown) – Sam Aloof (Designer);*
Client: *Various;* Materials: *Color-
plan, colorflute, coated box board;*
Manufacturing process: *Die cut, tab
locking; printing, litho printing,
debossing, gluing;* Year: *2005*

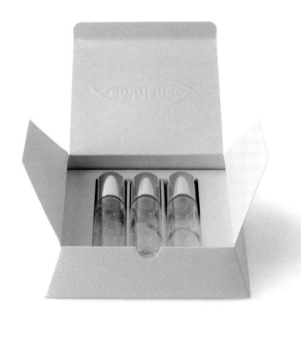

These packs represent a small selection
of Aloof's archive of work, developed in-house
as part of our ongoing self-initiated research
to explore the structural potential of sheet
materials. Aloof also have a range of innovative
packaging available to order in customised
production runs from x 250 units. Packs can
be sized to order, branded and produced in
a comprehensive range of papers, colours
and finishes.

Diese Verpackungen zeigen eine kleine
Auswahl der bisherigen Arbeiten von Aloof im
Bereich Verpackungsdesign. Sie wurden ohne
direkten Kundenauftrag im Haus produziert
und stellen Studien dar, die das Gestaltungs-
potenzial verschiedener Materialien testen.
Aloof verfügt über eine Kollektion von innovativen Verpackungen, die in Auflagen von 250
Stück produziert werden können. Die Packungen können nach Wunsch angepasst sowie
mit Markennamen versehen werden. Sie sind
in unterschiedlichen Farben sowie Papier-
und Kartonsorten und mit verschiedenen
Oberflächenbeschichtungen erhältlich

Ces boîtes représentent un petit échantillon
du travail qu'Aloof a réalisé en interne dans le
cadre de son exploration continue du potentiel
structurel des feuilles. Aloof propose également une gamme d'emballages innovants
disponibles à la commande en séries person-
nalisées de 250 unités. Ces emballages peuvent porter la marque du client, et peuvent
être fabriqués à la dimension désirée, dans
une vaste gamme de papiers, de couleurs
et de finitions.

HEAL'S (IDENTITY)
Design: *Lippa Pearce – Domenic
Lippa (Art Director), Paul Skerm
(Designer);* Materials: *White carton
board* ; Manufacturing process:
*litho, overall matt varnish with
spots of gloss UV;* Year: *2004*

Heal's has been at the forefront of stylish, contemporary design ever since it opened its first store nearly 200 years ago. Great supporters of the arts and craft movement, the Heal's family founded a company that has led the way in furniture and home design for years, bringing good, beautiful design to a wider audience through its growing number of UK stores. Over the past fifteen years, the existing logo for Heal's has reflected the history and heritage of the brand, but more recently, with a change in their product offer, a need to readdress who they are, as a company and as a retailer, has led to the necessary step of acquiring a new visual identity that can take the brand forward.

Seit Eröffnung des ersten Geschäfts vor fast 200 Jahren war Heal's immer ein Vorreiter auf dem Gebiet des stilvollen, modernen Designs. Als begeisterte Unterstützer der Arts-and-Crafts-Bewegung gründete die Familie Heal eine Firma, die seit Jahren in den Bereichen Möbel und Innenausstattung führend ist. Durch ihre stetig wachsende Zahl von Geschäften in Großbritannien bringt sie einem immer größer werdenden Publikum gutes und geschmackvolles Design näher. In den vergangenen 15 Jahren hat das bestehende Heal's-Logo die Geschichte und Tradition der Marke verkörpert. Durch einige Änderungen im Warenangebot in jüngster Vergangenheit wurde es notwendig, eine neue visuelle Identität zu entwickeln, die die Besonderheiten des Unternehmens veranschaulicht und seine Ziele fördert.

Heal's est à l'avant-garde du design élégant et contemporain depuis l'ouverture du premier magasin de la chaîne il y a près de 200 ans. En grands amateurs des arts et de l'artisanat, les membres de la famille Heal ont fondé une entreprise qui a depuis très longtemps une grande influence dans le domaine du mobilier et de la décoration d'intérieur, et qui met des objets esthétiques et de bonne qualité à la disposition d'un public de plus en plus vaste grâce à des magasins de plus en plus nombreux au Royaume-Uni. Ces quinze dernières années, le logo de Heal's a reflété l'histoire et les valeurs de la marque mais, plus récemment, avec un changement dans leur offre de produits, un besoin de redéfinir leur identité en tant qu'entreprise et distributeur les a conduits à acquérir une nouvelle identité visuelle qui permettra à la marque de continuer d'avancer.

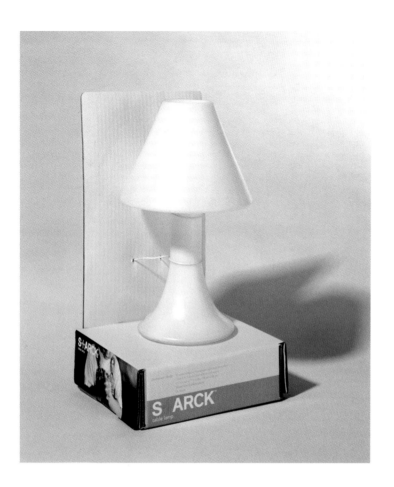

PHILIPPE STARCK
PACKAGING
Design: *Design Guys – Steve Sikora (Creative Director), John Moes, Gary Patch(Designers);* Client: *Target;* Awards: *Industrial Designers Society of America (Bronze);* Materials: *Corrugated and paperboard, shrink plastic, acetate windows;* Manufacturing process: *6-colour litho printing, die cut;* Year: *1999*

MICHAEL GRAVES
PACKAGING
Design: *Design Guys – Steve Sikora (Creative Director), Gary Patch, Steve Sikora, Scott Thares, Tom Riddle, Jerry Stenbach (Designers);* Client: *Target;* Awards: *Industrial Designers Society of America (Gold);* Materials: *Corrugated and paperboard;* Manufacturing process: *Litho printing, matte plastic laminating, die cutting, folding cartons;* Year: *1998*

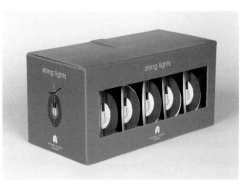

The original concept for Michael Graves Design packaging was inspired by the work of Michael Graves. The box concept was co-designed with Michael Graves Design. The blue colour is a hue derived from the product colour palette. Packaging, other than boxes, were often elaborate forms created to compliment the products they contained. At launch, Design Guys created packages for over 150 products in the kitchen, garden and decorative home accessories categories. Although product manufacturing took place in several countries, for consistency all printing was done at a single source in Hong Kong. This was the only way to match the blue, which belongs to no colour system. A dull laminate gives the boxes a velvety surface and softens the colour just a bit. Other than aesthetics the dull finish kept the packaging looking good despite the wear and tear of the store environment and dust from the floor polisher.

Das Originalkonzept für die Verpackungen für Michael Graves Design wurde durch Michael Graves' Arbeit inspiriert. Michael Graves Design war auch an dem Konzept für die Kartons beteiligt. Der Blauton wurde aus der Farbpalette der Produktreihe genommen. Die Verpackungen, die nicht aus Karton waren, hatten oftmals sehr komplizierte Formen, die das jeweilige Produkt ergänzten. Zum Start der Reihe entwickelte Design Guys Verpackungen für über 150 Produkte aus den Bereichen Küche, Garten und dekorative Accessoires. Obwohl die Produkte in den verschiedensten Ländern gefertigt wurden, übernahm eine Druckerei in Hongkong den gesamten Druck, um Einheitlichkeit zu garantieren. Nur so konnte die Qualität des Blaus durchgängig gewährleistet werden, denn der Ton ist eine Spezialfarbe, die keinem Farbsystem entnommen wurde. Die Kartonagen wurden matt laminiert, was ihnen einen samtigen Glanz verleiht und die Farbe ein wenig abtönt. Die Laminierung schützt die Verpackungen zudem vor den üblichen Abnutzungen und vor Staub im Verkaufsraum

Le concept original des emballages pour Michael Graves Design s'inspire du travail de Michael Graves. Le concept de la boîte a été créé en collaboration avec Michael Graves Design. Le bleu utilisé est une couleur dérivée de la palette de couleurs des produits. À l'exception des boîtes, les emballages ont souvent des formes assez compliquées, créées pour mettre le produit en valeur. Au moment du lancement, Design Guys a créé des emballages pour plus de 150 accessoires de cuisine, de jardin et de décoration intérieure. Bien que la fabrication soit réalisée dans plusieurs pays, un seul fournisseur s'occupe de l'impression, à Hong Kong, pour des questions d'uniformité. C'était la seule manière d'obtenir toujours le même bleu, car cette nuance n'appartient à aucun système de couleur standardisé. Une couche mate donne aux boîtes une surface veloutée et adoucit un peu la couleur. Outre le côté esthétique, cette surface mate permet également au produit de conserver un aspect satisfaisant malgré l'usure et les manipulations subies en magasin et la poussière.

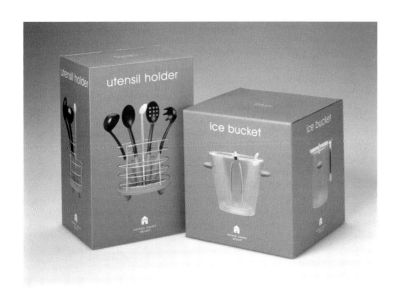

TUPPERWARE PACKAGING
Design: *Design Guys – Steve Sikora
(Creative Director)*, *Wendy
Bonnstetter*, *Gary Patch (Design-
ers)*; Client: *Tupperware*; Awards:
Industrial Designers Society of
America (Bronze); Materials:
Paperboard and label stock;
Manufacturing process: *Litho print-
ing, die cutting, folding cartons*;
Year: *2002*

Never before in the fifty year history of Tupperware had there been branded product packaging; this was due in part to the phenomenal success of their direct selling programme. When the time was right for a secondary sales strategy with key retail partners, Design Guys was enlisted to develop Tupperware packaging. The assignment was to create packaging for a wide variety of product forms as well as to design the visual personality of the brand, which would pull the various forms together. The objective was to keep the packaging as minimal as possible in order to be cost-effective and ecologically sensitive. The word most commonly associated with the Tupperware brand is "party." So naturally Design Guys wanted to do something convivial. The use of bright colours conveyed festivity as well as differentiated collections within the line. The form factors that were used were as innovative as the products inside. At the end of the fast track process, all of these ideas came together to create a vibrant shelf appeal for the newly visualised Tupperware brand.

In den 50 Jahren seit ihrem Bestehen hatte die Firma Tupperware nie ein markeneigenes Verpackungsdesign, was vermutlich auf den Direktvertrieb zurückzuführen ist. Als ein zweites Vertriebssystem mit ausgesuchten Verkaufspartnern aufgebaut werden sollte, wurde Design Guys beauftragt, Verpackungen für die unterschiedlichen Produktformen von Tupperware zu entwickeln. Die Gestaltung der Verpackungen sollte einen Markencharakter aufweisen und die Produktvielfalt optisch zusammenhalten. Zudem sollten die Verpackungen aus umwelttechnischen und wirtschaftlichen Gründen so minimal wie möglich ausfallen. Ein Wort, das die meisten Menschen mit Tupperware verbinden, ist „Party". Daher wollte Design Guys natürlich etwas Fröhliches entwerfen. Sie verwendeten leuchtende Farben, um einerseits festliche Stimmung zu vermitteln und andererseits die einzelnen Kollektionen farblich zu kennzeichnen. Die Formen, die sie einsetzten, waren ebenso innovativ wie die Produkte, die sie umhüllten. Am Ende des extrem schnellen Entwicklungsprozesses stand eine strahlende Verpackung mit auffälliger Regalpräsenz und ein neues optisches Erscheinungsbild für Tupperware.

En partie à cause du succès phénoménal de son programme de vente directe, tout au long de ses 50 ans d'histoire, Tupperware n'avait jamais eu besoin pour ses produits d'un emballage aux couleurs de la marque. Lorsque le moment est venu de passer à une stratégie de ventes secondaire avec des distributeurs choisis, Tupperware a chargé Design Guys de créer son emballage. Le travail consistait à créer un emballage pour des produits aux formes très variées ainsi qu'à concevoir la personnalité visuelle de la marque, pour faire le lien entre les différentes formes. L'objectif était que l'emballage soit aussi simple et dépouillé que possible, afin d'être économique et respectueux de l'environnement. Le mot le plus couramment associé à la marque Tupperware est « fête ». L'équipe de Design Guys a donc voulu faire quelque chose de convivial. Ils ont utilisé des couleurs vives pour exprimer cette notion festive, et pour distinguer les différentes collections au sein de la gamme. Les formes qu'ils ont utilisées pour l'emballage étaient aussi innovantes que les produits eux-mêmes. Au terme du processus de conception et de fabrication, toutes ces idées ont abouti à une expression visuelle de la marque Tupperware qui lui donne une présence en rayon très efficace.

RÖRSTRAND WINE GLASSES
Design: *Stockholm Design Lab;*
Client: *Rörstrand;* Materials:
Plastic; Manufacturing process:
Not disclosed; Year: *2005*

WASHAWAY
Design: *Alloy Ltd – Nina Warbur-
ton (Design Team Leader);* Client:
Concept; Materials: *Soluble film;*
Manufacturing process: *Concept/
not in production;* Year: *2005*

SIMPLE IS HARD
(RICHARDSON SHEFFIELD
REBRANDING)
Design: *Elmwood – James Back-
hurst (Design Director), Richard
Palmer (Project Manager);* Client:
*Richardson Sheffield – Andrew
Stokes (Brand Manager);* Awards:
*Roses Award for Brand Identity
Design;* Materials: *Various;*
Manufacturing process: *Various;*
Year: *2003*

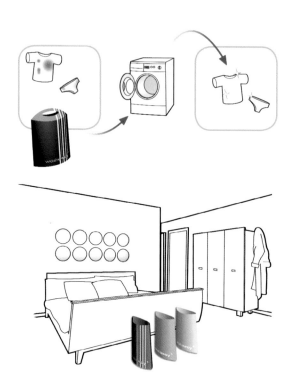

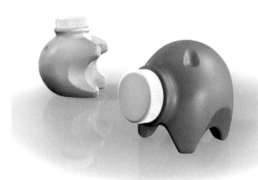

PUG
Design: *Tin Horse Design Team;*
Client: *Tin Horse;* Materials:
High density polyethylene (bottles),
polypropylene (closures);
Manufacturing process: *Injection*
moulded closures, blow moulded
bottles; Year: *2005*

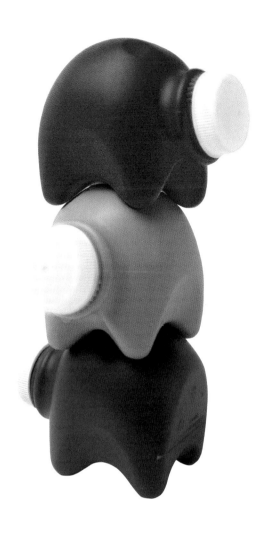

This particular bottle idea was conceived as a way of engendering the dullness of kids' drinks packaging with the personality of animals. The form is both highly feasible and hugely characterful; a chameleon form capable of becoming a range of animal types through colour and decoration. The bottles will stack for both play at point-of-sale and, of course, at home. The design has been tooled and awaits a suitable licensee, but the Tin Horse Design Team was interested in a differentiated product.

Mit dieser speziellen Flaschenidee wollte man den sonst langweiligen Getränkeverpackungen für Kinder die Gestalt von Tieren verleihen. Die Form ist nicht nur sehr gut umsetzbar, sondern auch besonders charakterstark. Zudem ist sie äußerst wandlungsfähig, da sie durch Farbgebung und Dekoration ganz unterschiedliche Tiere darstellen kann. Besonders praktisch für die Präsentation im Verkaufsraum, aber auch für die Verwendung als Spielzeug ist die Stapelbarkeit der Flasche. Das Design ist ausgearbeitet und wartet auf einen passenden Lizenznehmer, allerdings ist das Designteam von Tin Horse an einem differenzierten Produkt interessiert.

Ce concept de bouteille a été imaginé dans le but de remédier à l'insipidité des bouteilles de boissons pour enfants en utilisant la personnalité des animaux. La forme est à la fois très faisable et pleine de caractère, une forme caméléon qui, selon les couleurs et les motifs, peut représenter différents animaux. Les bouteilles peuvent s'empiler pour jouer sur le lieu de vente et, bien sûr, à la maison. Le processus de fabrication est prêt, il ne manque plus qu'une licence appropriée, mais l'équipe de design de Tin Horse cherche un produit original.

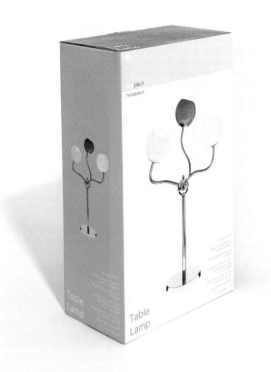

TABLE LAMP
AND TABLE PACKAGING
Design: *Design Guys;* Client:
Wave Pendant; Materials: *Carton
paper;* Manufacturing process:
Printing; Year: *2007*

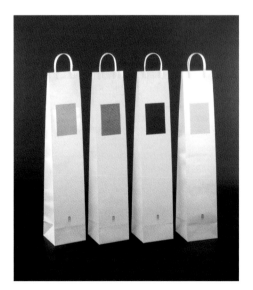

LONG STORE BAG
Design: *Okumura Akio;*
Client: *M USA,* Materials:
Carton; Manufacturing
process: *Various;* Year: *2002*

SO EAT CUTLERY
Design: *Elmwood;* Client: *So Eat;*
Materials: *Carton;* Manufacturing
process: *Printing;* Year: *2005*

GLOBAL PACKAGING PROJECT
FOR MONOPRIX BRANDS
Design: *CB'a Design Solutions –
Nathalie Jacquot, Philippe Delmotte
(designers);* Client: *Monoprix;*
Materials: *Paper, plastic;* Manufac-
turing process: *Various;* Year: *2005*

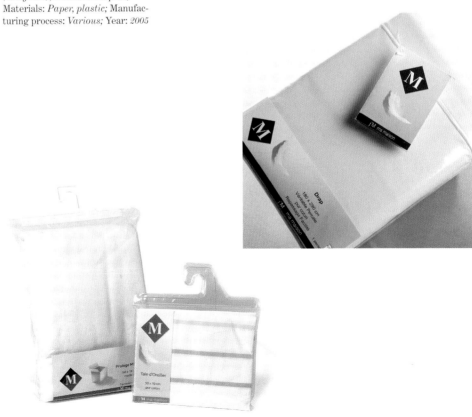

FILIPPA K UNDERWEAR
Design: *Stockholm Design Lab;*
Client: *Filippa K;* Materials:
Nylon bag, removable sticker;
Manufacturing process: *Various;*
Year: *2005*

FILIPPA K MUG
Design: *Stockholm Design Lab;*
Client: *Rörstrand;* Materials:
Plastic, paper, soft Styrofoam;
Manufacturing process: *Various;*
Year: *2005*

TYPE BOX
Design: *Sayuri Studio – Sayuri
Shoji;* Client: *Not disclosed;* Materi-
als: *Paper;* Manufacturing process:
Folding, gluing; Year: *2005*

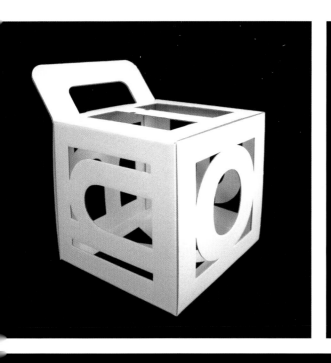
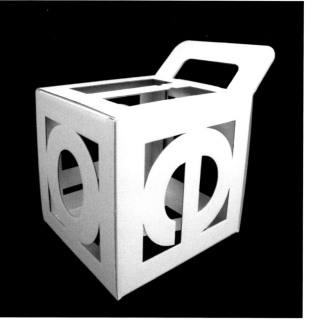

IKEA
(PACKAGING CONCEPT)
Design: *Stockholm Design Lab;*
Client: *IKEA;* Awards: *Core Design
(First Prize in Graphic Design/
Packaging Design);* Materials:
Carton; Manufacturing process:
Folding, gluing, printing;
Year: *2001*

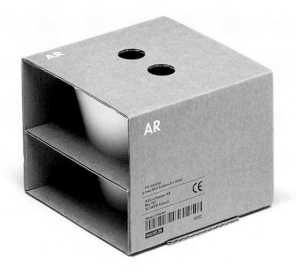

PAPER AIR PACKING
Design: *Tana-X;* Client: *Honda;*
Awards: *Japan Packaging Contest;*
Materials: *Cardboard;* Manufacturing
process: *Not discloosed;* Year: *2001*

IKEA asked Stockholm Design Lab to design a packaging concept for 8,000 non-furniture products. IKEA is widely known for flat, brown packages containing products for home assembly, yet also sells products in conventional packaging.

IKEA set out six criteria for the concept:
1. Make the packaging environmentally-friendly.
2. Provide for efficient production worldwide.
3. Cut costs.
4. Address the fact that IKEA packaging requires multi-language information.
5. Solve the problem of customers opening packages in the store to ensure that the product is the right colour, etc.
6. Create attractive packaging.

In collaboration with IKEA, Stockholm Design Lab devised a packaging concept based on a "wraparound" principle and a system for product information consisting of product name, pictogram/illustration and placement of barcode/logo. The design permits products to be visible, open sides through the packaging reveal the model and colour, and a hole makes it easy to carry. The new packaging is predominantly brown in colour to build on the existing positive packaging image of IKEA. A pictogram, illustration or photograph identifies the contents in closed packages. Some have a transparent front.

IKEA beauftragte das Stockholm Design Lab mit dem Entwurf eines Verpackungskonzeptes für 8.000 Non–Furniture–Produkte.

IKEA ist zwar weltweit für seine in flache braune Pakete verpackten Produkte bekannt, die der Kunde selbst montieren muss, doch das Unternehmen verkauft auch Waren in konventionellen Verpackungen.

IKEA stellte sechs Anforderungen an das neue Verpackungskonzept:
1. Die Verpackungen sollten umweltfreundlich sein.
2. Sie sollten weltweit effizient produziert werden können.
3. Sie sollten preisgünstig sein.
4. Das Konzept sollte beachten, dass IKEA-Verpackungen mehrsprachige Informationen bieten müssen.
5. Das Konzept sollte berücksichtigen, dass Kunden die Verpackung im Laden öffnen, um die Farbe des Produktes oder Ähnliches zu prüfen.
6. Die Verpackungen sollten attraktiv sein.

Gemeinsam mit IKEA entwickelte Stockholm Design Lab ein Verpackungskonzept, das auf dem „Einwickelprinzip" basiert und ein System für Produktinformationen, das Produktname, Piktogramm/Illustration und Barcode/Logo umfasst. Durch dieses Verpackungskonzept bleiben die Produkte sichtbar. Offene Seiten erlauben es, Modell und Farbe des Produktes zu sehen, ein Trageloch ermöglicht ein bequemes Transportieren. Die neuen Verpackungen sind vorwiegend braun, um sich dem positiven Image der bisherigen IKEA-Verpackungen anzupassen. Bei geschlossenen Paketen erleichtern Piktogramm, Illustration oder Fotografie die genaue Identifizierung des Produkts. Einige Verpackungen haben eine durchsichtige Front.

IKEA a demandé à Stockholm Design Lab d'imaginer un concept d'emballage pour 8 000 articles de décoration.

IKEA est bien connu pour ses paquets plats et marron contenant des produits en kit à monter soi-même, mais vend aussi des produits dans des emballages classiques.

IKEA a défini six critères pour le concept :
1. Respecter l'environnement.
2. Mettre en place un système de production efficace dans le monde entier.
3. Réduire les coûts.
4. Tenir compte du fait que l'emballage IKEA nécessite des informations en plusieurs langues.
5. Résoudre le problème des clients qui ouvrent les emballages dans le magasin pour vérifier la couleur, etc. du produit.
6. Créer un emballage attrayant.

En collaboration avec IKEA, Stockholm Design Lab a imaginé un concept d'emballage basé sur un principe « enveloppant » et, pour les informations sur le produit, sur un système qui comporte le nom du produit, un pictogramme/une illustration et l'emplacement du code barre/logo. L'emballage permet au client de voir le produit. Les ouvertures sur le côté de l'emballage révèlent le modèle et la couleur, et un trou permet de le porter facilement. Le nouvel emballage est essentiellement marron afin de profiter de l'image positive de l'emballage IKEA. Un pictogramme, une illustration ou une photographie identifie le contenu des paquets fermés. Certains ont une face transparente.

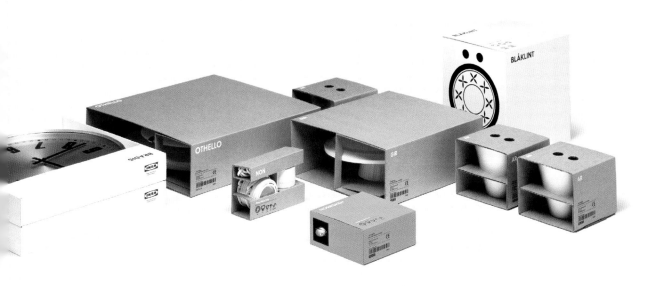

CANDLE BOX
Design: *Aloof Design;* Client: *Hush;*
Materials: *Carton;* Manufacturing
process: *Folding, gluing, printing;*
Year: *2006*

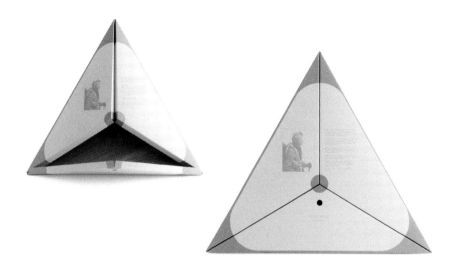

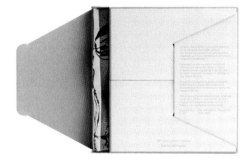

TEATOWEL & TRAY BOX
Design: *Aloof Design;* Client:
TTO; Materials: *Carton;*
Manufacturing process:
Folding, gluing, printing;
Year: *2006*

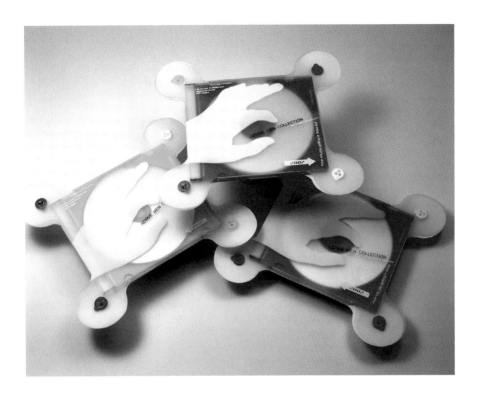

COMPACT DISK PACKAGING
Design: *Yasuo Tanaka;* Client:
Package Land; Materials:
Plastic; Manufacturing process:
Not disclosed; Year: *2002*

COSMOX
Design: *Yasuo Tanaka;* Client:
Honda; Materials: *Various;*
Manufacturing process:
Not disclosed; Year: *1998*

JAPANESE FIGURE
PACKAGING
Design: *Yasuo Tanaka;* Client:
Package Land; Materials: *Paper;*
Manufacturing process: *Not
disclosed;* Year: *2004*

BOTTLE PACKAGING
(STRUCTURAL PACK DESIGN)
Design: *Aloof Design – Sam Aloof;*
Client: *Hallmark on behalf of
Marks & Spencer;* Materials:
Colorflute; Manufacturing process:
*Handmade mock ups, die cut and
debossed with one glue line and
envelope base (proposed production
version);* Year: *2000*

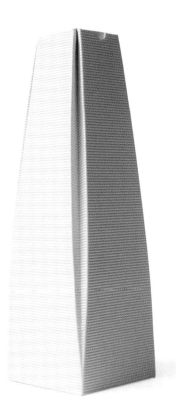

IX

MISCELLANEOUS

Cahan & Associates
Design Guys
Landor Design
Lewis Moberly
Lippa Pearce
Metaphase Design Group
Minale Tattersfield & Partners
PDD Group
Pentagram
PI3
Stockholm Design Lab
Tátil Design
Toyo Seikan Kaisha
The Ad Store
Tin Horse Design Team

P. 374+376
Z-END
Design/Client: *Toyo Seikan*
Kaisha; Materials:
aluminum; Year: *2005*

Z-END is a new method adopted for the opening of cans. This "universal design end" is much easier to open than that of the past SOT-END. Regardless of age or sex, this is a simple cap that is easy for anybody to use. Easy To Open Tab: The method adopted is an "easy finger insertion and simple pulling of the tab-ring", which basically eliminates the difficulty of prying open the SOT-END tabs with one's finger. Easy to Use Cap: The opening and re-closing of the cap can be done with ease. So there is no longer a need for concern if the can is knocked over on a desk, as the contents will not spill. This is a vacuum-sealed can.

Z-END ist eine neue Methode zum Öffnen von Getränkedosen. Dieses „Universal Design End" ist wesentlich einfacher zu öffnen als das frühere „SOT-END"; die Handhabung des neuen Designs ist kinderleicht. Easy To Open Tab: Da der neue Mechanismus mit einem Aufreißring funktioniert, der unkompliziert mit einem Finger bedient werden kann, ist das Öffnen wesentlich leichter als mit dem herkömmlichen Mechanismus. Easy To Use Cap: Durch den neuen Mechanismus kann der Deckel schnell geöffnet und wieder verschlossen werden. Es gibt also kein lästiges Auslaufen mehr, wenn die Dose einmal umfällt. Diese Dose ist vakuumversiegelt.

Z-END est une nouvelle méthode d'ouverture des cannettes, beaucoup plus facile à utiliser que la méthode précédente de la languette « stay-on tab ». Quels que soient l'âge ou le sexe de l'utilisateur, cette capsule toute simple est facile à utiliser pour tout le monde. Une languette facile à ouvrir. La méthode adoptée ne demande que d'insérer le doigt et de tirer sur la languette, ce qui élimine la difficulté des languettes « stay-on tab », qui obligent à faire levier avec le doigt pour ouvrir. Une capsule facile à utiliser: La capsule est facile à ouvrir et à refermer. Si la canette se renverse sur un bureau, pas d'inquiétude, son contenu ne s'écoulera pas. C'est une cannette fermée sous vide.

FRENCH RABBIT CARAFE
Design: *Cahan & Associates –
Erik Adams (Designer);*
Client: *Boisset, USA;* Materi-
als/Manufacturing process: *Concept;*
Year: *2006*

TRAVELER PLUS™ LID
Design: *Metaphase Design Group –
Bryce Rutter, Brian Bone, Heath
Doty (Designers), Colin McRae
(Photo credit);* Client: *Solo;* Awards:
*Red Dot Award, DuPont Silver
Award, Institute of Packaging
Professionals, I.D. Magazine
Annual Design Review;* Materials
and process: *Lid parts are thermo-
formed from sheets of polystyrene,
which are then die-cut to create the
individual parts;* Year: *2004*

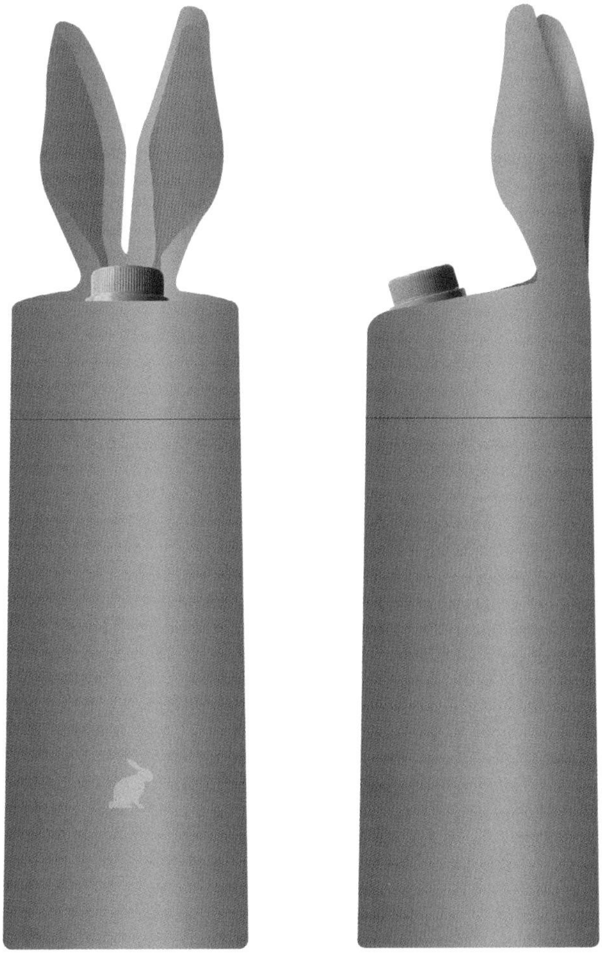

Q8 OIL (BRAND)
Design: *PI3;* Client: *Q8 Petroleum;*
Awards: *Starpack Award;*
Materials: *Bottle and wadded
cap – high density polyethylene. ;*
Manufacturing process: *Bottle –
extrusion blowing; Cap – injection
moulding;* Year: *2006*

CASPIAN (BRANDING
AND PACKAGING)
Design: *Minale Tattersfield &
Partners;* Client: *Fouman Chimie;*
Materials: *Plastic;* Manufacturing
process: *Blow moulding;* Year: *2005*

SYNGENTA PORT-A-PACK
Design: *PI3 – Jed O'Brien, Eric Connolly, Dave Salmon;* Client: *Syngenta Crop Protection;* Awards: *Starpack Award;* Materials: *High density polyethylene, polyethylene terephthalate, nitrile seals, polypropylene;* Manufacturing process: *Injection moulded components and inline filling and closure.* Year: *2006*

A unique problem demands a unique solution. Syngenta needed to find a cost-effective way to supply concentrated herbicides and insecticides to the estimated one billion small farm holders in China and India. Conventional packaging was too expensive and so they designed a refill system that cut the cost of packaging by encouraging multiple use of each of the packaging elements. This technically highly challenging design provides a number of functional design firsts, such as significantly improving state-of-the-art liquid dispensing and closed loop pack recycling.

Ein ausgefallenes Problem bedarf einer ausgefallenen Lösung. Syngenta musste eine kosteneffiziente Möglichkeit finden, konzentrierte Herbizide und Insektizide an etwa eine Milliarde kleiner Bauernbetriebe in China und Indien zu liefern. Da konventionelle Verpackungslösungen viel zu teuer waren, entwickelte man ein wiederbefüllbares System, das die Verpackungskosten senkte, indem es den mehrfachen Gebrauch der einzelnen Verpackungselemente ermöglichte. Bei der technisch höchst anspruchsvollen Entwicklung wurden auch einige funktionale Neuerungen wie etwa ein topmoderner, verbesserter Flüssigkeitsspender und eine höchst effektive, geschlossene Recyclingkette verwirklicht.

Un problème original demande une solution originale. Syngenta devait trouver un moyen rentable de fournir des herbicides et des insecticides concentrés à la population de petits fermiers de l'Inde et de la Chine, estimée à un milliard de personnes. Le conditionnement classique coûtait trop cher, alors l'équipe a inventé un système rechargeable qui diminue le prix du conditionnement en encourageant une utilisation multiple de chaque élément. Ce design très ambitieux du point de vue technique apporte plusieurs innovations en matière de design fonctionnel, comme le doseur de liquide ultra-moderne et le recyclage d'emballage en boucle fermée

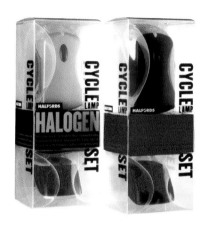

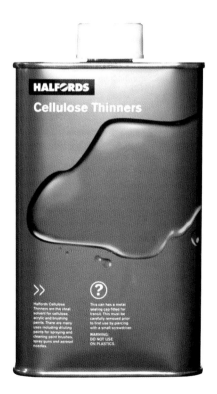

REAVER ADULT CYCLE
HELMET (TRAX)
Design: *Lippa Pearce;* Client:
Halfords; Materials: *Various;*
Manufacturing process: *Various;*
Year: *2003*

HALFORDS OWN BRAND
PACKAGING (CYCLE LIGHTS
AND CELLULOSE THINNERS)
Design: *Pentagram – Harry Pearce,
Jenny Allan, Christian Eves;*
Client: *Halfords Limited;* Materi-
als: *Various;* Manufacturing process:
Various; Year: *2007*

AR VISION
Design: *PDD Group – Ian Heseltine, Oliver Grabes, Dave Wykes (All PDD);* Client: *PDD Internal Futures Concept;* Materials/Manufacturing process: *Concept (not in production);* Year: *2005*

RCA SUSTAINABLE PACKAGING
Design: *Design Guys – Steve Sikora, Jerry Stenback, Shawn Hogland;* Client: *TTE Corporation;* Materials: *Bio Foam (corn starch based expanded foam), paperboard, natural; rubber bands;* Manufacturing process: *Molds are built and injected with the same material as used in water-soluable packing peanuts;* Year: *2007*

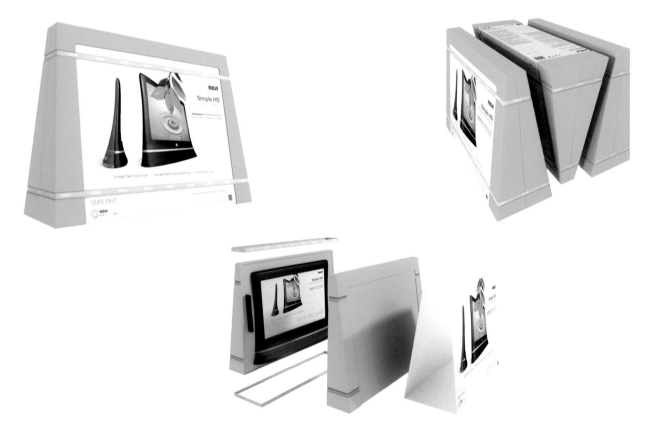

YU NO MI

Design: *PI3 – Magali Vitel*; Client: *Thirsty Minds Ltd / 2020 Organisation*; Materials: *Main container is a laminate structure incorporating printed OLED (Organic light-emitting diode) visual display and an elastomeric valve closure and refill port, polypropylene segmented structural spine; USB style ram* disk for media storage with Power Paper rechargeable flat batteries; Manufacturing process: *Injection moulded polypropylene spine with secondary moulding of elastomeric components, performance laminate refillable inner container produced on horizontal sealer with profile cutter, robotic assembly of pack elements*; Year: 2006

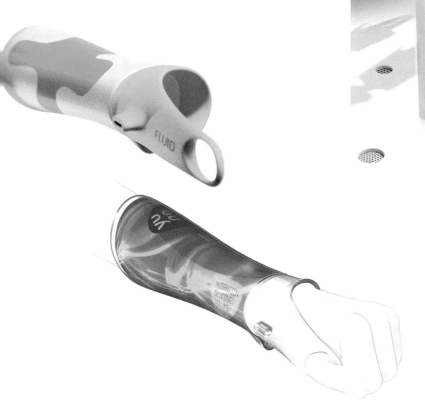

Yu No Mi is a projective design looking at how drinks brands might evolve (or mutate) over the next few years. Created as a design study for drinks company Thirsty Minds, and exhibited at the Total 2020 exhibition, Yu No Mi is a refillable, wearable pack that gives its owner access to refreshment in a variety of ways: drinks, images, sounds and interaction. The Yu No Mi brand suggests a future where the brand can be individually tailored to meet the needs of urban tribes requiring distinctive identities and rituals where the product becomes the experience, however it is delivered.

Yu No Mi ist eine Designstudie, die untersucht, wie sich Getränkemarken innerhalb der nächsten Jahre entwickeln (oder wandeln) können. Die Studie wurde im Auftrag der Getränkefirma Thirsty Minds erstellt und auf der Total 2020 Exhibition vorgestellt. Yu No Mi ist eine stabile, tragbare Verpackung, die dem Träger Erfrischung auf vielfältige Weise bietet: Getränke, Bilder, Klänge und Interaktion. Die Marke Yu No Mi beschwört damit eine Zukunft herauf, in der jede Marke individuell auf die Bedürfnisse, Identitäten und Rituale verschiedener urbaner Gruppierungen angepasst werden kann und in der jedes Produkt zum Erlebnis wird.

Yu No Mi est un concept projectif qui s'intéresse à la manière dont les marques de boissons pourraient évoluer (ou muter) d'ici à quelques années. Cette étude de design réalisée pour la société de boissons Thirsty Minds a été présentée à l'exposition Total 2020. Yu No Mi est un conditionnement de boisson portable et rechargeable qui permet à son propriétaire de se rafraîchir de différentes façons : par la boisson, par les images, par les sons et par l'interaction. La marque Yu No Mi suggère un avenir où la marque s'adapte sur mesure afin de satisfaire les tribus urbaines qui ont des besoins identitaires forts et qui veulent des rituels au sein desquels le produit devient une véritable expérience, quelle que soit la façon dont il est consommé.

The Easy Can package allows brush loading wiping/loading away from sealing the rim, has an easy to open and easy to pick up/close lid, a gripable body, and allows visibility for colour. For the first time in the category, polyethylene terephthalate technology was utilised to maximise the opportunity for creating shape, leading to unique closure and sleeving systems.

Die Easy-Can-Verpackung macht es möglich, den Pinsel abzustreifen, ohne dass der Verschlussring verschmutzt wird. Sie hat einen einfach wiederverschließbaren Verschluss, eine gut in der Hand liegende Form und erlaubt, den enthaltenen Farbton von anßen zu sehen. Mit dieser Verpackung wurde Polyäthylen zum ersten Mal im Bereich Farben verwendet, um die Formbarkeit des Materials für maximalen Nutzen einzusetzen, was zu einem einzigartigen Verschluss- und Etikettierungssystem geführt hat.

Le pot de peinture Easy Can permet de charger le pinceau et de l'essorer loin du bord de fermeture. Son couvercle est facile à ouvrir, facile à ramasser et facile à refermer. Il est facile à prendre en main et permet de voir la couleur de la peinture. Pour la première fois dans cette catégorie, le pot est fabriqué en PET, ce qui a permis de travailler sa forme et d'obtenir un système de fermeture et un système de gainage uniques en leur genre.

EASY CAN
Design: *Tin Horse Design Team;*
Client: *ICI Dulux;* Awards: *Star Pack (Gold), Good Housekeeping Innovation Award;* Materials: *Can – polyethylene terephthalate, shrink sleeve – polyethylene terephthalate; screw lid, and brush wipe – polypropylene, foil wad/liner;* Manufacturing process: *Can – injection blow moulded; lid and brush wipe – injection moulded;* Year: *2003*

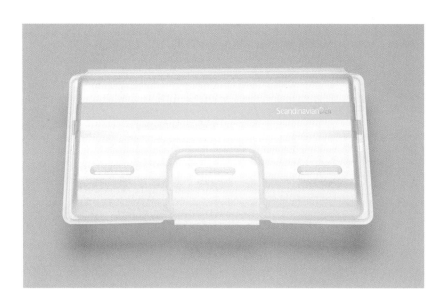

SNOWFLAKE
Design: *Stockholm Design Lab;*
Client: *SAS Scandinavian
Airlines;* Awards: *The Golden Egg
Award;* Materials: *concept;* Manu-
facturing process: *not in production;*
Year: *2006*

THE BLUE BAR
CD PACKAGING
Design: *Pentagram – John Rushworth (Designer); The Berkeley Hotel*; Materials: *various;* Manufacturing process: *various;* Year: *2007*

TESTONI PRESS KIT
"ITALIAN INSIDE" USA
Design: *The Ad Store;* Client:
A. Testoni; Materials: *Cardboard,
leather;* Manufacturing process:
*Rigid cardboard folder covered
inside and out using Stardream
Bronze 120gm screen printed UV
gloss on the cover;* Year: *2007*

THE SKIN OF OUR BOOK
(BOOK PACKAGING DESIGN)
Design: *Tátil Design – Fred Gelli, Ana Laet (Chief Designers), Aline Cohen, Felipe Aguiar (Designers), Rico Gelli, Guido Paternot, Tarso Ghelli (Photo credits)*; Client: *Tátil Design*; Awards: *IF Design Awards, XV Brazilian Promotional Festival – Packaging and Design (Grand Prix and Silver), HOW International Design Competition, 7th Brazilian Graphic Design Biennial*; Materials: *EVA leftovers from Cellsoft (a sandal manufacturer)*; Manufacturing process: *Die cutting*; Year: *2002*

When Tátil first thought of a packaging for their portfolio a few requisites were listed straight away. The packaging should be inventive, guaranteeing protection, and preferably made from recycled materials. Above all, it should guarantee a remarkable experience for the target; it should also refer to the inspiration of Tátil's origin: Fred Gelli's University project, studying the principles of packaging in nature –so much so that the fruits of his idea are now in other people's hands. After exploring pineapples, graviolas and pumpkins, the idea of having slices arose, enabling the creation of a distinctive and splendid form from only one piece. The chosen material was EVA, a kind of rubber that guarantees protection to the portfolio, apart from representing no cost as they used leftovers from recyclable materials.

Als Tátil zum ersten Mal über eine Verpackung für ihr Portfolio nachdachte, standen einige Kriterien sofort fest. Die Verpackung sollte ausgefallen sein, schützen und bevorzugt aus recycelten Materialien bestehen. Vor allem aber sollte sie der Zielgruppe ein außergewöhnliches Erlebnis bescheren. Gleichzeitig sollte sie aber auch einen Bezug zu Tátils Wurzeln haben: Fred Gellis Projekt an der Universität, bei dem er die Prinzipien der Verpackungen in der Natur studierte. Heute halten andere die Früchte seiner Idee in den Händen. Nach der Beschäftigung mit Ananas, Stachelannonen und Kürbissen kam die Idee auf, Scheiben zu verwenden. So können außergewöhnliche und herrliche Formen aus einem Stück geschaffen werden. Das Material der Wahl war EVA, eine Art Gummi, das Schutz für das Portfolio garantiert und praktisch nichts kostet, da Reste von recycelbaren Materialien verwendet wurden.

Lorsque Tátil a commencé à réfléchir à un emballage pour son portfolio, l'équipe a immédiatement défini plusieurs critères. L'emballage devait être inventif, garantir la protection du livre, et être fabriqué de préférence à partir de matériaux recyclables. Il devait surtout faire impression sur le public ciblé. Il devait également faire référence aux origines de Tátil : le projet de Fred Gelli à l'université, étudiant les principes de l'emballage dans la nature. À tel point que les fruits de ses réflexions se trouvent maintenant entre les mains d'autres personnes. Après avoir étudié les ananas, les graviolas et les citrouilles, l'idée survint de recourir à des tranches, permettant la création d'une forme splendide et originale, faite d'une seule pièce. Le matériau choisi est l'EVA, une sorte de caoutchouc qui garantit la protection du portfolio. De plus, il est gratuit, puisqu'ils ont utilisé des restes provenant de matériaux recyclables.

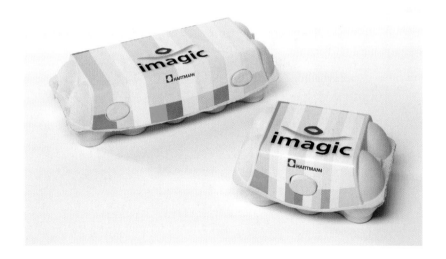

IMAGIC® PACKAGING
STRUCTURAL DESIGN
Design: *Landor Design – Nick Hackley (designer);* Client: *Hartmann Verpackung GmbH,* Awards: *World Star, CroPack, PakStar, Bronze Pack, Deutscher Verpackungsdesign Wettbewerb, Innov' Space;* Materials: *Moulded-fibre (using 100% recycling paper);* Manufacturing process: *Moulded-fibre packaging technology;* Year: *2003*

PANINI
Design: *Lewis Moberly – Mary Lewis (Creative Director), Sonja Frick (Art Director), Hideo Akiba, Fiona Verdon-Smith (designers and illustrators), Hideo Akiba (Typographer);* Client: *Grand Hyatt, Dubai;* Materials: *Paper;* Manufacturing process: *Printing, die cut;* Year: *2005*

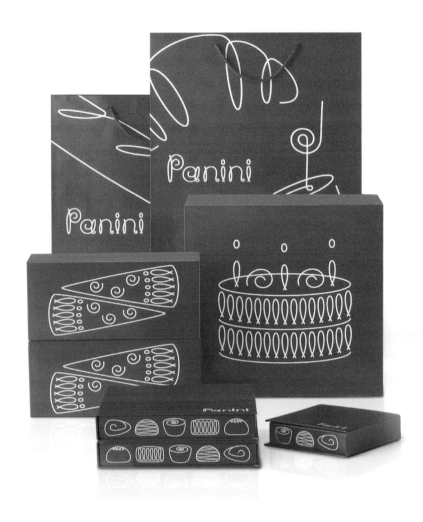

GLOBE LINK
Design: *Pentagram;*
Client: *Global Link;* Materials:
Paper; Manufacturing process:
Printing, die cut; Year: *2007*

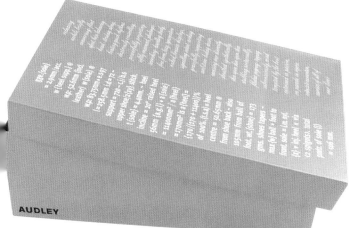

AUDLEY SHOES
Design: *Pentagram;* Client:
Audley Shoues; Materials: *Card-
board, paper;* Manufacturing
process: *Printing, box assenbling;*
Year: *2007*

A to Z of Technical Terms

SiebertHead (www.sieberthead.com)

As with all specialist subjects, the design of packaging has developed its own terminology. In order to assist those perhaps unfamiliar with the terms used, SiebertHead has prepared a guide to some of the most commonly used terms and abbreviations. The meanings given are those which are generally accepted within the industry, rather than strict definitions for the packaging specialists. This is a simple reference on packaging design terminology for the marketing executive. If you would like to know more or have the complete list, please contact SiebertHead at www.sieberthead.com.

Acetate *(cellulose acetate)* **– Material**
Transparent plastic used widely for window film in the carton industry and for presentation boxes.

Achromatic – Repro
One of many manufacturer specific names given to GCR (Grey Component Replacement). GCR removes the grey component from all colours in the image and increases the black to compensate. Used where heavy concentrations of blue, red and yellow exist to make the image clearer and sharper.

Acrylic *(acrylonitrile)* **– Material**
Synthetic material produced from acrylonitrile. One trade name is Perspex. It is clear or opaque, with or without colour. Used in solid form for models, point of sale and as a basis for some printing inks.

Additive colour – Computing
Reproducing colours by mixing light, as on a television or computer screen. Each of the three additive colours — red, green and blue

produce lighter colours in two combinations and pure white light in all three combinations (see also Subtractive Colour).

Against the grain – Manufacturing
The folding or cutting of any fibrous material at right angles to the grain.

Analox print – Printing
Rollers that convey the ink in flexographic printing to the printing plates. The rollers contain an engraved surface determining how much ink is transferred. This allows control of ink density, enabling further control of the flexographic printing quality.

Aseptic – Manufacturing
Factory packing for food and drink carried out in conditions which exclude microorganisms.

Barcode – Packaging
A pattern of printed vertical lines and 12/13 or 8 digit numbers that is read by a computer-linked laser sensor. In use at checkout points of supermarkets for pricing, stock control and ordering. There are numerous types of bar codes, the commonest being EAN (European Article Number), The American UPC (Universal Product Code) and ITF (Interleaved Two of Five) used for outer cases.

Bleed – Printing
The extension of an image area beyond the trim edge of an artwork to compensate for any mis-register during the finishing process of a job.

Blending – Computing
A blend produces a transition between shapes, colours or stroke widths by creating a group of intermediate paths between two original shapes, colours or stroke widths. A red square, for example, can be changed over a distance into a yellow circle by a specified number of steps.

Blister packs – Computing
A (usually) clear thermoformed film blister sealed onto a card backing, retaining the product within.

Boil in the bag – Packaging
Using temperature-stable and water-resistant film, food is packed in a bag and sold within a folded carton. The food is heated in the bag and only opened for serving. Film used is commonly Nylon 11. Often used for frozen meals heated in microwaves.

Box board *(folding boxboard)* **– Packaging**
A laminated board for printing cartons. It has a top layer of bleached cellulose, a central layer often of mechanical pulp and a reverse side of cellulose. Referred to as Duplex board.

Bronzing – Printing
Obtaining a metallic effect in printing by first applying an adhesive layer, then dusting it with metallic powder.

Buck – Design
Initial stage in 3D model making.

Butane – Manufacturing
Flammable gas often used in liquid form as an aerosol propellant. Although flammable

it has the advantage over PFCs and CFCs in being non-harmful to the ozone layer (see also PFC, CFC).

C-type – Design
A photographic colour print produced from a colour negative.

CAD/CAM *(computer aided design/ computer aided manufacture)* – Computing
A complete computer system allowing on-screen technical data criteria to be transferred to the production process, e.g. carton blank design on screen to production of multiple cartons, cutting and creasing forms.

Cellulose film *(regenerated cellulose film)* – Material
Produced from a pure wood pulp to produce clear film. Poor barrier to water vapour unless coated. Excellent as an odour barrier, used for confectionery and biscuit wrapping.

Champagne base – Packaging
Similar to petalloid base but uses a totally concave base shape. This type of base, although distinctive for designers, uses more material.

Check digit – Packaging
The final digit in a bar code. When the product is scanned in the supermarket the check digit confirms that the whole number has been registered correctly.

Chroma – Packaging
The degree of intensity or purity of any colour.

C0-extrusion moulding – Manufacturing
The process of extruding two or more different plastic materials simultaneously to produce one thickness possessing the characteristics of the combined materials. Used for squeeze bottles or sauces where gas barrier properties are required in addition to flexibility.

Coated paper – Material
Quality paper usually coated with china clay to provide a smooth surface for fine screen printing.

Colour gamut – Repro
A representation of the range and extent of colour that can be output by a particular system. For example the range or gamut of colour viewed on a transparency on a light box will

be almost twice that of the same image printed in ink on reasonable quality board.

Colour overlay – Repro
Artwork used to be prepared in black and white and handed over to origination houses or printers. Artworks therefore included a rough colour sketch to indicate colours and other details.

Colour separation *(separation)* – Repro
Film separation (one colour per film) by a scanner of full colour originals (transparencies, illustrations or colour prints). Usually as cyan, magenta, yellow and black in four colour printing. Linework colour separations are similarly achieved by using a camera.

Colour swatch – Repro
An actual colour sample, attached to the artwork that specifies a Pantone/Focoltone etc. number that the printer must match. If the designer cannot find a suitable colour reference that matches their requirements then a sample of the colour must be attached (see also Pantone/Focoltone).

Composite *(comp)* – Manufacturing
Different materials combined to make one pack e.g. paperboard drum with metal or plastic end caps.

Continuous tone *(contone, ct)* – Repro
An image containing colour/colours smoothly blending to provide a true representation of the original image. This image is not made up of varying sized dots (halftone). No print process can print continuous tone without a dot screen, except for collotype which uses a gelatin covered plate and is rarely seen today.

Control strips *(eurostandard)* – Repro
The control strip contains vital information concerning exposure, grey balance, density range, dot gain, slur, trapping and registration. It allows designers and printers to check that a proof has been properly produced and it enables the printer to identify the problem if the print does not match the proof.

Corrugated board – Material
A fluted or corrugated sheet between two flat parallel sheets (liners) glued together to provide a reinforced laminated structure for shipping cases.

CPET *(crystalline polyethylene terephthalate)* – Material
Derived from PET, frequently used for pre-cooked dinner and entrée plates as the material is capable of withstanding radiant oven temperatures without deformation (see also PET).

Crash lock base – Packaging
Glued-up base flaps, which automatically lock when the carton is erected. Used for heavy items such as bottles of spirits.

CRC *(child resistant closures)* – Packaging
Devices designed to restrict/ prevent opening by children. Some products are legally obliged to comply e.g. bleach, pharmaceuticals, chemicals etc.

Cutter guide – Packaging
A drawing of the die cut for any piece of artwork indicating the size, shape and vital measurements of the artwork. It is vital information required before the artwork process is started.

Cutting and creasing – Printing
Cutting the shape of the carton and making the creases in correct register in one operation (see also Die Cut).

Debossing – Packaging
Producing a sunken image into a surface as against a raised image in embossing.

Descender – Typography
The part of certain lower-case characters, such as g, p, q, y etc. which appears below the baseline.

Die cut – Manufacturing
A wooden sheet which incorporates the cutting and creasing lines (made of metal). Applied post print, these create the cutting and creasing shape of the pack.

Digital proof – Printing
One of various forms of digital printing used as a faster, more cost effective means of checking artwork/repro/photographic files. It is also used for small digital prints for mock-ups, brochures etc. Common digital machines are Digital Cromalin, Kodak Proofer, Indigo etc. There are limitations, but they are now commonly used as a suitable proof for printers.

Direct-to-plate – Printing

Also known as Straight to Plate, this dispenses with film separations. Digital information is passed straight to a plate plotter. For this process thinner plates are required.

Dot gain – Printing

The change in size of a halftone dot due to factors such as exposure in film, plate making and ink spread during printing. Using the Straight to Plate process, the only dot gain will occur on press.

Dot skip – Printing

With gravure printing the finest engraved dots hold very little ink, in some instances the ink dries too quickly and is not transferred to the substrate. On the printed item dots are missing or skipped.

Dry offset – Printing

Cylinders transfer each colour in turn to an offset (blanket) cylinder from which all colours together are printed onto an awkward, usually non porous surface. No colours can overprint. Used for toothpaste tubes, plastic drinking cups, margarine and yogurt tubs, bottles etc.

Duotone – Printing

A registered set of two halftones, in two colours. Varying effects can be achieved by giving one colour image more contrast than the other. Tritones use three colours.

Embossing – Printing

Producing a raised image on a surface by using an embossing plate, or in the moulding process on a bottle.

Euroslot – Packaging

Euroslot is a standardisation of peg mounting holes to guarantee that a product will hang on any standard peg in any country. No agreed international standard exists and the term has become generic for a hanging slot.

Extrusion blow moulding – Manufacturing

In extrusion blow moulding a hollow parison tube is clamped inside a mould, air under pressure inflates the parison to the shape of the mould. Used for hollow packaging, most commonly bottles (see also Injection Blow Moulding).

Eye marks – Printing

Small block or blocks of dark colour on wrappers, used to keep web fed material in register for printing, tension and trimming. Eye marks are "read" by an electronic eye.

Flange – Printing

A projecting collar, rim or rib on an object for fixing it to another object.

Flexible packaging – Packaging

Packaging provided from film, rolls and laminates e.g. sachets and pouches.

Flexo – Printing

Relief printing process using rubber or photo-polymer plates attached to a cylinder. Origination costs are lower than for gravure and the process is therefore suitable for medium length print runs. Its many uses in packaging include printing on corrugated boxes, folding cartons and flexible films/laminates and foils.

Focoltone – Printing

A numbered colour-matching system to select tint combinations of cyan/magenta/yellow/black with tint combinations of an additional special colour. This gives five colour work a greatly extended number of colour options. It is not the same as the Pantone system.

Foil (aluminium foil) – Material

Formed by rolling pure aluminium foil from a slab into a sheet. Used for trays, peel-off lids, laminates and decoration.

Foil blocking – Printing

Used to apply gloss or matt metal finish foils to printed items. A heated block presses and adheres the foil to the substrate. A costly process that is suitable only for expensive products such as perfumes and spirit beverages. Also referred to as Hot Foil Stamping.

Glassine – Material

A smooth, shiny form of greaseproof paper, glassine is used for wrapping products in baking and confectionery industries.

Grain direction – Printing

The main direction of fibres in paper and board. Paper is stronger under tension in machine direction and less liable to stretch or shrink.

Gripper edge – Printing

The edge of a paper sheet that is pulled first through the machine by a line of grippers.

HDPE (high density polyethylene) – Material

A derivative of PE which is stronger and more durable than LDPE due to greater crystallinity. HDPE is used widely for blow moulding (see also PE).

Header card – Packaging

Either the backing card on blister packs or hanging cards on bagged products. Thus creating a print area and space for euroslot.

Hickie – Printing

Debris that has become attached to a printing plate and shows up on the print as a haloed spot.

Hi-Fi screen/hexachrome – Printing

A very fine screen, often uniquely designed which allows more than the conventional 4 colours to be used. Hexachrome is Pantone's registered 6-colour system. In its truest sense. Hi-Fi screening allows any number of colours to be combined to produce the final image. Other proprietary systems also exist.

Highlight – Repro

The lightest area, containing detail, of an image.

Hips (high impact polystyrene) – Packaging

General purpose material very easy to form although clear HIPS is brittle.

Injection blow moulding – Manufacturing

Injection blow moulding is a two-stage process, used for precise neck designs on bottles. The neck is injection-moulded with a short sealed tube and then transferred to a blow moulding station (see also Extrusion Blow Moulding).

Key lines – Repro

Lines on traditional artworks that indicate the edge of a colour or photographic image, they do not print and are only position guides.

Kraft paper – Material

Made from sulphate pulp, kraft papers are heavy-duty paper. They can be bleached, coloured or left natural. Commonly used for corrugated board, sacks and bags. They can also be made water-repellent.

Laquer – Printing

Protective film in liquid form applied to a carton inside or out to provide protection to the carton. Lacquers can also be used on tinplate. However, there is not one lacquer suitable for all purposes.

Laminate – Packaging
A number of single ply materials adhered together to optimise physical and barrier properties. Supplied on reels.

Lamination – Printing
The technique of bonding together a number of layers of materials, giving a hard protective surface. Cookery cards are a common example of the use of this process which is more robust and more expensive than a varnish.

Letterpress – Printing
Printing process in which the ink impression is taken from a raised surface of type matter or blocks. The oldest of the printing processes, now less widely used. Like flexography it is a relief print process. It can be flat bed (sheet fed) or rotary (web fed).

Light weighting – Packaging
Reducing the amount of material used in a bottle by careful use of shape, i.e. rounded corners and smooth curves.

Line work – Printing
A term relating to the generation of artwork using solid elements rather than screened images.

Litho laminate – Printing
Used for printing on corrugated cases, it involves litho printing the graphics onto paper subsequently laminated to the outer liner of the case blank.

MAP (modified atmosphere packaging) – Packaging
Used primarily for pre-packed red/cooked meats. MAP packaging is a process where packed meats are sealed into their containers with a combination of gases to improve the shelf life of the product.

Metallised – Manufacturing
The deposition of metallic particles (commonly aluminium) onto a surface, usually a film. Provides a matt or gloss metallic appearance.

Micron – Packaging
Measurement: 1000µm (micron) = 1mm. Carton board is measured in microns.

MIPP (metallic integrated process printing) – Printing
In simple terms the processed image integrates dots of gold and silver ink with the 4 process colours wherever the original image has a metallic quality. By integrating gold and silver into the process set it is possible for the image to retain its continuous tonal values and to give realistic shadow and highlight detail, without losing either realism or reflective quality.

Misregistration – Printing
When two or more colours in a printed sample are incorrectly aligned horizontally and/or vertically. The resulting image looks blurred.

Mockups – Design
Simulation of a final article or pack in either 2D or 3D format.

Moiré – Repro
All four colours used to print full colour images are made up from lines of halftone dots. For each colour the lines must be set at different angles. If these angles are set incorrectly, the dots will clash and form distorting patterns that confuse the eye.

Object oriented image – Computing
An object oriented image is defined mathematically by means of curves, lines and geometric shapes rather than as pixels in a bitmapped image. This kind of graphics is often used in logos, types and technical drawings.

Opacity – Printing
The degree to which ink will obscure the colour of the material on which it is printed, or how much the paper will prevent "show-through" or "see through". A measure of how much light is stopped by a film or absorbed by an ink layer.

OPP (oriented polypropylene) – Material
A flexible plastic film for packaging, stronger than polypropylene as the molecular structure has been altered (oriented). (See also PP).

Oriented – Manufacturing
Orientation of plastics is altering the alignment of the molecules within the material, making it stronger, usually in a specific direction or directions.

Overprinting – Printing
Printing on an already pre-printed area e.g. batch codes, "use before" dates etc. or to achieve a colour using a combination of 2 colours i.e. blue overprinting yellow to create green.

Overwrap – Packaging
Protective film wrapped around a carton or box, e.g. chocolate boxes. Used also as a means of collating smaller packs.

Pallet – Manufacturing
Large wooden, wood and board or plastic trays for transporting goods. Pallets have a raised deck to allow fork lift trucks to carry and load them. They come in standard sizes and in two forms, two way and four way entry. This refers to how they may be picked up by a fork lift.

Pantone – Printing
Trade name of an industry standard colour identification system for matching and mixing specific ink colours (see also Colour Swatch, Focoltone).

PC (polycarbonate) – Material
Plastic material: PC is temperature resistant, clear, rigid and has a high impact strength. Due to cost, most commonly used for special applications e.g. high temperature resistance.

PE (polyethylene) – Material
Plastic material: there are two types of PE, LDPE (low density polyethylene) and HDPE (high density polyethylene). Both LDPE and HDPE are used for films and containers (bottles). HDPE is more rigid. Polyethylene is suitable for using with frozen foods.

PET (polyethylene terephthalate) – Material
Plastic material: used extensively in plastic blow moulded bottles. In film form PET is biaxially oriented polyester and is used in labelling and high performance films. The crystalline version (CPET) is suited to high temperature use, such as microwavable packaging trays.

PFC (polyfluorocarbon propellant) – Material
Non-inflammable propellant used in aerosol cans. Contains chemicals that are harmful to the ozone layer (see also Butane).

Pigment – Printing

Pigments are solid particles which give ink its colour.

Pillow pack – Packaging

A flow-wrapped pack, sealed at both ends with a seam down the back. Commonly used in crisp packaging.

Polymer – Material

Polymers are made up of monomers (molecules). A plastic is formed from a polymer through polymerisation. If only one kind of monomer is used in polymerisation, then it is homopolymer. If more than one kind of monomer is used, then it is a copolymer.

Pouches – Packaging

There are two main types of pouch packs (or sachets): fin-sealed and pillow. Fin-sealed pouches are sealed on all four sides. Pillow pouches are sealed at two ends with a vertical seam up the back, commonly used for crisp packets etc. Now available as stand up pouches.

PP *(polypropylene)* **– Material**

Probably the most versatile plastic combining excellent chemical resistance and good strength. It can be extruded, blow moulded, injection moulded, compression moulded and vacuum formed. Available as a fibre, film or foam in any colour and in clear.

Pre-printing – Printing

When printing on corrugated cases, pre-printing can be used. It is printing the graphic image on the outer liner of the board before the corrugation process.

Process colours – Printing

The colours (cyan, magenta, yellow) plus black that are combined to print full colour images. Process colours can produce the widest range of colours with the fewest inks.

Propane – Material

Flammable hydrocarbon gas used under pressure in liquid form as an aerosol propellant. Alternative to CFCs.

PS *(polystyrene)* **– Material**

Plastic material: used for crystal clear or coloured injection mouldings. Excellent but brittle moulding material. In expanded form, used for protective packaging.

Ptfe *(polytetrafluoroethylene – teflon)* **– Material**

Plastic material: it comes in two forms, low friction film, used on adhesive tape and solid form. In solid block form it retains its low friction properties and it can be machine shaped. However, it cannot be heat formed in any way.

PU *(polyurethane)* **– Material**

Plastic material: Polyurethane comes in two forms, foam and bonded chipfoam. Both are used for protective packaging. Foam is moulded around the article either in a mould or in-situ. Chipfoam is used in sheets, rolls, corner blocks and mouldings. Also an adhesive base.

Punt – Packaging

The recess in the base of a bottle.

PVA *(polyvinyl acetate)* **– Packaging**

Adhesive: used in the gluing of cartons.

PVC *(polyvinyl chloride)* **– Material**

Plastic material: clear film or sheet. In film form it is used for shrink wrapping of meat and fresh fruit. In sheet form it is good for vacuum forming. Granular form used for bottle production.

PVDC *(polyvinylidene chloride – saran)* **– Material**

Plastic material: it has good resistance to water, odour, flavour and gases. Often applied as a clear coating to films to improve barrier properties.

Quad bags – Packaging

A variant on a flow wrap bag, but where all corners are sealed, in addition to other areas, giving the pack a more rectangular stance.

Resin master – Manufacturing

Intermediate stage in tool production for moulded containers. Synthetic resin representation of container incorporating shrinkage factors used in production of metal mould.

Reverse printing – Printing

Where the print is placed on the inside of a (clear) film. The film acts as a protective layer to the print.

Rigid box – Packaging

Pre-erected box. Shoeboxes and assembled boxes ready for filling.

Rub down – Design

A system by which an image is transferred from one surface (usually polythene) to another substrate by rubbing with a pen or stylus.

Run off – Manufacturing

Excess material produced following the injection moulding process.

Run on – Printing

An item sometimes included in a print quotation giving the price for increasing the print quantity by a specific amount.

Shell and slide – Packaging

Pack design, often produced in carton board, where tray slides out, as with a matchbox. Shrink wrap packaging used primarily for packaging meat and poultry to produce a tight, tamper-evident wrap.

Skin pack – Packaging

A thin plastic film is heated and drawn around a carded product under vacuum. Provides secure component location and high visibility.

Sleeves wrap – Packaging

Sleeves are used mainly around bottles for labelling and come in two forms, shrink and stretch. Shrink sleeves are placed around a bottle and heated to shrink. Stretch sleeves are stretched cold and released once around the bottle where they try to return to original size. N.B. Card sleeves are also produced to enhance product communication on shelf.

Sot – Manufacturing

a) Stay-on-Tab. (a means of retaining the opening part of a beverage can to the can body).

b) Straight-on-Tray (a means of displaying products on-shelf in the retail environment).

Spectrophotometer – Print

A very accurate colour-measuring instrument. Used to define a colour accurately and measure or compare how different a colour is from another.

Spiral winding – Packaging

A laminate of paper wound round in a helix to form a strong tube. Used on toilet roll and kitchen roll cores.

Spreads and chokes – Repro

All printing presses have the potential to go out of register during a print run. If different colours "kiss-fit" then splinters of white will show through from the substrate if there is the slightest mis-register. To overcome this, two colours are made to overlap very slightly (usually .15 of a millimetre). The weaker colour always chokes inwards or spreads outwards under the stronger colour.

Stretch wrap – Packaging
The stretching of film around rigid items on pallets to hold in position. No heating is required.

Strip packaging – Packaging
Two rolls of heat-sealable material are sealed around the product. Both materials are flexible and are frequently aluminium foil based or plastics.

Structural design – Design
Design of three-dimensional packaging, not including surface graphics, e.g. design of a bottle.

Subtractive colour – Printing
All applications of ink to a surface, such as white paper, subtract (absorb) some portion of white light reflected from it. Cyan, magenta and yellow are the subtractive colours, ideally each one subtracting one third of the visible spectrum. Together they subtract the whole spectrum thereby making black (see also Additive colour).

Surface printing – Printing
Where the print is placed on the outer surface of the object to be printed.

Susceptor – Packaging
By including a metallic based component in the packaging — the susceptor — these areas reach a higher temperature than non-metallic areas and can be used to "crisp" and "brown" microwaved food.

Tamper evident – Packaging
Closure system or device designed to positively indicate that opening of a package has taken place. Often confused with "tamper proof" — which is seldom, if ever, achieved.

Tampo printing – Printing
Sometimes also know as "Tampon printing" outside the UK. This is a method of printing on to complex curved surfaces/curves. Ink from the printing plate is transferred to the object to be printed by a soft latex pad that can distort round the object to be printed.

Therimage – Printing
Heat transfer of a printed image from web to product. Often gravure printed image used, hence long runs needed. Typical use, plastic bottle printing where four colour halftone illustration is required.

Thermoforming – Printing
Moulding plastic sheet by forcing it into or over a mould. Main method of thermo-forming is vacuum forming.

Thermography – Printing
Technique in which heat-treated ink image produces a raised effect.

Throat – Packaging
The inside of the neck of a bottle.

Tint – Repro
Any solid colour can be weakened by printing it in a halftone screen of dots. The smaller the size of the dot the lighter the colour.

Trapping – Printing
The ink from the previous printed colour that is removed when the next colour on the press is applied. The pressman's aim is to reduce the trap factor to a minimum for the best printed result. This term has been incorrectly used by artwork software houses to replace the conventional print industries — "spreads and chokes" (see also Spreads and chokes).

Tynocolour print – Printing
Specialist patented printing process. Very thick ink is deposited and is very accurate for colour. It is used in particular medical disciplines where a colour is produced after a medical test and which has to be consistent and match a colour chart to aid diagnosis e.g. in a pregnancy test.

Ullage – Packaging
The total volume of a container is greater than the content, the difference is known as the ullage.

Fachausdrücke von A bis Z

SiebertHead (www.sieberthead.com)

Wie alle Fachgebiete hat auch das Verpackungsdesign seine eigene Terminologie entwickelt. Für diejenigen, die vielleicht nicht mit allen Begriffen vertraut sind, hat SiebertHead ein Glossar der gebräuchlichsten Begriffe und Abkürzungen zusammengestellt.

Die Erläuterungen entsprechen eher den Gheiten der Industrie als den strikt technischen Definitionen der Verpackungsspezialisten. Hier soll dem Marketing Manager ein einfacher Leitfaden für die Terminologie des Verpackungsdesigns an die Hand gegeben werden.

Weitere Informationen finden Sie unter www.sieberthead.com

Abreiben – Design

Ein Verfahren, bei dem durch Reiben mit einem Stift oder Stylus ein Bild von einer Oberfläche (in der Regel Polyethylen) auf ein anderes Medium übertragen wird.

Achromatische Korrektur – Reprografie

Eine der vielen proprietären Begriffe eines Herstellers für die Graukomponentenersetzung (GCR: Grey Component Replacement), bei der die Graukomponente aus allen Farben eines Bildes entfernt und zum Ausgleich der Schwarzanteil erhöht wird. Kommt dort zur Anwendung, wo starke Konzentrationen von Blau, Rot und Gelb vorhanden sind, um dem Bild mehr Schärfe zu verleihen.

Acryl *(Acrylnitril)* **– Material**

Synthetisches Material, das aus Acrylnitril gewonnen wird. Ein Handelsname ist Plexiglas. Es kann transparent, undurchsichtig, gefärbt oder farblos sein. In fester Form wird es für Modelle und Verkaufsdisplays und flüssig als Basis für einige Druckfarben verwendet.

Additive Farbmischung – IT

Die Farbdarstellung durch Lichtmischung, wie z. B. bei einem Fernsehgerät oder Computermonitor. Jede der drei Farben Rot, Grün und Blau ergibt in Zweierkombination hellere Farben und in Dreierkombination reinweißes Licht (siehe auch Subtraktive Farbmischung).

Anschnitt – Drucktechnik

Die Positionierung eines Bildbereichs jenseits der Schnittkante einer Druckseite, sodass der Passerversatz beim Druck kompensiert wird.

Aseptisch – Herstellung

Industrielle Verpackung von Lebensmitteln unter Bedingungen, die die Verunreinigung durch Mikroorganismen ausschließen.

Automatikboden – Verpackung

Verleimte Bodenlaschen, die sich beim Auffalten des Kartons automatisch verschränken. Wird für schwere Waren wie Flaschen verwendet.

Azetat *(Zellulose-Azetat)* **– Material**

Transparenter Kunststoff, der als Fensterfolie in der Kartonagenindustrie und bei Präsentationsverpackungen verwendet wird.

Barcode *(Strichcode)* **– Verpackung**

Ein Muster aus aufgedruckten Strichen und 12, 13 oder 8 Ziffern, das von einem Computerscanner gelesen werden kann. Wird von Verkaufsstellen zur Preisregistrierung und Fakturierung verwendet. Es gibt verschiedene Typen von Barcodes, die gebräuchlichsten sind EAN (früher: European Article Number, heute: International Article Number), der amerikanische UPC (Universal Product Code) und ITF (Interleaved Two of Five), die außen auf Verpackungen aufgedruckt werden.

Beschnittmarke – Verpackung

Markierung zur Beschneidung einer Form, die Größe, Form und andere wichtige Maße für die Grafik liefert. Muss festgelegt werden, bevor mit den grafischen Arbeit begonnen wird.

Beutel – Verpackung

Es gibt zwei Formen des Beutels (oder Sachets): an allen vier Seiten versiegelt oder an zwei Enden versiegelt und mit einem Rückensaum versehen. Die zweite Form heißt auch Kissenpackung und wird meist für Kartoffelchips u. Ä. verwendet. Es gibt sie mittlerweile auch in standfähiger Form.

Blisterpackung – Verpackung

Ein (meist) transparenter, thermogeformter Luftblasenfilm, der auf eine Kartonunterlage geklebt wird und das Produkt enthält.

Bronzierung – Drucktechnik

Das Aufbringen einer metallischen Oberfläche im Druck. Dazu wird eine Leimschicht aufgebracht, die mit einem metallischen Pulver bestäubt wird.

Buchdruck, Hochdruck – Drucktechnik

Druckverfahren, bei dem die Farbe von den erhabenen Bereichen der Druckplatte übertragen wird. Dieses älteste Druckverfahren ist heute nicht mehr sehr verbreitet.

Buck – Design
Erste Stufe des 3D-Modelling.

Butangas – Herstellung
Brennbares Gas, das in flüssiger Form häufig als Treibgas für Aerosolflaschen verwendet wird. Es ist zwar entflammbar, hat aber gegenüber PFC und CFC den Vorteil, dass es die Ozonschicht nicht schädigt (siehe auch PFC).

Butze, Partisane, Popel – Drucktechnik
Verunreinigung auf der Druckplatte, die im Druck als unscharf umrandeter Fleck erscheint.

CAD/CAM *(Computer Aided Design/Computer Aided Manufacture)* **– IT**
Ein vollständiges Computersystem, das die Übertragung virtueller Daten auf den Produktionsprozess ermöglicht, z. B. der Entwurf von Kartons am Bildschirm bis zur Produktion der Kartons mit Schnitt- und Falzanweisungen.

Champagne-Boden – Verpackung
Ähnlich wie der Petalloid-Boden, ist aber komplett konkav. Dieser Flaschenboden wird zwar von Designern gern verwendet, erfordert aber mehr Material.

Chroma – Verpackung
Das Maß der Intensität oder Reinheit einer Farbe.

CPET *(kristallines Polyethylenterephthalat)* **– Material**
Ein PET-Derivat, das regelmäßig für Verpackungen von Convenience Food verwendet wird, da das Material hitzebeständig ist und sich im Ofen nicht verformt (siehe auch PET).

C-Type Print – Design
Ein Farbfotoabzug von einem Farbnegativ.

Deckkraft – Drucktechnik
Das Maß, in dem eine Farbe die Farbe überdeckt, auf die sie gedruckt wird, oder in dem das Durchscheinen von Papier verhindert wird. Das Maß, wie viel Licht von einem Film abgehalten oder von einer Farbschicht absorbiert wird.

Digitalproof – Drucktechnik
Eine Form des Digitaldrucks, die zur kosteneffizienten Überprüfung von Druckdateien dient. Wird auch für Digitaldrucke von Dummies, Broschüren usw. eingesetzt. Gebräuchliche digitale Druckmaschinen sind Digital Cromalin, Kodak Proofer, Iris Indigo usw. Der Nutzen ist begrenzt, die Ausdrucke dienen Druckern meist als Proofs.

Direct-to-plate – Drucktechnik
Bei dieser Drucktechnik sind Filmseparationen überflüssig. Die digitalen Daten werden direkt auf eine Druckplatte übertragen. Für dieses Verfahren werden dünnere Druckplatten benötigt.

Doppeltondruck, Duotondruck – Drucktechnik
Ein passgenauer Satz von zwei Rastern in zwei Farben. Durch Verstärkung des Kontrasts in einem Farbbild lassen sich verschiedene Effekte erzielen. Der Dreitondruck verwendet entsprechend drei Farben.

Dot-Skip *(fehlende Punkte)* **– Drucktechnik**
Beim Tiefdruck nehmen die kleinsten Punkte nur sehr wenig Farbe auf, die manchmal zu schnell trocknet und nicht auf das Druckmedium übertragen wird. Dadurch fehlen im Druck einzelne Punkte.

Dummies – Design
Modell des fertigen Artikels in zwei- oder dreidimensionaler Form.

Duplexkarton – Verpackung
Ein laminierter Karton für bedruckte Verpackungen. Er besitzt eine Außenschicht aus gebleichtem Zellstoff, ein mittlere Lage aus Altpapiermaterial und eine Rückseite aus Zellstoff.

Europoolpalette *(Europalette)* **– Herstellung**
Große Palette aus Holz oder Kunststoff für den Warentransport. Paletten sind meist zweilagig, damit ein Stapler sie mit der Ladegabel aufnehmen und transportieren kann. Sie sind in Größe und Form genormt.

Euroschlitz – Verpackung
Der Euroschlitz ist eine standardisierte Ausstanzung für Aufhängelöcher, die dafür sorgt, dass ein Produkt innerhalb eines Landes an jeder Displaystange gleich hängt. Es gibt keinen internationalen Standard, und der Begriff ist zum Synonym für Aufhängelöcher geworden.

Extrusionsblasen – Herstellung
Beim Extrusionsblasen wird ein Schlauch in eine Form gespannt und mit Druckluft hineingepresst. Wird für Hohlverpackungen, meist Flaschen, verwendet (siehe auch Spritzblasen).

Farbmuster *(Farbfeld)* **– Reprografie**
Ein physisches Farbmuster, das einer Illustration beigelegt wird, um eine bestimmte Pantone-/Focoltone- oder ähnliche Farbe für den Druck vorzugeben. Wenn der Designer keine passende Farbreferenz für seine Bedürfnisse finden kann, muss er ein Beispiel der Farbe mitliefern (siehe auch Pantone, Focoltone).

Farbraum – Reprografie
Eine Beschreibung des Umfangs und der Bandbreite an Farben, die ein bestimmtes System darstellen oder ausgeben kann. So ist z. B. der Farbraum eines Diapositivs auf einem Leuchttisch doppelt so groß wie der Farbraum des Bildausdrucks auf einem hochwertigen Karton.

Farbschattierung – Reprografie
Jede Farbfläche kann durch Aufrasterung aufgehellt werden. Je kleiner die Punktgröße desto heller ist die Farbe.

Farbseparation *(Separation)* **– Reprografie**
Die Filmseparation (eine Farbe pro Film) einer Farbvorlage (Dia, Illustration oder Farbdruck) per Scanner. Normalerweise werden die vier Prozessfarben Cyan, Magenta, Gelb und Schwarz verwendet.

Faserverlauf – Drucktechnik
Die Hauptverlaufsrichtung von Fasern in Papier und Karton. Papier ist unter Spannung in Laufrichtung stabiler und neigt weniger zum Strecken oder Schrumpfen.

Flansch – Drucktechnik
Ein vorstehender Kragen, Rand oder Falz zur Verbindung eines Objekts mit einem anderen.

Flexible Verpackung – Verpackung
Verpackung aus Folie, Rollenmaterial und Laminaten, z. B. Tütchen und Taschen.

Flexodruck – Drucktechnik
Hochdruckverfahren mit Gummi- oder Foto-Polymerplatten, die auf eine Rolle aufgebracht sind. Die Vorlagenerstellung ist günstiger als beim Tiefdruck. Das Verfahren

eignet sich vor allem für mittelgroße Auflagen. Es wird z. B. für den Druck auf Wellpappenkartons, Faltkartons und flexible Filme, Laminate und Folien verwendet.

Focoltone – Drucktechnik
Ein auf Zahlen basierendes Farbabstimmungssystem zur Kombinationen der Prozessfarben Cyan, Magenta, Gelb und Schwarz mit einer zusätzliche Schmuckfarbe. Es erweitert die Auswahl verwendbarer Farben erheblich. Nicht mit dem Pantone-System zu verwechseln.

Folie (Aluminiumfolie) – Material
Sehr dünn ausgerolltes Aluminiumblech. Wird für Tabletts, Abziehdeckel, Laminate und Dekorationen verwendet.

Folienprägung – Drucktechnik
Das Aufbringen glänzender oder matter Metallfolie auf Drucksachen. Ein erhitzter Druckblock presst die Folie auf das Medium. Ein teures Verfahren, das sich nur für Luxusprodukte wie Parfüm oder Spirituosen lohnt. Wird auch als Heißfolienprägung bezeichnet.

Folienverpackung – Verpackung
Ein dünner Kunststofffilm wird erhitzt und im Vakuum über ein Produkt auf einem Kartonrücken gezogen. Sorgt für eine sichere Positionierung und hervorragende Erkennbarkeit des Produkts.

Gestrichenes Papier – Material
Hochwertiges Papier, das mit weißem Ton beschichtet ist, um eine möglichst glatte Oberfläche für den hochwertigen Siebdruck zu erhalten.

Gewichtsreduzierung – Verpackung
Reduzierung der Materialmenge einer Flasche durch optimale Formung, d. h. runde Schultern und glatte Kurven.

Greiferrand – Drucktechnik
Der Rand eines Papierbogens, der von Greifern zuerst in die Druckmaschine gezogen wird.

Halbtonbild – Reprografie
Ein Bild mit Farben, die nahtlos ineinander übergehen, um eine farbtreue Wiedergabe des Originalbildes zu erzielen. Das Bild besteht nicht aus unterschiedlich großen Punkten (Rasterbild). Kein Druckprozess kann Halbtonbilder ohne Rasterung drucken, mit Ausnahme der Kollotypie, die eine mit

Gelatine überzogene Platte verwendet, aber heute kaum noch zum Einsatz kommt.

HDPE (Polyethylen hoher Dichte, Niederdruck-Polyethylen) – Material
Ein PE-Derivat, das stärker und beständiger als LDPE ist. HDPE wird häufig in der Hohlkörperblasformung eingesetzt (siehe auch PE).

Header Card – Verpackung
Entweder der Trägerkarton einer Blisterpackung, oder die Aufhängekarte einer Beutelverpackung. Bietet als Aufhängekarte Platz für Aufdrucke.

Hi-Fi-Screening/Hexachrom – Drucktechnik
Ein sehr feines, häufig maßgeschneidertes Siebdruckraster, das den Druck mit mehr als 4 Farben zulässt. Das Verfahren ermöglicht die Kombination einer beliebigen Anzahl von Farben. Hexachrom ist ein von Pantone patentiertes 6-Farb-System. Daneben existieren noch weitere Markensysteme.

HIPS (High Impact Polystyrene; hochschlagzähes Polystyrol) – Material
Vielfältig verwendbares Material, das leicht formbar ist. Allerdings ist transparentes HIPS spröde.

Kaschierung – Drucktechnik
Die Verbindung mehrerer Materiallagen, um eine stabile und schützende Oberfläche zu erhalten. Kochrezeptkarten sind ein Beispiel für dieses Verfahren, das robuster als eine einfache Lackierung ist.

Kindersicherer Verschluss – Verpackung
Technische Vorrichtungen, die ein Öffnen der Verpackung durch Kinder verhindern sollen. Einige Produkte müssen aus gesetzlichen Gründen kindersicher verschlossen sein, z. B. Bleichmittel, Medikamente, Chemikalien usw.

Kissenpackung – Verpackung
Eine Schlauchpackung, die an beiden Enden versiegelt ist und einen Saum auf der Rückseite hat. Wird am häufigsten für Kartoffelchips u. Ä. verwendet.

Kochbeutel – Verpackung
Beutel aus temperaturbeständiger und wasserunlöslicher Folie, der ein Lebensmittel enthält und in einem Umkarton verkauft wird. Das Lebensmittel wird im Kochbeutel erhitzt und erst zum Servieren geöffnet. In der Regel wird hier das Material Nylon 11

verwendet. Wird häufig für Tiefkühlmahlzeiten, die für die Mikrowelle geeignet sind, eingesetzt.

Koextrusion – Herstellung
Die simultane Extrusion von zwei oder mehreren verschiedenen Kunststoffen, um einen Film mit den Eigenschaften der kombinierten Materialien zu erhalten. Wird für Quetschflaschen verwendet, wo neben der Flexibilität auch Luftdichtigkeit gefordert ist.

Kontrollstreifen – Reprografie
Der Kontrollstreifen enthält wichtige Informationen zu Belichtung, Grauabgleich, Dichteumfang, Tonwertzuwachs, Doublage, Überfüllung und Registrierung. Damit können Designer und Drucker überprüfen, ob ein Proof korrekt gedruckt ist, und Unregelmäßigkeiten schnell beheben, wenn der Druck dem Proof nicht entspricht.

Konturlinien – Reprografie
Striche auf traditionellen Reinzeichnungen die den Rand einer Farbe oder eines Fotos anzeigen. Sie werden nicht gedruckt und dienen ausschließlich der Positionierung.

Kraftpapier – Material
Kraftpapier ist ein hochstabiles Papier aus Sulfatzellstoff. Es kann gebleicht oder gefärbt werden oder naturbelassen bleiben. Wird meist für Wellpappe und Papiertaschen verwendet. Lässt sich auch wasserdicht imprägnieren.

Kunstharzmodell – Herstellung
Zwischenstufe bei der Werkzeugherstellung für formgezogene Behälter. Modell des Behälters unter Berücksichtigung der Schrumpffaktoren, der in der Herstellung einer Metallform zum Einsatz kommt.

Laminat – Verpackung
Zur Verbesserung der Stabilität und Schutzeigenschaften miteinander verbundene Materialschichten. Wird in Rollenform angeboten.

Lichter – Repro
Der hellste noch durchzeichnete Bereich eines Bildes.

Litho-Laminat – Drucktechnik
Wird zum Druck auf Wellpappenverpackungen verwendet. Die Grafik wird im Flachdruckverfahren auf Papier gedruckt und anschließend auf die Außenkaschierung des Kartons aufgeklebt.

Manipulationssicher – Verpackung

Verschlusssystem oder -gerät, das anzeigt, wenn die Packung geöffnet wurde. Nicht zu verwechseln mit einem – eher selten erreichbaren – physischen Schutz vor Sabotage oder Manipulation.

MAP-Verpackung *(Modified Atmosphere Packaging; Aromaschutzverpackung)* **– Verpackung**

Wird vorwiegend für abgepacktes rohes oder vorgegartes Fleisch verwendet. Bei der MAP-Verpackung wird das Fleisch unter Einsatz von Schutzgas in der Packung versiegelt, was die Haltbarkeit erhöht.

Maul – Verpackung

Die Innenseite eines Flaschenhalses.

Metallisierung – Herstellung

Das Aufbringen von Metallpartikeln (meist Aluminium) auf eine Oberfläche, in der Regel auf einen Film. Liefert ein mattes oder glänzendes metallisches Aussehen.

Mikrometer – Verpackung

Maßeinheit: 1000 µm (Mikrometer) = 1 mm. Karton wird in Mikrometern gemessen.

MIPP *(Metallic Integrated Process Printing)* **– Drucktechnik**

Einfach ausgedrückt enthält das bearbeitete Bild neben den vier Prozessfarben an allen Stellen goldene und silberne Farbtropfen, an denen das Originalbild einen metallischen Schimmer hat. Durch die Integration von Gold und Silber in den Druck kann das Bild seine Halbtonwerte behalten und eine realistische Zeichnung in den Tiefen und Lichtern bewahren, ohne an Realismus oder Reflexion zu verlieren.

Moiré – Reprografie

Alle vier für den Farbdruck verwendeten Farben bestehen entweder aus Linien oder Rasterpunkten. Die Linien und Punkte der verschiedenen Farben müssen in bestimmten unterschiedlichen Winkeln zueinander stehen. Sind diese Winkel nicht richtig eingestellt, entstehen Interferenzmuster, die das Auge stören.

Negatives Prägen – Verpackung

Aufbringen einer vertieften Prägung auf der Oberfläche im Gegensatz zur Reliefprägung.

Oberflächenbedruckung – Drucktechnik

Der Druck wird auf die äußerste Schicht des zu bedruckenden Objekts aufgebracht.

Objektorientiertes Bild – IT

Ein objektorientiertes Bild setzt sich im Gegensatz zum Bitmapbild aus mathematisch definierten Kurven, Linien und geometrischen Formen statt aus Pixeln zusammen. Diese Art der Grafik wird häufig für Logos, Schriften und technische Zeichnungen eingesetzt.

OPP *(Oriented Polypropylene; orientiertes Polypropylen)* **– Material**

Ein flexibler Kunststofffilm für Verpackungen, der dank einer veränderten Molekularstruktur (Orientierung) stärker als Polypropylen ist (siehe auch PP).

Orientierung – Herstellung

Bei der Orientierung von Kunststoffen wird die Ausrichtung der Moleküle innerhalb des Materials so verändert, dass sie in eine bestimmte Richtung oder in bestimmte Richtungen ausgerichtet sind.

Overlay – Reprografie

Reinzeichnungen wurden früher in Schwarz-Weiß angelegt und in Reprohäuser weiterbearbeitet. Man legte ihnen eine grobe Farbskizze bei, um Farben und andere Details zu beschreiben.

Pantone – Drucktechnik

Handelsname eines standardisierten Farbidentifikationssystems zur Abstimmung und Mischung bestimmter Druckfarben (siehe auch Farbmuster, Focoltone).

Passerfehler – Drucktechnik

Zwei oder mehr Farben, die im Druck vertikal und/oder horizontal falsch ausgerichtet sind. Das Ergebnis wirkt verwaschen.

Passermarken – Druck

Kleine dunkle Markierungen, die bei Druck und Beschnitt dazu dienen, beim Rollenoffsetdruck registerhaltig zu drucken. Die Marken werden elektronisch erfasst.

PC *(Polykarbonat)* **– Material**

Kunststoff. PC ist temperaturresistent, transparent, steif und hoch schlagfest. Wird häufig für Spezialanwendungen wie hitzebeständige Gefäße eingesetzt.

PE *(Polyethylen)* **– Material**

Kunststoff. Es gibt zwei Arten von PE: LDPE (Polyethylen niedriger Dichte) und HDPE (Polyethylen hoher Dichte). Beide werden für Filme und Behälter (Flaschen) verwendet. HDPE ist steifer. Polyethylen eignet sich für Tiefkühlkost.

Pergamin – Material

Ein glattes, glänzendes, fettundurchlässiges Papier, das zum Verpacken von Backwaren und Konfekten verwendet wird.

PET *(Polyethylenterephthalat)* **– Material**

Kunststoff. Wird massiv in der Hohlkörperblasformung von Flaschen eingesetzt. In Filmform ist PET ein biaxial ausgerichteter Polyester und wird für die Etikettierung und für Hochleistungsfilme eingesetzt. Die kristalline Version (CPET) eignet sich dank ihrer Hitzebeständigkeit für Mikrowellengerichte.

PFC *(Perfluorcarbon)* **– Material**

Nicht-entflammbares Treibgas für Sprayflaschen. Enthält Chemikalien, die die Ozonschicht schädigen (siehe auch Butangas).

Pigment – Drucktechnik

Pigmente sind Festpartikel, die der Farbe ihren Ton verleihen.

Polymer – Material

Polymere bestehen aus Ketten von Monomeren (Molekülen). Ein Kunststoff entsteht durch Polymerisation eines Polymers. Wird nur eine Art von Monomer bei der Polymerisation verwendet, spricht man von einem Homopolymer. Kommen mehrere Monomere zum Einsatz, spricht man von einem Copolymer.

PP *(Polypropylen)* **– Material**

Der wahrscheinlich vielseitigste Kunststoff, der eine hervorragende chemische Widerstandsfähigkeit mit einer guten Festigkeit vereint. Er kann extrudiert, hohlkörpergeblasen, spritzgeblasen, formgepresst und vakuumgeformt werden. Er ist als Faser, Film oder Schaum sowie farbig und farblos erhältlich.

Propan – Material

Entflammbares Kohlenwasserstoffgas, das in flüssiger Form unter Druck als Treibgas verwendet wird. Alternative zu CFC.

Prozessfarben – Drucktechnik

Die Farben Cyan, Magenta, Gelb und Schwarz, die für den Druck von Vollfarbbildern miteinander kombiniert werden. Prozessfarben ermöglichen die größte Farbbandbreite mit den wenigsten Druckfarben.

Prüfziffer – Verpackung
Die letzte Ziffer eines Barcodes. Beim Scannen im Supermarkt bestätigt die Prüfziffer, ob die gesamte Zeichenfolge richtig erfasst wurde.

PS *(Polystyrol)* **– Material**
Kunststoff. Wird für kristallklare und gefärbte Spritzgüsse verwendet. Hervorragendes, wenn auch sprödes Gussformmaterial. Wird in expandierter Form für Schutzverpackungen verwendet.

PTFE *(Polytetrafluorethylen)* **– Material**
Kunststoff. Kommt in zwei Formen vor, als reibungsarmer Film, der für Klebeband verwendet wird, und in solider Form. Behält als Block die Reibungsarmut und kann maschinell geformt werden. Er lässt sich aber nicht mit thermischen Verfahren formen.

PU *(Polyurethan)* **– Material**
Kunststoff. Kommt in zwei Formen vor, als Schaum und als Schaumstoff. Beide werden für Schutzverpackungen genutzt. Der Schaum wird entweder in einer Form oder frei um den Artikel geformt. Schaumstoff gibt es in Bahnen, als Rollen und in Blockform.

Punt – Verpackung
Englischer Fachbegriff für einen hohlen Flaschenboden.

PVA *(Polyvinylacetat)* **– Verpackung**
Klebstoff, wird zum Verkleben von Kartons verwendet.

PVC *(Polyvinylchlorid)* **– Material**
Kunststoff. Transparenter Film oder Bogen. Wird als Film für die Schrumpfverpackung von Fleisch und Frischobst verwendet. In Bogenform findet es in der Vakuumformung Verwendung. Als Granulat wird es zu Flaschen verarbeitet.

PVDC *(Polyvinylidenchlorid, Saran)* **– Material**
Kunststoff. Besitzt gute Widerstandsfähigkeit gegen Wasser, Geruch, Geschmack und Gase. Wird oft auf transparente Filme aufgetragen, um die Barriereeigenschaften zu verbessern.

Quad-Beutel – Verpackung
Eine Variante des Schlauchbeutels, bei dem alle vier Seiten versiegelt werden und der Beutel seine rechteckige Form behält.

Quer zur Faser – Herstellung
Das Falten oder Schneiden eines faserigen Materials im rechten Winkel zum Faserverlauf.

Rasterwalze – Drucktechnik
Rolle, die beim Flexodruck die Farbe auf die Druckplatten überträgt. Die Rolle besitzt eine gravierte Oberfläche, die den Farbauftrag steuert. Dadurch kann die Farbdichte und damit auch die Druckqualität gesteuert werden.

Reliefprägung – Drucktechnik
Die Erzeugung eines erhabenen Bildes durch eine Prägeplatte oder während des Formprozesses bei einer Flasche.

Rückseitendruck – Drucktechnik
Bedrucken der Innenseite eines (transparenten) Films. Der Film fungiert als Schutzschicht für den Druck.

Run on – Drucktechnik
Ein Angebotsposten im Druckgewerbe, der den Preis für die Erhöhung einer Auflage um eine bestimmte Menge angibt.

Schlauchverpackung – Verpackung
Schläuche werden vor allem zur Etikettierung um Flaschen gezogen. Es gibt sie in geschrumpfter oder gestreckter Form. Schrumpfschläuche werden über die Flasche gezogen und erhitzt, damit sie sich zusammenziehen. Ein Streckschlauch wird kalt gestreckt und losgelassen, sobald er um die Flasche liegt, wo er seine ursprüngliche Form annimmt.

Schutzlacküberzug – Drucktechnik
Schutzfilm, der in flüssiger Form auf Innen- oder Außenseite von Karton oder auch Weißblech aufgetragen wird. Es gibt allerdings keinen Allzweck-Schutzfilm.

Schwund – Verpackung
Das Gesamtvolumen eines Behälters ist größer als das des Inhalts. Dies nennt man Schwund.

Schieber und Hülse – Verpackung
Verpackungsform, meist aus Karton gefertigt, bei der eine innere Schublade wie bei einer Streichholzschachtel in einer stabilen Umverpackung steckt.

SOT – Herstellung
a) Stay-on-Tab, SOT-Lasche (eine Methode, dank der die Verschlusslasche einer Getränkedose am Blech verbleibt).

b) Straight-on-Tray (eine Methode, Produkte im Verkaufsregal zu präsentieren).

Spektralfotometer – Drucktechnik
Ein sehr genaues Farbmessgerät. Dient zur akkuraten Farbdefinition und zur Bestimmung der Unterschiede zwischen Farben.

Spiralwicklung – Verpackung
Ein Papierlaminat, das spiralförmig zu einer stabilen Röhre gewickelt wird. Dient als Trägerrolle für Toiletten- und Küchenpapier.

Spritzblasen – Herstellung
Spritzblasen erfolgt in zwei Stufen und dient der präzisen Formung von Flaschenhälsen. Der Hals wird mit einer kurzen versiegelten Röhre spritzgeblasen und dann in die Hohlkörperblasformung transferiert (siehe auch Extrusionsblasen).

Stabile Schachtel – Verpackung
Zusammengefaltete Schachtel, wie z. B. ein Schuhkarton.

Stanzen und Rillen – Drucktechnik
Das Ausschneiden der Packungsform und das Prägen der Falzlinien in einem Schritt (siehe auch Stanzform).

Stanzform – Herstellung
Ein Holzbrett, das die Stanz- und Falzlinien (in metallischer Form) trägt. Dient nach dem Druck zum Ausstanzen und Rillen der Verpackungsform.

Streifenverpackung – Verpackung
Das Produkt wird zwischen zwei Materiallagen eingeschweißt. Beide Lagen sind flexibel und bestehen meist aus Aluminiumfolie oder Kunststoff.

Stretchfolienverpackung – Verpackung
Umwicklung fester Waren auf einer Palette mit Stretchfolie, um sie zu sichern.

Stricharbeiten – Drucktechnik
Erzeugung von Grafiken aus soliden Flächen statt mit Rasterbildern.

Strukturelles Design – Design
Design einer dreidimensionalen Verpackung ohne Oberflächengrafik, z. B. einer Flasche.

Subtraktive Farbmischung – Drucktechnik
Alle auf eine Oberfläche (z. B. weißes Papier) aufgebrachten Farben subtrahieren

einen Teil des von ihr reflektierten weißen Lichts. Cyan, Magenta und Gelb sind die subtraktiven Farben, die idealerweise jeweils ein Drittel des sichtbaren Spektrums subtrahieren. Zusammen schlucken sie das gesamte Spektrum und erzeugen damit Schwarz (siehe additive Farbmischung).

Susceptor – Verpackung
Durch eine Verpackungskomponente auf Metallbasis wird ein Teil der Packung stärker erhitzt als die nicht-metallischen Teile. Dadurch können Mikrowellenspeisen gebräunt und knusprig werden.

Tampondruck – Drucktechnik
Ein Verfahren zum Druck auf komplex geformte Oberflächen und Kurven. Die Farbe der Druckplatte wird durch einen weichen Druckballen aus Latex auf das Objekt übertragen. Der Druckballen legt sich dabei um die Konturen des Objekts.

Therimage – Drucktechnik
Heißtransferverfahren für die Aufbringung eines gedruckten Bildes auf ein Produkt. Oft werden Tiefdruckbilder verwendet, sodass das Verfahren für große Auflagen geeignet ist. Kunststoffflaschen werden in diesem Verfahren mit Vierfarb-Halbtonbildern bedruckt.

Thermoformung – Drucktechnik
Die Formung eines Kunststoffbogens durch Druck auf oder in eine Form. Geschieht meist im Rahmen der Vakuumformung.

Thermografie – Drucktechnik
Technik, bei der ein hitzebehandeltes Farbbild einen Relieffeffekt erzeugt.

Tonwertzuwachs – Drucktechnik
Die Vergrößerung eines Rasterpunkts, die bei der Filmbelichtung, der Plattenherstellung und durch das Verlaufen der Druckfarbe auf dem Papier auftritt. Beim Direct-to-plate-Druckprozess tritt der Tonwertzuwachs nur in der Druckmaschine auf.

Trockenoffset, Letterset – Drucktechnik
Druckrollen übertragen eine Farbe nach der anderen auf eine Offsetrolle, von der alle Farben zusammen auf ein nicht-poröses Medium gedruckt werden. Keine Farbe kann überdrucken. Wird für Zahnpastatuben, Kunststofftrinkbecher, Margarine- und Joghurtbecher, Flaschen usw. genutzt.

Über- und Unterfüllung – Reprografie
Alle Druckmaschinen tendieren im Verlauf einer Auflage zu leichten Passerfehlern. Wenn unterschiedliche Farben auf Stoß aneinander grenzen, kann es dabei zu sichtbaren Blitzern, also einem Durchscheinen des Druckmediums kommen. Um dies zu vermeiden, lässt man die Farben leicht (meist 1/15 Millimeter) überlappen. Die schwächere Farbe wird immer nach innen unterfüllt oder überfüllt unter der stärkeren Farbe nach außen.

Überblendung – IT
Eine Überblendung erzeugt mittels Zwischenpfaden einen glatten Übergang zwischen zwei Formen, Farben oder Strichstärken. So kann zum Beispiel ein rotes Quadrat in einer vorgegebenen Anzahl von Zwischenschritten in einen gelben Kreis überblendet werden.

Überdrucken – Drucktechnik
Druck auf einem bereits bedruckten Bereich oder der Druck mit einer Kombination aus zwei Farben (z. B. Blau über Gelb, um Grün zu erhalten).

Überfüllung, Trapping – Drucktechnik
Die zuvor gedruckte Farbe, wird entfernt, wenn die nächste Farbe gedruckt wird. Das Ziel ist dabei, den Überschuss möglichst gering zu halten. Der Begriff wird fälschlicherweise auch von Grafiksoftwareherstellern verwendet (siehe auch Über- und Unterfüllung).

Überlauf – Herstellung
Überschüssiges Material, das beim Spritzguss entsteht.

Umverpackung – Verpackung
Schutzfolie um einen Karton oder eine Schachtel, z. B. mit Konfektwaren. Außerdem eine Sammelverpackung für mehrere kleinere Packungen.

Unterlänge – Typografie
Der Teil eines Kleinbuchstaben wie z. B. g, p, q, y usw., der über die Grundlinie hinausragt.

Verbundstoff – Herstellung
Unterschiedliche Materialien, die zu einer Verpackung verbunden werden, z. B. eine Papprolle mit Metall- oder Kunststoffdeckeln.

Vorbedrucken – Drucktechnik
Beim Bedrucken von Wellpappenkartons kann man die äußerste Schicht bedrucken, bevor die Wellpappe laminiert wird.

Wellpappe – Material
Ein gewelltes Blatt, das zwischen zwei parallele glatte Lagen geleimt ist, um ein stabiles Laminat für Versandverpackungen zu bilden.

Zellglas *(Cellophan)* – Material
Besteht aus reiner Zellulose, die zu einem transparenten Film verarbeitet wird. Ist unbeschichtet, durchlässig für Wasserdampf. Bietet hervorragenden Geruchsschutz und wird unter anderem zur Verpackung von Konfekt und Teigwaren verwendet.

Les termes techniques de A à Z

SiebertHead (www.sieberthead.com)

Comme pour toutes les spécialités, le design d'emballage a développé sa propre terminologie. Pour aider ceux qui ne sont pas forcément familiarisés avec les termes utilisés, SiebertHead a préparé un guide de certains des termes et des abréviations les plus fréquemment utilisés.

Les significations données sont celles qui sont généralement acceptées dans le secteur, plutôt que des définitions strictes réservées aux spécialistes de l'emballage. C'est un guide de référence simple sur la terminologie du design d'emballage, destiné aux responsables marketing.

Si vous souhaitez en savoir plus, ou avoir la liste complète, veuillez contacter SiebertHead sur www.sieberthead.com.

Acétate *(acétate de cellulose)* **– Matériau**

Plastique transparent très utilisé pour les fenêtres dans l'industrie du carton et pour les coffrets de présentation.

Achromatique – Reproduction

L'un des nombreux noms donnés par les fabricants au GCR (Grey Component Replacement, équilibrage électronique des gris). Le GCR élimine le composant gris de toutes les couleurs d'une image et augmente le noir pour compenser. Utilisé là où il y a de fortes concentrations de bleu, de rouge et de jaune, pour rendre l'image plus claire et plus nette.

Acrylique (acrylonitrile) – Matériau

Matériau synthétique fabriqué à partir de l'acrylonitrile. Perspex est l'un de ses noms commerciaux. Il est transparent ou opaque, avec ou sans couleur. Utilisé sous forme solide pour maquettes, sur les lieux de vente et comme base pour certaines encres d'impression.

Allégeage – Emballage

Réduction de la quantité de matière employée dans une bouteille grâce à une utilisation adaptée des formes, c'est-à-dire coins arrondis et courbes peu prononcées.

Aluminium en feuille – Matériau

Fine plaque ou feuille d'aluminium pur en rouleau. Utilisé pour fabriquer des plateaux, des couvercles, des matériaux stratifiés et pour la décoration.

Aseptique – Fabrication

Emballage d'usine pour la nourriture et la boisson, effectué dans des conditions qui excluent les microorganismes.

Bande de contrôle *(standard européen)* **– Reproduction**

La bande de contrôle contient des informations sur l'exposition, la balance des gris, la gamme de densité, l'élargissement du point, le piégeage et le repérage. Elle permet au designer et à l'imprimeur de vérifier qu'une épreuve a été produite correctement, et elle permet à l'imprimeur d'identifier le problème si l'impression ne correspond pas à l'épreuve.

Base à verrouillage automatique – Emballage

Base à rabats collés qui se verrouillent automatiquement quand le carton est debout. On utilise ce système pour les objets lourds, comme les bouteilles d'alcool.

Base champagne – Emballage

Semblable à la base pétaloïde, mais avec une forme totalement concave. Ce type de base, bien qu'apprécié des designers, est plus gourmand en matériau.

Blister – Emballage

Une plaquette thermoformée généralement transparente, scellée sur un support en carton et recouvrant le produit.

Boîte rigide – Emballage

Boîte préassemblée, comme les boîtes à chaussures ou toute boîte prête à remplir.

Bord d'entraînement – Impression

Dans une feuille de papier, le bord qui est tiré en premier par la machine, à l'aide d'une ligne de pinces.

Bronzage – Impression

Donne un effet métallique à l'impression grâce à l'application d'une couche adhésive puis d'une poudre métallique.

Butane – Fabrication

Gaz inflammable souvent utilisé sous forme liquide comme propulseur d'aérosol. Bien qu'inflammable, par rapport aux PFC et aux CFC il a l'avantage de ne pas être nocif pour la couche d'ozone (voir également PFC).

CAO/PAO *(conception assistée par ordinateur/ production assistée par ordinateur)* **– Informatique**

Un système informatique complet qui permet de transférer les données techniques affichées à l'écran vers le processus de production. On passe par exemple d'une boîte en carton sur l'écran à la production de multiples boîtes en carton, en découpant et en pliant les formes.

Carte en-tête – Emballage

Le carton qui sert de fond aux blisters, ou la carte accrochée aux produits emballés en sachets. Elle fournit une surface pour imprimer des informations et un espace pour l'euroslot.

Carton duplex – Emballage

Un carton stratifié pour les boîtes imprimées. Il est constitué d'une couche supérieure en cellulose blanchie, d'une couche centrale souvent en pâte à papier mécanique et d'un verso en cellulose.

Carton ondulé – Matériau

Une feuille cannelée ou ondulée collée entre deux feuilles plates parallèles, qui donne une structure stratifiée renforcée pour les boîtes de transport.

Chiffre de contrôle – Emballage

Le dernier chiffre d'un code-barres. Lorsque le produit est scanné dans le supermarché, le chiffre de contrôle confirme que le nombre entier a été enregistré correctement.

Chlorure de polyvinylidène (Saran) – Matériau

C'est un plastique qui résiste bien à l'eau, aux odeurs, aux goûts et aux gaz. Souvent appliqué comme revêtement transparent sur des films pour en améliorer les propriétés d'isolation.

Code-barres – Emballage

Un motif composé de lignes verticales imprimées et de 12/13 ou 8 chiffres, lu par un capteur laser relié à un ordinateur. Utilisé aux caisses des supermarchés pour afficher le prix, contrôler les stocks et réapprovisionner les stocks. Il existe de nombreux types de codes-barres. Les plus courants sont l'EAN (numéro d'article européen), l'UPC américain (code produit universel) et l'ITF (intercalé deux de cinq) utilisé pour les suremballages.

Collerette – Impression

Sur un objet, un col ou un anneau qui le fixe à un autre objet.

Composite – Fabrication

Différents matériaux combinés dans un emballage, par exemple un tambour en papier cartonné avec des extrémités en métal ou en plastique.

Conditionnement sous atmosphère contrôlée – Emballage

Principalement utilisé pour les viandes rouges/cuites préemballées. Les viandes emballées sont scellées dans leurs récipients avec un mélange de gaz pour améliorer la durée de conservation du produit.

Couleur additive – Informatique

La reproduction des couleurs par mélange de la lumière, comme sur un écran de télévision ou d'ordinateur. Les trois couleurs additives, rouge, vert et bleu, produisent des couleurs plus lumineuses combinées deux par deux, et de la lumière blanche pure combinées toutes ensemble (voir également Couleur soustractive).

Couleur soustractive – Impression

Toute application d'encre sur une surface, comme du papier blanc, soustrait (absorbe) une certaine portion de la lumière blanche qui l'atteint. Le cyan, le magenta et le jaune sont des couleurs soustractives. Dans leurs proportions idéales, chacune absorbe un tiers du spectre visible. Toutes ensemble, elles absorbent le spectre entier et créent ainsi du noir (voir également Couleur additive).

Couleurs de la quadrichromie – Impression

Les couleurs (cyan, magenta et jaune, plus noir) qui sont combinées pour imprimer des images en couleur. Les couleurs de la quadrichromie sont celles qui peuvent produire le plus grand nombre de couleurs à partir du plus petit nombre d'encres.

CPET (polyéthylène téréphtalate cristallin) – Matériau

Dérivé du polyéthylène téréphtalate, ou PET, souvent utilisé pour les assiettes des plats cuisinés car le matériau résiste aux températures des fours à chaleur rayonnante sans se déformer (voir également PET).

Cul de bouteille – Emballage

Le renfoncement au fond d'une bouteille.

Découpage et pliage – Impression

Découpe de la forme du carton et réalisation des plis aux bonnes mesures en une seule opération (voir également Découpe à l'emporte-pièce).

Découpe à l'emporte-pièce – Fabrication

Une plaque de bois qui reprend les lignes de découpe et de pliage (en métal). Appliquée après l'impression, elle crée la forme de découpage et de pliage du paquet.

Défaut d'alignement – Impression

Lorsque plusieurs couleurs d'un échantillon imprimé ne sont pas alignées correctement horizontalement et/ou verticalement. L'image semble floue.

Descendante – Typographie

La partie de certains caractères en bas de casse, comme g, p, q, y, etc. qui descend en dessous de la ligne de base.

Design structurel – Design

Le design de l'emballage tridimensionnel, sans les graphismes extérieurs. Par exemple, la forme d'une bouteille.

Direct à la plaque – Impression

Cette technique évite les séparations de films. L'information numérique est passée directement au graveur de plaques. Il faut utiliser des plaques plus fines.

Dorure à chaud – Impression

Technique utilisée pour appliquer des feuilles de finition en métal brillant ou mat sur les articles imprimés. Un bloc chauffé fait pression sur la feuille et la fait adhérer au substrat. C'est un procédé coûteux qui ne convient qu'aux produits chers, comme les parfums et les alcools. Également désigné sous le nom d'estampage à chaud.

Duotone (deux tons) – Impression

Un ensemble aligné de deux images en demi-teinte de deux couleurs différentes. On peut obtenir différents effets en donnant à l'une des images plus de contraste qu'à l'autre. Le tritone utilise trois couleurs.

Échantillon de couleurs – Reproduction

Un échantillon de couleurs réelles, joint à l'image, qui indique les références Pantone/Focoltone, etc. que l'imprimeur doit reproduire. Si le designer n'arrive pas à trouver une référence de couleur adaptée à ses besoins, il doit joindre un échantillon de la couleur (voir également Pantone, Focoltone).

Écran haute fidélité/Hexachrome – Impression

Un écran très fin, souvent conçu sur mesure, qui permet d'utiliser plus que les 4 couleurs habituelles. Hexachrome est un système à 6 couleurs, déposé par Pantone. En fait, les écrans haute fidélité permettent de combiner n'importe quel nombre de couleurs pour produire l'image finale. Il existe aussi des systèmes développés par d'autres entreprises.

Élargissement du point – Impression

Le changement de la taille d'un point tramé à cause de facteurs tels que l'exposition du film, la fabrication de la plaque ou l'étalement de l'encre pendant l'impression. Avec le procédé d'impression directe à la

plaque, l'élargissement du point ne se produi-
ra qu'au moment du passage sous presse.

Emballage en continu – Emballage

Deux rouleaux de matériaux thermoscel-
lables sont scellés autour du produit. Les deux
matériaux sont souples, et sont fréquemment
à base de papier aluminium ou en plastique.

Emballage souple – Emballage

Emballage fait de matériaux en feuilles
souples, par exemple un sachet ou une poche.

Emballage sous film étirable – Emballage

On étire un film autour d'articles rigides
posés sur des palettes pour les maintenir en
place. L'utilisation de ce film ne requiert
aucun traitement thermique.

En travers du fil – Fabrication

Le pliage ou le découpage de tout matériau
fibreux perpendiculairement au sens de la fibre.

Épreuve numérique – Impression

L'une des différentes formes d'impression
numérique, utilisée comme moyen rapide et
économique de vérifier des fichiers d'image/de
reprographie/de photographie. Elle est également employée pour les petites impressions
numériques pour les maquettes, les brochures, etc. Les machines numériques les plus
courantes sont Digital Cromalin, Kodak
Proofer, Indigo, etc. Elles comportent certaines limitations, mais sont maintenant fréquemment employées par les imprimeurs
pour produire des épreuves.

Euroslot – Emballage

Euroslot est un standard qui s'applique aux
trous des supports à crochets et qui a pour but
de garantir qu'un même produit pourra s'accro-
cher sur n'importe quel crochet standard dans
n'importe quel pays. Il n'existe aucune norme
internationale, et le terme est devenu une dési-
gnation générique pour ce type de support.

Fermeture sécurité enfant – Emballage

Dispositif conçu pour limiter/empêcher l'ouverture par des enfants. La loi oblige certains
produits à en être pourvus : eau de javel, produits pharmaceutiques, produits chimiques, etc.

Film rétractable

S'utilise surtout pour emballer la viande et
la volaille, afin d'obtenir un emballage serré.
Il permet aussi au consommateur de s'assurer que personne n'a touché le produit depuis
qu'il a été emballé, puisque toute ouverture
de l'emballage serait aussitôt visible.

Flexographie – Impression

Procédé d'impression en relief qui utilise
des plaques en caoutchouc ou en photopolymè-
re fixées sur un cylindre. Les coûts de départ
sont inférieurs à ceux de l'héliogravure, ce
procédé est donc adapté aux tirages moyens.
Il a de nombreuses applications dans l'emballage, dont l'impression sur les boîtes de carton
ondulé, les cartons pliables, les pellicules ou
les stratifiés souples et les feuilles de métal.

Focoltone – Impression

Un système numéroté de correspondance
des couleurs, pour choisir des combinaisons
de cyan/magenta/jaune/noir avec des combinaisons d'une couleur spéciale supplémentaire. Cela augmente considérablement le
nombre d'options pour les impressions en
cinq couleurs. Ce n'est pas la même chose
que le système Pantone.

Fond perdu – Impression

L'étirement des dimensions d'une image
au-delà du bord d'un document pour compenser toute erreur de repérage pendant le processus de finalisation d'un travail.

Fusion – Informatique

Une fusion produit une transition entre
des formes, des couleurs ou des épaisseurs de
trait différentes en créant un groupe de che-
mins intermédiaires entre les deux formes,
couleurs ou épaisseurs de trait initiales. Un
carré rouge, par exemple, peut se transformer en cercle jaune sur une certaine distance
et en un certain nombre d'étapes.

Gabarit en résine – Fabrication

Étape intermédiaire dans la mise au point
d'outils pour la fabrication de récipients moulés. Représentation du récipient en résine
synthétique, prenant en compte les facteurs
de rétrécissement utilisés dans la production
des moules en métal.

Gamme de couleurs – Reproduction

Une représentation de la gamme et de la
palette de couleurs qui peuvent être repro-
duites par un certain système. Par exemple,
la gamme de couleurs vue sur un transparent
grâce à un rétroprojecteur sera presque
deux fois plus importante que si la même
image est imprimée à l'encre sur un carton
de qualité moyenne.

Goulot – Emballage

L'intérieur du col d'une bouteille.

Guide de découpe – Emballage

Le schéma de découpe d'une image, indiquant sa taille, sa forme et ses mesures
essentielles. Ce sont des informations cru-
ciales, nécessaires avant de commencer le
processus de création de l'image.

Haute lumière – Reproduction

La zone la plus claire de l'image, mais qui
contient encore des détails.

HIPS *(High Impact Polystyrene, polystyrène antichoc)* – Emballage

Matériau multiusages très facile à façonner, bien que le HIPS transparent soit fragile.

Image orientée objet ou image vectorielle – Informatique

Une image orientée objet est définie
mathématiquement au moyen de courbes, de
lignes et de formes géométriques, par opposi-
tion aux pixels dans le cas d'une image en
bitmap. Ce type de graphisme est souvent
employé pour les logos, les caractères et les
schémas techniques.

Impression en surface – Impression

Lorsque le motif est imprimé sur la surface
externe de l'objet.

Impression en transparence – Impression

Lorsque le texte ou l'image est imprimé
sur la face interne d'un film (transparent).
Le film agit en tant que couche de protection
pour ce qui est imprimé.

Laque – Impression

Pellicule de protection sous forme liquide,
appliquée à l'intérieur ou à l'extérieur d'une
boîte pour la protéger. Les laques peuvent
également être utilisées sur le fer blanc.
Cependant, aucune laque n'est adaptée à
tous les supports à la fois.

Litho-laminé – Impression

Pour imprimer sur des boîtes en carton
ondulé. Avec cette technique, les graphismes
sont lithographiés sur du papier qui est ensuite stratifié sur des boîtes en carton brut.

Manchon – Emballage

Les manchons s'utilisent surtout sur les bouteilles, sur lesquelles ils servent d'étiquette. Ils
peuvent être rétractables ou étirables. Les
manchons rétractables se placent autour de la
bouteille et rétrécissent sous l'effet de la chaleur. Les manchons étirables sont étirés à froid
et placés autour de la bouteille. Lorsqu'on arrê-
te de les étirer, ils essaient de retrouver leur

forme d'origine et épousent les contours de la bouteille. N.B. : on fabrique aussi des manchons pour cartes, dont la fonction est de fournir une surface d'impression pour les informations relatives au produit.

Maquettes – Design
Simulation d'un article final ou d'un emballage en 2D ou en 3D.

Métallisé – Fabrication
Le dépôt de particules métalliques (généralement de l'aluminium) sur une surface, habituellement un film. Donne un aspect métallique mat ou brillant.

Micron – Emballage
Mesure : 1000µm (micron) = 1mm. Les planches de carton sont mesurées en microns.

MIPP *(Metallic Integrated Process Printing, impression à traitement métallique intégré)* – Impression
En termes simples, l'image traitée intègre des points d'encre dorée et argentée aux 4 couleurs, là où l'image d'origine a un fini métallique. Comme le doré et l'argenté sont entièrement intégrés au processus, l'image garde des valeurs tonales continues. Les ombres et les accents de lumière sont détaillés, et l'on ne perd ni en réalisme ni en réflexion.

Moiré – Reproduction
Chacune des quatre couleurs utilisées pour imprimer les images en couleur est composée de lignes ou de points tramés. Pour chaque couleur, les lignes doivent être placées selon des angles différents. Si ces angles ne sont pas corrects, les points forment des distorsions qui brouillent la vue.

Moulage par extrusion en couches multiples – Fabrication
Un processus d'extrusion simultanée de deux ou plusieurs matières plastiques différentes pour obtenir une épaisseur possédant les caractéristiques des matériaux combinés. Utilisé pour des bouteilles souples ou de sauces, qui doivent être résistantes au gaz en plus d'être souples.

Moulage par extrusion-soufflage – Fabrication
Dans le moulage par extrusion-soufflage, un tube creux, ou paraison, est maintenu à l'intérieur d'un moule. De l'air sous pression gonfle la paraison et lui donne la forme du moule. Ce procédé s'utilise pour les emballages creux, surtout des bouteilles (voir également Moulage par injection-soufflage).

Moulage par injection-soufflage – Fabrication
Le moulage par injection-soufflage est un processus en deux étapes, utilisé pour les cols de bouteille comportant des détails fins. Le col est moulé par injection avec un petit tube scellé, puis transféré à un poste de moulage par soufflage (voir également Moulage par extrusion-soufflage).

Offset à sec – Impression
Les cylindres transfèrent chaque couleur tour à tour sur un cylindre offset (blanchet) à partir duquel toutes les couleurs sont imprimées ensemble sur une surface habituellement non poreuse. Aucune couleur ne peut s'imprimer en excès. Technique utilisée pour les tubes de dentifrice, les tasses en plastique, les barquettes de margarine et les pots de yaourt, les bouteilles, etc.

Opacité – Impression
La mesure dans laquelle l'encre cache la couleur du matériau sur lequel elle est imprimée, ou dans laquelle le papier empêche que l'on voie à travers. C'est une mesure de la quantité de lumière arrêtée par une surface ou absorbée par une couche d'encre.

OPP *(polypropylène orienté)* – Matériau
Une feuille de plastique flexible pour emballage, plus résistante que le polypropylène parce que sa structure moléculaire a été modifiée (orientée). (Voir également PP).

Orienté – Fabrication
L'orientation des plastiques est la modification de l'alignement des molécules du matériau, ce qui le rend plus résistant, habituellement dans un ou des sens spécifique(s).

Palette – Fabrication
Larges plateaux en bois, en bois et carton ou en plastique pour transporter des marchandises. Les palettes ont une plate-forme surélevée pour permettre aux chariots élévateurs de les soulever et de les charger. On les trouve en plusieurs tailles standardisées, et de deux types : à deux ou à quatre entrées. Le nombre d'entrées fait référence au nombre de côtés par lesquels le chariot élévateur peut aborder la palette.

Pantone – Impression
Nom commercial d'un système standard d'identification des couleurs pour assortir et mélanger des couleurs d'encre spécifiques (voir également Échantillon de couleurs, Focoltone).

Papier cristal – Matériau
Un type de papier sulfurisé lisse et brillant. Le papier cristal s'utilise pour l'emballage des produits dans les secteurs de la pâtisserie et de la confiserie.

Papier enduit – Matériau
Papier de qualité, habituellement enduit de kaolin pour que la surface lisse se prête à une sérigraphie très fine.

Papier kraft – Matériau
Fabriqué à partir de pâte au sulfate, le papier kraft est très résistant. Il peut être blanchi, coloré ou laissé à l'état brut. Généralement utilisé pour le carton ondulé, les sachets et les sacs. Il peut également être hydrofuge.

PC *(polycarbonate)* – Matériau
Le PC est un plastique résistant à la température, il est transparent, rigide et présente une bonne résistance aux chocs. En raison de son coût, il est généralement utilisé pour des applications spéciales, par exemple pour résister aux températures élevées.

PE *(polyéthylène)* – Matériau
Le PE est un plastique. Il existe deux types de PE, le PEBD (polyéthylène basse densité) et le PEHD (polyéthylène haute densité). Ils sont tous deux employés pour fabriquer des films et des récipients (bouteilles). Le PEHD est plus rigide. Le polyéthylène peut être utilisé pour les aliments surgelés.

PEHD *(polyéthylène à haute densité)* – Matériau
Un dérivé du PE, plus solide et plus durable que le PEBD (polyéthylène à basse densité) grâce à un taux de cristallinité plus élevé. Le PEHD est très utilisé dans le moulage par soufflage (voir également PE).

Pellicule de cellulose *(pellicule de cellulose régénérée)* – Matériau
Pellicule transparente produite à partir de pulpe de bois pure. Barrière peu efficace contre la vapeur d'eau si elle n'est pas recouverte par un autre matériau. Excellente comme barrière anti-odeur, utilisée pour la confiserie et les biscuits.

Pelliplacage – Emballage
Une mince feuille de plastique est chauffée et appliquée sous vide tout autour d'un produit posé sur un fond en carton. Ce procédé permet de bien maintenir les éléments en place et permet au client de bien voir le produit.

PET *(polyéthylène téréphtalate)* – Matériau

C'est un plastique utilisé pour les bouteilles moulées par soufflage. Le film de PET est un polyester orienté bi-axialement et est utilisé pour l'étiquetage et les films à haute performance. La version cristalline (CPET) convient à une utilisation à haute température, comme les barquettes de plats pour micro-ondes.

Pétouille – Impression

Se forme lorsque des particules viennent se coller à une plaque d'impression, et apparaissent sur l'impression sous forme de tâche auréolée.

PFC *(propulseur au polyfluorocarbone)* – Matériau

Gaz propulseur non inflammable utilisé dans les aérosols. Contient des produits chimiques nocifs pour la couche d'ozone (voir Butane).

Piégeage – Impression

L'encre de la couleur que l'on vient d'imprimer doit s'enlever avant de passer à la couleur suivante sur la presse. Le but de l'imprimeur est de réduire le facteur de piégeage au minimum pour obtenir la meilleure qualité d'impression possible.

Pigment – Impression

Les pigments sont des particules solides qui donnent à l'encre sa couleur.

Point manquant – Impression

Avec l'héliogravure, les plus petits points gravés ne contiennent que très peu d'encre, et parfois l'encre sèche trop rapidement et n'est pas transférée au substrat. Sur l'impression, les points sont manquants.

Polymère – Matériau

Les polymères sont composés de monomères (molécules). Le plastique se forme à partir d'un polymère au moyen de la polymérisation. Si la polymérisation n'utilise qu'une seule sorte de monomère, il s'agit alors d'un homopolymère. S'il y a plus d'un monomère, c'est un copolymère.

PP *(polypropylène)* – Matériau

C'est sans doute le plastique le plus polyvalent. Il allie une excellente résistance chimique et une bonne solidité. Il peut être extrudé, moulé par soufflage, par injection ou par compression et formé sous vide. Disponible sous forme de fibre, de film ou de mousse de toutes les couleurs et en transparent.

Pré-impression – Impression

Pour imprimer sur des boîtes en carton ondulé, on peut employer la pré-impression. Il s'agit d'imprimer l'image sur la surface extérieure avant le processus de formation du carton ondulé.

Propane – Matériau

Gaz d'hydrocarbure inflammable utilisé sous pression et sous forme liquide comme propulseur d'aérosol. Peut remplacer le CFC.

PS *(polystyrène)* – Matériau

Plastique utilisé pour des moulages par injection transparents comme du cristal, ou colorés. Excellent matériau de moulage, mais fragile. Sous sa forme expansée, s'utilise comme protection dans l'emballage.

PTFE *(polytétrafluoroéthylène – téflon)* – Matériau

C'est un plastique que l'on peut trouver sous forme de film à faible cœfficient de friction, pour le ruban adhésif par exemple, et sous forme solide. Sous forme de bloc solide, il conserve son faible coefficient de friction, et l'on peut le façonner à la machine. Mais il n'y a aucun moyen de le thermoformer.

PU *(polyuréthane)* – Matériau

C'est un plastique qui se présente sous deux formes, en mousse et en mousse agglomérée. Les deux sont employées pour la protection en emballage. La mousse est moulée autour de l'article, dans un moule ou sur place. La mousse agglomérée est employée en feuilles, en rouleaux, en blocs de coin et en moulages. Elle sert aussi de base adhésive.

PVAC *(polyacétate de vinyle)* – Emballage

Adhésif pour coller les boîtes en carton.

PVC *(chlorure de polyvinyle)* – Matériau

Plastique transparent, en film ou en feuille. Sous forme de film il est employé pour l'emballage rétractable de la viande et des fruits frais. Sous forme de feuille il se prête bien au formage sous vide. Sous forme de granules, on l'utilise pour faire des bouteilles.

Recouvrement – Reproduction

Toutes les presses bougent un peu lors de l'impression et peuvent donc produire des décalages. Si des couleurs contiguës sont parfaitement ajustées, le moindre défaut d'alignement fera apparaître de fines bordures blanches. Pour éviter cela, on fait en sorte que les deux couleurs se chevauchent très légèrement (habituellement 0,15 mm).

La couleur la plus faible se rétracte toujours vers l'intérieur ou s'étend vers l'extérieur sous la couleur la plus forte.

Relief – Impression

Travailler une image en relief par rapport à la surface à l'aide d'une plaque en relief, ou dans le processus de moulage d'une bouteille.

Relief en creux – Emballage

Travailler une image en creux par rapport à la surface.

Repères – Impression

Petits blocs de couleur sombre sur les papiers d'emballage, qui servent à repérer le positionnement correct des matériaux distribués par bobines pour l'impression, la tension et la découpe. Ces repères sont « lus » par un œil électronique.

Résidu – Fabrication

Excédent de matériau restant après le procédé de moulage par injection.

Rouleau anilox – Impression

En flexographie, c'est le rouleau qui transporte l'encre vers les plaques d'impression. Ce rouleau a une surface gravée qui détermine la quantité d'encre transférée. Cela permet de contrôler la densité de l'encre, et donc de mieux contrôler la qualité de l'impression.

Sachet coussin – Emballage

L'emballage se fait en continu. Le sachet est thermoscellé aux deux extrémités, et tout le long du dos. Très utilisé dans l'emballage des chips.

Sachet de cuisson – Emballage

La nourriture est emballée dans un sachet fabriqué dans un film résistant à l'eau et à la chaleur, et les sachets sont vendus dans une boîte en carton. La nourriture est réchauffée dans le sachet, que l'on n'ouvre qu'au moment de servir. Le film utilisé est généralement du nylon-11. Souvent utilisé pour les plats surgelés réchauffés au four à micro-ondes.

Sachets – Emballage

Il y a deux types principaux de sachets d'emballage : thermoscellés sur deux côtés (sachet coussin) ou quatre côtés. Les sachets coussins sont scellés aux deux extrémités et tout le long du dos, et sont utilisé pour les paquets de chips, etc. On trouve maintenant des sachets qui tiennent debout tous seuls.

Sachets quad – Emballage

Une variante du sachet à conditionnement en continu, mais tous les coins sont scellés, ainsi que d'autres zones, ce qui donne au sachet une tenue plus rectangulaire.

Saturation – Emballage

Le degré d'intensité ou de pureté de n'importe quelle couleur.

Schéma des couleurs – Reproduction

Traditionnellement, les images étaient préparées en noir et blanc puis remises à l'imprimeur. Elles étaient donc accompagnées d'un croquis approximatif indiquant les couleurs et d'autres détails.

Sens du fil – Impression

Le sens principal des fibres du papier et du carton. Dans le sens du fil, le papier résiste mieux à la tension en machine et a moins tendance à s'étirer ou à rétrécir.

Séparation des couleurs (*séparation*) – Reproduction

Séparation des films (une couleur par film) par un scanner d'originaux en couleur (transparent, illustration ou impression couleur). Habituellement la séparation se fait en cyan, magenta, jaune et noir dans l'impression en quadrichromie. La séparation des couleurs unies (sans dégradés de tons) s'effectue de la même façon en utilisant un appareil photo.

SOT – Fabrication

a) Stay-On-Tab (à languette retenue). Un type d'ouverture de canette. La languette ne se détache pas de la canette.
b) Straight-On-Tray (debout sur plateau). Une façon de présenter les produits dans les rayons des magasins.

Spectrophotomètre – Impression

Un instrument qui mesure la couleur très précisément. On l'utilise pour définir une couleur avec exactitude et pour mesurer ce qui la différencie d'une autre couleur.

Stratification – Impression

Technique consistant à coller ensemble plusieurs couches de matériaux, pour obtenir une surface protectrice dure. Les fiches de cuisine sont un exemple courant de ce procédé, plus solide et plus cher que le vernissage.

Stratifié – Emballage

Plusieurs feuilles de matériaux d'épaisseur simple collées ensemble pour améliorer les propriétés physiques et de protection. Fourni en bobines.

Suremballage – Emballage

Film de protection autour d'un carton ou d'une boîte, par exemple des boîtes de chocolats. Également utilisé pour maintenir ensemble plusieurs petites boîtes.

Surimpression – Impression

Impression sur une surface déjà imprimée, par exemple des numéros de lot, des dates limites de consommation, etc. ou pour obtenir une couleur en utilisant une combinaison de deux couleurs, c'est-à-dire bleu avec surimpression de jaune pour créer du vert.

Suscepteur – Emballage

Si l'on incorpore à certaines zones de l'emballage d'un plat préparé à réchauffer au four à micro-ondes un composant à base de métal (le suscepteur), ces zones atteindront une température plus élevée que le reste de l'emballage, et pourront donc servir à dorer le plat.

Tampographie – Impression

C'est une méthode d'impression sur des surfaces incurvées complexes. L'encre de la plaque d'impression est transférée à l'objet au moyen d'un tampon en latex souple qui peut prendre la forme de l'objet.

Teinte – Reproduction

On peut affaiblir n'importe quelle couleur pure en l'imprimant en trame de points en demi-teinte. Plus les points sont petits, plus la couleur est claire.

Therimage – Impression

Transfert thermique d'une image de la bobine au produit. On utilise souvent une image héliogravée, il faut donc travailler sur de grands tirages. Utilisation type : impression sur une bouteille en plastique qui requiert une image en quadrichromie et en demi-teinte.

Thermoformage – Impression

Moulage d'une feuille de plastique appliquée dans ou sur un moule. La méthode la plus courante de thermoformage est le formage sous vide.

Thermographie – Impression

Avec cette technique, l'encre soumise à un traitement thermique gonfle et produit un effet en relief.

Tirés à la suite – Impression

Élément parfois inclus dans un devis d'impression, qui donne le prix pour l'augmentation du tirage en fonction d'une certaine quantité.

Ton continu – Reproduction

Une image qui comporte toutes les nuances entre les différentes couleurs, pour donner une représentation fidèle de l'image originale. Cette image n'est pas formée de points de différentes tailles (image en demi-teinte). Aucun processus d'impression ne peut imprimer en ton continu sans trame, sauf la collotypie qui emploie une plaque recouverte de gélatine, mais cela se fait rarement de nos jours.

Transfert – Design

Un système au moyen duquel on transfère une image d'une surface (habituellement en polythène) à un autre substrat en frottant avec un stylo ou un stylet.

Travail au trait – Impression

Un terme qui se réfère à la génération d'une image en utilisant des objets dessinés plutôt que des objets tramés.

Tube spiralé – Emballage

Du papier stratifié enroulé en spirale pour former un tube solide. Utilisé pour les rouleaux de papier toilette et d'essuie-tout.

Tynocolour – Impression

Procédé d'impression spécialisé et breveté, qui utilise une encre très épaisse et dont la couleur est très fiable. On emploie ce procédé dans certaines disciplines médicales, pour les tests médicaux dont le résultat est exprimé par une couleur qui doit ensuite être comparée à un tableau de couleurs de référence afin d'établir le diagnostic. Par exemple, pour les tests de grossesse.

Type C – Design

Une impression photographique couleur produite à partir d'un négatif couleur.

Typographie – Impression

Processus d'impression dans lequel l'encre est imprimée par la surface saillante de blocs de plomb, qui forment les caractères. C'est le plus vieux des procédés d'impression, et il est moins utilisé aujourd'hui. Comme la flexographie, c'est un processus d'impression en relief. Il peut s'agir d'une impression à plat (sur des feuilles) ou rotative (alimentation par bobine).

Index
Studios & Institutions

Starck Packaging), 356 (Michael Graves Packaging), 358 (Tupperware Packaging), 364 (Table Lamp and Table Packaging), 382 (RCA Sustainable Packaging)

Dew Gibbons
49 Tabernacle Street, London, EC2A 4AA, UK
http://www.dewgibbons.com
22 (Case 02 - Boots Essentials), 222-224 (De Beers), 310 (Danièle Ryman), 329 (Invent Your Scent)

DJPA Partnership Ltd. (UK)
88 Gray's Inn Road, London, WC1X 8AA, UK
http://www.djpa.com
184 (Amoy Premium Soy Sauce), 282 (Radox Shower, Bath and Handwash - Redesign)

DJPA Partnership (NL)
Lemelerbergweg 31A, 1101 AH, Amsterdam, Netherlands
http://www.djpa.com
193 (Leonidas Luxury Pralines)

Dragon Rouge
32, rue Pagès, BP 83, F-92152 Suresnes Cedex, France
http://www.dragonrouge.com
95 (Wyborowa Vodka), 112 (Ricar Spirit), 122 (Vittel Mineral Water), 123 (Perrier Pet), 216 (XO Cognac Martell), 283 (Palmolive Thermal SPA)

Elmwood
Ghyll Royd, Guiseley, Leeds, LS20 9LT, UK
http://www.elmwood.co.uk
361 (Simple is Hard - Richardson Sheffield Rebranding), 365 (So Eat Cutlery)

Forme Design Office Inc.
901, ICB Morinomiya Bldg. 1-14-17, Morinomiya Chuo, Chuo-ku, Osaka 540-0003 Japan
http://www.forme-design-office.co.jp
262 (Illume Cool Force UV), 265 (SK-II Skin Care Cosmetics), 265 (SK-II LXP Skin Care Cosmetics), 290 (Pucelle)

Fuseproject
528 Folsom St, San Francisco CA 94105
http://www.fuseproject.com
284 (Hip Holispa), 305 (Philou), 323 (Perfume 09)

Guerlain International
125, rue du President Wilson, F 92300 Levallois-Perret, France
http://www.guerlain.com
239 (KissKiss)

IDEO
White Bear Yard, 144a Clerkenwell Rd, London EC1R 5DF, UK
http://www.ideo.com
12 (Case 01 - NatureWorks)

Industrial Facility
Address: Pegasus House, 116/120 Golden Lane, London EC1Y 0TF, UK
http://www.industrialfacility.co.uk
155 (once)

Jones Knowles Ritchie
128 Albert Street, London, NW1 7NE, UK
http://www.jkr.co.uk
101 (Strongbow), 103 (Stella Demi Artois), 131 (J20), 166 (Sharwood's Noodle Box), 311 (Molton Brown Colour Cosmetics)

Kan & Lau Design Consultants
416 Innocentre, 72 Tat Chee Avenue, Kowloon Tong, Hong Kong
http://www.kanandlau.com
120 (Watson's Water - Centennial Anniversary and "Year of Hong Kong" Project), 138 (Geow Yong Tea),

Karim Rashid Inc.
357 West 17th Street, New York, NY 10011
http://www.karimrashid.com
202-204 (Method), 233 (Davidiff Echo Man & Echo Woman), 244-245 (Prada Multidose Skincare), 246 (Tommy Hilfiger), 322 (Metasense), 324 (Prescriptives), 330 (Kenzo Ryoko)

Kirin Brewery Company
10-1, Shinkawa 2-chome, Chuo-ku, Tokyo 104-8288, Japan
http://www.kirin.co.jp
92 (Fujisanroku Single Malt Aged 18 Years), 93 (Kirin Pure Blue), 106 (Kirin Chu-Hi Kyoketsu)

Kornick Lindsay
230 W. Huron, Chicago, IL 60610
http://www.korlin.com
145 (Motorola Pebl), 148 (Moto V-180),

K2design
3 Louka Bellou str., 115 24 Athens, Greece
http://www.k2design.gr

268 (Korres Face Care - Unisex Sophisticated Containers), 270 (Korres Coloured Pencils), 271 ((Korres Face Care - Unisex Sophisticated Containers), 272 (Total Care Toothpaste), 272 (Aromatic Chewing Gum), 273 (Krokos - Korres Greek Flora), 273 (Krokus - Mouthwash Natural Protection)

Kosé Corporation
1-9-9 Hatchobori, Chuo-ku, Tokyo 104-0032, Japan
http://www.kose.co.jp
242 (Jill Stuart), 308 (Stephen Knoll Collection), 314 (Fasio), 314 (Viseé)

Landor Associates
Klamath House, 18 Clerkenwell Greem, London EC1R 0QE, England
http://www.landor.com
90 (The Glenlivet - 21 Year Old and Cellar Collection), 124 (Maxens - The Four Elements), 125 (Evian Origine), 205 (Febreze Air Effects), 206 (Ariel Excalibur - Redesign of Ariel Packaging Identity), 390 (Imagic Packaging Structural Design)

Lewis Moberly
33 Gresse Street, London, W1T 1QU, UK
http://www.lewismoberly.com
122 (Belu Water), 170 (Waitrose Cheeses), 184 (Waitrose Mustards), 184 (Tamarind), 186 (Waitrose Cooks' Ingredients), 192 (Waitrose Belgian Chocolates), 309 (Seah Hairspa), 390 (Panini)

Lippa Pearce Design Ltd.
358a Richmond Road, Twickenham, London TW1 2DU, UK
http://www.lippapearce.com
89 (Cask Number 26.40 Limited Edition Single Malt Whisky), 280 (Naked - Brand Identity), 292 (Boots Botanics), 352 (Heal's - Identity), 381 (Reaver Adult Cycle Helmet - Trax)

Lloyd (+ co)
180 Varick St, Suite 1018, New York, NY 10014, USA
http://www.lloydandco.com
124 (Smart Water), 128 (Vitamin Water), 236 (Gucci Envy Me), 236 (YSL M7), 236 (Gucci Eau de Parfum), 240 (YSL M7 - Clean Bottle), 240 (John Varvatos), 240 (Gucci Rush), 245 (John Varvatos)

Marc Atlan Design, Inc.
434 Carroll Canal, Venice, CA 90291, U.S.A.
http://www.marcatlan.com
238 (Comme des Garçons Eau de Parfum),
320 (Comme des Garçons Cosmetic Line)

Marks & Spencer
27 Baker St, London W1U 8EQ, UK
http://www.marksandspencer.com
32 (Case 03 - Food to Go), 174 (Marks &
Spencer Flavoured Snacks), 176 (Full on
Flavour), 179 (Gastronomic Adventures)

Matsushita Battery Industrial Co., Ltd.
1-1 Matsuhista-cho, Moriguchi
City, Osaka 570-8511
http://panasonic.co.jp/mbi/en
Design Division: Panasonic Design Company,
Matsushita Electric Industrial Co., Ltd.
1-1 Matsushita-cho, Moriguchi City,
Osaka 570-8511
http://panasonic.co.jp/design/en
156 (Easy-to-distinguish Dry Battery
Package), 156 (Qoopaq)

Matsushita Electric Industrial Co., Ltd.
1006 Kadoma, Kadoma City,
Osaka 571-8501, Japan
http://panasonic.co.jp/global/
157 (New Easy-to-Use Hearing Aid Battery)

MetaDesign AG
Leibnizstrasse 65, 10629 Berlin, Germany
http://www.metadesign.de
146 (I-Mode Mobile Telephone)

Metaphase Design Group, Inc.
12 South Hanley Road, St. Louis,
Missouri 63105, USA
http://www.metaphase.com
134 (Gatorade E.D.G.E. - Ergonomically
Designed Gatorade Experience), 172 (Drink
'N Crunch), 172 (Scoopable 1 Gallon Salad
Dressing for the Food Service Market), 377
(Traveller Plus Lid)

Minale Tattersfield & Partners Ltd.
The Poppy Factory, 20 Petersham Road,
Richmond, Surrey TW10 6UR, UK
http://www.mintat.co.uk
173 (Espress Dairies - Structural Packaging),
378 (Caspian - Branding and Packaging)

Morinaga & Co., Ltd.
33-1, Shiba 5-chome, Minato-ku,
Tokyo 108-8403, Japan
http://www.morinaga.co.jp
178 (Morinaga Fried Potatoes), 195 (Koeda
Bitter Taste), 195 (Dars)

Mountain Design
Paleisstraat 6, 2514 JA DEN HAAG,
The Netherlands
http://www.mountaindesign.nl
134 (Coca-Cola Light Lemon (Visual
Executed in a 0,5 L PET), 157 (Push Braces)

Okumura Akio
IM-LAB: Commemorative Association For
The Japan World Exposition (1970): 1F
1-1 Senri Banpaku-Koen, Suita, Osaka,
565-0826, Japan
http://www.okumura-akio.com
89 (Budouka Grappa), 101 (Sake Hourin),
111 (Gomeyama), 201 (Fruit Jelly), 364
(Long Store Bag)

Parker Williams Design
Voysey House, Barley Mow Passage,
London, W4 4PT, UK
http://www.parkerwilliamsdesign.co.uk
127 (Llanllyr Source Organic Water)

Pearson Matthews
9 Princess Mews, Horace Road, Kingston
upon Thames, London KT1 2SZ, UK
http://www.pearsonmatthews.com
339 (Nurofen Mobile Pack), 340
(Clevername), 341 (Clearblue), 344
(Solutions for the Vitamins Market -
2020 Vision Design Challange)

PDD Group Ltd.
85-87 Richford St, London, W6 7HJ, UK
http://www.pdd.co.uk
147 (Helix), 160 (Platinum), 328 (Snif),
382 (Ar Vision)

Pearlfisher
50 Brook Green, London W6 7BJ, UK
http://www.pearlfisher.com
94 (Absolut Cut), 158 (Waitrose Ready
Meals - Restaurant Quality Meals), 164
(Waitrose Soups), 185 (Waitrose Olive Oils),
221 (Absolut Level), 261 (Cowshed), 286
(Waitrose Umi)

Pentagram
11 Needham Road, London W11 2RP, UK
http://www.pentagram.com
140 (Wistbray Dragonfly Tea), 168 (EAT),
252 (Langford), 381 (Halfords Own Brand
Packaging - Cycle Lights and Cellulose
Thinners), 387 (The Blue Bar CD Packaging),
391 (Globe Link), 391 (Audley Shoes)

PI3
1 Colville Mews, Lonsdale Road, London
W11 2AR , UK
http://www.pi3innovation.com
101 (Guinness Draft in a Bottle), 180
(Pringles Pop Box), 194 (Mr. Kipling),
276 (Oil for Olay), 340 (Imigran), 378
(Q8 Oil - Brand), 380 (Syngenta Port-a-Pack),
383 (Yu No Mi)

**Pola Cosmetics Inc. (Pola Chemical
Industries Inc.)**
2-2-3 Nishi Gotanda, Shinagawa-ku,
Tokyo 141-8523, Japan
http://www.pola.co.jp
259 (Pola Estima Altiva), 260 (Pola Wrinkle
Shot Essence), 311 (Pola the Make B.A.)

P&W design consultants
21 Ivor Place, Marylebone,
London NW1 6EU, UK
http://www.p-and-w.com
98 (Bambarria Tequila), 99 (Ron
Veracruzano), 211 (Olly/Ecolive
Washing Powder)

**PSAG (The Packaging Solutions
Advice Group)**
1 Wardour Mews, D'Arblay Street, London
W1F 8AH, UK
http://www.psag.co.uk
78 (Cse 08 - Package Materials)

Pure Equator
The Old School House, High Pavement, The
Lace Market, Nottingham NG1 1HN, UK
http://www.pure-equator.com
306 (Pure Equator)

R Design
420 Highgate Studios, 53 –79 Highgate stu-
dios, London NW5 1TL, UK
http://www.r-email.co.uk
162 (Selfridges), 165 (The Food Doctor), 178
(Tesco Breadsticks), 188 (Tesco Herbs), 195
(Cocoa Deli), 235 (SPA), 263 (Mea), 300
(Tesco Spa Body Therapy), 303 (Tesco Finest
Classic Health and Beauty Range), 317
(Mea), 327 (Micheline Arcier)

Sayuri Studio, Inc.
#101, 3-9-11 Ebisu Minami, Shibuya-ku,
Tokyo 150-0022 Japan
http://www.ss-studio.com
130 (Namacha Green Tea - Package
Renewal), 221 (Waterbottle), 250 (Pleats
Please Limited Edition Shopping Bag - Issey
Miyake), 251 (Fino Premium Touch
Shampoo), 283 (RMK Collection Kit - Sugar

Color), 293 (Kuyura Body Wash), 317 (Shu Uemura Cosmetics), 318 (Estée Lauder Prime FX), 346-348 (Candle 0015/0017), 348 (Felissimo Carton Box), 367 (Type Box)

SiebertHead Ltd.
80 Goswell Road, London EC1V 7DB, UK
http://www.sieberthead.com
94 (Somerfield Vodka Sherry and Port - Graphic Redesign), 113 (La Rustía Wine Bottle), 282 (Avon - Senses & Skin So Soft, Structural Redesign), 342 (Pharmassist - 2020 Vision Design Challenge), 343 (Profile - 2020 Vision Design Challenge), 392 (A to Z of Technical Terms)

slover [AND] company
584 Broadway [Suite 903],
New York, NY 10012, USA
http://www.sloverandco.com
196 (Dancing Deer Baking Company), 294 (Benefits - Bath & Body Works), 296 (Monde Sensuelle Bath & Body Collection), 299 (Desert Bambu - Wynn Las Vegas In-Room Amenities)

StickTea
Lovello Fausto, C.so C. Marx,
Alessandria, Italy
http://www.sticktea.com
139 (StickTea)

Stockholm Design Lab AB
Riddargatan 17d, SE-114 57,
Stockholm, Sweden
http://www.stockholmdesignlab.se
154 (Askul Batterier Batteries), 275 (Oriflane Cosmetics), 360 (Röstrand Wine Glasses), 366 (Filippa K), 368 (Ikea - Packaging Concept), 368 (Snowflake)

Strømme Throndsen Design
Holtegata 22, 0355 Oslo, Norway
http://www.stdesign.no
100 (Mozell Art Bottle), 103 (Ringnes Swing), 127 (Imsdal Bottle), 166 (Rakfish Snolked Salmon), 185 (Black Boy Premium)

Taku Satoh Design Office Inc.
1-14-11, Ginsho Bldg. 4F Ginza
Chuo-ku, Tokyo 104-0061, Japan
http://www.tsdo.jp/
60 (Case 06 - Package Design in Japan), 152 (± Carton), 188 (Spice & Herb Series), 193 (Pascal Caffet for ± 0 - Food)

Tana-X Inc.
277 Horinouchi-cho Takatsuji,
Shinmachi-Nishiiru Shimogyo-ku,
600-8446 Kyoto, Japan
http://www.tana-x.co.jp/
368 (Paper Air Packing),

Tangerine
9 Blue Lion Place, 237 Long Lane,
London SE1 4PZ, UK
http://www.tangerine.net
150 (MP3 Player Packaging)

Tátil Design
Rio de Janeiro: Estrada da Gávea, 712 / 101-104, São Conrado, Rio de Janeiro – RJ, CEP 22610-002
São Paulo: Rua Tenerife, 31 / 11° andar, Vila Olímpia, São Paulo – SP, CEP 04548-040
T. +55 11 3847 8660
http://www.tatil.com.br
149 (Nokia 3220 - Press Kit with Gift), 291 (Natura Kid - Redesign Proposal and Packaging Concept), 389 (The Skin of Our Book - Book Packaging Design)

Terumo Corporation
44-1, 2-chome, Hatagaya, Shibuya-ku, Tokyo, 151-0072 Japan
http://www.terumo.com
332 (Soft Bag for Infusion), 334 (Syringe)

The Ad Store
Viale Fratti 20/D, Parma, Italy
http://www.adstore.it
226 (Mandarina Duck Jewellery Box), 264 (Action Sublime Pack), 266 (Daviness - Confort Zone, Linea Man), 298 (Starhotel Night Confort Kit), 388 (Testoni Press Kit "Italian Inside" USA)

Third Eye Design
23 Newton Place, GLASGOW G3 7PY,
Scotland
http://www.thirdeyedesign.co.uk
220 (KSHOCOLÂT)

Tin Horse
Pelham House Pelham Court, London Road
Marlborough, Wiltshire SN8 2AG, UK
http://www.tinhorse.com
126 (Deep River Rock), 274 (Pond's), 335 (K-Haler), 363 (Pug), 384 (Easy Can)

Toyo Seikan Kaisha, Ltd.
1-3-1 Uchisaiwaicho, Chiyoda-ku,
Tokyo 100-8522 Japan
http://www.toyo-seikan.co.jp
304 (Gradation Bottle), 374-376 (Z-End)

Tridimage
Av. Congreso 4607, C1431AAB Buenos Aires, Argentina
http://www.tridimage.com
134 (Dragonfly Energy Drink - Brand Identity, Label Design and Structural Bottle Design)

WSdV – Webb Scarlett deVlam
12 Junction Mews, London W2 1PN, UK
felix.scarlett@wsdv.com
http://www.wsdv.com
180 (Pringles Single Serve), 207 (Dawn / Fairy Active), 208 (Downy Simple Pleasures), 209 (Lenor), 276 (Olay Daily Facials Clarity), 276 (Olay Regenerist), 293 (Olay Body - Quench), 311 (Covergirl Outlast)

Wolff Olins
10 Regents Wharf, All Saints Street, London N1 9RL, UK
http://www.wolff-olins.com
136 (Sen)

Wren & Rowe
4, Denbigh Mews, London SW1V 2HQ, UK
http://www.wrenrowe.com
http://www.brand-ignition.com
104 (G Port), 108 (Andresen Reserve Trio)

Yasuo Tanaka
Package land.,Ltd.
201 Tezukayama Tower plaza 1-3-2
Tezukayama-Naka, Sumiyoshi-Ku, Osaka 558-0053 Japan
http://www.package-land.com
190 (Coffee Package), 289 (Bathing Oil), 372 (Compact Disk Packaging), 372 (Cosmox), 373 (Japanese Figure Packaging)

Ziggurat Brand Consultants
8 – 14 Vine Hill, Clerkenwell, London EC1R 5DX, UK
http://www.zigguratbrands.com
130 (Sainsbury Flavoured Waters), 171 (Over the Moon), 182 (KP Nuts), 183 (Jonathan Crisp), 189 (Mrs Massey's)

Acknowledgements

First of all we would like to thank all the design offices and designers that have made incredible contributions to this publication, supplying us with cutting-edge materials from all over the world. Also the professionals who sent us all the in-depth case studies, making precious information available to a wider public, and without whose input this book would not have been possible.

We would especially like to thank Charlotte Raphael, from Marks & Spencer, who dedicated a lot of time and effort in her contributions; equally, Takashi Tsurumaki, who helped immensely with all the Japanese contacts.

Special thanks also go to Jutta Hendricks, who helped us a lot in the final rounds, considerably improving the publication throughout; and as well to Daniel Siciliano Brêtas and Stefan Klatte, who have been a constant support during the whole process.

Last but not least, big thanks go to Birgit Reber and Andy Disl, who did a superb job in designing the publication.

Imprint

Barnsley College
Honeywell
Learning Centre

© 2008 TASCHEN GmbH
Hohenzollernring 53
D-50672 Köln
www.taschen.com

To stay informed about upcoming TASCHEN titles, please request
our magazine at www.taschen.com/magazine or write to TASCHEN,
Hohenzollernring 53, D-50672 Cologne, Germany, contact@taschen.com,
Fax: +49-221-254919. We will be happy to send you a free copy of our
magazine which is filled with information about all of our books.

Design & Layout
Sense/Net, Andy Disl and Birgit Reber, Cologne
Production
Stefan Klatte

Editor
Gisela Kozak
Julius Wiedemann
Editorial Coordination
Jutta Hendricks
Daniel Siciliano Brêtas

German Translation
Wolfgang Beuchelt, Katrin Kügler, Brigitte Rüßmann
(Equipo de Edición, Barcelona)
French Translation
Aurélie Daniel (Equipo de Edición, Barcelona)

Printed in Italy
ISBN 978–3–8228–4031–3